STRUCTURES OF AG

STRUCTURES
OF AGENCY

Essays

Michael E. Bratman

UNIVERSITY PRESS

2007

OXFORD
UNIVERSITY PRESS

Oxford University Press, Inc., publishes works that further
Oxford University's objective of excellence
in research, scholarship, and education.

Oxford   New York
Auckland   Cape Town   Dar es Salaam   Hong Kong   Karachi
Kuala Lumpur   Madrid   Melbourne   Mexico City   Nairobi
New Delhi   Shanghai   Taipei   Toronto

With offices in
Argentina   Austria   Brazil   Chile   Czech Republic   France   Greece
Guatemala   Hungary   Italy   Japan   Poland   Portugal   Singapore
South Korea   Switzerland   Thailand   Turkey   Ukraine   Vietnam

Published by Oxford University Press, Inc.
198 Madison Avenue, New York, New York 10016

www.oup.com

Oxford is a registered trademark of Oxford University Press.

Library of Congress Cataloging-in-Publication Data
Bratman, Michael.
Structures of agency : essays / Michael E. Bratman.
p. cm.
Includes bibliographical references and index.
ISBN-13 978-0-19-518770-0; 978-0-19-518771-7 (pbk.)
ISBN 0-19-518770-9; 0-19-518771-7 (pbk.)
1. Intentionality (Philosophy)   2. Autonomy (Philosophy)   3. Agent (Philosophy)
I. Title.
B105.I56B74 2006
128'.4—dc22   2006043776

9 8 7 6 5 4 3 2 1

Printed in the United States of America
on acid-free paper

For Susan, Gregory, and Scott

Contents

STRUCTURES OF AGENCY

Chapter 1

INTRODUCTION

We are planning agents; our agency extends over time; and, sometimes at least, we govern our own actions. These essays aim at understanding important interrelations between these basic features of our agency—interrelations between our planning agency, our temporally extended agency, and our self-governance. Essays 2–11 explore basic elements of my proposed view concerning these matters. A final pair of essays draws on these theoretical resources for further philosophical purposes.

A conjecture that underlies these essays is that we can better understand at least one basic case of self-governed agency by reflecting on the roles of relevant planning attitudes in the cross-temporal organization of our action and practical thinking. This conjecture ties together earlier work of mine on the planning theory of intention[1] and the present foray into debates about autonomy and self-governance.[2] Taken together, these essays are a preliminary effort to see whether this link between the planning theory and issues of autonomy and self-governance can yield philosophical insight. While there remain both significant unanswered questions and some tensions between the essays, I have decided to put these essays together in one place so as to facilitate a focused consideration of their main themes.

---

1. *Intention, Plans and Practical Reason* (Cambridge, MA: Harvard University Press, 1987; reissued by CSLI Publications, 1999); *Faces of Intention: Selected Essays on Intention and Agency* (Cambridge: Cambridge University Press, 1999).

2. My first efforts to bring together some of these ideas are in "Identification, Decision, and Treating as a Reason," as reprinted in my *Faces of Intention*, pp. 185–206.

I. THEMES

I begin by sketching some central themes. What I say here will be sche-matic: details, arguments, and connections with the work of others are in the essays. But it is nevertheless my hope that this overview will be of some use in approaching these essays.

1. *Autonomy, self-governance, and agential authority.* Philosophical talk about human autonomy is multifaceted. It includes ideas about forms of agency that are considerably more demanding than those in-volved in merely purposive agency. And it includes ideas about conditions for culpability and accountability. One central idea is that of forms of agency that constitute self-governance. And that is the idea that takes center stage in these essays. When I talk of autonomy it is, in particular, this idea of self-governance that is my direct concern.

   What is self-governance? As an initial, basic step we can say that in self-governance the agent herself directs and governs her practical thought and action. Or anyway, that is the intuitive, pretheoretical idea, one that plays significant roles in our self-understanding and in associated social practices. But what is it for the agent to direct and to govern?

   Begin with agential direction. As a first step we can say that for the agent to direct thinking and acting is for relevant attitudes that guide and control that thinking and action to have authority to speak for the agent—to have agential authority. In this way, the idea of agential authority serves as a bridge between, on the one hand, appeal to attitudes that guide and control and, on the other hand, appeal to the agent as directing. When relevant attitudes with such agential authority appropriately guide and control, the agent directs.

2. *Subjective normative authority.* For the agent to *govern* her thinking and acting, however, it is not sufficient that she directs them. To govern is to direct in a way that is shaped by what the agent treats as justifying considerations, as reasons. In self-governance, attitudes that have agential authority need to guide relevant thought and action by way of articulating what has, for the agent, justifying significance—what

has subjective normative authority for that agent. So a model of self-governance needs to provide coordinated accounts of both agential authority and subjective normative authority.

3. *Temporally extended agency and agential authority.* What gives an attitude agential authority? To answer we need to appeal to relevant roles in the psychic economy. Which roles? Well, it is a deep and important feature of our agency that it is temporally extended: one and the same agent persists over time, and there are complex continuities and connections that help constitute the organized interweave of our action and practical thinking over time. Indeed, on a broadly Lockean approach to personal identity, the connections and continuities that are the back-bone of this psychological, cross-temporal quilt are constitutive of the identity of the agent over time, an identity that is presupposed in much of our practical thinking. And this suggests the conjecture that it is primarily its role in constituting and supporting this organized, cross-temporal, Lockean interweave of action and practical thinking that confers on a structure of attitudes a claim to speak for the agent—a claim to agential authority.[3]

4. *Intentions and the planning theory.* According to the planning theory, intentions are characteristically elements of larger, partial plans of action, and these plans play basic coordinating, organizing roles at a time and over time. Associated with these roles are distinctive rational pressures on intentions for consistency and coherence at a time, and stability over time.[4] And intentions help constitute and support the cross-temporal organization of our temporally extended agency in part by way of the kinds of cross-temporal ties—psychological, semantic, causal—that are, on a broadly Lockean approach, partly constitutive of personal identity. My conjecture is that this complex relation to the temporal extension of our agency is the key to arguing that certain intention-like attitudes have a significant claim to agential authority.

---

3. I say "primarily" to leave room for a condition of "satisfaction" that derives from Harry Frankfurt's work. See essay 2.

4. See *Intention, Plans and Practical Reason*, and for a more recent defense of these ideas, "Intention, Belief, Practical, Theoretical" in Jens Timmerman, John Skorupski, and Simon Robertson, eds., *Spheres of Reason* (forthcoming).

5. *Policies.* Which intention-like attitudes? Well, policies are intentions that are appropriately general in their content. They support treating, over time, like cases in like ways, and doing this as a matter of (and so, with reference to one's) policy. So their generality tends to give them a central role in Lockean cross-temporal organization. So, among intention-like attitudes, policies, in particular, can have a significant claim to agential authority.

6. *Self-governing policies.* Which policies? Here we need to recall the need, in self-governance, for guiding attitudes that articulate what one is to treat as a justifying reason in one's motivationally effective practical reasoning[5]—that articulate what has subjective normative authority. Policies that say what to treat as a reason, and with what weight and significance—and thereby help determine what has subjective normative authority—can bring together, in the way needed for self-governance, both agential and subjective normative authority. And such policies, in their characteristic functioning, will engage the norms of consistency, coherence, and stability highlighted by the planning theory. I call such policies *self-governing policies.*[6]

7. *Conative hierarchy.* There are significant pressures, within self-governance, for self-governing policies to be in part about relevant functioning in the psychic economy of first-order motivating attitudes—for self-governing policies to be hierarchical attitudes. These pressures toward conative hierarchy include, as Harry Frankfurt

---

5. If the content of these policies involves the idea that the agent treats something as a reason, if we then appeal to such policies to understand strong forms of agency, and if treating as a reason is itself a strong form of agency, there may seem to be a circle here. I address a version of this problem of circularity in essay 4, and return to it also in essays 5 and 9.

6. In "Identification, Decision, and Treating as a Reason," I highlighted the role in identification of *decisions* about whether to treat a desire as reason-giving. Such decisions are one source of self-governing policies. But the claim now is that the agential authority of these self-governing policies is grounded primarily in their Lockean role in cross-temporal organization, rather than in the very fact that these policies are the issue of (more or less reflective) decision. Indeed, it is not necessary, though it is common, that these policies are an upshot of a decision. This development in my view emerges in essay 2. Related issues about the theoretical significance of appeals to decision are discussed in the Appendix to essay 6. My thinking about this broadly Lockean picture has benefited greatly from a series of interactions with Gideon Yaffe. Yaffe imaginatively explores Locke's view of the relation between personal identity and agency and the relation of this view to a "retributivist conception of punishment" (p. 116) in his *Liberty Worth the Name: Locke on Free Agency* (Princeton, NJ: Princeton University Press, 2000), esp. chaps. 2 and 3.

emphasizes, the fact that self-governing agents characteristically step back and reflect on their motivation with an eye to a kind of self-constitution. But it is important that they include as well certain practical pressures in the direction of hierarchy—practical pressures that are engaged given that these self-governing policies do indeed have agential authority. These practical pressures derive in part from the importance in human lives of forms of self-management, given the independent status, in human agents, of many forms of motivation. And they include pressures that derive from the roles of these policies in supporting cross-temporal organization.[7] Finally, there are also pressures for a specific form of hierarchy—namely, reflexivity—that derive from pressures, within self-governance, for a distinctive kind of agential endorsement of self-governing policies: such agential endorsement is best understood by appeal to self-governing policies that reflexively favor their own functioning. It is not, at bottom, the hierarchical structure of these self-governing policies that explains their agential authority.[8] Agential authority is primarily a matter of Lockean cross-temporal organizing roles. Nevertheless, there are, as noted, significant pressures—including significant practical pressures—in the direction of hierarchy. And once hierarchy is on board, the hierarchical structure of self-governing policies helps realize and support these authority-grounding Lockean roles.

So there is a theoretical loop: Self-governing policies have agential authority grounded primarily in their cross-temporal organizing roles. Given this authority, there are practical pressures—including pressures of self-management—in the direction of hierarchy. And once these hierarchical structures are built into the self-governing policies, they contribute to the ways in which those

7. I note this second practical pressure, one associated with policy-guided cross-temporal organization, in essay II. Both these practical pressures involve a kind of transparency of certain forms of functioning to content, within the psychology of self-governance. I discuss this later in this Introduction and in essay 8.

8. So in this respect, I agree with Gary Watson that hierarchy does not guarantee (what I call) agential authority. But I do not agree with Watson about the implications of this point. See essays 10 and 11 for references and discussion.

policies play the cross-temporal roles that give them authority. Finally—and this is the next theme—the hierarchical structure of self-governing policies helps constitute a strong form of identification with—and ownership of—a first-order desire.

8. *Identification and hierarchy.* For an agent to identify with a certain first-order desire is, in a basic case, for that agent to have a self-governing policy that has agential authority and that says to treat that desire and/or what it is for as a justifying consideration in motivationally effective practical reasoning. Such identification involves a higher-order policy that is not merely about one's motivation but is also about one's practical reasoning. And such identification is central to a basic form of self-governance.

9. *Valuing and value judgment.* Given their roles in shaping practical thought and action, such self-governing policies constitute a form of *valuing*. Such valuing will frequently be responsive to judgments about what is good. And there are rational pressures against extreme forms of incoherence between valuing and value judgment. But there can be valuing, in this sense, without such value judgments. And even when valuing is coherently embedded in a psychic economy that includes related value judgments these attitudes need to be distinguished. Value judgments are tied to intersubjective pressures to which self-governing policies need not be directly accountable. And an agent's intersubjectively accountable value judgments may well significantly underdetermine what she values. Nevertheless, what an agent values, in this sense, engages relevant norms of consistency, coherence, and stability, and shapes ongoing practical thought and action.[9]

10. *Valuing and agential authority.* Valuings—self-governing policies—can have agential authority and determine what has subjective normative authority for the agent, even in cases in which they are, and

---

9. Compare Aurel Kolnai: "the ends we set up and stamp with the *fiat* of the 'sanctioning' imperative power of decision subject us to so many commitments and objectivizations, which are henceforth to circumscribe and govern our will though engendered by its ruling." "Deliberation Is of Ends," *Proceedings of the Aristotelian Society* suppl. Vol. 36 (1962) as reprinted in Elijah Millgram, ed., *Varieties of Practical Reasoning* (Cambridge, MA: MIT Press, 2001): 259–78, quotation from p. 274.

are recognized to be, underdetermined by intersubjectively accountable value judgment. Their agential authority is, at bottom, primarily a matter of their roles in the cross-temporal Lockean organization of agency, not of their responsiveness to judgments about the good, even though it is normally better if there is such responsiveness.

11. *How to be a wholehearted pluralist.*[10] A Platonic theory of self-governance sees as central practical reasoning and action that are determined by judgments about the good. A Frankfurtian theory highlights determination by higher-order attitudes that have agential authority, and the relation of these higher-order attitudes to judgments about the good is not central. The Platonic theory overstates the extent to which we can expect intersubjectively accountable value judgment to determine the shape of a person's life. The Frankfurtian model seems to understate the role of value judgment in self-governance. The present approach allows us to model important forms of self-governance that are in the theoretical space between these Platonic and Frankfurtian conceptions. We acknowledge the potential relevance, within a psychic economy that exhibits self-governance, of judgments about the good. Nevertheless, we also, in a broadly Frankfurtian spirit, reject the idea that the connection to these value judgments is at the heart of agential authority.

12. *Metaphysics, not "agency-at-its-best."*[11] Such self-governance may fail to be good agency if it is guided by commitments to treating as reasons considerations that should not be so treated. A certain kind of evil person may, on the theory, be self-governing. This is a model of the metaphysics of self-governance, not, on its own, an ideal of the best form of human agency—though self-governance is one element in important and powerful ideals of human agency. Some have thought that autonomy or self-governance requires at least a capacity, perhaps unexercised, to judge correctly about the good. I leave this issue open here. What I do say is that self-governance does not preclude being guided by considerations by which one should not be guided. (There

10. Thanks to Susan Wolf for this way of putting this idea.
11. The quote is from Gideon Yaffe, *Liberty Worth the Name: Locke on Free Agency,* 72.

are parallels here with the legal positivist's view that there can be legal governance even if the laws are bad laws.)

13. *The will.* This model of self-governance highlights intention-like commitments both to action and to modes of practical reasoning. And it highlights the cross-temporal organizing roles of these commitments. Given the ways in which these commitments are underdetermined by value judgment, and given their ties to decision and choice, it is natural and plausible to see these commitments as aspects of the will. These aspects of the will play a wide range of organizing roles in our lives: in this sense, this is a thick conception of the will. It is also a modest conception of the will in the sense that it understands the will in terms of familiar psychological roles and associated norms, and is, at least on its surface, compatible with the idea that the will is as fully embeddable as belief and desire in a natural causal order.

14. *Stability of intention.* Intention-like attitudes have a characteristic stability, and reasonably so. One idea here is that some form of stability is needed for intentions and plans to play their cross-temporal organizing roles, and these roles are significantly useful for agents like us in the pursuit of a wide range of ends. A related idea is that cross-temporal stability of commitments with agential authority is part of what is involved in the forms of cross-temporal integrity and self-government that we normally value.[12] There is also an intriguing, though as yet undeveloped, parallel between the stability of intention and the legal doctrine of *stare decisis.*[13]

The idea of reasonable stability is part of my effort to find a path between an overly Platonic view of our agency and certain features of a Frankfurtian theory. One way to see this is to note how, in recent work, Frankfurt has been led to understand a central form of stability by appeal to the idea that certain basic commitments are volitionally necessary. To be volitionally necessary is, in part, to be

12. This point goes a bit beyond what I explicitly say in these essays in this volume. I develop this point in "Anchors for Deliberation," in Christopher Lumer and Sandro Mannini, eds., *Intentionality, Deliberation and Autonomy* (Alsershot, etc.: Ashgate, forthcoming).

13. This is suggested by Robert Nozick's remarks about decisions and precedents. See essay 6. Shelly Kagan also noted this parallel in correspondence.

immune to change at will;[14] so this is a strong form of stability, one
that involves an incapacity of the will.[15] In contrast, I seek a model
of reasonable stability in self-governance that does not require
(though it does not preclude) such an incapacity of the will, but
also does not anchor the needed stability solely in Platonic judgments about the best.[16]

15. *Methodology.* In developing these views I am to some extent guided by
a quartet of methodological ideas. First, in articulating the structure
of increasingly complex forms of agency, we do well to exploit a
version of Gricean "creature construction." We build step-wise from
the simpler to the more complex: more complex structures build
on simpler structures and are introduced in response to specifiable
problems and issues that arise at the less complex level. Second, we
try to see to what extent models of strong forms of agency can be
constructed in a way that is neutral with respect to debates in
metaethics between cognitivist and expressivist views; though (as
Nadeem Hussain has emphasized) we need to remain alive to the
possibility that such neutrality will not be available at the end of the
day. Third, we focus primarily on claims about sufficient conditions
for strong forms of agency—forms of agency that include, especially, autonomy and self-governance. We can make progress while
leaving open the possibility that there are multiple modes of psychological functioning that can constitute such strong forms of
agency.[17] It is progress if we can articulate one such mode and see
how it might be an element in a broadly naturalistic psychic

14. See Harry Frankfurt, "On the Necessity of Ideals," in his *Necessity, Volition, and Love*
(Cambridge: Cambridge University Press, 1999).

15. There is a somewhat similar focus on impossibility in Joseph Raz's discussion of Peter
Winch's approach to the case of Vere in *Billy Budd.* See Raz, "The Truth in Particularism," in his
Engaging Reason: On the Theory of Value and Action (Oxford: Oxford University Press, 1999): 218–46, at
241–46. See however note 41 in this paper for a suggestion about the role of "commitments" that
is closer in spirit to the view I want to defend.

16. I discuss this middle way further in "Anchors for Deliberation," and briefly in "A
Thoughtful and Reasonable Stability: A Comment on Harry Frankfurt's 2004 Tanner Lectures,"
in *Taking Ourselves Seriously and Getting It Right*, ed. Debra Satz (Stanford: Stanford University Press,
2006): 77–90 and 114–15.

17. This third idea emerges in essay 7 and later. It represents a qualification of suggestions in
some of the earlier essays that the proposed model seeks to be a model of the unique form of
self-government.

economy. Fourth, we try to understand small-scale shared agency primarily in terms of the planning theory of the intentions of the individual participants supplemented by an account of the special contents and interrelations of those intentions that are characteristic of these forms of sociality. This is a version of the Gricean strategy of creature construction applied to the step from individual to shared agency.

2. THE ESSAYS

Now that these broad themes are on the table, I proceed to some brief remarks about each of the essays.

Essay 2: "Reflection, Planning, and Temporally Extended Agency" sketches connections between strong forms of agency, the planning theory, and Lockean cross-temporal organization. It introduces the idea of higher-order self-governing policies concerning what to treat as reason providing. And it draws on a version of Frankfurt's idea of satisfaction with such an attitude. What is basic is that these self-governing policies play relevant Lockean organizing roles in cross-temporal identity, not that their contents are explicitly a conception of one's "practical identity."[18] And there is also room in the theory to accord agential authority to attitudes that play these cross-temporal roles but are not, strictly speaking, policies. Such attitudes would be "quasi-policies."

Essay 3: "Valuing and the Will" sketches a model of valuing as a higher-order policy of weights in practical reasoning. It proceeds by way of a project of Gricean "creature construction": such policies about weights are a further development of planning structures, planning structures introduced earlier in the "construction" to support cross-temporal and social organization.

Essay 4: "Hierarchy, Circularity, and Double Reduction" addresses a potential circularity in the idea that to identify with a desire is, roughly, to have a self-governing policy in favor of treating that desire as reason-providing. It seems that for an agent to treat a desire in this way is already for the agent to identify with that desire. So we cannot, without circularity, simply appeal to

---

18. The quote is from Christine Korsgaard; see section 8 of essay 2.

such treatment by the agent in the content of the policy by appeal to which we aim to understand identification.[19] The solution is to appeal instead to a form of functioning of a desire—functioning as end-setting—that has two features. First, that functioning does not itself entail agential identification with that desire. But, second, if that functioning is in fact guided by a relevant self-governing policy in its favor, then the agent does identify with that desire and treat it as reason-providing. We thereby understand an agent's treating a desire as reason-providing primarily by appeal to the twin ideas of a desire's functioning as end-setting and an effective policy in favor of that. However, since a desire's functioning as end-setting involves the thought of that desire, or of what it is for, as a justifying reason, this is not yet an analysis of that very thought.

Essay 5: "Two Problems about Human Agency" distinguishes agential authority from subjective normative authority, argues that a theory of strong forms of human agency needs to provide a coordinated treatment of both, and explains how an appeal to higher-order self-governing policies aims to do this.

Essay 6 (and Appendix): "Nozick on Free Will." The idea of a reflexive self-governing policy that can be underdetermined by value judgment, and that plays a role in Lockean identity, is similar in important respects to Robert Nozick's idea of a "self-subsuming decision that bestows weights to reasons." Nozick develops this idea in his rich but understudied work, *Philosophical Explanations*.[20] My essay spells out this and related ideas from Nozick and argues that they do not depend on the forms of incompatibilism that are prominent in Nozick's treatment. The Appendix argues that there remains a serious issue, within Nozick's discussion, about how to explain agential authority and about the precise philosophical work that can be done by appeal to the very idea of a decision.

Essay 7: "A Desire of One's Own" addresses a Platonic challenge to a Frankfurt-type hierarchical theory of desire ownership and identification. My response aims to block this challenge by emphasizing important ways in which identification may be underdetermined by value judgment.

---

19. This is the concern about circularity anticipated above in note 5.
20. (Cambridge, MA: Harvard University Press, 1981). The quote is from p. 300.

Essay 8: "Autonomy and Hierarchy" explores multiple philosophical pressures in the direction of conative hierarchy as an element in autonomous agency. A central idea is that there is, in autonomy, a certain transparency of relevant psychological functioning of self-governing policies to their content. So the self-management function of self-governing policies leads to a hierarchical content of those policies. This might seem in tension with the idea that it is the *role* of self-governing policies in Lockean cross-temporal organization—not a *content* that is explicitly about one's identity—that is central to their agential authority.[21] But this tension is only apparent. Even in a case of autonomy in which its own role in Lockean identity is internalized in the content of the self-governing policy, it is not this content but this role that grounds the agential authority of that policy (though this content may contribute to this role). And an attitude whose content was a self-conception, but which did not play this role, would not have agential authority.

Essay 9: "Three Forms of Agential Commitment: Reply to Cullity and Gerrans." This essay explores the self-knowledge conditions on self-government. And it argues that a theory of autonomy needs to appeal both to psychological functioning in cross-temporal organization and to a kind of reflexivity of self-governing policy. This reflexivity is in part a response to concerns about circularity, and in part a response to pressures within self-governance in favor of a strong form of agential endorsement of governing policies.

Essay 10: "Planning Agency, Autonomous Agency" seeks to bring together many of the themes in essays 2–9. It highlights the basic connection, at the heart of these essays, between planning agency, agential authority, and self-government. And it returns to an important practical pressure in the direction of conative hierarchy.

Essay 11: "Three Theories of Self-Governance" continues the effort of essay 10 to bring the different threads together as a view in the middle of the field-defining debate between Harry Frankfurt and Gary Watson. It aims to deepen the account of how to be a wholehearted, pluralist, self-governing agent by drawing on Joshua Cohen's interpretation of the

---

21. In addressing this concern here I go beyond what I say explicitly in essay 8.

Rawlsian "idea of reasonable pluralism." And it develops further the central—and broadly Frankfurtian—claim that agential authority is a matter of non-Platonic psychological role in the Lockean organization of our temporally extended agency. This is true even for those evaluative attitudes that both have agential authority and track the good: their agential authority derives from their non-Platonic psychological role. And the normal hierarchical structure of self-governing policies helps them play these Lockean organizing roles.

Essay 12: "Temptation Revisited" extends the accounts of valuing and of agential authority to puzzles about rational willpower in the face of temptation. It explores two approaches, one that focuses on the agential authority of certain policies of action, and one that focuses on the reasonable stability of such policies. In each case we seek to understand the implications of basic features of our temporally extended planning agency for the rationality of certain forms of willpower.

Essay 13: "Shared Valuing and Frameworks for Practical Reasoning" extends the account of valuing to the case of shared valuing. It does this, in part, by drawing on the approach to shared agency that I have sketched in an earlier series of essays.[22] Central elements in this model of shared agency include ideas of (a) interlocking intentions, and of (b) intentions in favor of meshing subplans. (a) is an analogue of the semantic temporal cross-reference highlighted in the account of the Lockean ties central to agential authority in the individual case. (b) involves an analogue of the demand of consistency on an individual's intentions and plans. Shared valuing involves interlocking policies of treating, in ways that mesh, certain considerations as justifying in relevant shared deliberation and practical reasoning.

This extension to shared valuing points to an approach to shared governance that to some extent parallels the proposed theory of individual self-governance. Such an approach to shared governance would involve accounts of shared agential authority and of shared subjective normative authority that draw both on the accounts of agential authority and of subjective normative authority in the individual case, and on the general

22. *Faces of Intention*, essays 5–8.

approach to sharing developed in my earlier essays. These are, however, matters for further research.[23, 24]

3. ACKNOWLEDGMENTS AND SOURCES

This introduction, the appendix to essay 6, and essay 12 appear here for the first time. The remaining essays have been published previously. Within each of the two parts, the essays appear in more or less the order in which they were written. I have updated references and corrected an occasional minor infelicity; but I have refrained from substantive revision of already published essays. In leaving each essay capable of standing on its own, I also leave a certain amount of repetition across the essays, repetition for which I ask the reader's patience.

It will be clear to the reader that my efforts are deeply indebted to the work of Harry Frankfurt, J. David Velleman, and Gary Watson. In each case, their insightful and probing work has helped shaped our understanding of many of the problems and issues that I address in these essays. And I have also had the privilege of, and greatly benefited from, their philosophical friendship over the years. Throughout the entire course of my work on this project, I have also had the invaluable benefit of ongoing discussions and interactions with Gideon Yaffe. During roughly the second half of this project I benefited in significant ways from discussions with my Stanford colleagues Nadeem Hussain and Agnieszka Jaworska. And I want to thank Jennifer Morton for preparing the index.

Much of the work on these essays was done during two different fellowship years at the Center for Advanced Study in the Behavioral Science, made possible by financial support provided by the Andrew W. Mellon Foundation. Another substantial component of this work was made possible by a fellowship from the John Simon Guggenheim Memorial Foundation. I am deeply grateful to these wonderful institutions for their support. I am similarly grateful to Stanford University, and to my colleagues and students in the Philosophy Department, for their many forms of philosophical

23. I take some initial steps in "Dynamics of Sociality," *Midwest Studies in Philosophy* xxx (2006): 1–15.

24. Thanks to Agnieszka Jaworska and Gideon Yaffe for helpful comments on an earlier draft of this Introduction.

stimulation, encouragement, and support over the years. And, as before, my deepest thanks go to my family: Susan, Gregory, and Scott.

I am grateful for permission to reprint those essays that have been previously published. The original locations of the essays are as follows:

2. "Reflection, Planning, and Temporally Extended Agency," *The Philosophical Review* 109 (2000) : 35–61. By permission of *The Philosophical Review*.

3. "Valuing and the Will" *Philosophical Perspectives: Action and Freedom* 14 (2000): 249–65.

4. "Hierarchy, Circularity, and Double Reduction," in S. Buss and L. Overton, eds., *Contours of Agency: Essays on Themes from Harry Frankfurt* (Cambridge, MA: MIT Press, 2002): 65–85. By permission of The MIT Press.

5. "Two Problems about Human Agency," *Proceedings of the Aristotelian Society* 101 (2001): 309–26. © The Aristotelian Society 2001.

6. "Nozick on Free Will," in David Schmidtz, ed., *Robert Nozick* (New York: Cambridge University Press, 2002): 155–74. Reprinted with the permission of Cambridge University Press. Appendix: "Nozick, Free Will, and the Problem of Agential Authority" [Originally prepared for presentation at the University of Santa Clara Conference on the Philosophy of Robert Nozick, May 2005. Not previously published.]

7. "A Desire of One's Own," *The Journal of Philosophy* (2003): 221–42. By permission of *The Journal of Philosophy*.

8. "Autonomy and Hierarchy," in Ellen Frankel Paul, Fred D. Miller, Jr., and Jeffrey Paul, eds., *Autonomy* (New York: Cambridge University Press, 2003), 156–76. Reprinted with the permission of Cambridge University Press.

9. "Three Forms of Agential Commitment: Reply to Cullity and Gerrans," *Proceedings of the Aristotelian Society* 104 (2004), pp. 329–37. © The Aristotelian Society 2004.

10. "Planning Agency, Autonomous Agency" in James Stacey Taylor, ed., *Personal Autonomy* (New York: Cambridge University Press, 2005): 33–57. Reprinted with the permission of Cambridge University Press.

11. "Three Theories of Self-Governance." Forthcoming in *Philosophical Topics* 32:1 and 2 (2004). By permission of *Philosophical Topics*.

12. "Temptation Revisited." Not previously published. An earlier version was written for and presented at the 2002 Amsterdam Workshop on Intention and Rationality. This final version was written for and is forthcoming in a volume of essays associated with that workshop: Bruno Verbeek, ed., *Reasons and Intentions* (Aldershot, etc.: Ashgate, forthcoming). (A brief synopsis of some of the arguments in this paper, "Personal Rules and Rational Willpower," is in *San Diego Law Review* 42 [2005]: 61–68.)

13. "Shared Valuing and Frameworks for Practical Reasoning," in R. Jay Wallace, Philip Pettit, Samuel Scheffler, and Michael Smith, eds., *Reason and Value: Themes from the Moral Philosophy of Joseph Raz* (Oxford: Oxford University Press, 2004), 1–27. By permission of Oxford University Press.

PART I

Planning, Temporally Extended
Agency, and Self-Governance

Chapter 2

REFLECTION, PLANNING, AND TEMPORALLY EXTENDED AGENCY

I. CORE FEATURES OF HUMAN AGENCY

We are purposive agents; but we—adult humans in a broadly modern world—are more than that. We are reflective about our motivation. We form prior plans and policies that organize our activity over time. And we see ourselves as agents who persist over time and who begin, develop, and then complete temporally extended activities and projects. Any reasonably complete theory of human action will need, in some way, to advert to this trio of features—to our reflectiveness, our planfulness, and our conception of our agency as temporally extended. These are, further, features that have great significance for the kinds of lives we can live. For these two reasons I will say that these are among the *core* features of human

Thanks to Nomy Arpaly, Lawrence Beyer, David Copp, John Fischer, Matthew Hanser, Paul Hoffman, David V. Johnson, Keith Lehrer, Christopher McMahon, Elijah Millgram, Jennifer Rosner, Timothy Schroeder, J. David Velleman, the editors of the *Philosophical Review*, and audiences at Ohio State University, University of California at Riverside, University of Aarhus, University of Copenhagen, University of Lund, Stanford University, University of Michigan (during my visit as James B. and Grace J. Nelson Philosopher-in-Residence), University of California at Santa Barbara, University of Toronto, and the 1999 Inland Northwest Philosophy Conference for helpful comments. Very special thanks to Gideon Yaffe for a series of extremely useful and probing discussions. Initial work on this essay was done while I had the privilege of being a Fellow at the Center for Advanced Study in the Behavioral Sciences. I am grateful for financial support provided by the Andrew W. Mellon Foundation.

agency.[1] A theory of human action needs to say what these core features consist in and how they are related to one another. And such a theory needs also to clarify the relation between these core features of our agency and the possibility that we are fully embedded in an event causal order.

I begin by focusing on our reflectiveness about our motivation. But I am led fairly quickly to our planfulness and to our closely related conception of our agency as temporally extended, for it is in part by appeal to these latter features that we best understand our reflectiveness. Or so I argue.

2. THE AGENT'S REFLECTIVE ENDORSEMENT: AUTHORITY AND EXPLANATORY POWER

Begin with our reflectiveness. Many philosophers have emphasized that we have the capacity not merely to be moved by our desires and inclinations. We have the capacity to step back and reflect on our desires and inclinations.[2] We have the capacity to arrive at assessments of those desires and inclinations, assessments that can shape our deliberation, our motivation, and our conduct. One aspect of this capacity is the capacity to arrive at higher-order attitudes concerning a desire or inclination to act in a certain way.[3] Faced with a desire to stare at a scene whose very horror fascinates—as in the case of Leontius in Plato's *Republic*[4]—one might arrive, in particular, at a second-order desire that that desire neither play a reason-giving role in one's

---

1. Purposiveness, too, is such a core feature; but it is a feature we share with many other nonhuman agents. The trio of features just cited—reflectiveness, planfulness, and a conception of our agency as temporally extended—seems to be significantly closer to being distinctive of human agency. It may be, though, that we sometimes do things that are merely purposive and that do not involve these distinctive capacities.

Let me also note explicitly that I make no attempt here to provide a complete list of core features.

2. For important recent examples see, for example, Harry Frankfurt, *The Importance of What We Care About* (Cambridge: Cambridge University Press, 1988); J. David Velleman, "What Happens When Someone Acts?" *Mind* 101 (1992): 462–81; Christine Korsgaard, *The Sources of Normativity* (Cambridge: Cambridge University Press, 1996); Keith Lehrer, "Freedom, Preference and Autonomy," *Journal of Ethics* 1 (1997): 3–25; Stuart Hampshire, "Two Kinds of Explanation," in his *Morality and Conflict* (Oxford: Basil Blackwell, 1983), 69–81.

3. Such hierarchies of desires have been emphasized by, in particular, the work of Harry Frankfurt. See especially his *The Importance of What We Care About*.

4. *Republic* 4.440a: "overpowered in spite of all by his desire, with wide staring eyes he rushed up to the corpses and cried, There, ye wretches, take your fill of the fine spectacle!" (trans. Paul Shorey, in *The Collected Dialogues of Plato*, ed. Edith Hamilton and Huntington Cairns [New York:

deliberation nor control one's action. Other examples—most taken from
the recent literature—include higher-order desires concerning first-order
desires to seek revenge, to issue a cutting remark, to take a drug to which
one is addicted, to slap one's screaming two-year-old, to procrastinate, to
pursue certain sexual temptations, and to tell a lying promise.[5] But the
capacity to arrive at such higher-order desires is not all there is to our
reflective capacity.[6] We have what seems to be the further capacity to take a
stand, as an agent, with respect to relevant functioning of a given desire.[7] If,
like Leontius, I desire to stare at a particularly gruesome scene, but also desire
that this desire not control my conduct, then I have two relevant desires,
one first-order, the other second-order. My second-order desire manifests
one aspect of my capacity for reflection. But this second-order desire is itself
just one more desire in, as we might say, the psychic stew. By itself it does not
yet fully manifest my capacity for a kind of endorsement or rejection of my
first-order desire that constitutes *my* endorsement or rejection of—my
taking sides, my taking a stand with respect to—that desire.[8] After all, as
Gary Watson noted in response to Harry Frankfurt's early and seminal work
on these matters, we have as yet no reason for saying that, in the face of such
conflict, I am on the side of my second-order desire, rather than saying that I
am on the side of my first-order desire.[9]

Let us call the capacity to have higher-order pro or con attitudes concerning our first-order desires the capacity for *weak* reflectiveness. And let

---

Pantheon Books, 1966]). For an extremely helpful discussion of the case of Leontius see John M.
Cooper, "Plato's Theory of Human Motivation," *History of Philosophy Quarterly* 1 (1984): 3–21.

5. For what are more or less versions of examples 2–7 see respectively Harry Frankfurt, *The
Importance of What We Care About*, 67 and 17; Gary Watson, "Free Agency," in Gary Watson, ed. *Free
Will* (New York: Oxford University Press, 1982), 96–110, at 100–101; Thomas Schelling, "Ethics, Law
and the Exercise of Self-Command," in his *Choice and Consequence* (Cambridge, MA: Harvard
University Press, 1984), 83–112, at 90–91; John McDowell, "Are Moral Requirements Categorical
Imperatives?" *Proceedings Aristotelian Society* suppl. vol. 52 (1978): 13–29, at 27; Immanuel Kant,
Groundwork of the Metaphysic of Morals, trans. H. J. Paton (New York: Harper and Row, 1964), 89–90.

6. As Frankfurt has noted. See *The Importance of What We Care About*, 166.

7. Cp. Frankfurt's appeal to "where . . . the person himself stands" in *The Importance of What
We Care About*, 166; and see his similar remark in his "The Faintest Passion," *Proceedings and
Addresses of the American Philosophical Association* 66 (1992): 5–16, reprinted in his *Necessity, Volition, and
Love* (Cambridge: Cambridge University Press, 1999), 95–107, at 100.

8. Of course, even if I reflectively reject a desire, it remains my desire in a straightforward,
literal sense. See Frankfurt, *The Importance of What We Care About*, 18.

9. Watson writes: "the notion of orders of desires or volitions . . . does not tell us why or
how a particular want can have, among all of a person's 'desires,' the special property of being

us call the capacity to take a stand as an agent—to determine where *I* stand with respect to a given first-order desire—the capacity for *strong* reflectiveness.

A capacity for weak reflectiveness goes beyond what is strictly necessary for purposive agency. There can be purposive agents—cats and dogs, perhaps—who are not even capable of weak reflectiveness. But weak reflectiveness is, by itself, not yet strong reflectiveness.

Now, the idea of weak reflectiveness does seem fairly clear: a capacity for weak reflectiveness is a capacity for higher-order desires or other pro or con attitudes about one's first-order desires or inclinations. In contrast, the idea of strong reflectiveness can seem puzzling. How can we say in what strong reflective endorsement consists except by citing some complex of attitudes, including higher-order pro and/or con attitudes? But each such attitude seems itself to be just one more wiggle in the psychic stew. How could some complex of such attitudes constitute the agent's endorsement or rejection of a form of motivation? How could we get from the fact that certain *attitudes* favor a form of motivation to the fact that the *agent* endorses that motivation?

As J. David Velleman has emphasized, such reflections can lead us to a view—broadly in the spirit of work of Roderick Chisholm—that phenomena of an agent stepping back and endorsing or rejecting certain desires are simply not reducible to complexes of attitudes.[10] The agent who endorses or rejects a desire must be seen as a separate element in the metaphysics of our agency. Endorsement as a relation between agent and desire is, on this view, basic and not reducible to endorsements as relations among attitudes—endorsements as relations, for example, between second-order and first-order desires. But this seems a case of jumping from the frying pan into the fire. One problem is that it is difficult to know what it means to say that the agent—as distinct from relevant psychological events, processes, and

peculiarly his 'own,' " ("Free Agency," at 108; see also Watson, "Free Action and Free Will," *Mind* 96 [1987]: 145–72, at 149). Frankfurt acknowledges the point in *The Importance of What We Care About,* 166.

10. See Chisholm, "Freedom and Action," in *Freedom and Determinism,* ed. Keith Lehrer (New York: Random House, 1966), 11–44; *Person and Object* (London: Allen and Unwin, 1976), chap. 2; and "Comments and Replies," *Philosophia* 7 (1978): 597–636. Velleman's discussion is in his "What Happens When Someone Acts?"—an essay to which I am throughout much indebted.

states—plays such a basic role in the etiology and explanation of action. Second, and relatedly, in seeing the agent as a fundamentally separate and distinct element in the metaphysics of our action we seem to abandon the idea that our agency is as fully embedded in the event causal order as is the agency of purposive agents like dogs and cats. We are no doubt importantly different from dogs and cats; and the trio of core features of our agency that are my concern here are strong candidates for salient differences. But I would like to say what this difference is without abandoning the idea that we are all part of the same event causal order.

This is no easy task. Talk of the agent's strong endorsement of a desire points to a potential *explanation* of action, of why the agent acts as she does. Explanations of occurrences normally appeal to other occurrences—other events, states, processes, and the like.[11] That is a reason why appeals to the agent as cause seem problematic when offered as explanations. Yet when we make such appeals to other occurrences, we seem to risk giving up the idea that what explains action has, as we might say, the *authority* to ensure or constitute the *agent's* endorsement.[12] What ensures or constitutes the agent's endorsement needs to have both explanatory power and authority. Our problem is to explain how this could be.[13]

Chisholm's primary concern is with the idea of an agent bringing something about, as when—to use Chisholm's example—Jones kills his uncle. Chisholm believes that any adequate account of this will appeal to a nonreducible "residue of agent causation" ("Replies," 623). My concern here is with the idea of an agent's endorsement of her motivation. I want to know whether we can escape an analogous view that an account of such endorsement must appeal to a nonreducible "residue of agent causation." Velleman identifies these two issues about the agent ("What Happens When Someone Acts?" 470). This may not be quite right, since a weak-willed agent who acts on nonendorsed motivation may, it seems, still be an agent cause in Chisholm's sense. (Such a weak-willed agent may, it seems, "undertake" things, in Chisholm's sense; and that is enough to be an agent cause in Chisholm's sense ["Replies," 623–25].) Nevertheless, I agree with Velleman that the parallel between the two issues is close and revealing. Given this close parallel, it seems reasonable to describe the view, that there is a nonreducible role for the agent in endorsement, as broadly in the spirit of Chisholm's work. (Thanks to Randolph Clarke for raising this issue of interpretation.)

11. See Velleman, "What Happens When Someone Acts?" 467.

12. I do not say that the agent literally is those attitudes that ensure or constitute her endorsement. I seek, rather, necessary and sufficient conditions, among the agent's attitudes, for the truth of claims of the form "Agent *S* endorses desire *D*."

13. John Barth's novel *The End of the Road* (New York: Doubleday, Bantam edition, 1967) offers a fascinating example of this problem. My efforts here to solve this problem are to some extent a continuation and development (with changes) of my discussion in "Identification, Decision,

3. PLANNING AGENCY

A first step is to turn to the second of our core features: our planning agency. In earlier work I have focused on the central roles of plans and planning in our agency, and I have developed what I have called a planning theory of intention.[14] We do not simply act from moment to moment. Instead, we settle on complex—and, typically, partial and hierarchically structured—future-directed plans of action, and these play basic roles in support of the organization and coordination of our activities over time. In settling on a prior plan of action, one commits oneself to the plan— though of course one's commitment is normally not irrevocable, and new information can make it imperative to reconsider and abandon a prior plan. Prior plans have, in this sense, a certain stability: there is, normally, rational pressure not to reconsider and/or abandon a prior plan.[15] Prior partial plans are, further, subject to rational demands of consistency and of means-end rationality, demands—in the second case—for what I have called means-end coherence.[16] Because of these normative demands, plans

and Treating as a Reason," *Philosophical Topics* (1996): 1–18 [reprinted in my *Faces of Intention: Selected Essays on Intention and Agency* (New York: Cambridge University Press, 1999], 185–206). I also develop related ideas in "Valuing and the Will," *Philosophical Perspectives* 14 (2000): 249–65 [this volume, essay 3], and "Hierarchy, Circularity, and Double Reduction," in *Contours of Agency: Essays on the Philosophy of Harry Frankfurt*, ed. S. Buss and L. Overton (Cambridge, MA: MIT Press, 2002), 65–85 [this volume, essay 4].

14. See in particular my *Intention, Plans, and Practical Reason* (Cambridge, MA: Harvard University Press, 1987; reissued in 1999 by CSLI Publications, Stanford, California) and my *Faces of Intention*.

In his thoughtful review of *Intention, Plans, and Practical Reason*, J. David Velleman writes: "an understanding of intention requires an understanding of our freedom or autonomy. And I think that Bratman's account of intention falls short in some respects because he tries to study intention in isolation from such questions about the fundamental nature of agency" (*Philosophical Review* [1991]: 277–84, at 283). My strategy in the present essay is to some extent a partial response to this concern. I take as given my earlier defense of the planning theory as a theoretical approach to intention. I try to use this account of intention to shed light on other core features of our agency, though I stop short of a complete view about the nature of autonomy or self-determination. If I am successful, this would be a further argument in favor of the planning theory.

15. It is a difficult problem to say exactly what is involved in such stability for a rational agent. For my efforts on this problem, see my *Intention, Plans, and Practical Reason*, my "Toxin, Temptation, and the Stability of Intention," in *Rational Commitment and Social Justice: Essays for Gregory S. Kavka*, ed. Jules Coleman and Christopher Morris (New York: Cambridge University Press, 1998), 59–83 (reprinted in *Faces of Intention*, 58–90), and my "Temptation Revisited" [this volume, essay 12]. I think that the present discussion of the agent's endorsement may have implications for our view of rational stability. See "Temptation Revisited."

16. The idea of appealing to coherence constraints associated with one's intentions and plans derives from Gilbert Harman, "Practical Reasoning," *Review of Metaphysics* 29 (1976): 431–63.

introduce characteristic forms of practical reasoning: plans provide a somewhat stable background framework that needs to be filled in appropriately with specifications of means and the like.

Plans typically concern relatively specific courses of action extended over time. It is important, though, that sometimes one's commitment is to a certain kind of action on certain kinds of potentially recurrent occasions—for example, to buckling up one's seat belt when one drives, or to having at most one beer at dinner. Such general commitments are *policies*.[17]

In recognizing the organizing and coordinating roles of plans and policies, we go beyond a standard desire-belief conception of our agency.[18] Intentions, plans, and policies are all pro attitudes in a very general sense. But they differ in basic ways from ordinary desires: in particular, they are subject to distinctive rational norms of consistency, coherence, and stability. In giving plans and policies a basic explanatory role in our theory of human action we remain, however, within a causal view of human action, one that avoids seeing the agent as a distinct element in the etiology of action. We provide room for what we might naturally call "the will" without appealing to what Donald Davidson labels "mysterious acts of will."[19] In this sense, the planning theory partly constitutes a modest theory of the will.[20]

Harman, however, tried in that essay to do this in terms of a demand for explanatory coherence on the beliefs associated with intentions. I argued ("Intention and Means-End Reasoning," *Philosophical Review* 90 (1981): 252–65, esp. 255–56 n. 4) that such an appeal to *explanatory coherence* does not adequately capture the relevant demands of instrumental reason. That was the reason I introduced "means-end coherence" as a demand directly on the agent's plans, given his beliefs about how his plans need to be filled in to be executed successfully. For complexities about the very idea of an intended means see my *Intention, Plans, and Practical Reason*, chap 10; Gilbert Harman, *Change in View* (Cambridge, MA: MIT Press, 1986), chap. 9; and Michael Gorr, "Should the Law Distinguish between Intention and (mere) Foresight?" *Legal Theory* 2 (1996): 359–80, esp. 360–66.

17. See my *Intention, Plans, and Practical Reason*, 87–91, and my "Intention and Personal Policies," *Philosophical Perspectives* 3 (1989): 443–69, esp. 455–61. See also J. David Velleman, *Practical Reflection* (Princeton, NJ: Princeton University Press, 1989), 307–8.

18. This emphasis on the coordinating roles of plans and policies points toward a partial parallel with Allan Gibbard's "normative psychology" in his *Wise Choices, Apt Feelings: A Theory of Normative Judgment* (Cambridge, MA: Harvard University Press, 1990). Gibbard argues that "something like the ordinary notion of 'accepting a norm' must figure in an adequate human psychology." And Gibbard emphasizes the coordination functions of such norm acceptance (61).

19. See his "Intending," in his *Essays on Actions and Events* (New York: Oxford University Press, 1980), 83.

20. I make this point also in my introduction to *Faces of Intention*, at 5. Though I cannot develop the point here, I think this approach to the will is in tension with Kantian views that

Now, our planfulness and our reflectiveness may seem at first sight to be very different aspects of our agency. Our planfulness helps us project our agency in an organized way over time; our reflectiveness helps us, at any particular time, step back, assess our motivation, and take a stand. In each case there is a kind of hierarchy, but the hierarchies are different.[21] Our plans involve a hierarchy of ends and means; our reflective endorsements involve hierarchies of higher-order pro and con attitudes. One might be a nonreflective but planning agent. It also may seem that one might be reflective about one's motivation at any one time and yet not be a planner who projects her agency over time.

I believe, however, that this last appearance is misleading. I think that there is an important relation between our strong reflectiveness and our planfulness. To defend this idea, though, I need first to turn to the third of the core features noted at the outset: our understanding of our agency as temporally extended.

4. TEMPORALLY EXTENDED AGENCY

I see my activity of, say, writing a paper as something I do over an extended period of time. I see myself as beginning the project, developing it over time, and (finally!) completing it. I see the agent of these various activities as one and the same agent—namely, me. In the middle of the project I see myself as the agent who began the project and (I hope) the agent who will complete it. Upon completion, I take pride in the fact that *I* began, worked on, and completed this essay. Of course, there is a sense in which when I act, I act at a particular time; but in acting I do not see myself, the agent of

---

see a tie to universal principles of action as a crucial defining feature of the will. Korsgaard, for example, writes that "it is the claim to universality that *gives* me a will, that makes my will distinguishable from the operation of desires and impulses in me" (*Sources of Normativity*, 232). The planning theory, in contrast, cites other defining features of intentions that distinguish them from ordinary desires and impulses (though it can still acknowledge that in defending one's plans one will normally appeal to principles that are in some way general). A basic appeal of the planning theory is to connections and constraints across more-or-less singular intentions that are elements of larger coordinating plans for action over time. I develop this point a bit further in my "Hierarchy, Circularity, and Double Reduction," where I explore what I call "singular commitments."

21. I discuss this point in my "Responsibility and Planning," *Journal of Ethics* 1 (1997): 27–43 (reprinted in my *Faces of Intention*, 165–84, at 167–68).

the act, as simply a time-slice agent. I see my action at that time as the action of the same agent as he who has acted in the past and (it is to be hoped) will act in the future.[22] In this respect I differ importantly from those nonhuman agents who do not have the resources to understand their own agency as temporally extended.[23]

In understanding my agency in this way, I am getting at an important truth: one and the same agent—me—begins, develops, and completes temporally extended and coordinated activities and projects; my agency is, in this sense, temporally extended. How should we understand this truth?

Locke and today's Lockeans have argued that the identity of a person over time consists primarily in overlapping strands of various kinds of psychological ties—in Derek Parfit's terminology, overlapping strands of psychological connectedness.[24] Locke, as he is normally interpreted, focused on backward-looking memory. Today's Lockeans introduce, in addition to memory, forward-looking connections like those between a prior intention and its later execution, and continuities in desires and the like.[25]

There are, of course, many hard questions and problems to be confronted by such a broadly Lockean approach.[26] But for present purposes I am going to suppose that some such approach is available to us, at least provisionally, as part of a view of our temporally extended agency.

The next step is terminological. Parfit includes among "direct psychological connections . . . those which hold when a belief, or a desire, or

22. See my *Intention, Plans, and Practical Reason*, 78–79, and my "Responsibility and Planning," in *Faces of Intention*, at 179. Consider also Elijah Millgram's observation: "For first-person practical deliberation to have a point, the deliberating agent must be presumed to be around in the future in which the plans and policies that are deliberatively arrived at are to be implemented" (*Practical Induction* [Cambridge, MA: Harvard University Press, 1997], 66).

23. See J. David Velleman, "Well-Being and Time," *Pacific Philosophical Quarterly* 72 (1991): 48–77, at 68; and see John Locke, *An Essay concering Human Understanding*, bk. 2, chap. 27, sec. 9.

24. Derek Parfit, *Reasons and Persons* (New York: Oxford University Press, 1984), 206–8. Parfit, though, famously argues that "personal identity is not what matters" (217).

25. For an appeal to continuities of character see A. Quinton, "The Soul," *Journal of Philosophy* 59 (1962): 393–409, reprinted in *Personal Identity*, ed. John Perry (Berkeley: University of California Press, 1975), 53–72.

26. One question is whether a Lockean approach should see the persistence of a person over time as a case of what David Lewis calls "perdurance." (See Lewis's discussion of the contrast between "perdurance" and "endurance" in his *On the Plurality of Worlds* [New York: Basil Blackwell, 1986], 202–20.) I do not try to settle this question here.

any other psychological feature, continues to be had."[27] However, as Gideon Yaffe helped me see, it is a bit misleading to call such continuities of belief or desire "connections." In the case of a prior intention and its later intentional execution, each includes something like a reference to the other: the earlier intention refers to a relevant type of action, one instance of which is the later intentional execution; and the later intentional execution is understood by the agent as an execution of that prior intention.[28] In this sense there is a kind of referential connection in the case of earlier intention and later intentional execution that need not be present in the mere continuity of a desire. My later desire to be kind need not be connected in this sense to my earlier desire to be kind, though there is here a continuity of desire. Accordingly, I will label as "continuities" such continuities of desire or the like, and I will reserve talk of "connections" for those cases—like that of memory or of later intentional execution of an earlier intention—in which there really is some sort of temporal cross-reference.[29]

I want now to emphasize a feature of the Lockean approach that becomes more salient with the introduction into the picture of forward-looking psychological ties. The feature I have in mind is that, to some extent, the presence or absence of such psychological ties is a (sometimes intentional) result of the agent's activity.[30] Return to me and my ongoing project of paper-writing. I see the agent of the various temporal stages of this coordinated project as one and the same agent, me. But this need not be simply a passive observation. In pursuit of coordination I can help ensure appropriate psychological continuities and connections by sticking with and executing my prior plans and policies and by monitoring and

27. *Reasons and Persons*, 205–6.

28. Perhaps we should also say that the execution is intended by the agent to be an execution of that prior intention; but this is not a matter we need settle here. For a view along these lines see Carl Ginet, *On Action* (New York: Cambridge University Press, 1990), 143.

29. My memory of an earlier event involves some sort of reference to the past, and so involves a connection in the relevant sense. Note though that normally there is in the case of memory only a reference from present to past, whereas in the case of prior intention and later intentional execution there is normally reference in both directions.

30. Cp. Elijah Millgram: "unified agency is an achievement." See his "Incommensurability and Practical Reasoning," in *Incommensurability, Incomparability, and Practical Reason*, ed. Ruth Chang (Cambridge, MA: Harvard University Press, 1997), 151–69, at 162.

regulating my motivational structures in favor, say, of my continued commitment to philosophy.

We need, however, to be careful here. We do not want simply to say that *I* stand back from these motivational structures, monitor them, and, if they start to get out of line, intervene in pursuit of coordinating, Lockean ties; for this threatens to be just a temporally extended version of the picture of the agent as a separate and distinct element in the metaphysics of action. And that is a picture that we have tried to resist. We need, rather, to understand what constitutes my monitoring of motivational structures over time in pursuit of such Lockean ties. To do this we will want to appeal to relevant states and attitudes that play appropriate roles in the agent's psychology.[31] In particular, we will want to appeal to states and attitudes whose primary roles include the support of coordination by way of the constitution and support of connections and continuities, which, on a broadly Lockean view, help constitute the identity of the agent over time.

And now the point to note is that appeal to attitudes that play such roles can help us in our pursuit of the idea of an agent's reflective endorsement: if such attitudes were to support relevant functioning[32] of a given desire of the agent, there would be a case for saying that the *agent* endorses that desire. After all, the agent is not a time-slice agent. She is, rather, and understands herself to be, a temporally persisting agent, one whose agency is temporally extended. This makes it natural to suppose that for her to endorse a desire is, roughly, for that desire to be endorsed by attitudes whose role it is to support the temporal organization of her agency by way of constituting and supporting Lockean ties characteristic of her temporal persistence.[33]

31. This is in the spirit of Velleman's pursuit of "events and states to play the role of the agent" in "What Happens When Someone Acts?" 475. But Velleman and I identify different roles for this job.

32. I discuss which functioning is *relevant* functioning in section 7, below.

33. There are parallels here with aspects of Korsgaard's views about relations between reflection and the agent's conception of her identity over time. See her *Sources of Normativity*, esp. chap. 3. I discuss these parallels below in section 8. Gideon Yaffe discusses an alternative way of connecting conditions of, as he says, "agency at its best" and a Lockean view of personal identity in his *Liberty Worth the Name: Locke on Free Agency* (Princeton, NJ: Princeton University Press, 2000).

This is, so far, no more than a sketch. But I think it does point to a suggestive idea. The idea is first to determine what attitudes have it as a primary role to constitute and support Lockean ties of a sort that are characteristic of our temporally extended agency. We then appeal to the fact that the actor is, and understands herself to be, a temporally persisting agent whose agency is temporally extended to argue that some such attitudes can help determine where the agent stands at a time. We tackle the problem of where the agent stands *at a time* by appeal to roles of attitudes in creating broadly Lockean conditions of identity of the agent *over time*.

That is the idea. But what attitudes are these?

5. PLANS AND SELF-GOVERNING POLICIES

Return to our planfulness. A primary way in which we achieve organization and coordination of our activities over time is by way of settling on prior plans and policies. In the most straightforward cases, these are plans and policies that directly concern action: a plan for writing the paper, say, or a policy of writing every morning for at least two hours. Such plans and policies induce overlapping webs of cross-temporal connections and continuities. One's present intentional act may involve an intention that refers to a larger plan or policy in which it is embedded. I might, for example, see my writing this morning as embedded in a larger pattern of activity in which it is my policy to engage. Or I might see my writing chapter 2 as part of a larger planned project to write a book. My larger plan or policy involves references to past and/or future intentions and intentional activities. Further, the characteristic stability of such intentions and policies normally induces relevant psychological continuities of intention and the like. In these ways our plans and policies play an important role in the constitution and support of continuities and connections characteristic of the identity of the agent over time.

Indeed, this is part of what plans and policies are *for*. Such plans and policies have as their function the support of cross-temporal organization and coordination of action in part by inducing cross-temporal connections (for example, between prior plans or policies and later action, and between present intentional action and, later, planned activity) and continuities (for example, of stable plans and policies). A point of having plans and policies is to induce organization and coordination by way of such continuities and connections.

Now, in weak reflection, we arrive at higher-order pro or con attitudes concerning our motivation. When we add our planfulness to such weak reflection, we introduce the possibility that in some cases these higher-order pro or con attitudes will be, more specifically, higher-order policies.[34] And, indeed, we do seem on occasion to arrive at such higher-order policies. One might have, say, a policy of developing and supporting a strong concern with honesty in writing, of trying to be more willing to be playful or less inclined to be impatient with others, of trying not to be so attracted to chocolates or to other temptations, or of never acting on or treating as providing a legitimate consideration in one's deliberation a desire for revenge or a desire to demean. We may call such higher-order policies *self-governing* policies.[35] Such policies are, I think, a key to a solution to our problem about strong reflectiveness.

6. THE AGENT'S REFLECTIVE ENDORSEMENT: AN INITIAL PROPOSAL

We have been looking for attitudes whose endorsement or rejection of relevant functioning of a desire can constitute the agent's endorsement or rejection of that desire. The agent is, and understands herself to be, a temporally persisting agent whose agency is temporally extended. That is why we have been looking for higher-order attitudes whose roles are appropriately connected to the temporally extended structure of our agency. Our discussion suggests that relevant self-governing policies are such attitudes.

Self-governing policies are embedded in a planning framework whose organizing roles involve the constitution and support of Lockean continuities and connections characteristic of temporally extended agency. Further, such policies—unlike intentions and plans that concern only particular occasions—are explicitly concerned with the functioning of relevant desires

---

34. In my "Valuing and the Will," I treat this transition to higher-order policies as a step in Gricean "creature construction." See Paul Grice, "Method in Philosophical Psychology (From the Banal to the Bizarre)," *Proceedings of the American Philosophical Association* (1974–75): 23–53.

35. This is an extension of terminology I introduced in *Intention, Plans, and Practical Reason*, 159.

generally in one's temporally extended life. Their role includes the support of certain temporally extended and coordinated patterns of functioning of those desires. This suggests that the agent's reflective endorsement or rejection of a desire can be to a significant extent constituted by ways in which her self-governing policies are committed to treating that desire over time. She endorses or rejects a desire, roughly, when relevant self-governing policies endorse or reject relevant functioning of the desire.

But could one not have a self-governing policy from which one is estranged? This aspect of the problem of authority is endemic to appeals to hierarchies of higher-order attitudes. And ever since Frankfurt's early discussion of such hierarchies, we have known that we cannot respond simply by appealing to yet higher-order attitudes, for that would threaten a regress. But at this point we can draw on a different Frankfurtian move. In his American Philosophical Association Presidential Address, Frankfurt noted how such a regress could be blocked by appeal to a structural feature of the agent's psychology, a feature he called "satisfaction" with relevant attitudes.[36] Frankfurt focused on satisfaction with a hierarchy of desires: an agent is satisfied with such a hierarchy, roughly, when she is, on reflection, not moved to try to change it. Elsewhere I have appealed to cases of "enervation or exhaustion or depression" to argue that such satisfaction with a hierarchy of desires may not be sufficiently decisive to address problems about authority.[37] To this let me add that the addition of a satisfaction condition to hierarchies of *desires* still does not ensure an appropriate link to attitudes central to the temporally extended structure of our agency. But we can avoid both these difficulties, and make progress with worries about possible estrangement from one's policies, by appealing, instead, to satisfaction with a self-governing *policy*.

How should we understand such satisfaction? On the one hand, we do not want to preclude all psychological conflict. If satisfaction with one's policy is to be characteristic of strong reflective endorsement, it should be possible to be satisfied with a self-governing policy even though one

---

36. "The Faintest Passion," in *Necessity, Volition, and Love*, 103–5.

37. "Identification, Decision, and Treating as a Reason," in *Faces of Intention*, 195. For an influential but rather different appeal to cases of depression and the like see Michael Stocker, "Desiring the Bad: An Essay in Moral Psychology," *Journal of Philosophy* (1979): 738–53. J. David Velleman agrees that such cases of depression pose a challenge to Frankfurt. (See his introduction to *The Possibility of Practical Reason* [Oxford: Oxford University Press, 2000], 13.)

experiences some sorts of conflict and even violates the policy in a particular case. On the other hand, a conception of satisfaction does need to
preclude certain kinds of conflict. To say what is needed for satisfaction is
to get clear about the kinds of conflict that are compatible with, and the
kinds that are precluded by, strong reflective endorsement.

I think that, to a first approximation, what is important here is the
presence or absence of conflict with other self-governing policies. That is, to a
first approximation, one is satisfied with one's self-governing policy, P, when
one has no other self-governing policy with which P is in conflict.[38] But note
that sometimes the presence of a conflicting self-governing policy may not
actually interfere with the role of P in supporting coordination by way of
Lockean ties. Suppose, for example, an agent has both a policy, P_1, that
supports his inclination to be distrustful of strangers, and a conflicting policy,
P_2, that rejects that inclination.[39] But suppose the presence of P_2 nevertheless
does not lead him to be disposed to change P_1 and, more generally, does not
block the central organizing and coordinating roles of P_1. It is P_1 that controls
his relevant deliberation, planning, and action. His conflicting policies may
expose him to charges of criticizable inconsistency; but it still may be true
that he endorses his distrustful inclination. So let us say that self-governing
policy P^* *challenges* P when P^* is in conflict with P and, as a result, the presence
of P^* tends to undermine the role of P (perhaps by leading to a disposition to
change P) in supporting coordinating, Lockean ties. For one to be satisfied
with one's self-governing policy is, to a second approximation, for that policy
not to be challenged by one's other self-governing policies.[40]

In the end we will need a yet more complex understanding of
satisfaction. But it will be useful to work for now with the present proposal so as to see the shape of the theory that emerges.

The preliminary proposal, then, is that the agent's endorsement or rejection of a desire is ensured by the endorsement or rejection of relevant
functioning of that desire by a self-governing policy with which the agent is
satisfied. Such self-governing policies have it as part of their organizing role

38. This is similar to my treatment of satisfaction in "Identification, Decision, and Treating
as a Reason," 201.
39. This example is due to Lawrence Beyer.
40. Reflection leading to this move to a second approximation was first prompted by a
remark of Stephen Darwall. The details owe much to conversation with Gideon Yaffe.

to support a temporally extended pattern of functioning of relevant desires in ways that help constitute and support Lockean ties characteristic of our temporally extended agency.[41] And that is why they have authority to speak for the agent.

Self-governing policies are commitments that can, in an appropriate context, help determine where the agent stands with respect to certain motivation. This does not mean that these policies are immune to rational revision. One can sometimes reflectively reassess and revise where one stands. Our project is not to describe some irrevocable foundation at the bottom of all further practical reasoning; it is only to spell out what it is for an agent to take a stand in favor of or against certain motivations, a stand that can itself be subject to reexamination and revision. Self-governing policies might, so to speak, crystallize pressures from various elements of one's psychic stew into a more decisive attitude that can, in the relevant context, establish where one stands.[42] An agent's strong reflective endorsement or rejection can itself emerge—at times, tentatively—from a complex, underlying mix of thought, feeling, and inclination rather than be at the foundation of that complex mix.[43]

We wanted to explain both the authority and the explanatory power of that which ensures the agent's endorsement. Our initial proposal tries to do this by appeal to relevant self-governing policies in appropriate contexts of satisfaction. It tries to capture the authority of such policies to ensure the agent's endorsement by noting their special connection to the temporally extended structure of our agency. And it tries to capture the

41. But self-governing policies need not be full-blown plans of life in the sense developed by John Rawls in his *A Theory of Justice* (Cambridge, MA: Harvard University Press, 1971), 408–15; nor need they be what Korsgaard calls "practical conceptions of our identity" (*Sources of Normativity*, 129)—though a Rawlsian plan of life, or a Korsgaardian practical conception of one's own identity, might well involve such self-governing policies.

42. There may well be an important parallel here with Charles Taylor's talk of our efforts to arrive at "articulations" of our "largely inarticulated sense of what is of decisive importance" (Charles Taylor, "Responsibility for Self," reprinted in Gary Watson, *Free Will*, at 122–23)—though Taylor does not in this essay emphasize important coordinating roles of such, as I say, crystallizations.

43. I am sympathetic, then, to Joseph Heath's challenge to foundationalism about practical reason, though I do not endorse his proposed alternative. See his "Foundationalism and Practical Reason," *Mind* (1997): 451–73. Heath notes (463 n.)—correctly, I think—that much of Korsgaard's discussion in her *Sources of Normativity* has a foundationalist structure.

explanatory power of that which ensures the agent's endorsement in its appeal to policies that can shape reasoning and action.

7. MOTIVATION AND TREATING
AS REASON-PROVIDING

There remains a problem in spelling out the content of the relevant self-governing policies.

When a desire for X motivates an action of an adult human agent, that agent normally treats X as an end that provides at least some minimal justification for action, a justification that is available for relevant deliberation. This means that, in the normal case, the agent is to some extent aware that the desire for X is part of her motivation. It also means, I think, that the desire is not merely seen by the agent simply as something to be removed, as one might see an itch or a potential cause of future harm. Instead, the agent treats the achievement of the desired end as providing a (perhaps minimal) justification for the action, a justification that does not consist merely in the fact that the action is a way of removing that desire.

Normally, then, when one is motivated by a desire, one treats that desire as providing a justifying end. But there can also be cases in which these phenomena come apart.[44] Among such cases are ones in which a desire motivates but the agent is unaware of this,[45] and ones in which a desire motivates only because the agent aims at getting rid of the desire.[46]

---

44. For related discussions see J. David Velleman's discussion of a distinction between "the story of motivation" and "the story of rational guidance" in his "The Guise of the Good," *Noûs* 26 (1992): 3–26, esp. 3–7; and Michael Smith's discussion of the relation between the "intentional" and the "deliberative" perspectives in his "Valuing: Desiring or Believing?" in *Reduction, Explanation, and Realism*, ed. David Charles and Kathleen Lennon (Oxford: Oxford University Press, 1992), 323–59, esp. 323–29. (This essay is the basis of chapter 5 of Smith's *The Moral Problem* (Cambridge: Basil Blackwell, 1994). See also Philip Pettit and Michael Smith, "Backgrounding Desire," *Philosophical Review* 99 [1990]: 565–92.)

45. Such cases have been emphasized by J. David Velleman. In one of Velleman's examples from Freud, an agent knocks over an inkstand, and we can see that he does this as a means to his desired end of destroying the stand. But the agent is not aware that this desire to destroy the stand is motivating him. Given this lack of awareness, it seems that, though the desire motivates his purposive activity, the agent himself does not treat the desire as providing an end that to some extent justifies knocking over the stand. (See Velleman's introduction to *The Possibility of Practical Reason*. See also his "The Guise of the Good," 10, and his "The Possibility of Practical Reason," *Ethics* 106 [1996]: 694–726, at 724.)

46. See Sarah Buss, "Autonomy Reconsidered," *Midwest Studies in Philosophy* 19 (1994): 95–121, at 101–2.

This raises a question for our account of the agent's endorsement. For an agent to endorse a desire, in the sense we are after, is it enough for the agent to endorse that desire's functioning as an effective motive? Well, suppose an agent merely endorses a desire's functioning as an effective motive. So far, the agent seems to be seeing herself as a locus of causal forces and taking sides about which causal forces are to be effective. But the intuitive idea of an agent's endorsement of a desire seems to go beyond this and to include the endorsement of forms of deliberation and practical reasoning for which that desire sets an end, an end that is treated as justifying appropriate action.[47]

Suppose, for example, that I endorse the prospect that my powerful desire for an addictive drug motivate my action. I endorse this, let us suppose, only because I endorse my effort to rid myself, at least for a time, of that very desire and its threatened consequences. I endorse—as we might say—my letting off steam. But I do not endorse deliberation and practical reasoning in which I treat the end of getting the drug as an end that justifies action in a way that does not derive merely from the fact that the action will remove the desire. In such a case it seems to me that, while I endorse my letting off steam, I do not yet endorse my desire for the drug in the sense of strong endorsement we are trying to explain.

Another way to get at this point is to consider an objection to the hierarchical model that has been offered by Gilbert Harman.[48] On Harman's theory of intentional action, the involved intention is always, in part, about itself. It is an intention that this very intention issue in action. Such an intention is, among other things, a second-order pro attitude in support of that which is motivating action. If one acts intentionally one will have such a second-order pro attitude. But Frankfurt's unreflective "wanton," though he is not in the business of reflective endorsement, does act intentionally. So simply by appeal to second-order pro attitudes concerning what is to motivate one's action we do not distinguish unreflective wantons from reflective

47. There are signs that Frankfurt would agree. See, for example, *The Importance of What We Care About*, 170, where Frankfurt highlights conflicts in which what is at issue is whether a desire "is to be endorsed as a legitimate candidate for satisfaction or whether it is to be rejected as entitled to no priority whatsoever." Frankfurt's focus on desires that desires *motivate* (and in that sense be one's "will")—what he calls second-order "volitions"—may, however, be in tension with this. I return to related issues about Frankfurt's views in my "Hierarchy, Circularity, and Double Reduction."

48. "Desired Desires," in *Value, Welfare, and Morality*, ed. R. G. Frey and C. W. Morris (New York: Cambridge University Press, 1993), 138–57, at 146.

persons. Since Frankfurt supposes that it is precisely such second-order pro attitudes that distinguish unreflective wantons from reflective persons, there is a flaw in the hierarchical theory. Or so Harman maintains.

We might, of course, challenge Harman's story about the reflexivity of intention. But note that even if we accept such a story, the intention required for intentional action is not an intention that one treat one's intention as providing a justifying end. The required intention is at most an intention that it itself be an effective motive; at least, that is what we should say if we are going to apply Harman's story to the wanton's intentional action. So if the hierarchical theory of reflective endorsement appeals, in its model of the agent's reflection, to the higher-order endorsement of one's treatment of a desire as providing a justifying reason, it can avoid this objection.

Return now to the view of strong endorsement we have been developing. For the agent to endorse a desire is, to a first approximation, for that agent to have self-governing policies in favor of relevant functioning of that desire. Which functioning? Merely to endorse a desire's functioning as a motive seems not yet what we are after. Or so I have argued. But merely to endorse one's treating the desire as setting a justifying end in deliberation, without endorsing that desire's corresponding functioning as a motive (if that is possible) also seems too weak. Reflective endorsement is, after all, potentially explanatory of action. Nor will we want to understand the agent's endorsement of a desire in terms of independent endorsements of, on the one hand, its functioning as a motive and, on the other hand, one's treating it as providing a justifying reason. We want these two roles to be linked. It seems to me, then, that we should understand an agent's endorsement of a desire in terms, roughly, of a self-governing policy in favor of the agent's treatment of that desire as providing a justifying reason in motivationally efficacious practical reasoning.[49, 50] And it is, roughly,

---

49. Ideas to some extent similar to the idea of a policy that concerns one's treatment of a desire as providing a justifying reason can be found in a number of places. See, for example, Rachel Cohon, "Internalism about Reasons for Action," *Pacific Philosophical Quarterly* 74 (1993): 265–88; and Korsgaard, *Sources of Normativity*, lecture 3. There is an important discussion of related ideas in T. M. Scanlon, *What We Owe to Each Other* (Cambridge, MA: Harvard University Press, 1998), chap. 1, esp. 41–55. I have benefited from Scanlon's discussion, though I am more sanguine about the hierarchical model than he is.

50. The cited self-governing policy will frequently be associated with a policy to try to continue to have the desire; but such an associated policy is not necessary and may be absent in

a policy against treating a certain desire as providing a justifying reason in motivationally efficacious practical reasoning that is characteristic of the cases of Leontius, the unwilling addict, and the like—cases paradigmatic of the agent's rejection of a desire.

Now, Robert Nozick has highlighted the idea that certain decisions can bestow weights on various conflicting reasons under consideration: "The process of decision fixes the weights reasons are to have."[51] The self-governing policies to which I am appealing can play a similar role: they can specify whether a desired end is to be treated as justifying, and, if so, they can fix, perhaps roughly, a weight to be given to this desired end in deliberation.

To summarize the proposal so far: An agent's reflective endorsement of a desire is ensured by a self-governing policy—a policy with which the agent is satisfied—of treating that desire as providing a justifying end in motivationally effective practical reasoning.[52] Such a policy may establish relevant weights to be given to desired ends in deliberation.

Below in section 9 I will make one further modification to this proposal. But first I want briefly to consider some related work by Christine Korsgaard.

---

special cases. One may have a policy of treating a desire as reason-giving so long as one continues to have that desire, and yet not be committed to trying to maintain that desire. (Gilbert Harman discusses a case of both valuing and desiring something without desiring to continue to have that desire. He sees this case as an objection to the idea that valuing involves a higher-order pro attitude. But a corresponding objection to my account of reflective endorsement would not apply to the higher-order attitudes to which I am appealing. See Harman, "Desired Desires," at 151.)

51. See Robert Nozick, *Philosophical Explanations* (Cambridge, MA: Harvard University Press, 1981), 297. (Nozick notes relations to issues about personal identity on 306.) See also Allan Gibbard, *Wise Choices, Apt Feelings*, 163. And see this volume, essay 6.

52. Is there a criticizable circularity? An agent endorses a desire only if (roughly) she has a policy that favors her treating that desire as reason-giving in deliberation. But one might worry that for an agent to treat a desire as reason-giving essentially involves the agent's endorsement of that desire, and so there is an undesirable circularity in the account. In my "Hierarchy, Circularity, and Double Reduction," I respond to this objection. For an agent to treat a desire as reason-giving is, very roughly, for that desire to function appropriately because of the agent's intention or policy in favor of that functioning. This means that we need to say what the appropriate functioning is, and we need to do that without appeal to the very idea of the agent's endorsement. I think we can do that, and that what will be crucial will be appeal not merely to processes of motivation but also to processes of reasoning (though not to processes of reasoning that are of necessity endorsed by the agent); but I will not try to defend this here.

8. INTERLUDE: KORSGAARD, REFLECTION, AND PERSONAL IDENTITY

To solve the authority problem that is endemic to hierarchical theories, I have appealed to higher-order policies concerning what to treat as reason-giving. Such higher-order policies—understood in terms provided by the planning theory—help solve the authority problem in part because of their role in supporting organization and coordination over time by way of supporting Lockean ties at the heart of the agent's identity over time. In this way my proposal defends a version of the hierarchical approach by drawing on resources provided both by the planning theory and by a broadly Lockean approach to personal identity.

Now consider Korsgaard's work. In her discussion of a Kantian approach to related problems, Korsgaard remarks that "we impose the form of universal volitional principle on our decisions in our attempts to unify ourselves into agents or characters who persist through time."[53] In particular, universal principles that express conceptions of "practical identity"[54] are central to the agent's endorsement or rejection of a desire as "a reason to act."[55]

This approach to endorsement is developed within a Kantian framework, aspects of which I would want to eschew.[56] But there is nevertheless a way in which my proposal may echo some elements of Korsgaard's view. She cites principles of "practical identity" as essential to the agent's endorsement of a desire as a reason to act. I cite self-governing policies, concerning what to treat as reason-giving, as essential to the agent's endorsement of a desire. Such self-governing policies need not themselves be conceptions of one's identity. A policy not to treat as reason-giving one's recurring desire for a second beer, for example, is not itself such a conception. Nevertheless,

---

53. *Sources of Normativity*, 229. (Korsgaard later [231] expresses a qualification concerning the relevance of "a temporally later occasion." I discuss this apparent ambivalence in my review of *Sources of Normativity* in *Philosophy and Phenomenological Research* [1998]: 699–709 [reprinted in *Faces of Intention*, 265–78].) Korsgaard returns to related matters in her "Self-Constitution in the Ethics of Plato and Kant," *Journal of Ethics* 3 (1999): 1–29.

54. *Sources of Normativity*, 101. Cp. Nozick's emphasis on a "formed self-conception" in his *Philosophical Explanations*, 307.

55. *Sources of Normativity*, 97.

56. For example, my account need not hold that full reflection must lead one to embrace morality as overriding. Korsgaard indicates that on her view it must (*Sources of Normativity*, 256). See also notes 20 and 43.

it is the connection of such policies to the agent's identity over time that grounds their authority to determine where the agent stands. So I agree with Korsgaard in giving certain principles or policies a special connection to aspects of the agent's identity, and in seeing that connection as important to an account of the agent's endorsement.

It is important, though, that the connection envisaged between principles or policies and the agent's identity is different on the different theories. A Korsgaardian conception of "practical identity" explicitly includes in its content the very idea that it is a conception of one's identity. Self-governing policies, in contrast, need not have as a part of their explicit content the idea that they are a conception of one's practical identity (though of course they may). The primary connection between a self-governing policy and the agent's identity over time is grounded, instead, in the policy's characteristic role in coordinating and organizing the agent's temporally extended life in ways that constitute and support Lockean continuities and connections. In this way, on my view, a broadly Lockean approach to personal identity over time can help clarify the nature of the agent's reflective endorsement.[57]

9. QUASI-POLICIES

I want now to turn to a further complexity. The special status that is accorded certain self-governing policies is grounded in the fact that such policies have, as a matter of function, a special relation to our temporally extended agency. But this does not show that it is only such self-governing policies that have this special relation. So we can ask whether there are other attitudes that also, as a matter of function, have something like this special relation to our temporally extended agency and, if so, whether they also can play a role in the agent's endorsement.[58]

Consider, for example, an ideal of being a good citizen. Such an ideal might have a characteristic stability and might constitute and support various

---

57. Korsgaard criticizes Parfit's version of a broadly Lockean approach in her "Personal Identity and the Unity of Agency: A Kantian Response to Parfit," in her *Creating the Kingdom of Ends* (New York: Cambridge University Press), 363–97.

58. My discussion of this matter has been influenced especially by Paul Hoffman; I have also been influenced here by Nomy Arpaly, David Copp, and Jennifer Rosner.

Lockean cross-temporal continuities and connections. And this constitution and support of Lockean continuities and connections might plausibly be seen not merely as an effect but also as a function of such an ideal. A main point of having such ideals is that they, in these ways, help organize and structure one's life over time.[59] Further, the ideal might involve a higher-order concern with certain desires—for example, desires to avoid inconveniences associated with voting and other duties of citizenship. The ideal might, for example, eschew the prospect of one's treating such desires as providing justifying reasons in deliberation, and thereby support a pattern of thought and action that accords with the ideal.

Such higher-order concerns would then have, as a matter of function, a policy-like relation to temporally extended agency. Would those higher-order concerns simply be self-governing policies? Perhaps not, for they may perhaps not be subject to quite the same demands for consistency and coherence as those to which policies are subject. Suppose my ideal of good citizenship brings with it a stable concern not to give weight to a desire to avoid inconvenience by not voting. Suppose that this stable higher-order concern helps structure my temporally extended agency by way of its support for Lockean ties. But suppose that I nevertheless give into temptation and decide this time to give weight to my desire to avoid inconvenience by not voting. My decision goes against the higher-order concern built into my ideal. Nevertheless, this conflict with that higher-order concern may not bring with it the strong kind of inconsistency involved in deciding (and so intending) this time to X while *intending* generally not to X.

Not all concerns that constitute and support organizing, Lockean ties are themselves general intentions. So we do not want to assume that the cited higher-order, policy-like concerns will always be self-governing policies, strictly speaking. Let us call such higher-order policy-like concerns—when they are not, strictly speaking, general policies—self-governing *quasi*-policies. In this way we mark a significant similarity to self-governing policies while leaving room for differences in rational demands for consistency and the like. The structure of our argument then leads to a

---

59. This is compatible with granting that one can have an ideal while remaining imaginatively alive to the attractions of alternative ideals. See P. F. Strawson, "Social Morality and Individual Ideal," in his *Freedom and Resentment and Other Essays* (London: Methuen, 1974), 26–44, esp. 27–29.

natural extension: the agent's endorsement can be constituted by appropriate self-governing policies or quasi-policies in appropriate contexts
of satisfaction.[60]

This leads to a final modification of our account of satisfaction. To be
satisfied with a self-governing policy, we said earlier, is for that policy not
to be challenged by one's other self-governing policies. And now we see
the need for a more general account: to be satisfied with a self-governing
policy or quasi-policy is for that policy or quasi-policy not to be challenged
by one's other self-governing policies and quasi-policies. The agent's endorsement is ensured by appropriate self-governing policies or quasi-
policies with which the agent is satisfied.[61]

---

60. This discussion of quasi-policies overlaps in interesting ways with Harry Frankfurt's
discussion of caring in his essay "The Importance of What We Care About," in his book by that
name. In this essay, Frankfurt notes three distinguishing characteristics of caring.
First:

> The outlook of a person who cares about something is inherently prospective; that is,
> he necessarily considers himself as having a future. On the other hand, it is possible for a
> creature to have desires and beliefs without taking any account at all of the fact that he
> may continue to exist. (83)

Second:

> The moments in the life of a person who cares about something . . . are not merely
> linked inherently by formal relations of sequentiality. The person necessarily binds
> them together, and in the nature of the case also construes them as being bound
> together, in richer ways. (83)

And finally:

> Desires and beliefs have no inherent persistence. . . . But the notion of guidance, and
> hence the notion of caring, implies a certain constancy or steadiness of behavior; and
> this presupposes some degree of persistence. (84)

Caring about something involves a conception of the "prospective" role of the caring in one's
temporally extended life in the future, it involves a way of binding (as I would say, coordinating and organizing) these further futures, and it is an attitude that is itself inherently
persistent (as I would say, stable). Each of these three features of Frankfurtian caring has a
parallel with what I have said to be features of plans and policies. Such Frankfurtian carings, we
might then say, have policy-like roles in support of our temporally extended agency. And such
carings may include higher-order carings about the functioning of certain desires. There seems,
however, no guarantee that these higher-order carings will themselves always be general
intentions. So we can expect that certain kinds of carings will be self-governing quasi-policies.
    Frankfurt also discusses caring in his later essays, "On the Necessity of Ideals," "Autonomy,
Necessity, and Love," and "Caring and Necessity," all included in his *Necessity, Volition, and Love*.
Jennifer Rosner emphasizes the significance of caring to a plausible story about reflective
endorsement in her "Reflective Evaluation, Autonomy, and Self-Knowledge" (PhD diss.,
Stanford University, 1998).
    61. Let me note an important complexity here. In "Hierarchy, Circularity, and Double
Reduction," I discuss *singular* decisions and intentions in favor of relevant functioning of a desire.
Such singular higher-order decisions or intentions are not yet policies, but they do bring with

IO. A FINAL CONCERN ABOUT AUTHORITY

Consider a final concern. It seems that an agent might think to herself: "Well, from the viewpoint of my self-governing policies and quasi-policies I should not now treat D as providing a justifying reason in my deliberation. But why should I allow that viewpoint to determine where *I* stand on this present occasion?" This may seem a coherent thought. But if it is coherent, it suggests a challenge to the view I have been developing. It suggests there can be a gap between, on the one hand, being endorsed by relevant policies or quasi-policies and, on the other hand, being endorsed by the agent.

In response, we need to distinguish two different interpretations of the thought at issue. On one interpretation what is being challenged by the agent is her present package of self-governing policies and quasi-policies. Perhaps the agent finds herself newly impressed with considerations that have not yet been articulated by her as policies or quasi-policies. Perhaps the agent suspects that these considerations may suggest revisions in her self-governing policies and/or quasi-policies. The agent is wondering whether she should continue to be committed to these policies and quasi-policies or whether she should, instead, make changes in them. This is a perfectly coherent thought.

On a second interpretation, in contrast, the agent is thinking: "I do not want to, or see any reason to, change this current package of policies and quasi-policies. And I recognize that they clearly reject D. I just want to ask whether I should let them determine where *I* stand on the present occasion with respect to D." And this does not seem, at bottom, a coherent thought. It is, of course, possible for the agent to act contrary to the cited package of policies or quasi-policies. But this by itself does not change the fact that she is not a time-slice agent but, rather, is and understands herself to be a temporally persisting agent whose agency is temporally extended. So it does not change the fact that this package of plan-like

---

them distinctive normative demands of consistency and coherence. In cases of agency involving such singular commitments, the action is not grounded solely in the pushes and pulls of ordinary desires and aversions. So, though I maintain that the agent's endorsement of a desire involves a self-governing policy or quasi-policy, I also believe that our full theory of agency should make appropriate room for such singular commitments in its underlying story of the relevant intentional structures.

attitudes, in rejecting D, constitutes *her* rejection of D. If she is no longer to reject D, there needs to be a change in relevant aspects of this package—a point recognized by her thought on the first interpretation. To effect that change she needs to change relevant policies or quasi-policies—though that might involve criticizable instability.

II. CONCLUDING REMARKS

Our three core features are, then, interrelated in complex ways. In particular, our strong reflectiveness typically involves our planfulness and our related understanding of our agency as temporally extended.[62] This account adds support to the idea that this trio of core features is compatible with our being fully embedded in an event causal order. In this respect, these core features do not challenge an important commonality between us and merely purposive agents. But our reflectiveness, our planfulness, and our conception of our agency as temporally extended are also, taken together, prime candidates for inclusion in that which is special about human agency.

---

62. This approach to strong reflectiveness also suggests an associated approach to valuing, one that I discuss in my "Valuing and the Will."

Chapter 3

VALUING AND THE WILL

I. VALUING

In "Free Agency," Gary Watson argued that an account of free agency needs to distinguish what a person wants or desires—what a person is to some extent moved to do—from what a person values.[1] One may desire things one does not value—one example Watson gives is that of a "squash player who, while suffering an ignominious defeat, desires to smash his opponent in the face with the raquet."[2] And even when one values what one desires, the motivational strength of the desire may not correspond to the extent to which one values what the desire is for.

What is it to value something? Watson notes that it at least involves wanting it: "to value is also to want."[3] But it involves more than this. When Watson tries in this paper to say what more it involves, he tends to identify valuing with judging good.[4] He then goes on, in a tentative way, to offer a gloss on the idea of a person's values, a gloss that highlights a connection with one's reflective conception of a good life:

> an agent's values consist in those principles and ends which he—in a cool and non-self-deceptive moment—articulates as definitive of the good, fulfilling and defensible life.[5]

1. Gary Watson, "Free Agency," *Journal of Philosophy* 72 (1975): 205–20.
2. Ibid., p. 210.
3. Ibid., p. 215.
4. Ibid., p. 212.
5. Ibid., p. 215.

In a later essay, Watson continues to hold that "valuing cannot be reduced to desiring (at any level)" but grants that his earlier gloss on an agent's values "is altogether too rationalistic."[6] He writes:

> For one thing, it conflates valuing with judging good. Notoriously, judging good has no invariable connection with motivation. . . . One can in an important sense fail to value what one judges valuable.[7]

I think Watson was right on a number of counts. He was right to emphasize the centrality to our understanding of human agency (including especially forms of free agency and self-determination) of some notion of valuing. He was right to insist that to value is not merely to want, though valuing does involve wanting. And he was, I think, right later to note the need for a distinction between valuing and judging good. That said, we are still without a more detailed story about the nature of valuing.

I want to sketch such a story. My proposal draws on several papers of mine.[8] In these papers I try to bring together into a single framework structures emphasized by, on the one hand, hierarchical theories of our agency and, on the other hand, what I have called a planning theory of intention.[9] My account of an agent's valuing tries to draw on this proposed synthesis in a way that is responsive to the cited points of agreement with Watson and that highlights connections between a person's valuings and (what we might reasonably call) that person's will.[10]

---

6. "Free Action and Free Will," *Mind* (1987): 145–72, at p. 150.

7. Ibid. See also Michael Stocker, "Desiring the Bad: An Essay in Moral Psychology," *Journal of Philosophy* (1979): 738–53.

8. "Identification, Decision, and Treating as a Reason," *Philosophical Topics* (1996): 1–18 (reprinted in my *Faces of Intention: Selected Essays on Intention and Agency* [New York: Cambridge University Press, 1999]); "Reflection, Planning, and Temporally Extended Agency," *The Philosophical Review* 109 (2000): 35–61 [this volume, essay 2]; and "Hierarchy, Circularity, and Double Reduction," in S. Buss and L. Overton, eds., *Contours of Agency Essays on Themes from Harry Franto* (Cambridge, MA: MIT Press, 2002): 65–85 [this volume, essay 4].

9. For central discussions of hierarchical theories see Harry Frankfurt *The Importance of What We Care About* (Cambridge: Cambridge University Press, 1988). For my presentation of the planning theory see *Intention, Plans, and Practical Reason* (Cambridge, MA: Harvard University Press, 1987; reissued by CSLI Publications, 1999) and *Faces of Intention*.

10. As I note in "Reflection, Planning, and Temporally Extended Agency," I see the planning theory of intention as a modest theory of the will.

It will be useful to develop my proposal about valuing by exploiting certain Gricean ideas about, as he called it, "method in philosophical psychology."[11] So let me begin by saying what those ideas are.

2. GRICEAN CREATURE CONSTRUCTION

In his 1975 presidential address to the American Philosophical Association, Paul Grice sketched an approach to philosophical psychology that he labeled "creature construction." The idea, briefly, is

> to construct (in imagination, of course) according to certain principles of construction, a type of creature, or rather a sequence of types of creature, to serve as a model (or models) for actual creatures.[12]

Grice calls his creatures "pirots" and writes:

> The general idea is to develop sequentially the psychological theory for different brands of pirot, and to compare what one thus generates with the psychological concepts we apply to suitably related actual creatures.[13]

I find this methodology useful for present purposes.[14] I think that by proceeding with a process of broadly Gricean creature construction we can gain some insight into a number of theories and debates in the philosophy

---

11. Paul Grice, "Method in Philosophical Psychology (From the Banal to the Bizarre)" (Presidential Address) in *Proceedings and Addresses of the American Philosophical Association* (1974–75): 23–53.

12. Ibid., p. 37.

13. Ibid., p. 37.

14. Here I take myself to be in agreement with a number of other philosophers. One example is John Perry, who endorses this Gricean methodology in his "Perception, Action, and the Structure of Believing," in his *The Problem of the Essential Indexical and Other Essays* (New York: Oxford University Press, 1992): 121–49, at pp. 121–22. (See also his paper with David Israel, "Fodor and Psychological Explanations" in *The Problem of the Essential Indexical*: 301–21, at p. 306.) Another example is J. David Velleman, who points to a methodology that is Gricean in spirit in his "Introduction" to his *The Possibility of Practical Reason* (Oxford: Oxford University Press, 2000). Velleman's discussion helped rekindle my thinking about the use of Gricean creature construction in the present context.

of action. We can, in particular, learn something important about valuing and its relation to the will.

Let me make some brief remarks about how I will proceed. My aim is to see a number of different models of agency as reasonable stages in a sequence of creature constructions. At each stage in the sequence, I will try to identify an issue or problem that suggests some sort of modest addition to or extension of the earlier design.[15] The result will be a series of "just so stories." And this may give us pause. How does such a series of possible constructions tell us something about our own actual agency? Part of the answer is that the methodology depends on our arriving at a model of agency that recognizably applies to us—to adult human agents in a broadly modern world. We have a number of more or less articulated ideas about central features of our agency—what I have called "core" features of our agency.[16] A series of Gricean creatures is illuminating about our actual agency only if the series arrives at a model that does justice to these—or at least to many of these—core features. I hasten to add, though, that such a series need not be a unique route to a model of these core features; it need only be one intelligible route in which the steps along the way build appropriately on their antecedents.

But why not simply describe the final model of agency? Why bother with prior stages in the sequence of constructed creatures? The answer is that such a construction can help clarify how complex elements of our agency build on but differ from less complex elements. I think this is in particular helpful when we come to valuing. The model I arrive at in the end involves, as already indicated, a merger of hierarchical and planning structures. By seeing this model as an outcome of a sequence of constructed creatures we are in a position to identify different conceptions of valuing and to clarify their relations to each other.[17]

---

15. So I will try to respect Grice's "supposition that the psychological theory for a given type is an extension of, and includes, the psychological theory of its predecessor-type" ("Method in Philosophical Psychology," pp. 38–39).

16. In my "Reflection, Planning, and Temporally Extended Agency."

17. I see my remarks here about the significance of creature constructions as in the spirit of Grice's remarks in "Method in Philosophical Psychology" at p. 37. Let me add that, as will become clear below, this methodology also helps me articulate relations between several different ideas about planning agency that I have discussed elsewhere.

3. DESIRES, CONSIDERED DESIRES, AND DELIBERATION

I will begin considerably further along a "sequence of types of creature" than Grice begins. Let us suppose that *Creature 1* has both beliefs about its world and various desires concerning different possible states in that world, including different possible acts it might perform. These desires need not be organized in any systematic way and may well come into conflict in particular cases. When there is conflict, Creature 1 is moved to act by its strongest desire (or cluster of desires) at the time of action.

Creature 1 is pushed and pulled by its desires. It is an agent in only a minimal sense. Behavioral outputs are as much attributable to the particular desires that were, on the occasion, strongest, as they are to an agent in any important sense different from those desires.

In search of more robust forms of agency, let us consider a creature who is more reflective about its desires than creature 1. It acts only after it has considered what it desires in light of its beliefs, including beliefs about what relevant experiences are like. Sometimes such consideration changes what it desires. Perhaps it begins with a desire to fly to a distant land; yet, after consideration of what such an experience is really like, it comes to desire not to take the trip.

David Gauthier calls desires that pass such a test of reflection "considered."[18] Let us follow him in doing so. And let us construct a second creature, *Creature 2*. Creature 2 acts on the basis of its beliefs and *considered* desires. Because its desires are considered, it differs from Creature 1.[19] But it remains like Creature 1 in a basic way: its desires and beliefs at the time of action determine what it intentionally does (or, anyway, tries to do) then.

18. David Gauthier, *Morals by Agreement* (New York: Oxford University Press, 1986), pp. 29–33. Gauthier suggests (p. 30) that certain forms of inexperience preclude having a considered desire even if one fully reflects in light of beliefs one does have. This is a complexity I will put to one side here. Thanks to Sergio Tenenbaum for helpful discussion of Gauthier's vews.

19. To be more realistic, we might limit ourselves to saying that Creature 2 has the capacity to make the transition from unconsidered to considered desires but does not always do this. But it will keep the discussion more manageable to simplify and to suppose that all its desires are considered.

Creature 2's intentional efforts depend on the motivational strength of its considered desires at the time of action.[20] So far we have been seeing the process by which conflicting considered desires motivate action as a broadly causal process, a process that reveals motivational strength. But a creature—call it *Creature 3*—might itself try to weigh considerations provided by such conflicting desires in deliberation about the pros and cons of various alternatives. In the simplest case, such weighing treats each of the things desired as a prima facie justifying end. In the face of conflict it weighs such desired ends, where the weights correspond to the motivational strength of the associated, considered desire.[21] The outcome of such deliberation will match the outcome of the causal, motivational processes envisaged in our description of Creature 2. But in the process of weighing the desired ends are treated as justifying, and the deliberation tracks that.

Creature 3, then, has this capacity for a kind of deliberation in the face of conflicting desires. In this respect it goes beyond Creature 2. But since the weights it invokes in such deliberation correspond to the motivational strength of the relevant considered, desires (though perhaps not to the motivational strength of nonconsidered desires), the resultant activities will match those of a corresponding Creature 2 (all of whose desires, we are assuming, are considered). Each will act in ways that reveal the motivational strength of considered desires at the time of action. But for Creature 3 it will also be true that in some (though not all) cases it acts on the basis of how it weighs the ends favored by its conflicting, considered desires.

4. PLANNING AGENTS

It is time to note that many of Creature 3's considered desires will concern matters that cannot be achieved simply by action at a single time. It may, for example, want to nurture a vegetable garden or to build a house. Such

---

20. See Alfred R. Mele, "Motivational Strength," *Nous* 32 (1998): 23–36.

21. I do not say this is a principle that Creature 3 itself appeals to in its deliberation. The connection between weights in deliberation and motivational strength is a structural feature of Creature 3's psychology, not a principle the creature itself cites in its deliberations.

matters will require organized and coordinated action that extends over time. What it does now will depend not only on what it now desires but also on what it now expects it will do later given what it does now. It needs a way of settling now what it will do later given what it does now.

The point is even clearer when we remind ourselves, what we have so far ignored, that Creature 3 is not alone. It is, we may assume, one of some number of such creatures; and in many cases it needs to coordinate what it does with what others do so as to achieve ends desired by all participants, itself included. It needs others to be able reliably to predict what it will do later given what is done now.

There are, then, substantial pressures for mechanisms that support coordination and organization, both within the life of a particular creature and across the lives of a number of interacting creatures. Such mechanisms, further, need to respect basic limits we can expect to characterize the psychology of such creatures.[22] We can expect such creatures to have limited resources of time and attention for complex reasoning[23] and to be limited in what they know about themselves and their world. We need to add to the design of Creature 3 structures that support coordination, intrapersonal and interpersonal, in ways compatible with these limits.

A plausible strategy here would be to add capacities to settle in advance on complex but partial plans of action.[24] A creature who can settle in advance on partial plans of action, fill them in as time goes by and as need be, and follow through in the normal course of events is thereby in a better position to satisfy needs for coordination given basic cognitive limits. So let us add such planning structures to the structures of considered desires and beliefs characteristic of Creature 3. *Creature 4*, then, is a planning agent.

Creature 4's plans are plans for its own actions. Given their role in coordination, such plans will normally need to satisfy demands for consistency and coherence. They also will normally need to be stable, to be

22. Cp. Grice's remarks about the role of the "Engineer" in creature construction in "Method in Philosophical Psychology," at p. 38.

23. This is a general point of Herbert Simon. See, e.g., his *Reason in Human Affairs* (Stanford, CA: Stanford University Press, 1983).

24. This is a theme of my *Intention, Plans, and Practical Reason*.

resistant to being easily reconsidered and abandoned. Otherwise such plans would not play their needed role in organized activity. Further, in having such plans, our creature will need to be able to think of itself as the agent of actions at different times, of actions now and later. It will need to be able to think of itself as an agent who persists over time, one who begins and eventually completes temporally extended projects.

Creature 3, at any moment of choice, asks only what present action is best supported by its current beliefs and considered desires. Creature 4, in contrast, also has available plans of action settled on earlier. On some occasions of action, Creature 4 can simply continue with what it had earlier planned to do rather than step back and reconsider what present action is best supported by its current beliefs and considered desires. This is what is involved in having stable plans of action. In constructing Creature 4 we need to characterize this stability.

In the basic case of interest, Creature 4 has a prior plan to act in certain ways in its present circumstance, a prior plan formed on the basis, in part, of earlier beliefs about what its now-present circumstances would be. It is now faced with new information about its present circumstances, information that it did not anticipate when it formed its prior plan. When should it reconsider its prior plan in light of this new information? How stable should its plan be in the face of such new information?

These are questions about how to design the newly introduced planning structures. We want our answer to involve a modest extension from structures already present. One way to do this is to tie our account of plan stability directly to the creature's limits. We distinguish two different cases. There are, first, cases in which there is a present option that is known by the creature to be clearly favored by its present, relevant beliefs and considered desires. In such a case, it will simply do what it now knows to be favored by those present beliefs and desires. In a second case, it is not clear to the creature what the outcome would be of reconsideration of its prior plan in light of its new information. Now, there are costs of time and attention to stopping always to reconsider a prior plan in light of such new information. To the extent that a strategy of always reconsidering would make one less predictable to cognitively limited agents like oneself, there are further costs tied to needs for coordination. These costs are magnified for a creature whose various plans are interwoven so that a change in one element can have significant ripple effects that will need to be considered. So let us suppose that the general strategies Creature 4 has for responding in such a case to new information about its circumstances are sensitive to these kinds of costs. Its strategies are designed so that by following them, a limited creature with basic needs for coordination will tend to promote, in the long run, the satisfaction of its considered desires and preferences. We can suppose that in some instances of the second kind of case this will mean that Creature 4 follows through with a prior plan even though, had it explicitly reconsidered in light of its present considered desires and relevant beliefs, it would have acted differently.[25]

Creature 4 is a somewhat sophisticated planning agent. But it has a problem. It can expect that its desires and preferences, though considered, may well change over time in ways that tend to undermine its efforts at organizing and coordinating its activities over time. Perhaps in many cases this is due to the kind of temporal discounting emphasized by (among others) George Ainslie.[26] So, for example, Creature 4 may have a plan to exercise every day. This plan may be grounded in its considered preference for exercising every day over never exercising. Its problem, though, is that each day, when faced with exercising then, it tends (even after full consideration) to prefer a sequence of not exercising on the present day but exercising all days in the future, to a uniform sequence of exercising each day, the present day included. At the end of the day, it returns to its earlier considered preference in favor of exercising on each and every day. Nevertheless, its plan or policy[27] of exercising every day will be in trouble. Each day, when it comes time to exercise, it will prefer—and this will be a considered preference—not exercising that day.

25. See *Intention, Plans, and Practical Reason*, chap. 5, and my "Planning and the Stability of Intention," *Minds and Machines* 2 (1992): 1–16.
26. See his *Picoeconomics: The Strategic Interaction of Successive Motivational States within the Person* (New York: Cambridge University Press, 1992). I discuss Ainslie's views in my "Planning and Temptation," in Larry May, Marilyn Friedman, and Andy Clark, eds., *Mind and Morals: Essays on Ethics and Cognitive Science* (Cambridge, MA: Bradford/MIT Press, 1995): 293–310 (reprinted in my *Faces of Intention*). See also David Gauthier, "Resolute Choice and Rational Deliberation," *Nous* 31 (1997): 1–25, at p. 21.
27. I see policies as intentions that are general in relevant respects. See my *Intention, Plans, and Practical Reason*, at pp. 87–91, and my "Intention and Personal Policies," *Philosophical Perspectives* 3 (1989): 443–69.

Though Creature 4, unlike Creature 3, has the capacity to settle on prior plans or policies concerning exercise, this capacity does not yet help in such a case. This is not, after all, a case in which it is unclear at the time of action what would be the result of reconsideration, in light of new information, of the prior plan to exercise today. It is patently clear to the agent, at exercise time on each day, that it presently prefers not to exercise on the present day, though this considered preference will, it knows, change back later in the day. So Creature 4 will systematically undermine its prior exercise plan or policy.

Such cases of temptation, driven perhaps by temporal discounting, are likely to be quite common. Indeed, as Ainslie would emphasize, it seems an important fact about agents like us that such temptations systematically arise even when desires are considered. We can better equip our creatures for this fact about their own psychologies by providing for prior plans and policies that are stable in ways stronger than that envisaged in the construction of Creature 4.

How? Well, a planning agent sees itself as an agent who persists through time. In planning, it is planning for its own future. Built into the capacity and disposition to be a planning agent is a commitment to giving some sort of significance to how it itself will in the future see its present actions. This suggests that we construct a creature whose plans are stable in the following, further way: there is a tendency to stick with a prior plan, despite a present and considered preference to the contrary, when it knows that it would later regret abandoning the plan and would later welcome having stuck with the plan despite its now-present preference. The stability of this creature's plans is shaped in part by such a (other things equal) no-regret principle.[28]

In the temptation cases highlighted by Ainslie, Creature 4 acts on its present preference; but in acting in this way, it thereby frustrates a present and continuing preference for a uniform series of temptation-resisting actions over a uniform series of actions of giving in to temptation. To

28. This is, roughly, a view of plan stability I develop in "Toxin, Temptation, and the Stability of Intention," in Jules Coleman and Christopher Morris, eds., *Rational Commitment and Social Justice: Essays for Gregory S. Kavka* (New York: Cambridge University Press, 1998 [reprinted in my *Faces of Intention*]). In that paper I also discuss alternative models of stability proposed by David Gauthier and Edward McClennen. And see this volume, essay 12.

counteract this tendency to frustrate this present and continuing preference we build in a structure of plan stability that gives anticipated future
regret a role in present plan-or-policy execution. This modification in the
stability of the creature's prior plans and policies is grounded in commitments to some extent implicit in the planning structures already present in
Creature 4. And, without going into details, I think it is clear how plans and
policies that were stable in this further way might help in cases of temptation. A creature whose plans were stable in ways in part shaped by such a
no-regret principle would be more likely than Creature 4 to resist temporary temptations. So let us build such a principle into the stability of the
plans of Creature 5. Creature 5 is, like Creatures 3 and 4, an agent with
considered desires and preferences and an agent who deliberates in light of
those considered desires and preferences. Creature 5 is, like Creature 4, a
planning agent. But the stability of Creature 5's plans and policies is not
derived solely from facts about its limits of time, attention, and the like. It is
also grounded in the central concerns of a planning agent with its own
future, concerns that lend special significance to anticipated future regret.

5. HIERARCHY

Creature 5's desires and preferences are considered. Nevertheless, these
desires and preferences sometimes change over time in ways that lead to
problems about temptation and, more generally, to various forms of cross-
temporal incoherence. Such changes may well lead to conflict with prior
plans and policies. That was why we strengthened the stability of the plans
and polices of Creature 5 by adding a (other things equal) no-regret
principle. But these tensions between prior plans and policies, on the one
hand, and present, considered desires and preferences, on the other hand,
also elicit pressure to reflect further on those desires and preferences
themselves. Given the tension between these preferences and prior plans
and policies, there is reason to give the creature the ability to reflect further
and to ask itself whether it really wants a given desire or preference to play
the cited roles in its agency.[29]

29. The significance of a version of this question has been a major theme in work of Harry
Frankfurt. See esp. his *The Importance of What We Care About*.

Does this question really differ from the question that already arose in the construction of Creature 2, the question whether a desire would survive consideration in light of relevant beliefs? It seems that it does. A desire to smoke might in fact survive consideration even though it is a desire the creature, on reflection, would rather not have and would rather did not shape its deliberation and action.[30] In that sense it may still be a desire the creature does not reflectively support or endorse. So there is reason to add to our creature sufficient resources to arrive at its own reflective endorsements or rejections of its desires.

How should we understand such resources? In an important series of papers Harry Frankfurt has argued, roughly, that the relevant resources are primarily resources for arriving at higher-order desires: a desire concerning one's desire to smoke, for example.[31] More specifically, they are resources for arriving at higher-order desires concerning which first-order desires are effectively to control one's action, and in that sense be one's "will."[32] So let us add to Creature 5 the capacity and disposition to arrive at such hierarchies of higher-order desires concerning it's "will." This gives us a new creature, *Creature 6.*

6. MERGING HIERARCHICAL AND PLANNING STRUCTURES: PART ONE

There is, however, a problem with Creature 6, one that has been much discussed. It is not clear why a higher-order desire—even a higher-order desire that a certain desire be one's "will"—is not simply one more desire in the pool of desires. Why does it have authority to constitute or ensure the *agent*'s (that is, the *creature*'s) endorsement or rejection of a first-order desire?[33]

---

30. Cf. Gauthier: "Some persons prefer to smoke—and their preference may be fully considered and all too experienced—and yet they prefer to prefer not to smoke." *Morals by Agreement*, at p. 32.

31. See esp. his *The Importance of What We Care About.*

32. "Freedom of the Will and the Concept of a Person," in *The Importance of What We Care About*, p. 14.

33. See Watson, "Free Agency," pp. 217–19. Frankfurt's most recent response is in his "The Faintest Passion" (Presidential Address), *Proceedings and Addresses of the American Philosophical Association* 66 (1992): 5–16, reprinted in his *Necessity, Volition, and Love* (New York: Cambridge University Press, 1999): 95–107.

Applied to Creature 6 this is the question of whether, by virtue solely of its hierarchies of desires, it really does succeed in taking its own stand of endorsement or rejection of various first-order desires. Since it was the ability to take its own stand that we were trying to provide in the move to Creature 6, we need some response to this challenge.

A successful response will need to introduce further structure; but we will want to see whether that further structure need involve only a modest extension from features that are already present in Creature 6. Now, Creature 6 is both a hierarchical and a planning agent. Perhaps there are resources implicit in the planning structures that can be used to supplement the hierarchical structures in a way that addresses the cited problem of authority.

Indeed, I think there are. As a planning agent, Creature 6 has plans and policies concerning its actions. It is a short step to plans and policies concerning the functioning of its own desires. In particular, it is a short step to policies in favor of or against relevant functioning of relevant desires. Such policies, I think, help provide a plausible solution to the authority problem.

How? Let me briefly rehearse an argument for this that I have developed elsewhere.[34] The basic point is that Creature 6 is not merely a time-slice agent. It is, rather, and understands itself to be, a temporally persisting planning agent, one who begins, continues, and completes temporally extended projects. On a broadly Lockean view, its persistence over time consists in relevant psychological continuities (for example, the persistence of attitudes of belief and intention) and connections (for example, memory of a past event or the later intentional execution of an intention formed earlier).[35] Certain attitudes have as a primary role the constitution and support of such Lockean continuities and connections. In particular, policies that favor or reject various desires have it as their role to constitute and support various continuities both of ordinary desires and of the policies themselves. Such policies also have it as their role to support various

34. "Reflection, Planning, and Temporally Extended Agency."

35. I will simply take such a broadly Lockean view for granted in the present context. The terminology of connections and continuities comes from Derek Parfit, *Reasons and Persons* (New York: Oxford University Press, 1984), 204–9. I note a divergence in my use of these terms in my "Reflection, Planning, and Temporally Extended Agency."

connections across time, as when one self-consciously follows through with a previously formed policy. So such policies have it as their role to help constitute and support the temporally extended structure of agency, as that structure is understood on a broadly Lockean approach. Indeed, it is in part by way of supporting and constituting such Lockean ties that such policies play their role of supporting broad forms of cross-temporal co-ordination and organization of motivation and action. For this reason such policies are not merely additional wiggles in the psychic stew. Instead, these policies have a claim to help determine where the agent—that is, the temporally persisting agent—stands with respect to its desires. Or so it seems to me reasonable to say.

Let us then give *Creature 7* such higher-order policies. Creature 7 has the capacity to take a stand with respect to its desires by arriving at relevant higher-order policies concerning the functioning of those desires over time. Creature 7 exhibits a merger of hierarchical and planning structures. Like Creature 6 it is reflective in ways that involve higher-order pro and con attitudes concerning its lower-order desires. But the higher-order attitudes of Creature 7 specifically include higher-order policies.[36] We understand such policies by appeal to the planning theory; and we ground their authority in their connection to the temporally extended structure of agency.

7. MERGING HIERARCHICAL AND PLANNING STRUCTURES: PART TWO

Creature 7 takes a stand concerning its desires by way of higher-order policies concerning relevant functioning of those desires. What functioning? Since we are seeking continuity with Creature 6, let us suppose that for Creature 7 these policies concern which desires are effectively to motivate, are to be one's "will" in Frankfurt's technical sense.

---

36. So the psychology of Creature 7 continues to have the hierarchical structure of pro attitudes introduced with Creature 6. The difference is that the higher-order pro attitudes of Creature 6 were simply characterized as desires in a broad, generic sense and no appeal was made to the distinctive species of pro attitude constituted by plan like attitudes. That is the sense in which, following Grice, the psychology of Creature 7 is an "extension of" the psychology of Creature 6.

This brings us to a problem, however. Recall Creatures 3–5. They weigh conflicting ends for which they have conflicting, considered desires. They assign weights to those desired ends, weights that correspond to the motivational strengths of the considered desires. Creature 7 goes beyond Creatures 3–5 in part because Creature 7 has higher-order policies that favor or challenge motivational roles of its considered desires. When Creature 7 engages in deliberative weighing of conflicting, desired ends, it seems that the assigned weights should reflect the policies that determine where it stands with respect to relevant desires. But the policies we have so far appealed to—policies concerning what desires are to be one's will (in Frankfurt's technical sense of "will")—do not quite address this concern. The problem is that one can in certain cases have policies concerning which desires are to motivate and yet these not be policies that accord what those desires are for a corresponding justifying role in deliberation.[37] My policy may be to allow a certain desire to motivate as a way of letting off steam, or because I find such a motivational process itself to be charming; but I need not thereby have a policy of treating what is desired as a justifying end in deliberation. It is one thing to favor a state of affairs that involves a desire and an action motivated by that desire; it is another thing to favor treating the included desire as providing a justifying end.[38] In being limited to higher-order policies that concern solely which desire is to motivate, Creature 7 seems not yet fully to have the capacity to take a stand concerning how he will treat his desires as reason-providing in deliberation.

A solution is to give our creature—call it *Creature 8*—the capacity to arrive at policies that express its commitment to being motivated by a desire *by way of its treatment of that desire as providing, in deliberation, a justifying end for action*.[39] Creature 8 has policies of treating (or not treating) certain desires as providing

<hr/>

37. For related discussions see J. David Velleman, "The Guise of the Good," *Nous* 26 (1992): 3–26, esp. 3–7; Michael Smith, *The Moral Problem* (Oxford: Blackwell, 1994): 131–36.

38. I make this point also in "Hierarchy, Circularity, and Double Reduction."

39. I try to say more about what it is for an agent to treat a desire as, in the relevant sense, reason-providing in my "Hierarchy, Circularity, and Double Reduction." A consequence of my view there is that such treatment involves an intention or policy in favor of relevant functioning of the desire. This means that a policy of treating a desire as reason-providing is higher-order in two ways: first, it concerns the desire: second, it concerns a mode of treatment that itself involves an intention or policy.

justifying ends—as, in this way, reason-providing—in motivationally effective deliberation.[40]

Creature 8, like Creature 7, brings together both hierarchical and planning structures. Unlike Creature 7, though, Creature 8 has higher-order policies that concern not only the motivational role of its desires, but also its treatment of its desires as reason-providing in motivationally effective deliberation.[41] These are policies concerning what weight, if any, is to be given to desired ends in motivationally effective deliberation. Following a discussion of related matters by Robert Nozick, we can say that such policies involve a "commitment to make future decisions in accordance with the weights it establishes."[42]

Let us call such policies *self-governing* policies. Now such a creature might have self-governing policies that conflict with and challenge one another. This would introduce complexities I want to put to one side here. So I will suppose that Creature 8's self-governing policies are mutually compatible and do not challenge one another.[43]

The grounds on which Creature 8 arrives at (and on occasion revises) such self-governing policies will be many and varied. We can see these policies as crystallizing complex pressures and concerns, some of which are grounded in other policies or desires.[44] These self-governing policies

---

40. See my "Identification, Decision, and Treating as a Reason," and my "Reflection, Planning, and Temporally Extended Agency." Somewhat related ideas can be found in Rachel Cohon, "Internalism about Reasons for Action," *Pacific Philosophical Quarterly* 74 (1993): 265–88; Allan Gibbard, *Wise Choices, Apt Feelings* (Cambridge, MA: Harvard University Press, 1990), at p. 163; T. M. Scanlon, *What We Owe to Each Other* (Cambridge, MA: Harvard University Press, 1998), chap. 1; and Christine Korsgaard, *The Sources of Normativity* (Cambridge: Cambridge University Press, 1996), esp. chap. 3.

41. In this way Creature 8 involves, as Grice would want, an "extension" of structures already present in Creature 7.

42. Robert Nozick, *Philosophical Explanations* (Cambridge, MA: Harvard University Press, 1981), at p. 297.

43. In terminology drawn from Frankfurt, "The Faintest Passion," we can say that the creature in such a case is "satisfied" with its self-governing policies. I develop the idea of satisfaction in a way that is a bit different from Frankfurt's version in my "Reflection, Planning, and Temporally Extended Agency." In this latter essay, I also note—a further, important complication I will not discuss here—the need also to introduce what I call "quasi-policies."

44. This may be in the spirit of Charles Taylor's remarks about our efforts to arrive at "articulations" of our "largely inarticulated sense of what is of decisive importance." See his "Responsibility for Self," reprinted in Gary Watson, ed., *Free Will* (New York: Oxford University Press, 1982), at pp. 122–23.

may be tentative and will normally not be immune to change. Nevertheless, given their role in the creature's temporally extended agency, we can say, roughly, that for the creature to be in control is for such policies to be in control.

Now, in describing Creature 8 we have focused on cases in which its first-order desires precede its formation of relevant higher-order self-governing policies. But we may suppose that Creature 8's capacity to arrive at new self-governing policies also includes the capacity to arrive, on reflection, at a new package of self-governing policy and associated first-order desire. For example, Creature 8 might, as a result of a powerful personal experience of helplessness, newly come both to desire to help others and to have a policy of treating that desire as reason-providing. Indeed, Creature 8 might thereby arrive at a new first-order *policy* of helping others, together with a higher-order policy of treating that first-order policy as reason-providing. (A first-order policy is itself a kind of first-order desire, in the broadly generic sense of "desire" I am using here.) In such a case the creature may arrive at a reflexive policy to help others by way of treating this very policy of helping others as setting a justifying end for deliberation.[45]

My pursuit of Gricean creature construction stops here, at least for now.[46] Creature 8 is an agent with considered desires and beliefs, stable plans and policies, and higher-order self-governing policies, some of which may be reflexive in the way just highlighted. In these respects, our model of Creature 8 seems to me to capture important core features of *our* agency.

This much in hand, it is time to return to our query about the nature of valuing.

---

45. Keith Lehrer discusses a related (but different) idea of a reflexive higher-order preference. See his *Self-Trust: A Study of Reason, Knowledge, and Autonomy* (New York: Oxford University Press, 1997), pp. 110–12.

46. Further discussion would need more fully to address issues raised by various kinds of conflict. We might, in addition, also go on to consider what happens when our creatures join with one another to form *shared* intentions, plans, and policies. I discuss some of the issues raised by this possibility in a quartet of papers on shared agency included in my *Faces of Intention*. It might be that the story I go on to tell here about valuing could usefully be extended (using resources from my account of shared intention) to creatures who systematically join with one another in shared intentions and policies, at times thereby arriving at shared values. But that is an issue for another occasion. (See this volume, essay 13.)

8. MODELS OF VALUING

Begin by asking at what point in our series of constructed creatures something like valuing can be discerned. The answer, I take it, is: Creature 3. Creature 3's desires are considered; and it treats what those considered desires are for as justifying ends in deliberation. It would be natural to say that Creature 3 values what it, after consideration, desires, and it values such things to the extent that, after consideration, it desires them.[47] Such valuing involves wanting, but is more than that, as Watson wanted.

Valuing in this sense continues to be present in Creatures 4 and 5. What is added in the construction of those creatures is not a new structure of valuing, but rather a structure of more or less stable plans built on top of the same structure of valuing. For example, the story about regret in our discussion of Creature 5 led to a change not in the basic account of valuing but, instead, in the account of the stability of plans and policies.

Note, however, that once we introduce hierarchical structures—as we did with Creatures 6–8—these matters begin to change. Consider, in particular, Creature 8. Creature 8 has certain higher-order planning structures, including higher-order self-governing policies concerning its treatment of its own desires (including its own first-order policies) as reason-providing. These higher-order planning structures, in contrast with the planning structures introduced with Creatures 4 and 5, are not simply built on top of a separate structure of valuing. Instead, these higher-order planning structures themselves feed back to and help shape what such a creature can plausibly be said to value. I proceed to explain.

Suppose Creature 8 has a considered (though temporary) preference in favor of not exercising today. But suppose it has a higher-order policy that discounts the weight of this preferred end in deliberation, given its conflict with its considered preference for regular exercise over regular nonexercise.

---

47. Cp. Gauthier: "value is a measure of considered preference" (*Morals by Agreement*, at p. 33). Michael Smith criticizes Gauthier's view about valuing in his *The Moral Problem*, at pp. 141–42. But his criticism simply assumes, contrary to Watson's proposal, that valuing need not involve wanting. (Gilbert Harman makes a related point in response to Smith in his "Desired desires," in R. G. Frey and C. W. Morris, eds., *Value, Welfare, and Morality* [New York: Cambridge University Press, 1993]: 138–57, at p. 150.) My reason for providing, below, a different model of valuing is different from Smith's reason and is compatible with Watson's constraint that valuing involves wanting.

Suppose that this policy is not in conflict with some other self-governing policy of that creature. And suppose this creature deliberates about whether to go to the gym today. What weight will it assign to exercise: the weight associated with its considered (though temporary) preference in favor of not exercising today? or the weight associated with its self-governing policy? Given the authority of such a self-governing policy to speak for the agent—an authority grounded in ties to Lockean conditions of persistence of the agent over time—I think that it is this policy-determined weight that will be relevant to Creature 8's deliberation about what to do now. It is when this policy is effective and its policy-determined weight is operative in deliberation that we can say not only that there is a deliberative process but also that the agent is deliberating and the deliberation is its own.

If we ask what Creature 8 values in this case, the answer seems to be: what it values is constituted in part by its higher-order self-governing policies.[48] In particular, it values exercise over nonexercise even right now, and even given that it has a considered (though temporary) preference to the contrary. Unlike Creatures 3–5, what Creature 8 now values is not simply a matter of its present considered desires and preferences. It is in part a function of its higher-order self-governing policies. The introduction of these self-governing policies has changed the structure of its valuing.

This points toward a story about one important kind of valuing for a creature as complex as Creature 8. Roughly speaking, such an agent values X (in the relevant sense) when it has a desire for X (a desire that may itself be a first-order policy) and a self-governing policy in favor of treating that desire as providing an end that is justifying (perhaps to a certain, specified degree) in motivationally effective deliberation.

Now, this model of Creature 8 seems in relevant respects to be a (partial) model of us. So we arrive at the conjecture that one important

48. Another philosopher who has pointed in the direction of a connection between valuing and policies is David Copp. Copp claims that one's "values" consist, roughly, in policies concerning the course of one's life. Copp, though, does not focus on the kinds of higher-order policies that have been my concern here. See David Copp, *Morality, Normativity & Society* (New York: Oxford University Press, 1995), esp. pp. 177–78. It was Copp, too, who first suggested to me that my account of identification in my "Identification, Decision, and Treating as a Reason" might yield an account of valuing. Gilbert Harman, in a helpful conversation, also once suggested that he might favor some sort of close connection between valuing and policies.

kind of valuing of which we are capable involves, in the cited ways, both our first-order desires and our higher-order self-governing policies. In an important subclass of cases our valuing involves reflexive policies that are both first-order policies of action and higher-order policies to treat the first-order policy as reason-providing in motivationally effective deliberation.[49]

This may seem odd. Valuing seems normally to be a first-order attitude. One values honesty, say. The proposal is that an important kind of valuing involves higher-order policies. Does this mean that, strictly speaking, what one values (in this sense) is itself a desire—not honesty, say, but a desire for honesty? No, it does not. What I value in the present case is honesty; but, on the theory, my valuing honesty in part consists in certain higher-order self-governing policies.

Could one have a policy of treating, say, helping others as a justifying end in motivationally effective deliberation, and yet still not have a first-order desire in favor of helping others? I think the answer is yes. However, actually to treat helping others in this way in motivationally effective deliberation will, I think, involve some such first-order desire (in the broadly generic sense of "desire"). In the absence of such a desire, then, the cited policy will involve a commitment to coming to have the desire.[50] Should we say that such a higher-order policy, in the absence of the first-order desire, suffices for valuing? Well, it is not by itself a kind of valuing characteristic of self-determined activity, for that requires valuing that really does control action. But we might still say that this is a kind of (somewhat attenuated) valuing, related in indicated ways to the motivationally more robust valuing I have highlighted.[51]

49. Michael Smith has argued against a hierarchical account of valuing, sketched by David Lewis, according to which "valuing is just desiring to desire" (David Lewis, "Dispositional Theories of Value," *Proceedings of the Aristotelian Society* suppl. vol. [1989]: 113–37, at p. 115). Smith's main criticism is, in effect, that Lewis does not solve the authority problem for hierarchical theories. I agree with this criticism of Lewis's account. But if I am right that appeal to planning structures helps solve the authority problem, then Smith's objections to Lewis need not apply to my account. See Michael Smith, *The Moral Problem*, at pp. 142–47.

50. Here I depart from Frankfurt's decision to consider only higher-order desires concerning first-order desires one already has. See "Freedom of the Will and the Concept of a Person," in *The Importance of What We Care About*, pp. 15–16.

51. In this paragraph, I am indebted to conversation with Fred Schueler and Sergio Tenenbaum.

9. VALUING AND THE WILL

Our proposal ties an important kind of reflective valuing to the will of an agent whose agency is temporally extended. Intentions, plans, and policies were initially introduced on top of prior structures of considered desires. Those structures of considered desires were, at these preliminary stages, structures of valuings. Intentions and the like were introduced in response to pressures for coordination in the pursuit of what was, in that sense, valued. Such intentions involve a commitment to action, and so could reasonably be said to constitute structures of the will. Once such structures of the will were on the scene, there was pressure for them to include reflection on the very desires that grounded the introduction of those structures in the first place. Such pressure led us to Creature 7, and then to Creature 8. Given their ties to the temporally extended structure of agency, these structures fed back into the determination of what the agent values. This led us to our conclusion: the agent's reflective valuing involves a kind of higher-order willing.[52]

52. Thanks to Lori Gruen, Agnieszka Jaworska, Keith Lehrer, Elijah Millgram, Peter Railton, Fred Schueler, Sergio Tenenbaum, J. David Velleman, Gideon Yaffe, and audiences at the University of Michigan and the University of New Mexico. Many of the ideas in this essay come from work done while I was a Fellow at The Center for Advanced Study in the Behavioral Sciences. I am grateful for financial support provided by The Andrew W. Mellon Foundation.

Chapter 4

HIERARCHY, CIRCULARITY, AND DOUBLE REDUCTION

I. THE FIRST REDUCTION

A major element in Harry Frankfurt's groundbreaking work in the philosophy of action has been an emphasis on our capacity for "reflective self-evaluation"—in particular, our capacity to step back and reflectively assess our motivation.[1] Such reflective self-evaluation sometimes issues in "identification" with a form of motivation, sometimes in "withdrawal."[2] I might, on reflection, identify with my desire to help you. In contrast, a drug addict might reflectively reject and withdraw from his powerful desire for the drug,[3] and a person may despair of her extreme competitiveness and reject her powerful desire to win.[4] In this respect, we may suppose, our agency differs significantly from that of many nonhuman animals and of very young human children.

Frankfurt has been concerned to explain in what an agent's reflective identification with, or withdrawal from, such desires consists. Though the

1. The quote is from Harry Frankfurt, "Freedom of the Will and the Concept of a Person," in *The Importance of What We Care About* (Cambridge: Cambridge University Press, 1988), 12.
2. Frankfurt, "Freedom of the Will and the Concept of a Person," 18. Frankfurt remarks in "Three Concepts of Free Action" that "this notion of identification is admittedly a bit mystifying.... In my opinion, however, it grasps something quite fundamental in our inner lives" *The Importance of What We Care About*, 54.
3. Frankfurt, "Freedom of the Will and the Concept of a Person," 17.
4. I briefly discuss this example (which derives from an example of T. M. Scanlon) in my "Identification, Decision, and Treating as a Reason," in *Faces of Intention: Selected Essays on Intention and Agency* (New York: Cambridge University Press, 1999), 196–97.

details have varied, Frankfurt's basic strategy has included an appeal to a
hierarchy of higher-order pro or con attitudes. The project, I take it, has
been to provide an account of the *agent's* identification with, or withdrawal
from, a first-order desire in large part in terms of relations of support or
rejection between higher-order pro or con *attitudes* and that first-order
desire.[5] That is, concerning cases in which the agent has a first-order desire
D, we seek to provide truth conditions for

(1) The agent identifies with first-order desire D

primarily in terms of certain higher-order attitudes of the agent in support
of D. (We proceed in an analogous way in explaining the agent's withdrawal from a desire.) In this way, we seek a reduction of the agent's
identification with a desire, primarily to the support of that desire by
relevant higher-order attitudes of that agent. For reasons that will become
clear, I will call this effort to reduce agent identification to higher-order-
attitude support an effort to achieve the *first* reduction.

Frankfurt once noted that a psychiatrist might desire to have a desire for a drug without desiring that that desire move her to act.[6] Frankfurt would not, I take it, suppose that such a psychiatrist identifies with
that desire in the relevant sense. A lesson we can draw from this example
is that identification, in the relevant sense, with a desire does not
merely concern the presence of that desire. But, then, what does it concern?

Consider the following fascinating passage in "Identification and Wholeheartedness":

> There are two quite different sorts of conflicts between desires. In
> conflicts of the one sort, desires compete for priority or position
> in a preferential order; the issue is which desire to satisfy *first*. In

5. See Frankfurt's reflections on "where (if anywhere) the person himself stands" in "Identification and Wholeheartedness," in *The Importance of What We Care About*, 166. And see J. David Velleman,
"What Happens When Someone Acts?" *Mind* 101 (1992): 461–81. I discuss in more detail the sequence of
views that Frankfurt has proffered in my "Identification, Decision, and Treating as a Reason." I also
discuss views of my own that are closely related to the present paper in my "Reflection, Planning,
and Temporally Extended Agency," *Philosophical Review* (2000): 35–61 [this volume, essay 2], and my
"Valuing and the Will," *Philosophical Perspectives* 14 (2000): 249–65 [this volume, essay 3].

6. Frankfurt, "Freedom of the Will and the Concept of a Person," 14–15. Thanks to John
Fischer for reminding me of this example.

conflicts of the other sort, the issue is whether a desire should be given *any* place in the order of preference at all—that is, whether it is to be endorsed as a legitimate candidate for satisfaction or whether it is to be rejected as entitled to no priority whatsoever. When a conflict of the first kind is resolved, the competing desires are *integrated* into a single ordering, . . . Resolving a conflict of the second kind involves a radical *separation* of the competing desires, one of which is not merely assigned a relatively less favored position but extruded entirely as an outlaw. It is these acts of ordering and rejection—integration and separation—that create a self out of the raw materials of inner life.[7]

The suggestion, I take it, is that in identifying with a desire, one endorses it "as a legitimate candidate for satisfaction"; in withdrawing from a desire, one separates it from those desires that one endorses as such legitimate candidates.[8] The psychiatrist who just wants to know what it is like to experience a desire for the drug does not thereby endorse that desire "as a legitimate candidate for satisfaction."

But what is it for an agent to endorse a desire "as a legitimate candidate for satisfaction"? To answer we need to reflect on two potentially interrelated roles a desire may play in action. So that is what I will do in the next four paragraphs. I will then return to our question about endorsing a desire "as a legitimate candidate for satisfaction."

Begin by noting that a desire may function as an effective motive of intentional action. When a desire for E so functions, it is—at the least, and roughly speaking—part of a mechanism that cognitively tracks and thereby tends to promote (given true beliefs) bringing about or realizing E.[9] Now, Donald Davidson has supposed that when a desire functions in this

---

7. Harry Frankfurt, "Identification and Wholeheartedness," in *The Importance of What We Care About*, 170. See also his "Identification and Externality," in *The Importance of What We Care About*, 67, though in this earlier discussion Frankfurt does not use the term "legitimate."

8. Though in the quoted passage Frankfurt does not explicitly say that this is a view about identification, I think it is clear from the context that this is his intent. See, e.g., the immediately preceding paragraph on p. 170.

9. I put to one side cases in which the desire motivates not by providing an end but in some other way, for example, by providing a side-constraint. The terminology of "tracking" comes from Robert Nozick, *Philosophical Explanations* (Cambridge, MA: Harvard University Press, 1981), chaps. 3 and 4. See also Harry Frankfurt, "The Problem of Action," in *The Importance of What We Care About*, 69–79, esp. 74–75.

way something else is also true, namely, the agent "sets a positive value on" E and in part because of that has "attitudes and beliefs from which, had he been aware of them and had the time, he *could* have reasoned that his action was desirable (or had some other positive attribute)."[10] When a desire functions in this latter way it provides, by way of its "natural propositional expression,"[11] a premise for "a piece of practical reasoning the conclusion of which is, or would be if the conclusion were drawn from the premises, that the action actually performed is desirable."[12]

Davidson's idea, I take it, is that when a desire for E motivates intentional action, the agent is at least disposed to engage in practical reasoning in which the desire motivates by way of her treating E as a *justifying* consideration or reason in favor of her action. It will be useful to have a label for the case in which this disposition is realized—the case in which the desire for E motivates by way of the agent's treatment of E as a justifying end in her deliberation or practical reasoning. Let us say that in this case the agent treats that desire as providing a justifying reason for action. I will below (in section 8) try to say a bit more about this idea; but for now I think it clear enough to proceed.

In particular, we can reflect on Davidson's idea that these two roles of desire always go together; for one thing we have learned from the critical reaction to Davidson's philosophy of action is that it is not clear that they do.[13] That is, it is not clear that whenever

(i) a desire functions as an effective motive of intentional action

it is also true that

10. Donald Davidson, "How is Weakness of the Will Possible?" and "Intending," in *Essays on Actions and Events* (New York: Oxford University Press, 1980), 31, 85. (Though compare "Actions, Reasons, and Causes," in *Essays on Actions and Events*, 4.)

11. Davidson, "How is Weakness of the Will Possible?" 31.

12. Davidson, "How is Weakness of the Will Possible?" 33. I take it that the desire may so function because the agent holds that E is desirable whether or not he desires E; indeed, that may be, at least in part, why he desires E. Alternatively, the agent may see the desirability of E as dependent on the presence of the desire. Finally, the desire need not be in the "foreground" of the practical reasoning, in the sense introduced by Pettit and Smith. See Philip Pettit and Michael Smith, "Backgrounding Desire," *Philosophical Review* 96 (1990): 565–92.

13. See Michael Smith, *The Moral Problem* (Cambridge: Basil Blackwell, 1994), 137–41; J. David Velleman, "The Guise of the Good," *Nous* 26 (1992): 3–26; and J. David Velleman, Introduction to *The Possibility of Practical Reason* (Oxford: Oxford University Press, 2000), 5–10.

(ii) the agent is disposed to treat that desire as (in the indicated sense) providing a justifying reason for action.

One problem is that the existence of a motivational connection between desire and action is a general phenomenon, one that we see in both human and certain nonhuman animals. Once we grant this point, it seems that the presence of such a motivational connection between desire and action may or may not involve a conception, on the part of the actor, of the desired end as justifying. After all, the desires of young children (and certain other Frankfurtian "wantons")[14] motivate intentional action; yet it is not plausible that these children (and other wantons) must have associated dispositions to treat those desires as providing a justifying reason.[15] It is a remarkable achievement of human agency that many cases of motivation really do involve some such disposition. But we should not be so impressed with this achievement that we lose track of the potential gap between (i) and (ii).

I think Frankfurt would agree. A distinction between (i) and (ii) seems implicit in his approach to motivation by first-order desire, as a phenomenon that is present in both wantons and persons. After all, in both cases, first-order desires motivate, yet it is unlikely that all motivation in wantons involves (ii). The distinction also seems suggested by Frankfurt's discussion of the unwilling addict: it is natural to see such an agent as moved by a desire for a drug though he is not disposed to treat that desire as reason-providing.[16] And the idea that motivation by first-order desire is a general phenomenon present both in human and in nonhuman agents is in keeping with Frankfurt's advice that "we are far from being unique either in the purposiveness of our behavior or in its intentionality."[17]

---

14. "Freedom of the Will and the Concept of a Person," 16–18.

15. See Velleman, "The Guise of the Good," 7.

16. This is, pretty much, Smith's understanding of the example. See Smith, *The Moral Problem*, 134. For an alternative understanding of some versions of this case, see Sarah Buss, "Autonomy Reconsidered," in Peter A. French, Theodore E. Uehling Jr., and Howard K. Wettstein, eds., *Midwest Studies in Philosophy XIX: Philosophical Naturalism* (Notre Dame, IN: University of Notre Dame Press, 1994), 101. For a subtle and suggestive sketch of a general approach to addictive motivation, see Gary Watson, "Disordered Appetites: Addiction, Compulsion, and Dependence," in Jon Elster, ed., *Addiction: Entries and Exits* (New York: Russell Sage Foundation, 1999), 3–28.

17. Frankfurt, "The Problem of Action," 78. Frankfurt also emphasized this advice in his comments at the "Contours of Agency" Conference.

So let us distinguish these two related but different roles a desire might play in action: as a motive, and treated by the agent as reason-providing. Equipped with this distinction, let us now return, as promised, to our question about what it is for an agent to endorse a desire "as a legitimate candidate for satisfaction." When an agent endorses a desire in this way (and so identifies with that desire), does she merely endorse that desire's functioning as an effective motive? Or must she as well endorse her treating that desire as providing, in deliberation and practical reasoning, a justifying reason for action?

I think that one natural reading of the cited passage from "Identification and Wholeheartedness" supports the latter reading. Talk of a *legitimate* candidate for satisfaction points to a connection with the practical reasoning and deliberation that frequently lies behind action. On this way of thinking about identification with a desire, what it involves is not merely taking sides in favor of a certain motivational pressure; it involves as well a commitment to associated forms of deliberation and practical reasoning. Deliberation and practical reasoning play fundamental roles in our agency. If identification is central to the constitution of the "self out of the raw materials of inner life," it is reasonable to expect it to involve a commitment not merely to forms of motivation but also to associated modes of practical reasoning.

However, though I think there is much to be said in its favor, Frankfurt has indicated that this is not his approach.[18] And we can see signs of this in other essays. In "Identification and Externality," for example, Frankfurt emphasizes that a "person may acknowledge to himself that passions of which he disapproves are undeniably and unequivocally his."[19] If this is a case of identification, then identification, so understood, may only involve a resigned and perhaps grudging willingness to be moved by a desire.[20]

18. In his comments on an earlier draft of this essay at the "Contours of Agency" Conference. In my earlier discussion of these matters in "Identification, Decision, and Treating as a Reason," I was unsure about how to interpret Frankfurt on this point. (See note 33 in the version in my *Faces of Intention*.)

19. Frankfurt, "Identification and Externality," in *The Importance of What We Care About*, 65.

20. It does seem to me, though, that seeing such cases as ones of identification is in tension with the idea that identification with a first-order desire always involves a higher-order desire in its favor.

But even if identification, as Frankfurt understands it, need not involve a commitment to associated forms of practical reasoning, it remains plausible that there is an important, related phenomenon that does. Given the importance of practical reasoning to our agency, we can expect that this related form of identification will be an important target for a theory of human action.

We can, that is, try to begin by interpreting

(1) The agent identifies with first-order desire D

roughly along the lines of

(1a) The agent endorses D's functioning as an effective motive.

But, given the kind of agents we are—agents whose actions are normally tied to practical deliberation and the like—at some point we will need also to turn to a version of (1) along the lines of

(1b) The agent endorses her treating D as providing a justifying reason for action in motivationally effective practical reasoning.

The hierarchical model should at least be extendible to identification along the lines of (1b). We want to know, then, how to approach such identification within the framework of the hierarchical model. I want to sketch an answer. While my answer will be broadly in the spirit of aspects of Frankfurt's hierarchical model, it will also need to draw on further conceptual resources.

2. A THREAT OF CIRCULARITY

We seek an account of agent identification in a sense that involves (1b). From now on when I speak of identification, it is this kind of identification I shall have in mind—though I will occasionally allude to (1b) as a friendly reminder. The first reduction, as I understand it, aims at an account of such identification primarily in terms of relevant higher-order attitudes of the agent.

What type of higher-order attitudes? I will later describe a view that takes the relevant higher-order attitudes to be certain higher-order policies or the like. But the issues I want to focus on at this point concern, instead, the precise *content* of these higher-order attitudes. And the questions about content that I want to raise do not depend on focusing in particular on higher-order policies. So let us for now simply say that the first reduction seeks an account of the agent's identification (in a sense that involves [1b]) with a desire, D, along the lines of

(2) The agent has X-type higher-order attitudes in support of D.

Later we can consider in more detail what type X is. What I want now to note is a problem about the content of the higher-order attitudes to be cited in (2).

We have distinguished between a desire's functioning as an effective motive and a desire's being treated by the agent as providing a justifying reason. So we need to ask whether the higher-order attitudes to be cited in a fleshed-out version of (2) are simply to support the desire's functioning as an effective motive or are to support the agent's treating that desire as providing a justifying reason in motivationally effective deliberation. That is, should we fill in (2) along the lines of

(2a) The agent has X-type higher-order attitudes in support of D's functioning as an effective motive.

Or should we instead fill in (2) along the lines of

(2b) The agent has X-type higher-order attitudes in support of her treating D as providing a justifying reason.

The first reduction—from, so to speak, the 1-level to the 2-level—is a reduction of agent identification to higher-order attitude support. In carrying out this first reduction, we seem to face a choice between a reduction to (2a) and a reduction to (2b). Consider an appeal to (2b). A problem here is that an agent's treating a desire as providing a justifying reason in deliberation seems to involve the agent's identification with, or endorsement of, that desire: when the agent treats what is desired as a justifying consideration in her practical reasoning, she seems to be identifying with that desire.[21] But then, in the absence of further analysis, it seems that the

---

21. I say only "seems" because my final view allows for some qualification. (See below, section 8.) But for now we can work with the unqualified, but I think intuitively plausible, idea that one's treatment of a desire as providing a justifying reason in one's deliberation itself involves one's identification with that desire. After all, it seems that in so treating that desire, one is treating it as a "legitimate candidate for satisfaction."

contents of the higher-order attitudes cited in (2b) will themselves involve the very idea of the agent's identification with the desire. So if we simply appeal to (2b) without further analysis of the relevant contents, we are threatened by circularity.[22] We are seeking a reduction of agent identification to higher-order attitude support but then seem to be invoking in the content of those higher-order attitudes the very idea of agent identification.

3. FOUR STRATEGIES AND A SECOND REDUCTION

Consider four strategies of response. First, we could appeal directly to (2b) and just acknowledge that analysis stops here: a hierarchical theory needs also, at bottom, to appeal to a basic notion of one's treating a desire as reason-providing in deliberation. The problem here, however, is that an agent's treatment of a desire as reason-providing in deliberation seems itself to involve her identification with that desire. If this is right, then the appeal to hierarchy is not doing the work it was supposed to do in an account of agent identification. Second, we could appeal to (2b) as part of a hierarchical theory of agent identification but then go on to provide some sort of hierarchical account of an agent's treating a desire as reason-providing. Third, we could avoid direct appeal to (2b) and instead appeal directly to (2a) in our hierarchical theory of agent identification. Fourth, we could seek to appeal to a mode of functioning that is, in a sense to be discussed, in the space between that alluded to by (2a) and by (2b).

Which of these strategies is closest in spirit to Frankfurt's development of the hierarchical model? Well, a main idea of Frankfurt's essays has been that the higher-order attitudes central to agent identification concern whether or not a first-order desire is to be one's "will"—where to be one's "will" is to be an effective desire, a desire that "moves (or will or would move) a person all the way to action."[23] So one natural way to try to

22. I discussed an ancestor of this concern in "Identification, Decision, and Treating as a Reason," in *Faces of Intention*, 198.
23. Frankfurt, "Freedom of the Will and the Concept of a Person," 14. See also "Identification and Wholeheartedness," 164. Note though that in other discussions, Frankfurt employs a considerably broader notion of the agent's will. See, e.g., Harry Frankfurt, "Autonomy, Necessity, and Love," in *Necessity, Volition, and Love* (Cambridge: Cambridge University Press, 1999).

extend Frankfurt's theory would be to try to analyze identification in a sense that involves (1b), along the lines of

(2a) The agent has X-type higher-order attitudes in support of D's functioning as an effective motive.

This would be a version of the third strategy—the strategy of direct appeal to (2a). But there might also be available a version of the second strategy, one that allows initial appeal to

(2b) The agent has X-type higher-order attitudes in support of her treating D as providing a justifying reason.

but then seeks to explain an agent's treating a desire as reason-providing in terms of the effectiveness of a hierarchy in favor of that desire's being one's "will." In either case, the suggested proposal would include a *second* reduction. The first reduction is a reduction (from the 1-level to the 2-level) of agent identification to attitude support. Frankfurt's use of his technical notion of "will," when extended in the envisaged ways, suggests a second reduction, a reduction from the b-level to the a-level—a reduction, roughly, of the agent's treating a desire as reason-providing to that desire's functioning as effective motive because of higher-order attitudes in favor of that functioning.

I am, however, skeptical about such a second reduction. A desire for E may motivate action without any thought that E is a justifying consideration. This is, for example, a plausible story about the motivation of the actions of young children or certain other wantons; and it may be a plausible story about certain unwilling addicts. But, then, it seems that merely desiring that such a motivational process occur may still not bring into the story any thought of E as a justifying consideration. Indeed, it seems that one might even desire that the motivational process involving the desire for E in no way involve a thought of E as justifying. So it is not clear how identification, in a sense that involves (1b), could consist solely of hierarchical structures of a sort characterized by (2a).

This problem raises the question whether the use of the hierarchical model in understanding such identification should be made to depend on the success of this second reduction. I think the answer is no, and that we can instead give the hierarchical model something else to say.[24]

4. A WAY BETWEEN?

If we try to reduce the agent's identification with a desire all the way to (2a), we face objections along the lines just sketched. If we seek only a reduction to (2b), then—in the absence of further analysis—we face a threat of circularity. A response to this problem—and this is the fourth strategy mentioned earlier—is to try to locate a path between these two extremes.

An account of the agent's identification with a desire along the lines of (2a) is one version of a more general strategy. The general strategy is to characterize a mode of functioning of a desire such that, first, that mode of functioning does not itself entail that the agent identifies with the desire, and yet, second, we can understand the agent's identification with a desire in terms of higher-order attitude support of such functioning. We have described an extension of Frankfurt's work that involves a particular version of this strategy, one according to which the relevant mode of functioning is that of being an effective motive. I have argued that, when seen as an approach to (1b), this version of a double reduction runs into difficulties.[25] But perhaps we can find an alternative, and more successful, account of the relevant mode of functioning.

A more successful account would characterize a mode of functioning, F, of a desire—a mode of functioning that satisfies three desiderata. First, it goes beyond functioning merely as an effective motive. Second, by itself it does not entail the agent's identification with the desire. And third, it allows us to analyze the agent's identification with a desire—in a sense that involves (1b)—primarily along the lines of

(2-schema) The agent has X-type higher-order attitudes in support of D's functioning in way F.

24. J. David Velleman also eschews this second reduction in his introduction to *The Possibility of Practical Reason.*

25. For a further difficulty, see my "Identification, Decision, and Treating as a Reason," in *Faces of Intention,* 195–96.

If we take "D's functioning in way F" in (2-schema) to be "D's functioning as an effective motive," we get (2a); if we take "D's functioning in way F" to be "D's being treated by the agent as providing a justifying reason," we get (2b). We have seen reason to be wary of either such version of this general strategy. So, as part of the fourth strategy, we are looking for a conception of F that locates a way between.[26]

Now, we should remain alive to the possibility that there is no such F. We may discover that an F that is sufficiently demanding to make a version of (2-schema) work will itself also entail the agent's identification. Such a result would show the limits of the hierarchical approach. But I think we can do better.

5. FUNCTIONING AS END-SETTING
   FOR PRACTICAL REASONING

What we need is a mode of functioning of a desire for E, such that the thought of E as justifying plays a role in the motivational efficacy of that desire, but there remains the possibility that the agent does not endorse that functioning.

It is useful here to turn to Allan Gibbard's distinction between "accepting a norm" and "being in the grip of a norm."[27] As Gibbard understands these ideas, to accept a norm, or to accept that a certain norm "outweighs another in a given situation," is, roughly and in part, to be disposed explicitly to appeal to that norm (and/or its relative weight) in one's practical reasoning and in one's "normative discussion" with others, and to be, as a result, moved accordingly to action. Gibbard contrasts with this the case of merely being in the grip of a norm, one he explains in part by way of reflection on Stanley Milgram's famous experiment.[28] Many subjects in that experiment reluctantly go along with an experimenter's apparently authoritative orders to do

---

26. The situation here to some extent parallels an analogous problem for the causal theory of action. See, e.g., H. A. Prichard, "Acting, Willing, Desiring," in his *Moral Obligation* (New York: Clarendon Press, 1949), 187–98; and H. Grice, "Intention and Uncertainty," *Proceedings of the British Academy* 57 (1971): 263–79, at 275–78. The solution I go on to sketch, however, has a different structure than that proposed, in the action-theoretic cases, by Prichard and Grice.

27. Gibbard, *Wise Choices, Apt Feelings* (Cambridge, MA: Harvard University Press, 1990), 60. The discussion throughout chapter 4 is relevant here.

28. Ibid., 58–60.

that which appears to inflict suffering on a third party (though it in fact does not inflict suffering). Gibbard supposes that these subjects do not accept that norms of doing one's job override, in such a case, norms against the infliction of harm. Nevertheless, these subjects are in fact moved to act by their norms of doing their job. Gibbard says that these subjects are in the grip of (though they do not accept) that norm and/or its priority over harm avoidance.

Now, it seems likely that at least some obedient subjects in Milgram's experiment do not act without relevant thinking. Their actions are, instead, influenced by thoughts like: "Oh dear. He is the authority, and he told me to do this job, and I really should do my job I guess."[29] These are not cases of being motivated by a rule of which one is simply unaware, as in the case, cited by Gibbard, of the adjustment of conversational distance.[30] The actions of such subjects in Milgram's experiment are influenced by a kind of attenuated reasoning that tracks conformity to the norm of doing their job. For such subjects, thoughts such as "I guess I should cooperate with such an authority" function as end-setting premises in a kind of attenuated reasoning.

This seems a not-uncommon phenomenon. Suppose that I have a strong desire for revenge. This may simply move me to act, perhaps without my even being aware that this is why I am doing what I am doing. But it also may move me by way of powerful thoughts such as: "That creep! He harmed me and now he deserves to pay!" Such a thought about desert may exert a motivational influence by way of its role as end-setting in processes of reasoning. And it may do this even though, on reflection, I do not accept revenge as a justifying end. Again, my desire to procrastinate may involve wistful thoughts such as "Wouldn't it be nice to wait until next week." This may lead to practical reasoning that appeals to procrastination as a justifying end. This may happen even though, on reflection, my higher-order attitudes reject such reasoning.

R. Jay Wallace explores a related phenomenon in his effort to describe certain kinds of irrational guilt. In some such cases, Wallace avers, agents are prone "to entertain evaluative thoughts of disfigurement that they need not accept, but that they tend to find natural." One is disposed "to

---

29. Or so it seems to me. At this point, though, I may be going beyond Gibbard's intended interpretation of the idea of being in the grip of such a norm.
30. Ibid., 69–70.

entertain negative evaluative thoughts one does not necessarily endorse"—
and this "does not require that one be fully committed to [those] evaluative thoughts, either in practical deliberation or as a basis for public
discussion."[31] In these cases of irrational guilt, the negative thoughts provide
structure for the emotion. In the cases in which I am interested, thoughts
of ends as justifying provide structure for processes of reasoning. In neither case, however, need there be full commitment, on the part of the agent,
to these thoughts as elements in deliberation or public justification.[32]

Let us say that a desire for *E functions as end-setting for practical reasoning* when
that desire motivates by way of a process of practical reasoning that appeals
to *E* as a justifying end. For a desire to function as end-setting for practical
reasoning is not merely for it to function as an effective motive: such
functioning also involves thoughts of the desired end as justifying.[33] Nevertheless, a desire may function as end-setting for practical reasoning in the
absence of a higher-order attitude in favor of that functioning. This is what
is common to the Millgram case (as I have interpreted it) and to the cited
cases of revenge and procrastination. So a desire can function as end-setting
for practical reasoning even though the agent does not endorse this
functioning. It is then plausible to suppose that a desire can function as
end-setting for practical reasoning even though the agent does not identify
with that desire. And that is a possibility we wanted to keep open.

We have been trying to understand the agent's identification with a
desire along the lines of

(2-schema) The agent has *X*-type higher-order attitudes in support of *D*'s
functioning in way *F*.

We asked what *F* should be for this to work. The fourth strategy seeks a
version of *F* in the space between (2a) and (2b). We now have the conceptual

31. R. Jay Wallace, *Responsibility and the Moral Sentiments* (Cambridge, MA: Harvard University
Press, 1994), 46.
32. Lawrence Beyer has usefully explored related phenomena in theoretical reasoning. One
of Beyer's many examples is the functioning of certain racist stereotypes. Beyer suggests that
such stereotypes may in the absence of belief nevertheless shape actual thinking and reasoning. See Lawrence Beyer, *The Disintegration of Belief* (PhD thesis, Stanford University, 1999).
33. Might Frankfurt say that, as he is understanding the idea of motivation, motivation by
a first-order desire essentially involves that desire's functioning as end-setting for practical
reasoning? I do not see that this move is available given his understanding of motivation in
young children and certain other wanton agents.

resources to articulate a version of this fourth strategy. We can say that for
D to function in way F is for D to function as end-setting for practical
reasoning. This leads us to the conjecture that we can understand the
agent's identification with a desire along the lines of

> (2c) The agent has X-type higher-order attitudes in support of D's func-
> tioning as end-setting for practical reasoning.

Does this conjecture work?

6. SELF-GOVERNING POLICIES
AND IDENTIFICATION

We need to return to the question: what is type X? In essay 2 I focus on
higher-order policies concerning relevant functioning of one's desires.[34]
I call such higher-order policies *self-governing policies*. I argue that self-
governing policies can have authority to help constitute where the agent
stands with respect to his desires. They can have this authority because of
the central role of such policies in the constitution and support of the
psychological continuities and connections highlighted by broadly Lockean
approaches to the agent's identity over time.[35] Such policies support such
cross-temporal connections, for example, when they concern future deliberation and action, and when one later carries out a prior policy; and the
characteristic stability of such policies is an important kind of psychological
continuity. Such policies have as a characteristic function the support of
coordination and organization of action over time,[36] in part by way of
support for such cross-temporal, Lockean continuities and connections.
This characteristic role of such policies gives them a claim to speak for the
agent, to help settle where the agent stands with respect to a particular

34. "Reflection, Planning, and Temporally Extended Agency." I see policies as intentions
that are appropriately general, and I understand intentions along the lines developed in my
Intention, Plans, and Practical Reason (Cambridge, MA: Harvard University Press, 1987; reissued by
CSLI Publications, 1999).

35. Talk of continuities and connections comes from Derek Parfit, *Reasons and Persons* (New
York: Oxford University Press, 1984), 204–9. I note differences in my use of these terms in
"Reflection, Planning, and Temporally Extended Agency."

36. Frankfurt alludes to the coordinating roles of decisions in "Identification and Wholeheartedness," 175.

form of motivation. This is because the agent is not a time-slice agent but, rather, is—and in practical reasoning and action understands herself to be—a temporally persisting agent whose agency is extended over time.

There is an important qualification. For a higher-order self-governing policy to have such authority, it needs to be free from significant challenges from other relevant higher-order policies. Borrowing both an idea and a term from Frankfurt I have called this a condition of being "satisfied" with the policy.[37]

This suggests that the type of higher-order attitude needed in (2c) is, in the basic case, a higher-order self-governing policy with which the agent is satisfied. Here I will not try to add to the defense of this proposal.[38] Instead, my concern will be to bring this appeal to higher-order policies together with our reflections on the appropriate content of relevant higher-order attitudes.

Begin by considering a higher-order self-governing policy in support of one's treating D as providing a justifying reason.[39] We have seen that if we simply leave matters here in our account of agent identification, we face a concern about circularity. Our reflections on the fourth strategy suggest

37. See Frankfurt, "The Faintest Passion," in *Necessity, Volition and Love*. I develop the idea of satisfaction in a way that is slightly different from Frankfurt's in my "Identification, Decision, and Treating as a Reason," and in "Reflection, Planning, and Temporally Extended Agency."

A second qualification is that the relevant Lockean role can also be played by what I call higher-order "quasi-policies." Though important to the overall story I want to tell, we can safely put this qualification to one side here.

38. I see my discussion in "Reflection, Planning, and Temporally Extended Agency" as a partial defense, though more still needs to be said. Let me note here that, on my view, for a self-governing policy to have the relevant authority, it is not required that that policy be volitionally necessary or part of the person's "essential nature," in the senses recently developed by Frankfurt. (See his "On the Necessity of Ideals," in *Necessity, Volition, and Love*, 108–16, quotation at 113. And, for critical discussion, see J. David Velleman, "Identification and Identity," in S. Buss and L. Overton, eds., *Contours of Agency: Essays on Themes from Harry Frankfurt* (Cambridge, MA: MIT Press, 2002): 91–123.) Self-governing policies have a special relation to the agent's identity over time, not because they are volitionally necessary or essential, but rather because of their roles in organizing thought and action by way of constituting and supporting relevant Lockean ties.

39. This is where I left matters in "Reflection, Planning, and Temporally Extended Agency," noting that I would return later to concerns about circularity. For somewhat related ideas about policies or principles concerning whether to treat a desire as reason-providing, see Rachel Cohon, "Internalism about Reasons for Action," *Pacific Philosophical Quarterly* 74 (1993): 265–88; Christine Korsgaard, *The Sources of Normativity* (New York: Cambridge University Press, 1996); and T. M. Scanlon, *What We Owe to Each Other* (Cambridge, MA: Harvard University Press, 1998), 41–55.

that we consider instead a higher-order self-governing policy in support of
D's functioning as end-setting for reasoning. Is this the kind of higher-
order attitude to be cited in our version of (2-schema)?

Not quite. There are, I think, two further complexities. Let me indicate—
albeit briefly and without a full defense—what I think they are. First, we will
want the relevant policy to be in favor of such functioning *as a matter of
policy*.[40] The relevant policy should include the idea that D so function in
part because it is one's policy that it so function. A natural way to capture
this idea is to suppose that the policy is reflexive: it is a policy that D so
function by way of this very policy.[41]

Second, we will want the relevant higher-order policy to be noninstrumental in the following sense: it is not to be held solely because such
functioning of the desire is seen as a causal means to some further end
distinct from the end specified by the desire itself.[42] This will allow us to
preclude, for example, cases in which one has a policy in favor of such
functioning of a desire solely because one believes that when the desire
functions in this way it tends as a result to go away, thereby saving one
from pain and frustration.[43]

These adjustments in hand,[44] we arrive at an account of agent identification with desire D along the lines of

(3) The agent has a noninstrumental higher-order self-governing policy,
with which she is satisfied, in support of D's functioning, by way of that
very policy, as end-setting for practical reasoning.[45]

40. I owe this way of putting the point to Keith Lehrer.

41. See Gilbert Harman, "Practical Reasoning," *Review of Metaphysics* 29 (1979): 431–63, at 441–45.

42. Peter Railton, Michael Ridge, Michael Smith, and Gideon Yaffe have each helped
convince me of the need for this second modification. The issue goes back to a challenge once
posed to me by Alfred Mele.

43. Note, though, that a policy in favor of Y will be noninstrumental if one has it because
one sees Y as partly constitutive of an ideal one embraces.

44. For reasons Gilbert Harman has discussed, we may also want the policy not to be held
solely because it is thought that such functioning of the desire for E is evidence of (but not a
cause of) some further desired end distinct from E. But this is a complexity we can put to one
side here. See Gilbert Harman, "Desired Desires," in R. G. Frey and C. W. Morris, eds., *Value,
Welfare, and Morality* (Cambridge: Cambridge University Press, 1993), 149.

45. Such policies may go on to assign relevant weights to be given in practical reasoning to
the end set by D. See Nozick, *Philosophical Explanations*, 297; and Gibbard, *Wise Choices, Apt Feelings*,
163. These policies might also see the desire as associated with a kind of side-constraint, though
we do not need to examine this complexity here.

This is a double reduction, but it is one that is more modest than that sketched earlier. We analyze an agent's identification with a desire in terms of support by a relevant higher-order policy in favor of the functioning of that desire as end-setting for practical reasoning. This is a Frankfurtian reduction of agent identification to higher-order attitude support. But this account diverges from a second reduction that tries to appeal solely to the functioning of a desire as a motive. In (3) we explicitly appeal to processes of reasoning involving thoughts of ends as justifying, though to processes of reasoning that do not themselves ensure the agent's identification.

7. SINGULAR COMMITMENTS

An agent identifies with her desire only if she has a noninstrumental self-governing policy, with which she is satisfied, in favor of that desire's functioning, by way of that policy, as end-setting for practical reasoning. Suppose now that she has no such general policy. But suppose that on this particular occasion she does have a noninstrumental *singular* intention in favor of such functioning. That is:

($3_{singular}$) The agent has a noninstrumental intention that D function this time, by way of that very intention, as end-setting for practical reasoning.

Suppose further that

(SC) D functions this time as end-setting for practical reasoning because of ($3_{singular}$).

(SC) goes beyond the mere fact that D functions this time as end-setting for practical reasoning. A desire for revenge, or to cooperate with an authority, may, it seems, function this time as end-setting for practical reasoning even in the absence of an intention that it so function this time. One may in this way be "in the grip" of certain thoughts about desert, or authority. The addition of an instance of ($3_{singular}$) and (SC) to such a case brings with it a way in which the agent is committed to this functioning of the desire.[46] After

---

46. See G. A. Cohen's remarks about "singular edicts" in his "Reason, Humanity, and the Moral Law," included in Korsgaard, *The Sources of Normativity*, 176.

all, the intention in (3_{singular}), though singular, is still—by virtue of being an intention—subject to characteristic normative demands for consistency and coherence. These demands involve constraints that connect even a singular, present-directed intention with other intentions and plans. In that sense, even such a singular intention involves a commitment, on the part of the agent, to such treatment of the desire.[47]

We have, then, three increasingly demanding cases in which higher-order noninstrumental, reflexive plan-like attitudes support the functioning of a desire as end-setting for practical reasoning. One might intend this time that it so function; one might, further, have a policy in favor of its so functioning; and one might have such a policy and also be satisfied with that policy. These are three increasingly demanding ways in which higher-order intentions and policies, and their associated normative structures, can enter into our agency.

There is a tendency in the philosophy of action to limit attention to two main types of theory. There is, on the one hand, a broadly Humean theory that sees action as the output of the causal functioning of desires, and will as, at most, a mere spin-off. There is, on the other hand, a broadly Kantian theory that sees agency and will as essentially involving, and as embedded in, a system of universal principles. On the latter view, it is only when the role of one's desire has been "incorporated" into a system of universal principles that there is an agent and a will, and not merely a system of pushes and pulls.[48]

The present account of possible roles of higher-order plan-like attitudes points toward a conception of agency and will in territory midway between these Humean and Kantian models.[49] This is another respect in which it is indebted to Frankfurt's work, for that work has, as I see it, mapped some of the "contours"[50] of this middle ground. On this middle view, agency and

47. That intentions involve commitments is a theme of my *Intention, Plans, and Practical Reason.*
48. See Henry E. Allison's discussion of what he calls the "Incorporation Thesis" in *Kant's Theory of Freedom* (Cambridge: Cambridge University Press, 1990), 40. And consider Christine Korsgaard's remark that "it is the claim to universality that *gives* me a will, that makes my will distinguishable from the operation of desires and impulses in me" (*The Sources of Normativity*, 232).
49. I discuss a related point in my "Review of Korsgaard's *The Sources of Normativity*," in my *Faces of Intention* at 276–77.
50. To borrow from the apt title of this conference.

will can involve various kinds of higher-order commitments embedded in a system of intentions and plans. Such commitments can be singular and yet still bring to bear characteristic normative demands. But there are also substantial pressures—grounded in the temporal extension of our agency and captured in the idea of the temporally persisting agent's identification with a desire—in the direction of higher-order policies.

8. TREATING A DESIRE AS REASON-PROVIDING

We can now return to the idea of an agent's treating a desire as reason-providing. The conceptual resources we have introduced allow us to describe three increasingly strong cases that may merit the characterization "agent treats desire as reason-providing." The strongest case is one in which the general policy in (3) is effective: the desire functions as end-setting for practical reasoning because of the policy, in (3), in favor of that functioning of the desire.[51] The weakest case is one in which the singular intention in $(3_{singular})$ is effective. The intermediate case is one in which the relevant self-governing policy is effective this time (as in the strongest case), but it is not a policy with which the agent is satisfied. In all cases, treating as reason-providing involves a noninstrumental, reflexive intention or policy in favor of relevant functioning as end-setting for practical reasoning. So on all three views there is a gap between a desire's merely functioning as end-setting and its being treated by the agent as reason-providing. Further, these accounts of treating as reason-providing do not themselves explicitly appeal to the very idea of agent identification—though, on the theory, the strongest case does ensure such identification.[52]

51. If this is what it is for the agent to treat the desire as reason-providing, then by making the cited policy reflexive we ensure that it is, in effect, a policy in favor of one's treating the desire as reason-providing.

52. At this point, we might try to use some such account of the agent's treating a desire as reason-providing in a version of the second strategy noted in section 3. However, this version of the second strategy, like the version of the fourth strategy I have sketched, would be modest with respect to the second reduction: it would not try to understand treating D as reason-providing solely in terms of higher-order support for D's functioning as a motive. So such a version of the second strategy would still cohere with the central claim that such modesty is a better strategy for a hierarchical theory.

9. CONCLUSION

Frankfurt has emphasized hierarchical relations among desires of different orders. In earlier work I have emphasized planning structures—structures whose primary functions concern the coordination and organization of the temporally extended thought and action of a temporally persisting agent.[53] The present essay is part of an effort to bring together into a single theoretical conception both hierarchical and planning structures.[54] Here my primary concern has been to understand and to respond to a worry about circularity that appears to arise for hierarchical theories of identification in the sense of (1b). I have argued that one natural extension of Frankfurt's work to this phenomenon brings with it an overly ambitious double reduction. I have tried to replace this with a strategy for pursuing a less problematic, because more modest, double reduction. Finally, by bringing together both hierarchical and planning structures, we have been able to describe a complex range of ways in which higher-order intentions and policies can structure phenomena of agency and will.

ACKNOWLEDGMENTS

Thanks to John Fischer, Harry Frankfurt, Thomas Hofweber, Keith Lehrer, Alfred Mele, Elijah Millgram, Peter Railton, Michael Ridge, Jennifer Rosner, J. David Velleman, Gideon Yaffe, members of my 1998 Fall Graduate Seminar in the Philosophy of Action, audiences at the University of Michigan and the "Contours of Agency" Conference, and, in particular, the organizers of this conference, Sarah Buss and Lee Overton. Work on the issues discussed in this essay was begun while I was a Fellow at The Center for Advanced Study in the Behavioral Sciences. I am grateful for financial support provided by The Andrew W. Mellon Foundation.

53. See esp. my *Intention, Plans, and Practical Reason.*
54. See also my "Identification, Decision, and Treating as a Reason," "Reflection, Planning, and Temporally Extended Agency," and "Valuing and the Will."

Chapter 5

TWO PROBLEMS ABOUT HUMAN AGENCY

I

In recent work I have highlighted the role in our agency of higher-order "self-governing" policies that say which desires to treat in one's motivationally effective deliberation as associated with justifying reasons for action.[1] A basic role of such policies is the support of the cross-temporal organization of the deliberation and action of temporally persisting agents like us. A recognition of such policies, and of their role in the temporally extended structure of agency, is a key to a plausible account of kinds of agency and deliberation central to our lives. In the present essay I want to say how one can be led to these ideas by reflection on two interrelated problems in the philosophy of action, and on recent work on these problems by Harry Frankfurt and Christine Korsgaard.

1. See my "Reflection, Planning, and Temporally Extended Agency," *Philosophical Review* 109 (2000): 35–61 [this volume, essay 2]: "Valuing and the Will," *Philosophical Perspectives: Action and Freedom* 14 (2000): 249–65 [this volume, essay 3]; and "Hierarchy, Circularity, and Double Reduction," in S. Buss and L. Overton, eds., *Contours of Agency: Essays on Themes from Harry Frankfurt* (Cambridge, MA: MIT Press, 2002) [this volume, essay 4]. My discussion draws from ideas discussed in these essays.

I have sometimes also called "self-governing" higher-order policies that concern only the motivational efficacy of a desire. Here, however, I limit the term, as indicated, to policies about deliberation. My understanding of the very idea of a policy is grounded in the planning theory of intention I develop in my *Intention, Plans, and Practical Reason* (Cambridge, MA: Harvard University Press, 1987—reissued by CSLI Publications, 1999).

2

The first problem concerns deliberation. Intentional action is, I take it, normally motivated in part by what the agent wants or desires—in a suitably broad, generic sense of these notions.[2] It is also true that intentional action is sometimes the issue of deliberation in which the agent considers what she sees as reasons—that is, as justifying, normative reasons—for and against her alternatives. This raises the question: how is motivation of action by the agent's desires or pro attitudes related to motivationally effective normative deliberation of the agent of which action is sometimes the issue?

One response is that whenever there is motivated intentional action, the agent is in a position to deliberate, in a motivationally effective way, to a conclusion that she has normative reason so to act.[3] This entails that whenever there is motivated intentional action the agent both has the capacities needed for such normative deliberation and accepts relevant premises. As others have argued, however, this seems to tie motivation of intentional action too tightly to normative deliberation.[4] Motivating desires may be sudden urges or emotions or influences of which the agent is unaware at the time of action or aspects of addiction or powerful appetites or cravings or forms of anger or competitiveness or simply the desires of children who do not yet have the conceptual resources for normative deliberation. In some such cases it seems there can be motivation of intentional action even though the agent either does not have the capacity for normative deliberation or, though she has this capacity, does not accept relevant normative premises. Adult human agents are typically motivated by desires because they see these desires as associated with justifying reasons; but it does not follow, and it does not seem to be true, that this is a necessary feature of all motivation.

2. In a sufficiently abstract, broad, generic sense of "desire" or "pro-attitude," we can classify intentions as a kind of pro attitude. But on my view it is important that intentions are a distinctive kind of pro attitude and must be distinguished from ordinary desires that may favor or oppose various conflicting considerations. See my *Intention, Plans, and Practical Reason*.

3. This is one way to understand Donald Davidson's view in his "How Is Weakness of the Will Possible?" and "Intending" in his *Essays on Actions and Events* (Oxford: Oxford University Press, 1980). See e.g., 31, 86.

4. See Michael Smith, *The Moral Problem* (Oxford: Blackwell, 1994), chap. 5; and J. David Velleman, "Introduction," and "The Guise of the Good," in his *The Possibility of Practical Reason* (Oxford: Oxford University Press, 2000). The examples to follow are drawn from these and other essays in this recent literature.

If this is right, we need a more nuanced understanding of the relation between desire-based motivation and the agent's motivationally effective normative deliberation. This is a question about the relation between having a desire or pro attitude in favor of X, and seeing oneself, in one's motivationally effective deliberation, as having normative reason to promote X. It is a question about the relation between desiring X and treating X, or one's desire for X, as having normative authority in one's motivationally effective deliberation. So let us call this the problem of *subjective normative authority.*[5]

The second problem I want to discuss is a problem about the metaphysics of agency. When a person acts because of what she desires or intends or the like, we sometimes do not want to say simply that the pro attitude leads to the action. In some cases we suppose, further, that the *agent* is the source of, determines, directs, governs the action, and is not merely the locus of a series of happenings, of causal pushes and pulls.

A skeptic might doubt that there really is an important distinction between (merely) motivated behavior and action determined or governed by the agent.[6] And it is true that in any case of motivated behavior the agent in some sense acts. Nevertheless, many of the cases that suggest a gap between desire-based motivation that is and that is not appropriately related to the agent's normative deliberation also suggest a distinction between (merely) motivated behavior and, as I will call it, full-blown agency. An agent moved by desires of which he is unaware, or on which he is incapable of reflecting, or from whose role in action he is, as we sometimes say, estranged, seems himself less the source of the activity than a locus of forces.

I believe such intuitions do point to something important about our agency. The problem is to say what that is. In particular, we need to know whether this phenomenon of agent (or, self-) determination consists in

5. The label "subjective" is intended to indicate that this is a question about the agent's view of what has normative authority for her deliberation.

6. Actually, there are three different skeptics lurking. One is skeptical about the distinction between (merely) motivated behavior and action determined by the agent but not about the distinction between desire-based motivation that is and that is not appropriately related to the agent's normative deliberation. A second is skeptical about both distinctions. A third is skeptical about the distinction between two varieties of desire-based motivation but not about the distinction between (merely) motivated behavior and action determined by the agent. It is a skeptic of one of the first two varieties that is the concern of this paragraph.

some, perhaps complex, causal structure involving events, states, and processes of a sort we might appeal to within a broadly naturalistic psychology.[7]

We can sharpen the question. What we want to know is whether there is a kind of psychological functioning, a kind we can characterize without presupposing the very idea of agent determination of action, such that agent determination of action consists in such functioning. Can we uncover truths along the lines of

(A) S is the full-blown agent of X iff X is the issue of psychological functioning of type T.

What (A) would tell us is that psychological functioning of type T has authority to constitute the *agent's* determination of action. So let us call this the problem of *agential authority*. The problem of agential authority is the problem of specifying T or, alternatively, arguing that no such account is available.

So these are my two problems: the problem of subjective normative authority and the problem of agential authority.[8] I do not say these are the only relevant issues about authority that confront the philosophy of action. Indeed, I will turn at the end of this essay to yet a further issue about authority. But my main concern will be to explain how appeal to self-governing policies can advance our understanding of both agential and subjective normative authority. I begin by reflecting on work by Harry Frankfurt and Christine Korsgaard.

3

Frankfurt's work on higher-order desires suggests the following approach to the problem of agential authority:[9]

7. See J. David Velleman, "What Happens When Someone Acts?" in his *The Possibility of Practical Reason*, at 132. Velleman refers to related discussions of John Bishop in his *Natural Agency* (Cambridge: Cambridge University Press, 1989). See also Velleman's "Introduction" to *The Possibility of Practical Reason*, and R. E. Hobart's remarks about "the analytical imagination," in his "Free Will as Involving Determination and Inconceivable without It," *Mind* 93 (1934): 1–27.

8. The idea of formulating these problems in terms of two notions of authority to some extent derives from a conversation with Christopher McMahon.

9. See both his *The Importance of What We Care About* (Cambridge: Cambridge University Press, 1988) and his *Necessity, Volition, and Love* (Cambridge: Cambridge University Press, 1999).

(F) Agent S determines action X just when (roughly):
    (1) S's desire to X motivates X,
    (2) S desires that (1),
    (3) S has no yet higher-order desire in conflict with (2),
    (4) (1) because (2), and
    (5) S identifies with her desire in (2).[10]

Appeal to the second-order desire in (2)—what Frankfurt calls a second-order volition—is a hallmark of Frankfurt's hierarchical model. The need for something like (5) is indicated by Gary Watson's response to Frankfurt's original discussion. As Watson said, "Since second-order volitions are themselves simply desires, to add them to the context of the conflict is just to increase the number of contenders; it is not to give a special place to any of those in contention."[11] We need something like condition (5) to explain why the second-order volition in (2) has authority to constitute where S stands.

A great deal, then, depends on how we understand (5). And this has been a concern of much of Frankfurt's work. As I see it, two different accounts of (5) have emerged. The first is along the lines of

(5a) The agent is satisfied with (2).[12]

The second is along the lines of

(5b) (2) is grounded in a volitional structure that has, for that agent, a "volitional necessity" that the agent is wholehearted about and that is "constitutive of his nature or essence as a volitional being."[13]

---

10. Qualifications are in order. First, in (1) we should allow for a case in which the desire at issue is for something other than X that the agent sees X as promoting. Second, we should add to (3) the disjunct that if there are yet higher-order, conflicting desires, the highest-order desire favors (2). Third, there are complexities about the interpretation of the "because" in (4) that would need to be sorted out in a more complete discussion. Fourth, in having the desire in (2) the agent needs to understand that, in at least a minimal sense, he himself is S. And, fifth, we can allow that an agent capable of such agency acts in some strong sense when, in the particular case, there is not sufficient reflection to satisfy (1)–(5) but such reflection is (in ways that would need to be explained) sufficiently in the background. But to keep things manageable I will here bracket these further complexities.

11. Watson, "Free Agency," *Journal of Philosophy* 72 (1975): 205–20, at 218. Watson is responding to Frankfurt's "Freedom of the Will and the Concept of a Person," reprinted in *The Importance of What We Care About*.

12. "The Faintest Passion," in *Necessity, Volition, and Love*. I discuss some Frankfurtian steps along the way to this idea in my "Identification, Decision, and Treating as a Reason," in my *Faces of Intention: Selected Essays on Intention and Agency* (New York: Cambridge University Press, 1999), 185–206.

13. "On the Necessity of Ideals," in *Necessity, Volition, and Love*, at 111–12.

Concerning (5a): As understood by Frankfurt, satisfaction with (2) is not a further attitude toward (2) but, rather, a structural feature of the agent's psychology.[14] The agent is satisfied with (2) when he has no interest in changing this fact about himself, and this lack of interest "derive[s] from his understanding and evaluation of how things are with him."[15] Concerning (5b): A volitional structure is volitionally necessary when the agent is, at the time, unable to will otherwise. He is wholehearted about this when his higher-order attitudes favor this inability and are themselves volitionally necessary. And the necessity is "constitutive of his nature or essence as a volitional being" when the agent would in some appropriate sense cease to be the person he is in the absence of this volitional structure.[16]

I have argued elsewhere that (5a) is too weak to play the needed role in (F).[17] Frankfurtian satisfaction with a desire may itself be rooted in a background of enervation, depression, exhaustion, or the like. In some such cases, conditions (1)–(4) and (5a) will not ensure that there is a fact about where the agent stands, and so will not ensure full-blown agency.

What about (5b)? While this is not the occasion to argue this in detail, I do think that (5b) is too strong.[18] There seem to be significant commitments— for example, my commitment to scholarship—that are sufficient to ground full-blown agency but that are not volitional necessities of the relevant sort.

So I doubt that either way of spelling out (5) will solve the agential authority problem. Nevertheless, there is an important lesson to learn from these efforts. Frankfurt tries to solve the agential authority problem by appeal to certain forms of psychological functioning of the higher-order desire in (2) (and of related volitional attitudes). Frankfurt requires, in particular, that the higher-order desire in (2) be embedded in a psychology in which pressure for change is absent, or in which certain aspects are volitionally necessary in the cited way. As indicated, I am skeptical that these are precisely the right kinds of functioning to which to appeal in

14. "The Faintest Passion," 104.
15. "The Faintest Passion," 105.
16. This, anyway, seems to me one reasonable reading of "On the Necessity of Ideals," 111–12.
17. "Identification, Decision, and Treating as a Reason," in *Faces of Intention*, at 194–95; "Reflection, Planning, and Temporally Extended Agency," at 48–49 [this volume, p. 94].
18. This is in the spirit of Jennifer Rosner's discussion of Frankfurt's views in her "Authority, Individuality, and Caring" (unpublished manuscript). For reasons discussed below, there is also a way in which (5b) is too weak to solve the problem of subjective normative authority.

solving the agential authority problem: one seems too weak, the other too strong. Rather than reject the strategy outright, however, we can seek an alternative form of functioning to play the needed role in agential authority. I return to this quest below.

Consider now the problem of subjective normative authority. Frankfurt's framework may suggest that the connection between motivating desires and the agent's normative deliberation is provided primarily by the higher-order desire in (2). To see myself as having normative reason to X is, very roughly, to desire that my desire to X motivate my action.[19]

There is an important insight here. We are creatures who are not merely motivated to act in various ways; we also have the capacity to step back and critically reflect on that motivation. Some version of such higher-order critical reflection seems central to the agent's normative deliberation.[20]

But there is, I think, a problem with the specific way just proposed of articulating this insight. The higher-order volition in (2) is a desire that a certain first-order desire *motivate*. It is not a desire to *reason* or *deliberate* in a certain way; it is not a desire that one treat the target of the first-order desire as *justifying*. We have noted that motivational processes need not involve normative deliberation. Once we note this, it seems unclear how yet another desire simply in favor of such a motivational process can on its own be enough to provide the materials for such normative deliberation.

Frankfurt may well agree. While he sees his hierarchical model as part of a solution to the agential authority problem, it isn't clear he would offer it, in the absence of further resources, as a solution to the problem of subjective normative authority.[21] Nevertheless, since it is natural to think of the hierarchical model as at least part of an effort to solve this problem, it is important to be aware of the issue just noted. Further, a theory of agential authority needs at least to be coordinated with an associated account of subjective normative authority. We are, after all, agents whose actions are

19. Cp. David Lewis's proposal that "valuing is just desiring to desire" in his "Dispositional Theories of Value," *Proceedings of the Aristotelian Society* suppl. vol. 73 (1989): 113–37, at 115. Note, though, the difference in the precise content of Lewis's second-order desires and Frankfurt's second-order volitions.

20. This is also a main theme of Korsgaard's work.

21. Frankfurt suggested in conversation (November, 1999) that he would not.

frequently the issue of normative deliberation; and we are frequently agents of such deliberation. For agents like us, these interconnections between agency and deliberation are significant.

4

Indeed, we can see Christine Korsgaard's work as aiming at simultaneous solutions to both problems of authority.[22] A basic move in this proposed joint solution is an appeal to the idea of a "conception of your practical identity."[23] Given a desire to act in a certain way, a reflective agent asks whether she has a normative reason for so acting.[24] She answers, in part, by seeing whether a conception of her practical identity grants this normative status to that desire, or to what that desire is for.[25]

It is not enough, however, simply that some entertained conception of one's identity regard the desire as reason-giving. After all, an agent may on occasion find attractive a certain conception of herself—say, as fabulously wealthy—and yet this only be a passing fancy. Or the agent may be tempted by conflicting and competing self-conceptions. For such a self-conception to play its role in a "source" of normativity, that conception must itself be endorsed by the agent—the agent must "identify" with that conception.[26] Further, it is when action is the issue of normative deliberation anchored in such an endorsed conception of practical identity that there is full-blown agency and not merely an outcome of causal pushes and pulls. The agent determines action just when conceptions of practical identity that are endorsed by the agent shape deliberation out of which action issues.

22. See Korsgaard's *The Sources of Normativity* (Cambridge: Cambridge University Press, 1996), esp. 100–104 and 227–32. Except as noted, I limit my brief discussion of Korsgaard's views to this book. A fuller treatment would also consider her more recent "Self-constitution in the Ethics of Plato and Kant," *The Journal of Ethics* 3 (1999): 1–29.

23. *Sources*, 101.

24. *Sources*, 97.

25. *Sources*, 101. See also 113.

26. *Sources*, 103–4. Rachel Cohon ("The Roots of Reasons," *Philosophical Review* 109 [2000]: 63–85) argues that further endorsement of the conception of practical identity may not be needed for that conception to ground a reason for action. The point I go on to make is, instead, that an appeal to this further endorsement brings us back to the need to say in what sense it is the *agent's* endorsement.

The problem is that we still need to be told what it is for *the agent* to endorse a conception of practical identity; for otherwise we are helping ourselves to the idea of agency that we were trying to explain. This problem may not be obvious, because the cited attitudes are conceptions of one's practical identity—of who one is to be—and this may suggest that there is no further issue of whether these attitudes speak for the agent. But that would be a mistake. Even if the content of the conception is about who the agent is to be, it is a further question whether that conception has authority to speak for the agent. This is at least in part because it is a further question whether that conception is located in the relevant way in the agent's psychological functioning.

Korsgaard might reply that a conception of practical identity speaks for the agent just when it functions in the indicated way in motivationally effective normative deliberation. And, indeed, this is true *if* by normative deliberation we mean deliberation directed *by the agent*. But then we need a way to distinguish deliberation directed by the agent from reasoning processes in the agent that mimic such deliberation but are not directed or endorsed by the agent.[27] And that returns us to the problem of agential authority.

What about the problem of subjective normative authority? Here Korsgaard's theory seems in one respect more apt than Frankfurt's theory. Frankfurt appeals to higher-order desires in favor of forms of motivation that need not themselves involve normative thought. Korsgaard appeals to conceptions of practical identity that explicitly concern what is to count in one's deliberation as reason for action. In this respect Korsgaard's conceptions are more explicitly directed at the problem of subjective normative authority.

However, Korsgaard's conceptions of practical identity cannot by themselves provide a full solution to that problem. A full solution must explain

---

27. In my "Hierarchy, Circularity, and Double Reduction," I suggest that certain cases of what Allan Gibbard calls being in the "grip" of a norm will involve processes in the agent that mimic such deliberation even though they are not endorsed by the agent. See Allan Gibbard, *Wise Choices, Apt Feelings* (Cambridge, MA: Harvard University Press, 1990), 60. According to Stephen Darwall, Ralph Cudworth made a related distinction between, as Darwall puts it, a "process *in* the person" connecting evaluative belief and action, and "something the agent can, in some suitable sense, himself direct." See Stephen Darwall, *The British Moralists and the Internal "Ought"* (Cambridge: Cambridge University Press, 1995), at 134.

the connection between motivational structures and normative deliberation *by the agent*. So a full solution must also solve the agential authority problem; and, as we have seen, we do not do that simply by appeal to conceptions whose content concerns a "practical identity."

5

I began this essay by pointing to the significance of the temporally extended structure of our agency. It is time to return to this idea.

Begin by recalling an aspect of Frankfurt's strategy. Frankfurt tried to identify a feature of full-blown agency that could anchor agential authority: satisfaction, on one account; or a form of volitional necessity, on another. He then asked what functioning of what higher-order attitudes constituted such a feature. My proposal will be that we pursue a similar strategy but highlight a different feature of our agency.

An agent acts at a particular time. But adult human agents are not simply time-slice agents. Adult human agents persist over time, and their practical thinking concerns itself with and plays central roles in the organization and coordination of their activities over time. In this sense their agency is temporally extended.

Such temporal extendedness is a deep feature of our agency.[28] A creature whose thought, in contrast, did not function to impose forms of cross-temporal organization on its moment-to-moment activities would be an agent of a very different sort, one who would be incapable of many of the forms of living we most value. The capacity for temporally extended agency is, to use Rawls's term, a primary good, useful in the pursuit of an enormously wide range of human ends.[29] So let us ask what happens if we let the temporal extendedness of our agency play a theoretical role, in the account of agential authority, analogous to that played in Frankfurt's theory by satisfaction or forms of volitional necessity. Well, we should then look for modes of psychological functioning, of relevant higher-order attitudes, that

28. Cp. Korsgaard: "When the person is viewed as an agent, no clear content can be given to the idea of a merely present self." "Personal Identity and the Unity of Agency," in Christine M. Korsgaard, *Creating the Kingdom of Ends* (Cambridge: Cambridge University Press, 1996): 363–97, at 372.

29. John Rawls, *A Theory of Justice*, rev. ed. (Cambridge, MA: Harvard University Press, 1999), 54.

help constitute and support this temporal extension of our agency. The conjecture would be that such higher-order functioning is central to the agent's determination of her action.

This conjecture would not be very far from Frankfurt's appeals to volitional necessity or to satisfaction.[30] Both these Frankfurtian phenomena are connected to forms of stability important to the cross-temporal organization of our agency.[31] What this conjecture does is explicitly characterize the constitution and support of such cross-temporal organization and coordination as a form of functioning that provides a ground of agential authority.

This conjecture would also share with Korsgaard the idea that agential authority is somehow tied to the agent's identity over time.[32] Korsgaard develops this idea by appeal to agentially endorsed conceptions whose content concerns the kind of agent one is to be. The present conjecture, in contrast, appeals to the role or function of certain higher-order elements in supporting and constituting the temporal extension of agency.[33] If we take a broadly Lockean view of the agent's temporal persistence—a view that sees various psychological connections and continuities as constituting temporal persistence—we will see such functioning as tied tightly to the agent's identity over time.

The conjecture, then, is that the ground of agential authority involves higher-order attitudes whose function includes the constitution and support of the temporal extension of agency.

Well, what attitudes are these? In earlier work I have argued that our intentions, plans, and policies have it as a characteristic role to help constitute and support the organization and coordination of our activity

30. Indeed, I believe that a full theory will also need to appeal to a kind of satisfaction with the higher-order attitudes that play such roles in the temporal extension of agency. See my "Reflection, Planning, and Temporally Extended Agency," 48–50 [this volume, pp. 33–36].

31. Cp. Frankfurt, "Identification and Wholeheartedness," in *The Importance of What We Care About*, 175.

32. Note also Frankfurt's allusion to issues of personal identity in condition (5b).

33. A psychological structure can have causal tendencies that are not included in its function, in the sense of "function" we need here. To return to an earlier example, a depression that leads to an absence of interest in changing one's desires may tend to result in certain cross-temporal continuities; but this is not, I take it, a function (in the relevant sense) of such depression any more than it is a function of a flat tire to keep a car from moving.

over time.[34] They play these roles in part by way of constituting and supporting kinds of psychological connections and continuities that are, on a broadly Lockean view, central to the agent's persistence over time.[35] In playing these roles intentions, plans, and policies involve distinctive forms of commitment to relevant planning and action, forms of commitment that go beyond what is ensured by ordinary desires. If we combine these views with the strategy just sketched we arrive at the conjecture that the ground of agential authority involves higher-order intentions, plans, and policies.[36]

What, precisely, would the contents of these higher-order intentions, plans, and policies be? To answer, we need to return to subjective normative authority.

6

Suppose we follow Frankfurt and see hierarchy as central to full-blown agency. Suppose, however, that when we turn to subjective normative authority, we agree that Frankfurt's hierarchical structures fall short because of their exclusive focus, in their content, on the motivational functioning of first-order desires. Should we then bypass the hierarchical story in our approach to deliberation and subjective normative authority? This would, I think, be a mistake. The thought, that our normative deliberation is tied to higher-order reflection on our motivation remains a powerful idea. I do not think that we can adequately develop this idea by appeal solely to higher-order volitions, in Frankfurt's technical sense. But we should be careful not to throw out the baby with the bath water. Further, we know that in the end the responses to each problem of authority must mesh; for we need to model the *agent's* deliberation. These

34. See *Intention, Plans, and Practical Reason* and *Faces of Intention.*
35. See "Reflection, Planning, and Temporally Extended Agency."
36. The claim is not that higher-order intentions, plans, and policies are necessary for the temporal persistence of the agent; the claim is that these higher-order attitudes have the constitution and support of temporally extended agency as part of their function.

A further point is that we shall, I believe, need to extend this view to include, in the grounds of agential authority, what I have called "quasi-policies." [See "Reflection, Planning, and Temporally Extended Agency," at 57–60 (this volume, pp. 42–44).] But we can safely ignore this complexity here.

considerations suggest that a natural step, in approaching subjective normative authority, would be to exploit hierarchical structures that are going to be needed in the story of full-blown agency. But we have seen that these cannot be limited to Frankfurtian structures of higher-order volitions that solely concern motivational functioning.

At this point we can draw on a more Korsgaardian idea: we appeal to higher-order attitudes concerning what desired ends to treat as justifying considerations in motivationally effective deliberation. Now, the hierarchical story I have been developing appeals to higher-order intentions, plans, and policies. So the idea would be to give these higher-order attitudes contents that concern what desired ends to treat as justifying reasons. We try to solve the problem of subjective normative authority, and to say what constitutes the agent's deliberation, by appeal to higher-order intentions, plans, and policies, about which desired ends to treat as reasons in motivationally effective deliberation. This seems a promising strategy in part because such higher-order intentions, plans, and policies have, as a matter of function, tight connections to the temporal extension of agency. That is why they are candidates for attitudes that, because of their role in our agency, can speak for the agent.

In particular, higher-order *policies* about which desired ends to treat as reasons are intimately tied to the cross-temporal organization and systemization of one's deliberative agency over time; for such policies concern one's deliberation and deliberative action in repeated occurrences of situations of certain types.[37] And this brings us, as promised, to the idea of a self-governing policy—that is, a higher-order policy about which desired ends to treat as reasons in one's motivationally effective deliberation. Such self-governing policies provide a structural connection between motivation and normative deliberation. And such policies help ground agential authority because of their tie, by way of their function, to the organization of deliberative agency over time. They can thereby play, as promised, central roles in interlocking accounts of agential authority and of subjective normative authority.

37. A more detailed discussion would also need to consider higher-order singular intentions to treat, this time, a desired end as justifying in deliberation. I discuss these matters in my "Hierarchy, Circularity, and Double Reduction."

Now, it is Korsgaard's view that it is only from the practical point of view of deliberation and decision that our full-blown agency is discernible. She writes:

> it is only from the practical point of view that actions and choices can be distinguished from mere "behavior" determined by biological and psychological laws.[38]

In contrast, while the proposal I am sketching highlights the first-person perspective of the reflective agent, it still allows for third-person judgments, made from a theoretical point of view, that there is sufficient reflective structure to constitute self-government of action. So we can continue to see full-blown agency as part of a natural order that is available to shared, third-person, theoretical investigation.

7

Does our appeal, within the content of self-governing policies, to the *agent's* treating something as justifying draw on the very idea of agency that poses the problem of agential authority? Are we moving in a circle?

There is, I believe, a way to avoid such circularity.[39] We first characterize a mode of functioning of a desire for E in terms of two ideas. First, this mode of functioning issues in an intention in favor of a believed means to E, and it does this in a way that suitably depends on the thought of E as a justifying end. This mode of functioning is a kind of (perhaps, attenuated) reasoning. Nevertheless, and this is the second idea, though this functioning takes place in the agent, the agent may or may not direct or endorse it. So, for example, perhaps for some subjects in the famous Milgram experiments all of the following was true: they had desires to conform to the orders of the experimenter; these desires motivated intention and action by way of attenuated reasoning involving thoughts such as "I guess I should do what the authority tells me to do"; and yet the subjects did not direct or endorse that reasoning.[40]

---

38. "Personal Identity and the Unity of Agency," at 378.
39. See "Hierarchy, Circularity, and Double Reduction."
40. See Allan Gibbard's discussion of these experiments in his *Wise Choices, Apt Feelings*, at 58–61. Lawrence Beyer discusses cases of theoretical reasoning that are to some extent analogous in his *The Disintegration of Belief* (PhD thesis, Stanford University, 1999).

Let us say that when a desire for E functions in the cited way it *functions as end-setting for practical reasoning*. Since this functioning may fail to be directed or endorsed by the agent, it need not be an instance of full-blown agency. We can then say that a policy of one's treating a desired end, E, as a reason in one's motivationally effective deliberation consists, in the basic case, of a policy in favor of that desire's functioning, by way of this very policy, as end-setting for practical reasoning. In this way the explicit content of the self-governing policy need not appeal to a prior notion of full-blown agency. However, while the cited functioning of the desire as end-setting need not be an instance of full-blown agency, its occurrence by way of such a reflexive policy is.

While this helps avoid circularity with respect to agency, it may seem to bring into the open a different threat. A self-governing policy appeals in its content to processes involving the thought of E as *justifying*. But what is it to think of E as justifying? Without an answer have we really made progress with the problem of subjective normative authority?

I think that we have made progress; for we have provided a noncircular story about how this thought needs to be enmeshed in the agent's psychology for there to be motivationally effective normative deliberation by the agent. While not a reductive analysis of thinking of E as a justifying consideration, it is a model of agency and deliberation within which to locate such thinking.[41]

8

A self-governing policy to treat a desired end E as a justifying consideration is, on analysis, a reflexive policy in favor of the functioning of the desire for E as end-setting for practical reasoning. I have appealed to characteristic roles of such policies in the temporal extension of our agency as support for their claim to agential authority.[42] This aspect of my story is broadly Frankfurtian, for it sees a certain kind of functioning in our agency (though

---

41. I think this model allows for either a cognitivist or an expressivist understanding of such thinking. See T. M. Scanlon, *What We Owe to Each Other* (Cambridge, MA: Harvard University Press, 1998), 58.
42. Though recall complexities cited above in notes 30, 36, and 37.

a kind of functioning different from those emphasized by Frankfurt) as grounding a claim to agential authority. But, in contrast with Frankfurt's discussions, the content of these policies involves the very idea of a justifying reason for action. This joint appeal, in the story of self-governing policies, to function and to content provides resources for a coordinated solution to both our problems about authority.

There may seem, however, to be a further kind of authority for which we have not yet provided. Suppose an agent's relevant self-governing policy favors giving her desired end E deliberative preference over her desired end F in case of conflict. Given this policy,[43] if she were to intend this time to pursue F rather than E, her web of policies and more specific intentions would involve an important incoherence. She can avoid this incoherence by either (a) eschewing the intention to pursue F this time, or (b) changing her self-governing policy. But, further, it also seems that there is an important sense in which, within the agent's perspective, there is a (perhaps defeasible) presumption in favor of (a) rather than (b).[44] Within the agent's perspective, the self-governing policy seems to have a *presumptive normative authority*.[45] And the worry is that we have so far failed to explain this.

One point to make here is that we can normally expect general policies to be, other things equal, subject to stronger demands for stability than are temporally specific intentions. This is at least in part because their generality is normally the result of prior reflection.[46] But there is, I think, a further point in the offing, and our account of agential authority allows us to say what it is. Begin by asking: what constitutes the perspective of the agent within which the self-governing policy is seen as having presumptive

43. And her satisfaction with it.

44. This formulation is intended to allow for cases in which, from the outside, we would be more critical of (a) than of (b). (Suppose the self-governing policy is morally corrupt.) It is also intended to leave open the possibility of cases in which other features of the agent's overall psychology override this presumption. For a discussion of related matters, see Nomy Arpaly, "On Acting Rationally against One's Best Judgment," *Ethics* 110 (2000): 488–513.

45. In his discussion of authority in the political domain, Christopher McMahon distinguishes (i) subordinating authority from (ii) authorized authority. When we turn from the political to the psychological we can say that (ii) corresponds roughly to agential authority, whereas (i), when seen within the agent's perspective, corresponds roughly to presumptive normative authority. See his *Authority and Democracy: A General Theory of Government and Management* (Princeton, NJ: Princeton University Press, 1994), chap. 2.

46. In this sentence I have benefited from discussion with Harry Frankfurt and Robin Jeshion.

normative authority? Well, so long as we are talking about agents like us, the agent of the action is an agent who persists over time and whose agency is temporally extended. And this is a deep fact about the kind of agents we are; or so I have averred. So it is natural to understand the relevant, agential perspective as the perspective of the temporally persisting agent whose agency is temporally extended. And that may well be what we are thinking when we say that within the agent's perspective the self-governing policy has presumptive normative authority. This thought would be explained and justified by the tight connection between such self-governing policies and temporally extended agency. Since self-governing policies have, be-cause of this tight connection, agential authority, they play a central role in constituting the very perspective that is at issue in such talk about pre-sumptive normative authority. Since these policies in part constitute the relevant perspective, it is no surprise that within this perspective they have a special authority.[47]

47. My thinking in this essay has benefited from a series of conversations with Harry Frankfurt and Gideon Yaffe. Thanks also to David Copp, Christoph Fehige, Govert den Hartogh, Agnieszka Jaworska, Ariela Lazar, Michael Ridge, Michael Smith, J. David Velleman, and participants in discussions of this paper at colloquia at University of Soutern California, Northwestern University, Bowling Green State University, and The Aristotelian Society. My work on this essay was supported by a fellowship from the John Simon Guggenheim Memorial Foundation.

Chapter 6

NOZICK ON FREE WILL

Robert Nozick's *Philosophical Explanations*[1] is a rich and wide-ranging explo-
ration of some of the deepest issues in philosophy. Nozick examines
fundamental questions about, among other things, personal identity,
knowledge, free will, value, and the meaning of life. In this chapter, my
primary concern will be with Nozick's discussion of free will: What is it,
might we have it, and why should we want it? Nozick says much about free
will that is fascinating, suggestive, and worth our further reflection.[2] His
discussions of free will also are linked with many of his other views in this
book—especially about personal identity and value. This presents both an
opportunity and a problem. The opportunity is to see a sketch of one way
we might profitably conceptualize some of the interrelations among these
issues.[3] The problem is that Nozick's views about personal identity and
value themselves raise a host of difficult questions; yet in each case the

1. (Cambridge, MA: Harvard University Press, 1981) (hereafter *PE*). Parenthetical page references in the text are to this book.
2. See esp. *PE*, pp. 291–362.
3. Recently, a number of theorists have explored ways of understanding connections
between forms of free will, autonomy, or self-determination, on the one hand, and personal
identity, on the other. This makes Nozick's early discussion of such connections of particular
interest. For recent discussions of different versions of such connections, see Christine Korsgaard, *The Sources of Normativity* (Cambridge: Cambridge University Press, 1996); Harry Frankfurt,
"On the Necessity of Ideals," in his *Necessity, Volition and Love* (Cambridge: Cambridge University
Press, 1999): 108–16; Gideon Yaffe, *Liberty Worth the Name: Locke on Free Agency* (Princeton, NJ:
Princeton University Press, 2000); J. David Velleman, "Identification and Identity," in S. Buss and
L. Overton, eds., *Contours of Agency: Essays on Themes from Harry Frankfurt* (Cambridge, MA: MIT Press,
2002); and my own "Reflection, Planning, and Temporally Extended Agency," *Philosophical Review*
109 (2000): 35–61 [this volume, essay 2].

examination of those questions would require an essay of its own. My strategy will be to try to take advantage of the opportunity while avoiding the temptations to write yet another paper.

I. FREE WILL AND DIGNITY

What is free will and why do we want it? As Nozick notes, many have been interested in free will because they believe that some form of free will is necessary for a person to be an appropriate target of moral praise or blame, or of forms of criminal punishment. While recognizing the importance of such matters (indeed, there is an extended discussion of punishment in *PE*, pp. 363–97), however, Nozick's primary concern lies elsewhere. Nozick believes that the absence of free will would "undercut human dignity" (291). So he seeks to "formulate a conception of human action" that sees us as having a kind of free will sufficient to ground human dignity (291). And here Nozick grapples with a familiar, traditional puzzle.

Ignoring some subtleties, we can put the puzzle this way: An event, E, is causally determined if conditions prior to that event, together with causal laws of nature, ensure that E occur. Determinism is the view, roughly, that every event is causally determined by prior conditions. Suppose that determinism is true and so that every choice, decision, and action is determined by prior conditions that were causally sufficient for its occurrence. In this case, it seems that when one acts one is not free to act otherwise, and so there is no free will.[4]

Suppose, in contrast, that determinism is false and that some choice, decision, or action is not determined by prior conditions. Given all prior conditions and all relevant causal laws that choice, decision, or action might not have happened. But then it seems that the occurrence of that choice, decision, or action was a matter of chance—a random, unexplainable event. Such a random event is not a ground for human dignity. But, given any choice, decision, or action either it is determined by prior conditions or it is not. In either case it does not involve a kind of free will that could ground human dignity. So there is no such free will.

4. See Peter van Inwagen, "The Incompatibility of Free Will and Determinism," *Philosophical Studies* 27 (1975): 185–99.

That is the traditional puzzle. There are, of course, traditional lines of response. Libertarians agree that the causal determination of a decision is incompatible with its being free. They then try to construct a model of free, nondetermined choice or decision, a model that shows how choice, decision, or action can be nondetermined and free, and yet not happen at random, as a matter of chance.[5] Note that a libertarian need not deny that free choices and decisions have causes; she need only deny that these causes, if such there be, function deterministically.[6]

Compatibilists try instead to answer by constructing a model of free choice and action such that a choice or action can be both free (in the relevant sense) and causally determined by prior conditions.

Nozick's response is complex and does not fit neatly into either of these categories (though he would very much like to be a libertarian). Nozick presents three different models of human action. The first is offered as a form of libertarianism; the other two are seen by Nozick as the best we could do in a deterministic world. Nozick is not confident that the first successfully answers worries about randomness; but he also doubts that the latter two—which he sees as "second best" (293)—even taken together, fully capture what we want when we want free will.

I turn first to Nozick's proposed libertarian model of human agency.

2. MODEL #1: SELF-SUBSUMING DECISIONS TO BESTOW WEIGHTS

We are frequently faced with conflicting considerations that favor conflicting options. In an effort to decide what to do, we need to weigh these conflicting considerations. One model of such weighing is that we consult "previously given precisely specified weights" (294). But on Nozick's first model of human agency, we sometimes instead *decide* what the relative weights of these considerations are to be in our deliberation. Such a deliberative process "not only weighs reasons, it (also) weights them" (294).

---

5. For recent defenses of a libertarian conception, see Robert Kane, *The Significance of Free Will* (New York: Oxford University Press, 1998), and Timothy O'Conner, *Persons and Causes: The Metaphysics of Free Will* (New York: Oxford University Press, 2000).

6. *PE*, 295. And see G. E. M. Anscombe, *Causality and Determination* (Cambridge: Cambridge University Press, 1971).

Our decision bestows weights for our deliberation, weights that thereby settle the decision problem with which we were faced. Furthermore, the decision to bestow these weights is normally in part about itself: It is a decision to give these weights to these considerations in this very decision. In this sense the decision is "self-subsuming." Such a decision also can set up a framework of weights to be used in future deliberation. Later decisions may then stand to such an earlier decision in something like the way a later court decision stands to an earlier, precedent-setting decision: "The decision represents a tentative commitment to make future decisions in accordance with the weights it establishes" (297). Sometimes the earlier weight-bestowing decision is a decision in favor of a general principle concerning such weights.[7] In especially reflective cases, the decision is a decision to be a certain kind of person, one who lives a life that involves bestowing such weights. In these cases, the "self-subsuming" decision to bestow certain weights is a decision in favor of a certain "conception of oneself" (300).

Now, suppose one acts on the basis of such a self-subsuming, weight-bestowing decision in favor of a conception of oneself. Suppose such a decision were not itself determined by prior conditions. Given the kind of decision that it is, it seems it nevertheless need not thereby be a random decision, one that is a matter of chance. The decision is a decision to bestow weights in a way that makes that very decision reasonable and understandable: "Such a self-subsuming decision will not be a random brute fact; it will be explained as an instance of the very conception and weights chosen" (300–301). So Nozick conjectures that this model of self-subsuming decisions can serve as a model of libertarian free agency: it is a model of a kind of agency that can at the same time be nondetermined, free, and nonrandom.[8] And that is what the libertarian wants.

7. In a later work (*The Nature of Rationality* [Princeton, NJ: Princeton University Press, 1993] Ch. 2) (hereafter *NR*), Nozick considers principles of decision that confer different weights to expected causal utility, expected epistemic utility, and what Nozick calls symbolic utility. Nozick suggests that there is a range of possible weight-bestowing principles here, and we are in effect faced with a choice. As Elijah Millgram suggested to me, we can see the choice of one such weight-bestowing principle as an example of the kind of weight-bestowing decision highlighted in *PE*.

8. Nozick briefly suggests an analogy between such a weight-bestowing decision and measurement in quantum mechanics, as understood in "the currently orthodox interpretation of quantum mechanics" (298).

An important question here is whether Nozick's claim is that such a self-subsuming, weight-bestowing decision cannot be determined by prior conditions, or only that it need not be determined. Nozick does toy with the idea that such a self-subsuming decision could not be determined (308–9). But in the end, so far as I can tell, he does not endorse this claim. He grants the possibility of a weight-bestowing self-subsuming decision— even one involving a decision in favor of a conception of oneself—in a deterministic world.[9] And this seems right: If we suppose, as Nozick does, that thought and action might, in general, be embedded in a deterministic web, it is not clear why self-subsuming, weight-bestowing decisions could not be. But then we need to reflect on the significance of the issue of whether such a self-subsuming weight-bestowing decision is determined by prior conditions.

Suppose for the moment that we agree that such a weight-bestowing decision, given its self-subsuming structure, would be intelligible and non-random even if nondetermined. And now consider such a self-subsuming decision in a deterministic world. It would seem that a determined but self-subsuming decision would also be intelligible in just the way (whatever that is) a nondetermined self-subsuming decision would be. But then, if a nondetermined self-subsuming decision is a source of dignity, why isn't a determined self-subsuming decision also a source of dignity? But if we say that a determined self-subsuming decision is also a source of dignity then we have left the libertarian, incompatibilist framework.[10]

9. "Suppose that in certain types of situations, we did reconsider our weighting of reasons, our self-conception, and our lives, but the new position we arrived at was causally determined— we always would arrive at precisely that position in precisely those circumstances. . . . How significant is the difference between this deterministic situation and its indeterministic mate?" (PE, 310). There are, however, places in the text where Nozick seems to be thinking that such a process is of necessity not determined by prior conditions. See, for example, p. 448, where he labels his view of "weighting values" "indeterminist."

10. Indeed, we might then be moving in the direction of the sort of view I sketch in "Reflection, Planning, and Temporally Extended Agency." I appeal there to "self-governing policies" of treating certain desired ends as reasons to a certain extent. Such policies may be the upshot of a decision. So these self-governing policies share important similarities with Nozick's self-subsuming, weight-bestowing decisions. My understanding of such policies is grounded in the planning theory of intention I develop in Intention, Plans, and Practical Reason (Cambridge: Harvard University Press, 1987; reissued by CSLI Publications, 1999). And it is no part of my understanding of such self-governing policies that they cannot be determined by prior conditions.

This is a version of one traditional worry about libertarian theories. Most such theories agree that a mere absence of prior causal determination is not yet enough for the kind of free will we want. After all, it may be that the disintegration of a uranium atom is nondetermined; but that is not a promising model for a source of human dignity. Libertarians standardly respond with a further, positive condition on free will. (In Nozick's case, the positive condition is the role played by a self-subsuming, weight-bestowing decision.) But then one may ask whether this positive condition might not by itself be enough for free will, even in a deterministic world.[11]

Now, it is common to hold that moral responsibility and accountability for doing something requires the ability to do otherwise. This is a view that is standardly called the principle of alternate possibilities. It is also common, although controversial, to hold that the relevant ability to do otherwise, properly understood, is itself incompatible with causal determinism. Someone who held both these views would see the absence of causal determinism as a necessary condition for moral responsibility and accountability.[12] On such a view, no positive condition that was itself compatible with causal determination could by itself be sufficient for moral responsibility.

It is important to see, though, that this cannot be Nozick's primary response to the present challenge. Nozick has made it clear that his interest is not primarily in the claim that the absence of causal determinism is necessary for moral responsibility and accountability; he is instead interested in the claim that the absence of causal determinism is necessary for the kind of free will that grounds human dignity.[13] We must look elsewhere, then, for Nozick's response to this challenge.

11. See Gary Watson's "Introduction" to his *Free Will* (New York: Oxford University Press, 1982), at p. 11.

12. Nozick thinks justified retributive punishment is compatible with the causal determination of action (393–97). And he seems in general to understand the ability to do otherwise in an incompatibilist way. So he probably does not accept the principle of alternate possibilities. This interpretation is also supported by Harry Frankfurt's reference to Nozick's lectures in Frankfurt's "Alternate Possibilities and Moral Responsibility," in *The Importance of What We Care About* (New York: Cambridge University Press, 1988), p. 6 n. 2.

13. Gary Watson distinguishes between concerns about "accountability" and concerns about "attributability." Watson suggests that the former are the main source of pressure for a demand for alternate possibilities (Gary Watson, "Two Faces of Responsibility," *Philosophical Topics* 24 [1996]: 227–48, esp. p. 237). Nozick's concerns, in contrast, are in the spirit of a concern with attributability.

3. ORIGINATIVE VALUE

The place to look is Nozick's appeal to what he calls originative (or, sometimes, originatory) value. Here is what Nozick says:

> something's originative value ... is a function of the value it newly introduces into the world, the new instrumental or intrinsic value it introduces that was not presaged by or already fully counted in previous instrumental value. (311)
>
> What causal determinism does not allow is originatory value. (313)
>
> [I]t is originatory value that is crucial to the problem of free will. (315)

The idea, I take it, is that we can see that our human dignity depends on our having a special kind of value—originatory value—and that we also can see, on reflection, that we would not have this value in a deterministic world. In particular, agency in which the weight-bestowing self-subsuming decision was causally determined by prior conditions would not have originatory value. And that is why such agency in a deterministic world would not ground special human dignity.

But what exactly is originative value? Nozick expresses one of the intuitive ideas here in this way:

> "A being with originative value, one whose acts have originative value, can make a difference." (312)

What does it mean to make a difference? One natural understanding is this: for x to make a difference is for x to be a cause of some effect such that, in the absence of x, that effect would not have occurred. But a decision can, in this sense, make a causal difference even if it is determined by prior conditions; for a decision, even if determined, can be a cause of downstream effects, and it can be true that those effects would not have occurred in the absence of the decision.

Nozick's response would be that if the decision is determined by prior causes then the good downstream deterministic consequences of that decision are also deterministic consequences of the prior causes. So those good consequences are "already fully counted in previous instrumental value," namely, the instrumental value of those prior, upstream causes. This is true even though the decision itself makes a causal difference in the sense that the downstream good consequences depend causally on that decision. The decision would have what Nozick calls "contributory value," but not originatory value.[14]

But does our human dignity really depend on the idea that the good we cause is not also a deterministically causal effect of yet earlier conditions? A random disintegration of a uranium atom in a nondeterministic world would, it seems, have originative value if it results in something of value. How could a feature we would share with such a nondeterministic system be so central to an account of our distinctive dignity? Why shouldn't we instead see our special dignity as grounded in the very special role we play (but the uranium atom does not) in the causal route to downstream good consequences? And once we see the matter this way, it will be an open question whether this role can be played in a deterministic world.

To be sure, we would need a story about that role, a story that helps us understand its special, distinctive features. But such a story might well defuse the temptation to think that in a deterministic world we simply would be like puppets manipulated by the past.[15] (Indeed, I think that much of what Nozick says about human agency can be seen as a contribution to such a project—a point to which I will return.)

We can put the point as a challenge: Why must our dignity depend on the failure of conditions prior to our choices and actions also to have related forms of instrumental value? Why should we care so much about that? We don't care, I take it, that our parents and background social institutions are recognized as having instrumental value for helping us lead good lives. Indeed, it would be a mistake—a kind of hubris—to refuse to ascribe such

14. *PE*, p. 313. This raises the question of whether Nozick's concern with originatory value should lead him to want not merely that decisions not be determined but, further, that they not be caused. After all, if there are prior causes of a decision, which in fact leads to later good consequences, won't those prior causes get credited with the instrumental value of causing (although not determining) those later consequences? In the main text, though, I focus on the idea that our dignity requires the absence of deterministic causation.

15. Nozick invokes the metaphor of puppethood on pp. 310 and 313. See also Susan Wolf, "The Importance of Free Will," *Mind* 90 (1981): 386–405, at 404–5.

instrumental value. So why should we care, in general, that prior determining causes also turn out to have instrumental value when we do good things?[16] (Of course, if the prior causes do not involve persons in the right way, this will not amount to assigning moral credit to those prior causes.) Granted, we might well care that certain kinds of causes not be operative—for example, forms of coercion, brainwashing, and the like.[17] But we may care about that without thinking that our dignity is undermined simply by the existence of prior determining causes that get credited with instrumental value when we do good things.

There may be other reasons to hope that our world is not deterministic. Perhaps we think that this is needed if we are fairly to hold people morally accountable and subject to retributive punishment.[18] But, as we have seen, Nozick is not arguing in this way.[19] Nozick is, rather, seeking to articulate conditions of our human dignity. And it is not clear that we think, or should think, our dignity really does depend on our having, in Nozick's technical sense, originative value. So it is not clear that Nozick's appeals to originative value can play the role he wants them to play in his views about free will.

This may be one of those fundamental matters on which reasonable people will, in the end, disagree.[20] But, however we decide this issue, we also will be faced with a further challenge to Nozick's libertarian conception. This further challenge echoes a second common objection to libertarian theories. Is it true that a nondetermined, self-subsuming, weight-bestowing decision would not be, at bottom, random and unexplained? After all, an alternative self-subsuming decision to bestow weights in an alternative way

16. Cf. Harry Frankfurt's remark, about a related matter, that "there is a difference between being *fully* responsible and being *solely* responsible." "Freedom of the Will and the Concept of a Person," in *The Importance of What We Care About* (Cambridge: Cambridge University Press, 1988), at p. 25 n. 10.

17. Cf. Nozick's remarks about coercion on pp. 49, 520. There are hard questions about cases involving some such untoward form of causation—the work of a nefarious neurosurgeon, perhaps. See the discussion of related issues about moral responsibility in John Martin Fischer and Mark Ravizza, S.J., *Responsibility and Control* (New York: Cambridge University Press, 1998), pp. 194–201.

18. See the critical discussion of this idea in R. Jay Wallace, *Responsibility and the Moral Sentiments* (Cambridge, MA: Harvard University Press, 1994), esp. chaps. 4 and 7.

19. Indeed, as noted earlier, he thinks justified retributive punishment is compatible with determinism (393–97).

20. See *PE*, p. 21.

would also, if it occurred, make itself intelligible in this reflexive way. And we are supposing that it is fully compatible with the past and the causal laws of nature that this alternative decision occur instead. So does not the occurrence of the actual decision remain, at bottom, random and un-explained?

Nozick himself expresses some uncertainty on this point (301, 305), though he thinks this is the best chance for a libertarian model of free will. To arrive at a considered view on this matter, though, it will be helpful first to turn to other elements of Nozick's overall view of our agency.

4. MODELS #2 AND #3: TRACKING BESTNESS AND EQUILIBRIUM

Nozick sees his first model as a libertarian model of free will in the absence of determinism. But he also wants a model of action that is the best we can do in a deterministic world; for he fears that determinism may well be true (317). He believes that in a deterministic world we would not have all we want: we would not have originative value, and so, he claims, would not have the special dignity that goes along with that value. But we still might have an important and distinctive value.

Nozick sketches two distinctive kinds of agency possible in a determin-istic world. First, our actions might, as he says, track bestness or rightness in roughly the sense that if one intentionally does A, then A is right or best; and if A weren't right or best, one would not intentionally have done it.[21] This is not yet to say what makes an act right or best. It is only to say that there is, in such agency, this systematic interdependence between such deontic or axiological features and what one intentionally does.

One's decision and action might track bestness in a deterministic world. Furthermore, there seems no necessary connection, in either direction, between tracking bestness and acting on the basis of self-subsuming, weight-bestowing decisions. The latter involves a certain process of choice, one that might issue in wrong choices; the former is a condition of subjunctive dependency between choice and bestness/rightness (327, 352), a

---

21. *PE*, pp. 317–20. There are complexities here about cases in which several conflicting options are each permissible; but we can put these matters aside for now.

dependency that, it seems, may arise from a process that did not involve self-subsuming, weight-bestowing decisions. Nevertheless, there may in some cases be a mesh of these two conditions; one might, for example, arrive at and successfully execute a self-subsuming decision in favor of a policy of tracking bestness (300).

Nozick's third model focuses on how we would see our actions if we knew their causes. Many times we are ignorant of causes of our actions, but if we had known them at the time of action we would have wanted to act differently. If, for example, I had known that my chastizing you was grounded in an old resentment, not—as I think—my present assessment of your work, I wouldn't have done it. But sometimes an act may be in "equilibrium" in the sense that even if one fully knew its causes, one would not want any less to do it than one did want to do it when one did it: "An act in equilibrium withstands knowledge of its own causes."[22]

Nozick's second and third models are models of agency possible in a deterministic world. Nozick does not, in the end, offer these as models of free will. As I understand him, he remains, in the end, an incompatibilist about free will and causal determinism.[23] But he does suggest that we can combine these two models and arrive at a model of the best agency available to us in a deterministic world: "We would want our causally determined acts to be in (unfrozen) equilibria, tracking bestness."[24]

These two conditions might come apart. Perhaps my mode of thinking does support agency that tracks bestness, but I would want to change it if I knew what its causes were. But Nozick can simply grant this possibility and insist that what we most want, in a deterministic world, is agency in which these conditions do not come apart but are jointly realized.

22. *PE*, p. 349. Nozick returns to this idea of equilibrium in his discussion of symbolic meaning in *NR*, at p. 31.
23. Nozick writes:
we are left with the feeling that the notion of "tracking bestness or rightness" has not gotten to the heart of the free will problem. . . .
Though it leaves the issues of free will dark, nevertheless, the situation of tracking bestness or rightness may be a very desirable and valuable mode of action, the best we can hope to achieve. (332)
See also pp. 328–29.
24. *PE*, p. 352. Nozick explains the idea of "frozen" as follows: "an action is frozen if no possible knowledge of its causes can lead a person not to (want to) do it or to want (to want) it less" (716, n. 62).

5. A THREE-PRONGED, COMPATIBILIST MODEL?

Why not combine all three models into a compatibilist model of agency that is possible in a deterministic world? Why not consider agency in a deterministic world, agency that involves self-subsuming, weight-bestowing decisions in favor of self-conceptions, that thereby tracks bestness and that is in equilibrium? The need to track bestness would limit which self-conceptions are available. And we have noted that the second and third prongs might come apart, but need not. The idea that agency in a deterministic world might exhibit all three features depends on the possibility of self-subsuming, weight-bestowing decisions in a deterministic world. But we have seen that, in the end, Nozick appears to grant this possibility.

The idea need not be that all three prongs are necessary for free will, self-determination, or the like. We may want to allow that there can be self-determined but evil agents who do not track bestness. The idea is, rather, that the three prongs, taken together, give us a sketch of a compatibilist story about sufficient grounds for human dignity. An agent whose motivation is in equilibrium, whose actions are grounded in self-subsuming weight-bestowing decisions,[25] and who thereby tracks bestness is a very special kind of agent. Many purposive agents—including, probably, the nonhuman animals with whom we are familiar—do not instantiate this three-pronged model.

So we can ask: Would such a three-pronged model of agency in a deterministic world capture grounds sufficient for human dignity in the absence of Nozickian originatory value?[26] One advantage to a positive, compatibilist answer is that we would then be protected from the worries about randomness that challenge the libertarian project.[27] Although

25. And policies. See note 10.

26. Gideon Yaffe discusses a way of putting together our concerns with forms of agency roughly along the lines of the first two prongs in his "Free Will and Agency at its Best," in *Philosophical Perspectives: Action and Freedom* 14 (2000): 203–29. Yaffe calls a concern (roughly) with the first prong a concern with "self-expression" and a concern with the second prong a concern with "self-transcendence."

27. Recall that Nozick himself is unsure abut the success of his libertarian response to worries about randomness.

I don't mean to say, by the way, that a compatiblist theorist can simply borrow these models

Nozick does not consider such a three-pronged model of agency in a deterministic world, however, it is clear he would answer in the negative; for such agency would still not have originatory value, in Nozick's technical sense. So this returns us both to the issue of the significance of such originatory value and to the issue of Nozick's success, in his first model, in responding to worries about randomness.

To make further progress with these matters, it will be useful first to turn to Nozick's views about personal identity and value.

6. NOZICK ON PERSONAL IDENTITY
AND VALUE

Begin with a question brought powerfully to our attention by John Locke: What is it for one and the same person to persist over time? In Locke's famous case of the prince and the cobbler, one person at a later time has the cobbler's body but seems to remember the prince's earlier experiences.[28] We can also suppose that the person at the later time with the prince's body seems to remember the cobbler's earlier experiences. Which of the two later persons is the prince and which the cobbler? To answer, we seem to need to say what is more important to the identity of a person over time: bodily continuity or (as Locke concluded, in his so-called memory theory of personal identity) the kind of psychological continuity involved in (at least, apparent) memory.

Nozick would approach this example with the idea that the later prince-body person and the later cobbler-body person are each a "continuer" of the earlier cobbler person (35). They each have certain qualitative similarities with the earlier cobbler person: in one case (the case of the later cobbler-body person) the similarities are physical, and in the other (the case of the later prince-body person), psychological. And in

---

from Nozick without further ado. In particular, there will be questions about why such self-subsuming decisions count as fully the agent's own, in contrast with other psychological elements—for example, a desire for revenge that one does not reflectively endorse—that seem not to have authority to speak for the agent. The philosopher who has contributed the most to our understanding of these issues is Harry Frankfurt. See esp. his *The Importance of What We Care About*. I discuss related matters in my "Reflection, Planning, and Temporally Extended Agency."

28. *An Essay Concerning Human Understanding*, Book II, Ch. XXVII, Section 15.

each case, some properties of the later person are causally connected to those of the earlier cobbler person.

Nozick's idea (which he calls the "closest continuer theory") is that if the earlier cobbler person persists to the later time,[29] the later person who is identical to the earlier cobbler person is the *closest* continuer of that earlier person. But who is the closest continuer? To answer, we need a way of measuring closeness, a way that would assign relevant weights to such physical and psychological continuities. We can see Locke's memory theory as assigning all weight to certain psychological continuities: Thus, Locke concludes that the prince persists with the cobbler's body. But, according to Nozick, other metrics are theoretically possible:

> Does psychological continuity come lexically first; is there no tradeoff between the slightest loss of psychological continuity and the greatest gain in bodily continuity; is bodily continuity (to a certain degree) a necessary component of identity through time; ... what are the relevant subcomponents of psychological continuity or similarity (for example, plans, ambitions, hobbies, preferences in flavors of ice cream, moral principles). (69)

Nozick does not try to provide a single, objective story about "closeness" for personal identity. Instead, he claims that there is no such single story:

> What is special about people, about selves, is that what constitutes their identity through time is partially determined by their own conception of themselves, a conception which may vary, perhaps appropriately does vary, from person to person. (69)

Nozick later puts this idea as follows:

> The self's conception of itself will be, in the terms of the closest continuer theory, a listing and weighting of dimensions. This provides, implicitly, a measure of closeness. (105)

---

29. This condition serves to leave room for cases in which the closest continuer is not close enough for the earlier person to survive at all.

The metric of closeness needed for a closest continuer theory of personal identity is partially provided by the person herself, in her "self-conception."[30]

We are not free to adopt just any such self-conception and thereby individuate selves in radical ways. I cannot successfully "synthesize" myself as including both Moses Mendelsohn and Michael Jordan.[31] There are objective constraints on "self-synthesis." But there is also some latitude, some room for personal decision:

> there is not simply one correct measure of closeness for persons. Each person's own selection and weighting of dimensions enter into determining his own actual identity, not merely his view of it. (106)

Let me stop here to emphasize a structural feature of this view of the person. Persons persist through time; the conditions of their actual persistence involve a metric of closeness; this metric has objective constraints; but its details are also to some extent a matter of decision for the person, a decision of how to weigh "dimensions [that] enter into determining [one's] own actual identity." Personal identity is, in this sense, a *hybrid* phenomenon.

Turn now to Nozick's approach to value, to what it is that an action tracks when it tracks bestness. Here Nozick's views come in three stages. Nozick begins not with the question of whether there are "objective

---

30. Nozick arrives at this idea by reflection on the special knowledge we seem to have in identifying ourselves. When I think or say "I seem to remember being a cobler" it seems I can't be wrong about the reference of "I": the reference of "I" is, of course, me. But why is it that I am, as Shoemaker puts it, "immune to error through misidentification" (quoted in *PE*, 90)? Nozick's answer is that I am immune to such error because the use of "I" in my thought in a way individuates its referent:

> I know that when I say "I," the reference is to myself, because myself is synthesized as the thing which that act refers to, as the tightest and greatest organic unity including the act, and referred to by the act because including it. (90)

Nozick call this "the theory of the self as reflexively synthesized" (91). Nozick then extends this view about the referent of "I" at the present time to the persistence of the self, or person, over time. This leads him to the idea that "the I's self-synthesis includes a self-conception which projects itself into the future" (105).

For a different approach to such self-knowledge, see John Perry's discussion of what he calls "self-attached knowledge" in his "Myself and I" in Marcelo Stamm, ed., *Philosophie in Synthetisher Absicht* (Stuttgart: Klett-Cotta, 1998), pp. 83–103.

31. Nozick suggests, boldly, that these limits may be, at bottom, social (107–8).

values" but, rather, with the question how objective values are "even possible": "the project is to sketch what an objective ethics might look like, to understand how there (so much as) could be such a thing" (400). Here Nozick arrives at the view that if there are things that have intrinsic value, their degree of value is determined by what Nozick calls "degree of organic unity" (418). The idea of degree of organic unity is drawn from concerns in aesthetics with "the virtues of unifying diverse and apparently unrelated . . . material" (415).

> Holding fixed the degree of unifiedness of material, the degree of organic unity varies directly with the degree of diversity of that material being unified. Holding fixed the degree of diversity of the material, the degree of organic unity varies directly with the degree of unifiedness. (416)

Nozick's conjecture is that a generalized notion of organic unity captures "the basic dimension of intrinsic value" (418). "Something is intrinsically valuable in accordance with its degree of organic unity."[32]

Nozick then notes that this view about intrinsic value allows for an "ineradicable plurality of values" (446). Many things have intrinsic value, and there is no reason to think that they can all be realized in a single life. Indeed, Nozick believes that "these diverse values cannot be (tightly) unified, that there are ineradicable conflicts, tensions, needs for tradeoffs, and so on" (447). So an agent who is trying to respond to value will need to make choices among the plurality of values, will need "to formulate her own package of value realization" (447).

This has, for Nozick, two important implications. First, it blocks "the threat that the objectivity of values might appear to pose to individuality" (448). We need not worry that a world of objective values dictates a single way to live to all agents. Instead, "individuality is expressed in the

---

32. *PE*, p. 446. Note that this is a claim about *intrinsic* value and so, I take it, is not offered directly as an account of originatory value.

In a later work, Nozick notes that principles can function in a person's life in ways such that "through them, one's actions and one's life may have greater coherence, greater organic unity. That may be valuable in itself" [*NR*, 13]. I would want to make a similar claim about the role of intentions, plans, and policies in our lives. See my *Intention, Plans, and Practical Reason*.

interstices of the objective rankings of value, in the particular unified patterning chosen and lived" (448).

Second, the plurality of values means that one *must* make decisions about which values to weigh in one's deliberation, and how to weigh them:

> each person must (within the objective limits) arrive at her own weighting. That giving of weights is not something we happen to do, it is necessitated by the pluralist nature of the realm of values. (448)

The weights that one invokes in one's deliberations will, then, have a hybrid structure. On the one hand, they will be accountable to "objective limits." On the other hand, they will be shaped partially by the agent's own decisions.[33]

So far, Nozick's discussion has "bracketed the ontological question about the existence of value" (562). Nozick returns to this ontological question toward the end of PE. He suggests there that once we see what value would be like and how it would fit into our agency, if there were value, we can just choose to live as if there is value. And if we make such a choice, then there is value. Or so Nozick avers. Here is how he puts the view:

> We know what value would be; we have only to bring it to life, to value it, to seek and pursue it, contouring our lives in accordance with it. We have only to choose that there be value. What is needed to bring value to our universe is our reflexive choice that there be value. (563)

What is it to "choose that there be value"? It is to value things in the way described by Nozick's theory: "The choice that there be value is made in valuing things" (558). The deliberative process of bestowing weights, within objective constraints provided by the significance of organic unity in any world in which there is value, is enough to "bring value to our universe."

---

33. As I understand him (although I am unsure about this), Nozick does not claim that in giving weights within "the objective limits" one thereby makes it the case that it is objectively best to act in accord with those weights.

I am not sure how best to interpret Nozick's talk here of "bring[ing] value to our universe" simply by "valuing things." For present purposes, however, we can limit our attention to the question of how these hybrid approaches to valuing and personal identity can help buttress Nozick's defense of his libertarian model in response to a concern about randomness.

7. WEIGHT-BESTOWING DECISIONS REVISITED

The concern, recall, is that if a self-subsuming, weight-bestowing decision were nondetermined, then, even given the kind of decision that it is, it would remain, at bottom, arbitrary or random. After all, "there are different and conflicting self-subsuming decisions that could be made." So we may wonder: "Is it not arbitrary then that one-self-subsuming decision is made rather than another" (301)?

Nozick's response, we have seen, is that a self-subsuming, weight-bestowing decision provides a kind of explanation of itself: for it is intelligible in light of the weights it itself bestows (304). The point to note now is that Nozick's hybrid accounts of personal identity and valuing allow him to deepen this response.

First, in the most basic case the self-subsuming, weight-bestowing decision is a decision in favor of a "self-conception." Nozick's view is that such a self-conception helps in part structure who one in fact is, by providing, to some extent, weights for the metric of closeness of continuer (306). Given the hybrid nature of personal identity, the provision of such weights, by way of a self-subsuming decision, is an essential element in what is involved in the persistence of the person over time.

Second, such self-subsuming, weight-bestowing decisions are a needed response to value pluralism, a response that is to respect "the objective limits." And the bestowal of such weights itself has objective value, for a "life based upon such weightings will be unified by them, and so more valuable than one that exhibits no weighting or ignores value altogether" (449).

So, the theory is that a self-subsuming, weight-bestowing decision that favors a self-conception helps to some extent both determine who the agent is and, in a way that is responsive to "the objective limits" and is itself needed and valuable, what the agent does. Of course, it remains true that if the decision is not determined, then it is consistent with the past and the causal laws that a (to some extent) different agent, and different weightings, instead emerge. But the tight connections provided by the theory between the (partially self-constituted) agent, her (partially self-constituted) weightings, and the action performed may provide as strong a form of intelligibility and nonarbitrariness for a nondetermined decision as a libertarian can aspire to.

There is a possible problem here, as Nozick notes (306). In the case of a fundamental decision in favor of a self-conception—say, in Sartre's famous case, a decision to fight with the Free French rather than stay with one's mother[34]—it seems that the decision may, on the theory, be so tightly connected to who the agent is that it will not be true that *that very agent* could have decided otherwise. I am not sure what to say here; perhaps we can simply see this as an insight of the theory.[35]

Another point is that the connection between weight-bestowing decisions and personal identity has a further dimension that Nozick does not highlight but that may be useful to note. Recall Nozick's idea that some weight-bestowing decisions set a framework for later decisions, much as precedent-setting decisions do in the courts. One function of such weight-bestowing decisions may be, then, to create associated continuities over time. And these are kinds of psychological continuities that will be, on many versions of the closest continuer theory, partly constitutive of the person's persistence over time. To have this role in creating continuities, a weight-bestowing decision need not itself be a decision about a metric of closeness of continuer. Instead, a function of such weight-bestowing decisions can be to create the very continuities that are frequently a concern of such a metric.[36]

---

34. "Existentialism Is a Humanism," in W. Kaufmann, ed., *Existentialism from Dostoevsky to Sartre*, rev. and expanded (New York: Meridian/Penguin, 1975), pp. 345–69; at 354–56.

35. Nozick's discussion of this possible problem on pp. 306–7 does not seem to provide a direct response.

36. This distinction between two ways such decisions can shape conditions of personal identity parallels a distinction Nozick suggests in his later discussion of principles in *NR*. He says there that "principles may be one way a person can define her *identity*.... Further, principles followed over an extended period are a way a person can integrate her life over time and give it more coherence" (*NR*, 13–14). It is this second, integrating role that I want to emphasize here. To play this role a weight-bestowing decision need not itself be a decision about a "metric" of closeness.

The resulting action will be an issue of a decision whose function it is to induce continuities that are, on most relevant metrics, partly constitutive of the persistence of the person.

We have now arrived at a full Nozickian response to worries about randomness for the libertarian model. A self-subsuming, weight-bestowing decision provides an explanation of itself and its ensuing action as intelligible in light of the weights it itself bestows. Furthermore, this source of intelligibility, in ways noted, both partly constitutes basic features of the agent and is a needed, valuable response to the pluralism of value. So there is significant intelligibility of action despite the absence of prior determining conditions.

Is the response adequate? I am unsure. Here, again, we may have arrived at one of those fundamental matters on which reasonable people will disagree. What I would like to emphasize at this point, however, is that nothing about the story just told about how such decisions make actions intelligible, nonarbitrary, or the like, depends on the condition that the decision is not determined by prior conditions. If this story of intelligibility of decision and action works for the case of such self-subsuming decisions when they are not determined, it will work also for the case in which the decision is determined.

This is to return to the general worry that libertarianism is unstable: It needs a positive condition on free will in order to avoid seeing free will as merely the absence of causal determination; but then we can ask why that positive condition is not sufficient, on its own, for the kind of agency we seek. In the present case, we can ask why it is not sufficient for human dignity that we have the capacity to act on the basis of a self-subsuming, weight-bestowing decision that is a decision in favor of a self-conception. This concern is made more pressing when we see that the features of such decisions that are needed to provide the best answer to concerns about randomness are equally available to a compatibilist theory.

We can deepen the point. We have just noted that the explanatory, intelligibility-bestowing role played by self-subsuming decisions within

---

In my "Reflection, Planning, and Temporally Extended Agency," I make the related point that (what I call) self-governing policies organize our lives in part by creating psychological continuities and connections that are partly constitutive of the identity of a person over time. And self-governing policies can play this role without themselves being "self-conceptions."

Nozick's first model is one that may be played by such decisions in a deterministic world. We can add to this the idea, broached earlier, that this model may be wedded to Nozick's other two models: that of tracking bestness, and that of equilibrium in light of knowledge of causes. We can then offer such a three-pronged model as the beginnings of a compatibilist model of the grounds of human dignity.[37]

In his thoughtful survey of the literature on free will, Gary Watson observes that "the structure of an adequate libertarian account of freedom must be such that the condition of self-determination itself entails indeterminism."[38] Nozick's model of self-subsuming, weight-bestowing decisions is his version of a libertarian account of self-determination. So far as I can see, however, it is not true that this model of self-determination "itself entails indeterminism."

Nozick's response, I believe, would be that Watson's requirement is misguided; for there is independent reason to ask that the most basic decisions of an agent with dignity not be determined. After all, only then would the agent have originative value. This returns us to the fundamental question of whether we really think, or should think, that our special human dignity is a hostage to a concern with this special value. An agent who tracks bestness, whose motivation is in equilibrium, and whose actions are grounded in self-subsuming weight-bestowing decisions and (as I would say) policies is a distinctive kind of agent. If we are, sometimes, such agents, is that a sufficient ground for human dignity? Or does our dignity really depend, further, on whether or not our world is deterministic? Nozick would answer this last question in the affirmative. Even if, on reflection, we are not convinced by Nozick on this matter, we are in his debt for his suggestive discussions of forms of agency that even a compatibilist will value.[39]

---

37. As Nozick remarks (p. 448), we need to interpret tracking bestness in a way that is compatible with his value pluralism. I take it that this means that to track bestness is to track "the objective limits." And this three-pronged model will also continue to face issues about authority noted above (n. 27).

38. "Free Action and Free Will," at p. 165.

39. Thanks to John Fischer, Elijah Millgram, David Schmidtz, Manuel Vargas, and Gideon Yaffe for helpful comments.

Appendix

NOZICK, FREE WILL, AND THE PROBLEM OF AGENTIAL AUTHORITY

Robert Nozick's effort to construct a defensible libertarian position about free will and autonomy depends, at bottom, on the idea of "a self-subsuming decision that bestows weights to reasons on the basis of a then chosen conception of oneself and one's appropriate life, a conception that includes bestowing those weights and choosing that conception (where the weights also yield choosing that self-conception)."[1] The idea is that such a self-subsuming decision can anchor autonomy even if that decision is not determined by prior conditions. And Nozick believes that for such a decision to have "originatory value," it needs *not* to have been determined by prior conditions.

If the self-subsuming decision is indeed not determined by prior conditions, is it in an important sense random or arbitrary? This is a basic challenge for any libertarian theory. Nozick's initial response is as follows:

> Such a self-subsuming decision will not be a random brute fact; it will be explained as an instance of the very conception and weights chosen. . . . A self-subsuming decision does not happen inexplicably, it is not random in the sense of being connected to no

1. *Philosophical Explanations* (Cambridge, MA: Harvard University Press, 1981), p. 300. Hereafter *PE*.

weighted reasons (including the self-subsuming ones then chosen). (*PE*, 300–301)

Nozick is, however, not satisfied with this response. He goes on:

But although it doesn't happen just randomly, still, there are different and conflicting self-subsuming decisions that could be made; . . . Is it not arbitrary then that one self-subsuming decision is made rather than another? Won't it be left inexplicable why this one was made (rather than another one)? (*PE*, 301)

So how does Nozick respond? In my essay, "Nozick on Free Will," I offer the following interpretation:

First, in the most basic case the self-subsuming, weight-bestowing decision is a decision in favor of a "self-conception." Nozick's view is that such a self-conception helps in part to structure who one in fact is, by providing, to some extent, weights for the metric of closeness of continuer. . . .
    Second, such self-subsuming, weight-bestowing decisions are a needed response to value pluralism. . . .
    So . . . the tight connections provided by the theory between the (partially self-constituted) agent, her (partially self-constituted) weightings, and the action performed may provide as strong a form of intelligibility and nonarbitrariness for a non-determined decision as a libertarian can aspire to. (p. 167)

I then went on to argue that this way of modeling our freedom is also available to a compatibilist theory, since it is not essential to this model that the cited self-subsuming decisions not be determined by prior conditions. Nozick, of course, did not see things this way, since he assumed that autonomy must have "originatory value." In this appendix, though, I want to pursue a different though related issue, one that has come to the fore in the recent Frankfurt-inspired literature.

The issue I have in mind was noted in a footnote in my "Nozick on Free Will":

there will be questions about why such self-subsuming decisions count as fully the agent's own, in contrast with other psychological elements—for example, a desire for revenge that one does not reflectively endorse—that seem not to have authority to speak for the agent. (note 27)

Recall that Nozick's primary focus was on explaining why these self-subsuming decisions can be nonarbitrary and explicable even if nondetermined. But it is one thing to say that a decision is explicable and not arbitrary, another to say that it is a decision that is fully the agent's own, a decision that has authority to speak for the agent—"agential authority," as I have said.[2] So even if Nozick has provided for a form of explicability for such self-subsuming decisions, we need also to ask for an account of their agential authority.

This idea of agential authority earns its place primarily by way of its role in a model of self-government. Self-governed agency is agency that is deliberatively guided in an appropriate way by attitudes that, in that context, speak for the agent and have agential authority. In that context, the guidance by those *attitudes* constitutes the *agent's* governance of action.[3] Though Nozick does not, of course, use the language of "agential authority," I think it is clear that he implicitly supposes that the cited self-subsuming decisions about weights have agential authority in the sense that their guidance constitutes the agent's self-governance. Nevertheless, the main target of his reflection is their explicability. So we need to ask why we should suppose that they do have this authority.

This question of agential authority does not arise in the same way for a libertarian theory that appeals nonreducibly to the agent as cause. On such a view, the agent appears as a separate element in the metaphysics. So we need not worry whether certain attitudes speak for the agent; we can just appeal to the agent herself. Of course, there are many perplexities about how to understand such an appeal to the agent as cause. But in any case, this is not the kind of libertarian theory Nozick seeks. He seeks to

2. The basic ideas here come from Harry Frankfurt, *The Importance of What We Care About* (Cambridge: Cambridge University Press, 1988). My talk of agential authority comes from my "Two Problems about Human Agency," *Proceedings of the Aristotelian Society* (2001): 309–26 [this volume, essay 5].

3. Or anyway, this is the basic story. Qualifications can be put to one side here.

understand free agency not in terms of some primitive phenomenon of agent causation, but rather in terms of the (nondeterministic) functioning of a psychic economy by way of relevant self-subsuming decisions. So we need to know why it is that when such a self-subsuming decision guides thought and action, the agent governs.

You can get a feel for this Frankfurtian question by recalling Frankfurt's unwilling addict. He acts on a desire for the drug, though he desires not to act on that desire. His desire for the drug, while motivating, does not have agential authority. Now suppose that the addict's desire for the drug is not simply for the drug; it is, in addition, a desire to take the drug because of this very desire. Indeed, let us further suppose it is a desire to be a drug-taking person, one who takes the drug by way of this desire to be a drug-taking person and to take the drug. So it is self-subsuming and in favor of a self-conception. Even so, we can still ask whether it speaks for the agent: does it articulate a practical stance that is fully the agent's own in the sense that when it guides the agent governs? And I think that in the present example the answer may well be no.

This suggests that the reflexive structure of self-subsumption—even if what is reflexively supported is a self-conception—does not yet ensure agential authority, though it may ensure a kind of explicability.

Nozick, however, appeals not merely to a self-subsuming desire, but to a self-subsuming decision. So we need to ask: What happens when we move from a self-subsuming desire to a self-subsuming decision? Does that get us to agential authority?

Well, perhaps it does, at least in many cases. But we still need a theory that explains why. I'll return to this point below. What I want to emphasize now is that this issue about agential authority—an issue that goes beyond the issue of explicability and nonarbitrariness—is a basic problem for any account that seeks to model autonomy, self-government, by appeal to relevant functioning of a psychic economy. It is a problem whether or not the account seeks—as does Nozick's account—to be libertarian or, in contrast, to be compatibilist. We need to know how Nozick, or at least a Nozickian theory, should try to solve this problem.

One place where Nozick seems to be grappling with something like this issue is in the context of yet another response to worries about arbitrariness:

> Another way in which bestowal of weight upon reasons can be
> nonarbitrary is that the self can synthesize itself around this be-
> stowing: "I value things in this way." If in that reflexive self-reference,
> the I synthesizes itself (in part) around the act of bestowing weight on
> reasons, then it will not be arbitrary or random that *that* self bestowed
> those weights. (*PE*, 306)

Nozick says here that he is responding to worries about arbitrariness, but
what he says may also seem relevant to worries about the agential authority of the bestowal. The suggestion might be that the bestowal of
weights has agential authority because "the I synthesizes itself" as including
that bestowal of weights.

I think there are two ways to read this appeal to the idea that "the I
synthesizes itself." On the most straightforward reading, the problem is
that it does not seem to follow from the idea that this "self" includes the
bestowal that that bestowal has authority to speak for the agent, in the
sense that when it guides the agent governs. After all, in this sense
Frankfurt's unwilling addict's "self" includes his desire for the drug—
though it also includes his desire that that desire not motivate.

Granted, if I say or think "I desire that drug," I ineluctably succeed in
referring to none other than me. This is Shoemaker's point about being
"immune to error through misidentification," a point Nozick embraces
(*PE*, 90). But it does not follow from this that when I say or think "I desire
that drug" this desire has agential authority in the sense that when it
guides I govern.

One way to see this is to recall how Nozick interprets Shoemaker's
point:

> I know that when I say "I," the reference is to myself, because myself
> is synthesized as the thing which that act refers to, as the tightest
> and greatest organic unity including the act, and referred to by the
> act because including it. (*PE*, 90)

Without endorsing this way of understanding Shoemaker's point, we can
see that even if we follow Nozick here, we do not yet have a theory of
agential authority. Even if the thought "I want that drug" is an element of

a bestowal of weights that "synthesizes" me in a way that includes this very thought, it does not follow that the overall psychic economy included in "the tightest and greatest organic unity including the [thought], and referred to by the [thought] because including it" supports the agential authority of that thought. After all, that overall structure might also involve other elements that reject that thought and/or block its guidance of my practical thinking. Presumably, this is what happens when Frankfurt's unwilling addict thinks "I want that drug": he no doubt refers to none other than himself; and this "self" does want the drug; but this does not mean that the desire for the drug has agential authority.[4]

I said there were two readings of Nozick's appeal to the idea that "the I synthesizes itself"; and it is time for the second reading. On the second reading, what Nozick is talking about here is what Frankfurt would call identification. The "I" "identifies" with some rather than other motivating elements, and this is why the former have agential authority and the latter do not. This interpretation of what Nozick says is in tension with his apparent idea that what is at stake is the reference of "I"—since, again, the unwilling addict can well think "I want that drug." But, in any case, one of the main lessons of the last thirty years of Frankfurt-influenced philosophy of action is that this talk of identification itself needs careful analysis. Familiar problems about regress and about the relative significance of desiderative hierarchy and value judgment loom large here. So it is a mistake to think that we can simply appeal to identification, without further analysis, in a theory of freedom and self-government.

Return now to our question of whether it helps to remind ourselves that the bestowals in question are *decisions*. Well, why exactly would that help? One natural idea is that these bestowals—these decisions—are the active *doings* of the person and that this somehow supports their agential authority. Indeed, this may be one of the issues at stake in a passage in which Nozick raises the question, concerning decisions to bestow weights:

---

4. In his *Liberty Worth the Name: Locke on Free Agency* (Princeton, NJ: Princeton University Press, 2000), at 126–27, Gideon Yaffe notes a somewhat similar problem for the Lockean theory he sketches. Yaffe's proposed Lockean solution is on pp. 127–34.

whether the bestowal that did occur was a doing or merely a happening? Maybe it is possible for weights somehow to just happen to get bestowed on reasons; however, when the bestowal is anchored and tied in the way we have described, to a formed self-conception (even if formed just then), if it is self-subsuming and reflexive, leading to later (revocable) commitment, then it is a doing, not a happening merely. (*PE*, 307)

Note that Nozick does not appeal here to the idea that a decision to bestow weights is a doing in a sense that is fundamental and nonreducible. Rather, he aims here to say why certain bestowals—where these are, I take it, decisions— are doings and not mere happenings. Now, not all doings have or express agential authority; after all, when the unwilling addict takes the drug, he does something. But perhaps we can find in these remarks of Nozick an account of why certain bestowals, because they are doings, have agential authority.

One complexity in interpreting this passage as contributing to an account of agential authority involves its appeal to "later . . . commitment." One natural reading of this remark about commitment is that it alludes to a commitment *on the part of the agent*. And I agree with Nozick that certain self-subsuming decisions about weights do lead to such commitments on the part of the agent. But this is, in part, because they have agential authority. So we need to ask if there would here be an unacceptable circularity in explaining the agential authority of such a decision by appeal to its involved commitments. I will return to this matter below.

A second problem with the use of this passage for our purposes is that there is no further argument for the crucial claim that what Nozick has described is sufficient for the kind of agential authority we are after. Nozick does go on to say that "[i]f all that context and stage setting (compare Wittgenstein) does not make it an action, what alternative conception of action is being presupposed?" (*PE*, 307). But this is far from a constructive story that makes positive sense of the idea that central features of Nozickian self-subsuming decisions about weights give them authority to speak for the agent.

I think that to make progress here we need to distinguish two different ways in which issues about personal identity might enter into an account of agential authority. The way Nozick highlights—at least to the extent that he implicitly touches on this issue of agential authority—is that the *content* of the self-subsuming decision includes, in the central case, a "self-conception"—where this self-conception involves a "metric" for Lockean persistence. This is clear, I think, in Nozick's appeal, quoted earlier, to "a self-subsuming decision that bestows weights to reasons on the basis of a then chosen conception of oneself and one's appropriate life." And the problem here is that such an appeal to a self-conception in the content does not seem enough to ensure agential authority. This is what we saw when we considered the addict's desire to be a drug-taking person in part by way of this very desire. The content of the desire involves a self-conception; but the desire still may not have agential authority.[5]

If we are going to draw on a broadly Lockean approach to personal identity in our account of agential authority we do best, I think, to structure the appeal to personal identity in a different way in our theory of agential authority. We do best to appeal not primarily to such contents about a self-conception, but rather to Lockean *roles* in the psychic economy. Very roughly, an attitude has a claim to agential authority when its role in the psychic economy is to support the cross-temporal organization and Lockean unity of practical thought and action. This is a matter of role or function in Lockean identity, not essentially a matter of a content that is explicitly about Lockean identity; though this role or function may well normally be played by bestowals that do include in their content relevant self-conceptions. In self-government, relevant practical thought and action is under the guidance of attitudes whose role it is to organize practical thought and action over time in ways that involve the kinds of Lockean ties that, as both Nozick and I would agree, are central to personal identity over time. It is in significant part because these attitudes have these roles that they speak for the agent. Decisions to bestow weights—and their normal upshots, which are certain kinds of intentions and policies about such weights—normally play such organizing and unifying roles in our temporally extended, thoughtful agency; and that is a basic reason why they have agential authority. Or so I conjecture.[6]

5. I make a related point about Korsgaard's views in my "Two Problems about Human Agency," at p. 317 [this volume, p. 97].

6. See my "Reflection, Planning, and Temporally Extended Agency," *The Philosophical Review* 109 (2000): 35–61 [this volume, essay 2]. My thinking about these Lockean ideas owes much to numerous, temporally extended interactions with Gideon Yaffe.

This is not the place to defend this conjecture in detail; but let me say a bit by way of clarification. First, recall Nozick's remark that the relevant decisions about weights lead "to later (revocable) commitment." I raised the question of whether the relevant commitment is a commitment of the agent, and I wondered if there was a looming circularity here insofar as we appeal to such commitments to explain the agential authority of such decisions. Now, the present proposal is that such a decision about weights plays an appropriate Lockean cross-temporal role. That is why it has a claim to agential authority; and that is why its commitments have a claim to being the agent's commitments. The idea, then, is to avoid an unacceptable circularity in roughly the following way. First, we see such decisions as commitments to future reasoning and action in that they engage relevant norms—norms of stability over time and of consistency and coherence—that apply to such decisions. The acceptance of such norms is part of the story of how these decisions play their central Lockean cross-temporal roles. Once this Lockean story is in place, we can then conclude that these decisions have agential authority. We can then conclude, without circularity, that the cited commitments are, indeed, agential commitments.

The second point I want to make begins by recalling Nozick's analogy between agency and the functioning of a legal system.[7] I agree that there are natural and illuminating parallels here. In particular, the question about law that seems especially relevant to our present concerns with agential authority is: why do certain rules have legal authority?

Now, H. L. A. Hart's famous answer is—very roughly—that law is a "union of primary and secondary rules."[8] Certain primary rules have legal authority because they are accorded that authority by relevant secondary rules—which, these include "secondary rules of recognition, change and adjudication."[9] And the basic secondary rules have authority because of the way they are embedded in the functioning of the legal system, by way of their acceptance by the legal officials. Further, this functioning involves,

---

7. See *PE*, p. 297 where Nozick highlights parallels with the role of "precedents within a legal system."

8. H. L. A. Hart, *The Concept of Law* (second edition) (New York: Oxford University Press, 1994). The quote comes from the title of chapter 5.

9. *The Concept of Law*, p. 98.

inter alia, support for the continuity of that system over time. My proposal about the agential authority of bestowals of weights to some extent parallels this legal positivist answer about the legal authority of secondary rules: in each case we appeal, in part, to roles in the cross-temporal organization of the practical thought and action of the same (individual or institutional) agent engaged in that thought and action over time.

Self-subsuming decisions about weights can stand in two different relations to Lockean personal identity: their content can be explicitly about such identity; and they can shape, as a matter of their role or function, Lockean ties of practical thought and action. Granted, these two phenomena will frequently go together; but they remain different in analysis; and, for reasons I have sketched, the appeal to role seems to me the more fundamental appeal for a theory of self-government. Nozick is, I think, aware of this distinction; and (as I pointed out in "Nozick on Free Will," footnote 36), a related distinction appears in his later book on rationality. But in *PE*, this distinction does not get sufficient attention. Insofar as Nozick has a theory of agential authority, it is a theory that appeals, at bottom, to decisions that are explicitly about a self-conception, decisions that are explicitly Lockean in their content. If I am right, we do better to highlight the Lockean unifying roles of decisions about weights.

Nozick's path-breaking—if underdiscussed—views about free will generate a range of important ideas. And versions of these ideas have reemerged in various forms in the more recent literature. It is important to see, however, that these Nozickian ideas face a deep problem about agential authority and that there is work to be done before we can be confident that we fully understand how a theory that is broadly in the spirit of Nozick's—whether libertarian or compatibilist—should best respond to these basic issues about the metaphysics of our agency.

Chapter 7

A DESIRE OF ONE'S OWN

In his 1971 article, "Freedom of the Will and the Concept of a Person," Harry G. Frankfurt[1] pointed to a deep problem in the philosophy of action and sketched an attractive proposal for a solution. The problem arises when we take seriously the idea that you can sometimes have and be moved by desires that you in some sense disown. When such a desire moves you to act, the action is an issue of a desire that is, in one straightforward sense, yours—after all, whose desire is it if not yours? But in a deeper way, the desire's motivational impact on your action does not constitute your direction or governance of the action. As Frankfurt put it, though you do what you want you do not act of your own free will.[2] The problem is whether we can make sense of these ideas of—as I will say—ownership and

Thanks to John Fischer, Harry Frankfurt, Joshua Gert, Carl Ginet, Elizabeth Harman, Terence Irwin, Agnieszka Jaworska, Alfred Mele, Elijah Millgram, Geoffrey Sayre-McCord, T. M. Scanlon, Jeffrey Seidman, Michael Smith, Ralph Wedgwood, Susan Wolf, and audiences at MIT, Cornell, and Florida State University Philosophy Colloquia, the Utrecht Conference on Reasons of One's Own, the Jowett Lecture at the University of Oxford, the Bowling Green Conference on Reason and Deliberation, the University of London Workshop on the Philosophy of Action, the Ethics Workshop at the University of Zurich Ethics Center, and the 2001 Urbino Workshop on Moral Philosophy. I am particularly indebted to thoughtful written comments from John Broome, Peter Railton, Aaron Zimmerman, to extremely helpful conversations with Nadeem Hussain, and to extremely helpful conversations and correspondence with Gideon Yaffe. Much of my work on this essay was supported by a fellowship from the John Simon Guggenheim Memorial Foundation. I dedicate this essay to the memory of my parents, Anne and Harry Bratman.

1. *The Journal of Philosophy* LXVIII, 1 (January 14, 1971): 5–20; reprinted in his *The Importance of What We Care About* (Cambridge: Cambridge University Press, 1988), pp. 11–25.

2. The "will" for Frankfurt (in this 1971 article) is, roughly, one's effective desire. My own approach rejects this Hobbesian view.

rejection of a desire, without appeal to a little person in the head who is looking on at the workings of her desires and giving the nod to some but not to others. And what we have learned from Frankfurt is that our response to this problem has significant implications for our overall view of human agency and autonomy.[3]

I. OWNERSHIP, HIERARCHY, AND THE PLATONIC CHALLENGE

Frankfurt's proposed solution to this problem, sketched in his 1971 article, has come to be called the *hierarchical model*. A desire to *A* (where *A* is something you might do) is yours, in the strong sense we are after, when (roughly) it is a desire you want to move you to act (and so be your "will"). Frankfurt calls this latter, higher-order desire—the desire that the desire to *A* effectively motivate—a *second-order volition*.

Even in 1971, however, Frankfurt saw that this proposal, as just stated, would not work on its own. We need some further story about why certain higher-order desires establish where *you* stand—why they have, so to speak, *agential authority*.[4] And we need to do this without involving ourselves in a criticizable regress. This issue was pressed with insight by Gary Watson[5] in his 1975 reply to Frankfurt's essay; and I have discussed it elsewhere.[6] In those articles, I propose a version of a hierarchical model

---

3. As I will sometimes say, human agents are capable of strong forms of agency. In addition to being purposive agents, human agents have capacities for more complex forms of agency. They are reflective about their motivation and about what is of value. They have long-term plans and policies that organize their practical thought and action over time. Their motivations, value judgments, plans and policies at any one time have normally been shaped in part over time by on-going exercises of these capacities. My talk of strong forms of agency is intended to allude to capacities such as these. An adequate philosophy of action needs to help us understand these capacities, their interrelations, and their relations to self-government and autonomy. As I see it, the idea of ownership of desire earns its place by helping us in this project.

4. For this terminology, see my "Two Problems About Human Agency," *Proceedings of the Aristotelian Society* 101 (2001): 309–26 [this volume, essay 5].

5. "Free Agency," *Journal of Philosophy* LXXII, 8 (April 24, 1975): 205–20.

6. "Identification, Decision, and Treating as a Reason," reprinted in my *Faces of Intention* (New York: Cambridge, 1999), pp. 185–206; "Reflection, Planning, and Temporally Extended Agency," *Philosophical Review* 109 (2000): 35–61 [this volume, essay 2]; and "Two Problems About Human Agency."

that draws on my views about planning agency.[7] One of the main ideas is that the relevant higher-order attitudes will include higher-order intentions and policies concerning what considerations are to be treated as reasons in motivationally effective deliberation. These intentions and policies involve distinctive commitments concerning associated forms of practical thought and action, and play central roles in the cross-temporal organization of our temporally extended lives. I argue that such a view provides us with resources for a response to these worries about agential authority.[8]

In the present essay, however, I largely put to one side these differences between my view and Frankfurt's versions of a hierarchical theory. Though these differences are significant, and I will at times appeal specifically to my own account, my focus here will be on an issue that arises quite generally for a hierarchical theory. It seems that the relevant higher-order attitudes—whether Frankfurtian desires or higher-order intentions and policies—will themselves normally be to some extent grounded in and constrained by reflection on what one takes to be of value. Indeed, it seems that, normally, if an agent's relevant higher-order attitudes are not to some extent shaped by her evaluative reflections and judgments, her agency will be flawed.[9] But this suggests a challenge to the hierarchical account of ownership. The challenge is to explain why we should not see such evaluative judgments—rather than broadly Frankfurtian higher-order attitudes—as the fundamental basis of ownership or rejection of desire: it is when the role of desire in practical thought and action is determined by such evaluative judgments that one's action is self-determined

7. I develop the planning theory of intention primarily in *Intention, Plans, and Practical Reason* (Cambridge, MA: Harvard, 1987; reprint, Stanford: CSLI, 1999).

8. The argument for this draws on distinctive ways in which such intentions and policies organize our temporally extended lives by way of relevant psychological continuities and connections—see "Reflection, Planning, and Temporally Extended Agency." I say more about why such policies about practical reasoning normally involve hierarchy in my "Autonomy and Hierarchy," *Social Philosophy & Policy* 20 (2003): 156–76 [this volume, essay 8].

9. Eleonore Stump emphasizes a need for some such evaluative grounding in her "Sanctification, Hardening of the Heart, and Frankfurt's Concept of Free Will," *Journal of Philosophy* LXXXV, 8 (August 1988): 395–420. And see Susan Wolf, "The True, the Good, and the Lovable: Frankfurt's Avoidance of Objectivity," in Sarah Buss and Lee Overton, eds., *Contours of Agency: Essays on Themes from Harry Frankfurt* (Cambridge, MA: MIT, 2002), pp. 227–44.

or autonomous or performed of one's own free will. Call this the *Platonic challenge.*[10]

One response to this challenge might be to sever the supposed link between Frankfurtian higher-order attitudes and evaluative judgment.[11] My own view, however, is that we should retain some such link while blocking the Platonic challenge. I do not say that such an evaluative backing is, in general, necessary for agential authority or desire ownership or rejection. But I do think that a systematic absence of connection between higher-order Frankfurtian attitude and evaluative judgment would be a breakdown in proper functioning. I want to explain how we can grant this point and still block the Platonic challenge.

2. FEATURES OF FRANKFURTIAN HIERARCHY

Suppose Green has treated you badly, and so you are angry at him and have an associated desire to express this anger.[12] On a Frankfurtian theory, you might nevertheless reject this desire. On Frankfurt's 1971 view, this rejection would consist primarily of a second-order volition that this desire not move you to action. Other versions of a broadly Frankfurtian hierarchical view are available however, so it would be useful to point to features that will be common to such theories.

I think we can say that on a broadly Frankfurtian view, your rejection of your angry desire will have at least the following features. First, it will

---

10. This is one of the challenges posed by Watson's Platonic proposal in his "Free Agency." (Watson, however, qualifies this proposal in his discussion of "perverse cases" in his "Free Action and Free Will," *Mind* XCVI [1987]: 145–72.) Jan Bransen points to a closely related challenge in "True to Ourselves," *International Journal of Philosophical Studies* VI (1998): 67–85, at p. 76. Michael Ridge has pressed this issue in correspondence, as have Agnieszka Jaworska and Govert den Hartogh in conversation.

11. This seems to be Frankfurt's view. For example, as Jennifer Rosner has emphasized, in his 1971 article, Frankfurt held that "a person may be capricious and irresponsible in forming his second-order volitions and give no serious consideration to what is at stake" (p. 19n). More recently, Frankfurt says that higher-order "support or rejection of first-order desires need not include, or be based upon, any favorable or unfavorable attitude concerning how desirable or worthy of approval those desires may be"——"Reply to Michael E. Bratman" in Buss and Overton, eds., *Contours of Agency: Essays on Themes from Harry Frankfurt*, pp. 86–90, see p. 87. Frankfurt does, however, note that "needless to say, it is better for us to care about what is truly worth caring about"; "On Caring," in his *Necessity, Volition, and Love* (Cambridge: Cambridge, 1999), pp. 155–80, see p. 162.

12. I leave open the issue whether this desire is in some way essential to the anger.

involve a second-order attitude that is about that desire.[13] Second, this second-order attitude will itself be a conative attitude, in the broad, generic sense of a motivating attitude. Third, this second-order conative attitude will concern certain kinds of further functioning, from now on, of the first-order desire. The content of this second-order attitude will be in this sense forward-looking. Fourth, this forward-looking second-order conative attitude will include in its own functioning the guidance, from now on, of the functioning of the first-order desire. In short: the theory will appeal to a higher-order attitude that is conative, forward-looking in its content, and guiding in its function.

There is also a fifth feature that such theories try to capture. The higher-order, forward-looking, and guiding conative attitude is to constitute—at least in part, and given relevant background conditions—a commitment on the part of the agent concerning the role of the target desire in her own agency: the agent is appropriately settled on this. When we try to say what is needed for such agential commitment, we face issues about agential authority noted earlier. For now, though, it will suffice just to note that hierarchical theories at least aim at capturing some such commitment.

This quintet of features has remained constant throughout many discussions of hierarchical models. For example, in 1987, Frankfurt suggested that the higher-order pro attitude should concern not directly whether the first-order desire motivates but whether the first-order desire is "to be endorsed as a legitimate candidate for satisfaction."[14] This involved a change (from the earlier appeal to second-order volitions) in the precise content of the higher-order attitude;[15] but that content nevertheless remained forward-looking, and the attitude retained a downstream guidance

13. To keep the discussion manageable, I put to one side yet-higher-order attitudes.

14. "Identification and Wholeheartedness," in *The Importance of What We Care About*, pp. 159–76, on p. 170. I think Frankfurt's later appeals to satisfaction and to volitional necessity also fit into the cited mold, though they aim at a kind of commitment that—in contrast with the 1987 view—need not involve decision, see Frankfurt's "The Faintest Passion," "On the Necessity of Ideals," and "Autonomy, Necessity, and Love" in his *Necessity, Volition, and Love*.

15. This change allows Frankfurt to say that one can decide in a particular case not to act on a desire for X and still not reject that desire: one might simply give it a lower priority than a competitor in the present circumstance. See Frankfurt's remarks about two different kinds of conflict in "Identification and Wholeheartedness," see p. 170. I discuss this point in "Identification,

function. And Frankfurt's talk in this 1987 essay about decisive commitment makes clear the aim of capturing the kind of agential commitment
we have noted.[16]

More recently, in articles to which I alluded earlier, I have tried to
understand ownership of a first-order desire for X primarily by appeal to a
higher-order policy in favor of treating that desire as reason-providing in
motivationally effective practical reasoning. Such a policy favors the
motivational functioning of the first-order desire by way of practical
reasoning whose content involves the thought of X, or of the desire for X,
as a justifying consideration.[17] Despite differences from Frankfurt's accounts, appeal to such policies remains an appeal to a higher-order attitude that is conative, forward-looking in content, and guiding in function.
Such policies are intentions that are appropriately general; so they involve
distinctive commitments and bring with them distinctive norms of consistency, coherence, and stability over time. In these ways the theory aims
to shed light on the kind of agential commitment that is a concern of
hierarchical theories.

I do not mean to say that the cited quintet exhausts the features of
interest in hierarchical theories. Indeed, I will later emphasize yet a further
feature. We can nevertheless use this quintet for an initial characterization
of the kind of theory of interest. Our concern, then, will be with hierarchical theories of desire ownership and rejection in which basic theoretical
work is done by higher-order attitudes that are conative, forward-looking
in content, guiding in function, and purportedly constitute, in context, a
relevant commitment on the part of the agent concerning the role of the

---

"Decision, and Treating as a Reason," pp. 192, 195–98. See also Joseph Raz, "When We are
Ourselves: The Active and the Passive," in his *Engaging Reason: On the Theory of Value and Action*
(New York: Oxford, 1999), pp. 5–21, see p. 18.

16. "Identification and Wholeheartedness," p. 170.

17. The agent also needs to be, to use Frankfurt's term, satisfied with the policy. I propose
a way of understanding such satisfaction in "Reflection, Planning, and Temporally Extended
Agency," at pp. 48–50 and pp. 59–60 [this volume, pp. 33–36, 44]. My proposal there allows for
satisfaction with such a policy even in the face of certain strongly felt, first-order desires to the
contrary. This feature of the proposal might be challenged, but this is a challenge we need not
address here. What is important for present purposes is, rather, that such satisfaction need not
in general involve the kind of strong evaluative judgment cited by the Platonic challenge; more
on this below.

desire in her agency. Let us call such theories, and the higher-order attitudes they highlight, *Frankfurtian*.[18]

Now, I have maintained that such Frankfurtian attitudes will normally be to some extent grounded in and constrained by reflection on what one takes to be of value. Your higher-order rejection of your angry desire is, let us suppose, anchored at least in part in your view that it is good to be a person who turns the other cheek. The Platonic challenge is that once we note this grounding role of evaluative judgment, our account of what constitutes ownership of desire can dispense with essential appeal to such Frankfurtian attitudes. In the example, perhaps we can say that the fact that the desire to express your anger is not fully your own consists in its failure to cohere with your value judgment in favor of being a person who turns the other cheek. That, anyway, is the challenge.

One might respond by emphasizing that issues of ownership also arise concerning value judgments.[19] It seems, though, that the Platonic challenger can grant this point. She claims that ownership of desire consists, at bottom, in value judgment; to this she can add that the relevant value judgments need to be, in an appropriate sense, the agent's own. But she can claim that for a value judgment to be an agent's own is not for it to be supported by a higher-order Frankfurtian attitude. After all, even a Frankfurtian theory will at some point appeal to features of a Frankfurtian attitude that do not involve a yet-higher-order attitude but help give it agential authority. This is where appeals to, for example, satisfaction and/or a cross-temporal organizing role can take center stage.[20] The Platonic challenger can herself draw on similar resources but apply them to value judgment rather than to Frankfurtian higher-order attitude.[21]

---

18. Such theories can allow that there are cases in which desire leads to action in the absence of any higher-order attitude, pro or con. The claim is only that we should appeal to such higher-order attitudes in a model of strong forms of agency, including self-determination and autonomy.

19. This was Frankfurt's response in conversation. See also J. David Velleman, "What Happens When Someone Acts?" in his *The Possibility of Practical Reason* (New York: Oxford, 2000), pp. 123–43, on p. 134.

20. See "Two Problems about Human Agency," pp. 318–19 [this volume, pp. 98–99].

21. Though her explanation of the organizing role of relevant value judgments will differ from the analogue offered within a Frankfurtian theory.

For this reason, my strategy here will be to allow the Platonic challenger to appeal to such value judgments, but to argue that in important cases these judgments nevertheless leave open basic issues of desire ownership.

3. WEAKNESS OF WILL AND WATSONIAN PERVERSE CASES

An initial move appeals to cases of weakness of will and the like—cases in which value judgments do not bring with them relevant commitments, and relevant commitments go against one's value judgments. Perhaps I think it strictly better to be a person who forgives and turns the other check but nevertheless, in a kind of self-indulgence, allow into my life a willingness to express reactive anger. Though this role of my desire to express my anger diverges from my relevant evaluative judgments, it is not a desire I reject or disown. Indeed, in some versions of such a case—cases Watson calls "perverse cases"—I really am fully behind the expression of such reactive anger. As Watson says, "There is no estrangement here."[22] So, value judgment is one thing, and ownership another.

I think this is right as far as it goes; but it does not yet go far enough. After all, it seems that these are not cases of a well-functioning agent. A defender of the Platonic challenge might still offer his view as a view about a well-functioning agent: at least for such an agent, desire ownership and rejection are constituted by value judgment rather than by Frankfurtian higher-order attitude. I think, however, that even this qualified Platonic challenge does not work.

4. THREE EXAMPLES AND AN OBJECTION

Suppose that you and I both like to drink alcohol. We both think that there is some value in drinking alcohol when that is what one wants to do. We have both reflected also on the impact of such drinking on our lives, and we both see that there would also be a certain value in systematically

22. "Free Action and Free Will," p. 150.

abstaining from alcohol. So far, we are alike. But suppose that you go on reflectively to reject your desire to drink alcohol, whereas I do not. In what does your rejection consist? The answer offered by a Frankfurtian theory is that it consists in a higher-order, conative attitude, one that is forward-looking and guiding, and one that partly constitutes a commitment not to build that desire and its targeted activity into your life. A natural picture here is that this Frankfurtian attitude is to some extent grounded in your judgment of the value of abstinence, but it goes beyond that judgment. You arrive at this higher-order attitude, but I do not; yet we share the cited judgments of value. The fact that your lingering desire to drink is one you disown does not consist solely in those judgments, but essentially involves a Frankfurtian attitude.

Granted, once you arrive at the cited Frankfurtian attitude, there may be available a further judgment of value—namely, a judgment that it is good to stick with this commitment.[23] There is room here for disagreement about just how important a value this is. But we can grant the Platonic challenger that such a commitment to abstinence can be sufficiently integral to the agent's life for there to be a distinctive value of living in accord with it. Nevertheless, an appeal to such a value judgment to explain your rejection of your desire for alcohol would not support an effort to dispense with the Frankfurtian apparatus in the account of ownership and rejection.[24]

For a second case, return to you and your anger at Green.[25] Suppose that Green has also treated me badly and that I too am angry and want to express my anger at Green. Suppose that both of us think that anger, resentment, and their expression are in some ways fitting and appropriate reactions to such untoward behavior. We both also see the good in being a person who turns the other cheek. Where we differ is that after reflection you, in part on the basis of the latter judgment, come to reject your angry

23. See Raz's important discussion of related ideas in his *The Morality of Freedom* (New York: Oxford, 1986), chap. 14, especially pp. 385–90.
24. I discuss a related complexity below in section 7.
25. My thinking about this case benefited from discussion of related ideas in a meeting of the Bay Area Forum for Law and Ethics [February 2001], in which Samuel Scheffler presented his "Doing and Allowing" (which has now appeared in *Ethics* CXIV [2004]: 215–39). Scheffler too emphasizes the significance to our agency of our need to respond to diverse values and notes that this is a central theme in work of Joseph Raz.

desire, whereas I do not. We share a complex evaluative judgment of such anger and its expression; but you go on, and I do not, to a higher-order Frankfurtian commitment not to build the expression of such anger into your life. If your angry desire were to linger it would be one you disown; not so for me. And it seems that what accounts for this difference is not a difference in value judgment but a difference in commitment, a difference of a sort that a Frankfurtian theory is well positioned to capture.

Again, there is the complexity that given your Frankfurtian rejection of your angry desire, there is a further judgment of value that may be available—namely, a judgment that it would be good to stick with this commitment. But, again, this is not a way of undermining the significance of the Frankfurtian hierarchy.

For a third case, consider two people faced with a wartime draft. Each, let us suppose, sees value in resisting the call to arms; but each also sees value in loyally serving in one's country's military. Let us suppose that person 1, at the time of decision and after much soul-searching, arrives at a forward-looking and guiding Frankfurtian commitment in favor of resisting military service and rejecting his desire to serve: the desire to serve is not to play its normal, end-setting roles in his deliberation and action. Person 2, in contrast, decides in favor of military service. The nagging tug person 1 continues to experience in the direction of loyal military service is one he disowns even though he acknowledges the value in such service. And the fact that he rejects this desire seems to consist in part in his Frankfurtian commitment; for that is what seems to distinguish him from person 2. Granted, once this conscientious objector has arrived at this Frankfurtian commitment, a further judgment of value may be available, one that appeals to the value of being true to this prior commitment. But this does not give us reason to dispense with appeal to Frankfurtian attitudes.

In each of these examples, there are relevant judgments of value on both sides of a practical issue; and a Frankfurtian commitment is to some extent grounded in some of those judgments. But the presence of these evaluative grounds does not entail that there is no further work to be done by the Frankfurtian commitment. In some such cases it is only when one arrives at a Frankfurtian commitment that one has, in the relevant sense, taken a stand with respect to the issues raised for one's life.

This suggests an answer to the Platonic challenge. We can accept that in a well-functioning agent, Frankfurtian attitudes will normally be to some extent grounded in and constrained by judgments of value that do not themselves appeal to those Frankfurtian attitudes. We can, nevertheless, still reject the claim that these value judgments by themselves in general fully constitute the basis of ownership and rejection.

There is, however, an objection to this. Consider our conscientious objector. It might be claimed that if he is rationally to arrive at a Frankfurtian rejection of his desire to serve in the military, he must judge not only that resistance has value but also that resistance is strictly better than military service, and perhaps also that it is strictly better to be a person who resists. And similarly in the other examples. Once such strict comparative value judgments are available, however, we can appeal to them, rather than to Frankfurtian higher-order attitudes, in a Platonic account of ownership and rejection. Or so the Platonic challenger might claim.

If this is to support the Platonic challenge, the cited strict comparative value judgments must not themselves make essential appeal to prior Frankfurtian attitudes. It seems to me, however, that even in a well-functioning agent, desire ownership or rejection does not in general require the backing of such independent, strict, comparative value judgments. I proceed to explain why.

5. THE WILL

A number of years ago, Donald Davidson[26] proposed that intending is an "all-out" evaluative judgment. In my 1985 discussion, I interpreted this as the claim that to intend to A is to judge that A is strictly better than its relevant alternatives.[27] I then noted that when we see intention as such a strict comparative evaluation we face a Buridan problem; for there are cases in which one decides in favor of one of several conflicting options even

26. "Intending," originally published in 1978 and reprinted in his *Essays on Actions and Events*, second edition (New York: Oxford, 2001), pp. 83–102.

27. See my "Davidson's Theory of Intention," reprinted in *Faces of Intention*, pp. 209–24. I argued there that if we were instead to cite a weaker evaluative judgment—say, that there is something good about A, or that A is as good as its alternatives—we would run into difficulties concerning the rational agglomerativity of intention.

though, prior to one's decision, one only judges that the option one decides on is as good as (but is not strictly better than) its relevant alternative.[28]

An analogous point can be made in the present context. Perhaps, prior to his decision, our conscientious objector thinks that military service and resistance to such service really are, everything relevant considered, each as good as the other. Still, life must go on. One way for him to settle the issue would be to settle on a Frankfurtian commitment that rejects his desire for military service as no longer fully his own.[29]

Granted, he might simply make a decision about what to do on the present occasion and not arrive at a higher-order commitment that rejects his desire to serve.[30] Or he might only decide to give military service a lower priority in his practical reasoning but not reject his desire for military service as no longer his own. Given the significance to his life of the decision he faces, however, one intelligible response might be not simply to decide not to enlist, and not simply to give one option a lower priority, but to decide quite generally not to treat his own participation in loyal military service as a consideration of positive significance in his own life.[31] Still, one may think that such cases of apparent evaluative ties are rare. So let us extend the point. The next place to look will be cases in which the agent is, prior to his decision, uncertain about which course of action, or way of life, is better.[32] This, too, might be the plight of our conscientious objector. Yet here, again, he really must settle the issue and get on with his life. And he might do this by way of arriving at a Frankfurtian commitment that rejects his desire for military service.

Finally, an agent might think that there is something of value in both alternatives but that there is no further, relevant comparative evaluation

28. See "Davidson's Theory of Intention," and Edna Ullmann-Margalit and Sidney Morgenbesser, "Picking and Choosing," *Social Research* XLIV (1977): 757–85.

29. Rejecting the desire need not involve a commitment to getting rid of it; the commitment is, rather, to rejecting relevant functioning in practical reasoning and action. As Elizabeth Harman emphasized in conversation, it might even be important to the agent to retain the desire while blocking such functioning.

30. As Aaron Zimmerman has emphasized.

31. As I would put it, the relevant decision would be a decision not to treat this consideration as a reason in his relevant practical reasoning.

32. Thanks to Nadeem Hussain for emphasizing this case.

to be made—at least until he makes a relevant commitment. This, too, may be the plight of our conscientious objector. He may think there is value in resistance and value in loyal military service, but there is, at least prior to his relevant commitment, no further truth about which is better. Still, he must get on with his life.

What these cases have in common is that the agent's value judgments by themselves underdetermine his stance in response to the practical issues raised about how he is to live.[33] For a well-functioning agent in this predicament, Frankfurtian commitments can—and, indeed, need to—go beyond prior value judgment. Such commitments do not require the backing of strict comparative value judgments that do not themselves make essential appeal to such commitments.

A by-now familiar complexity is that, once the agent arrives at a Frankfurtian commitment, this may bring to bear the value of living in accord with such commitments. But the Platonic challenge cannot appeal to that further value judgment—a judgment that itself appeals to a prior, distinct Frankfurtian commitment—to support the claim that such commitments are no essential part of desire ownership.

Could such Frankfurtian commitments, without the backing of strict comparative value judgments that do not themselves make essential appeal

33. Consider Stuart Hampshire's description of a person who makes a decision in the face of a certain kind of conflict:

he will probably recognize that his choice of a way of life is undetermined by the arguments that support his decision. . . . He often would not wish to say that his decision on the right course is objectively right, in the sense that in making the decision he is at the same time claiming universal agreement for it. . . . But the word "commitment" carries a more positive implication; the implication is that he has himself recognized that his choice is undetermined by the reasons that support it, and, secondly, that he accepts responsibility for the choice as being his and his alone, without the support of any external authority. *Two Theories of Morality* (New York; Oxford 1977), p. 52.

David Wiggins points to related ideas in his discussion of the "doctrine of cognitive underdetermination"; see his "Truth, Invention, and the Meaning of Life" in *Need, Values Truth: Essays in the Philosophy of Value*, third edition (New York: Oxford, 1998), pp. 87–137, especially p. 124. See also Wolf, "The True, the Good, and the Lovable: Frankfurt's Avoidance of Objectivity," at pp. 234–35; Richard Holton, "Intention and Weakness of Will," *The Journal of Philosophy* XCVI, 5 (May 1999): 241–62, at p. 245; and Robert Nozick's suggestive discussion in *Philosophical Explanations* (Cambridge, MA: Harvard, 1981), pp. 446–50. (I discuss these views of Nozick in "Nozick on Free Will," in David Schmidtz, ed., *Robert Nozick* (New York: Cambridge, 2002), pp. 155–74. [this volume, essay 6]). Keith Lehrer also highlights the relation between hierarchical theories and a kind of underdetermination in his *Self-Trust: A Study of Reason, Knowledge, and Autonomy* (New York: Oxford, 1997), chap. 4.

to such commitments, nevertheless have agential authority? I think the answer is yes. This is because we can expect such commitments normally to be stable, and reasonably so, and to play appropriate roles in the agent's practical thought and action over time. On my version of such a theory, for example, these commitments consist primarily in higher-order policies concerning the role of various desires in one's motivationally effective practical reasoning. Such policies will normally have a distinctive stability and will support the cross-temporal organization of the agent's practical thought and action.[34] (I return to this matter below in section 8.)

In the kind of case of underdetermination I am emphasizing, one may arrive at a Frankfurtian commitment by way of reflection that is responsive to a wide range of relevant thoughts, feelings, and inclinations. And there is probably an important role here for what John Dewey called "dramatic rehearsal (in imagination) of various competing possible lines of action."[35] The claim is not that one's arriving at such a commitment need be simply a matter of unreflective, brute picking.[36] In reflectively arriving at the commitment, however, one may well go beyond one's value judgments that are independent of such commitments.

A further complexity is that the agent may arrive at a new Frankfurtian commitment in a way that draws on connections or parallels or analogies with other preexisting Frankfurtian commitments. This may sometimes have a structure analogous to an appeal to precedent in certain forms of legal reasoning.[37] And perhaps this is one way of understanding Charles Taylor's appeal, in such contexts, to "our sense of the shape of our lives."[38] But such reasoning does not support a Platonic rejection of the role of those prior commitments.

Yet another complexity concerns the significance to this story of an act of decision. It has been useful to think of our examples as involving a moment of decision; but this is not essential to the point I want to make.

34. See my "Reflection, Planning, and Temporally Extended Agency."
35. Dewey, *Human Nature and Conduct: An Introduction to Social Psychology* (New York: Random House, 1957), p. 179.
36. See E. Ullmann-Margalit and S. Morgenbesser, "Picking and Choosing."
37. See Nozick, *Philosophical Explanations*, p. 297.
38. Taylor, "Leading a Life," in Ruth Chang, ed., *Incommensurability, Incomparability, and Practical Reason*, (Cambridge, MA: Harvard, 1997), pp. 170–83, at p. 183.

What is central is the idea of a kind of attitude that, in the context, constitutes the relevant form of agential commitment. Decision is sometimes a way of arriving at such an attitude; but such an attitude may also emerge from a more complex, inchoate, and extended process of reflection. Further, if one were to think one has decided to reject a certain desire, but one did not thereby actually arrive at a relevant attitude, then one would not have arrived at the relevant commitment.[39]

6. COMPARATIVE VALUE JUDGMENT AND INTERSUBJECTIVITY

What conception of value judgment makes the most sense of these observations? This is a big issue. Here I limit myself to remarks about comparative value judgments and intersubjectivity, remarks that are intended to get at a feature of such judgments that will be acknowledged by a wide range of theories.

It is natural to see a judgment that X is better than Y as not merely expressing a personal ranking, but as being in the domain of the intersubjective. There are different ways of trying to articulate this idea. We might say that a judgment that X is better than Y is made from, as Hume would say, a "common point of view,"[40] or is at least, in part, a judgment that from a common point of view one would favor X over Y. Or we might say that such a judgment tracks a certain kind of interpersonal convergence. Or we might see such a judgment as, in part, the expression of an associated demand on others. And other views are possible. Here I want to remain neutral concerning how best to articulate this connection between value judgment and intersubjectivity; for I think that the main point I want to make will be available on any acceptable interpretation of this connection.[41]

It will help keep things manageable, however, to work with a particular interpretation. So let us consider an interpretation of this idea suggested by work of Michael Smith. On Smith's view, a judgment that X is desirable is a judgment about "convergence in the desires of fully rational agents"

---

39. Cf. Frankfurt, "The Faintest Passion," p. 101.
40. *An Inquiry Concerning the Principles of Morals*, section 9.
41. In particular, I want to remain neutral in the debate between cognitivist and expressivist treatments of this connection.

concerning "what is to be done in the various circumstances in which they might find themselves."[42] A corresponding view about comparative evaluations would be that a judgment that X is better than Y in certain circumstances involves a judgment that such fully rational advisors would converge on an all-considered preference for X over Y in those circumstances. On such a view, for our conscientious objector to judge that in his circumstances resistance is better than military service, he needs to judge that fully rational advisors would converge on an all-considered preference that people, in such circumstances, resist rather than join the military.

Will our conscientious objector think this? The answer will likely depend on how the cited circumstances are described. Our conscientious objector may think as follows: "If the cited circumstances are as my circumstances were before I decided in favor of resistance, then there seems little reason to expect such convergence among all rational advisors specifically in favor of resistance.[43] If, however, the circumstances include the agent's Frankfurtian commitment to resistance, then perhaps I would expect that rational advisors would converge on an all-considered preference in favor of the agent's resistance."[44]

This may be oversimplified. Perhaps there would be reason to expect such convergence concerning circumstances that do not include a commitment specifically to resistance, so long as those circumstances include certain other related Frankfurtian commitments of the agent. Even if our conscientious objector were to recognize this complexity, however, he still might have no relevant comparative evaluative judgment that satisfies the intersubjectivity constraint, does not appeal to prior Frankfurtian commitments, and yet settles the practical issue.

This suggests a general point. Judgments of comparative value are subject to an appropriate intersubjectivity constraint. Here we have considered an interpretation of this constraint that sees the judgment as

---

42. *The Moral Problem* (Cambridge: Blackwell, 1994), p. 173. See also Michael Smith, "In Defense of *The Moral Problem*: A Reply to Brink, Copp, and Sayre-McCord," *Ethics* CVIII (1997): 84–119, at pp. 88–90.

43. Cf. Wiggins: "Often we have to make a practical choice that another rational agent might understand through and through, not fault or even disagree with, but (as Winch has stressed) make differently himself," ("Truth, Invention, and the Meaning of Life," p. 126).

44. Though see below, section 7.

concerned with a convergence in the preferences of fully rational advisors; and one might question this particular story. But it seems in any case that some version of the connection with intersubjectivity will apply to the comparative evaluative judgments relevant here. And what our case of the conscientious objector suggests is that in some cases, an agent's comparative evaluative judgments that respect relevant intersubjectivity constraints, but do not appeal to prior Frankfurtian commitments, will be by themselves too weak to settle the practical issue that is at stake. In such cases, Frankfurtian attitudes can settle the practical issue; but—and this is the further feature of such attitudes to which I alluded earlier—they do not seem to be subject in the same way to corresponding intersubjectivity constraints. After all, the primary role of Frankfurtian commitments is to settle where *that agent* stands. This will, I think, require something roughly along the lines of what Frankfurt calls "wholeheartedness" on the part of the agent.[45] It does not, however, seem to require an assumption by that agent that all rational advisors would converge on (or an injunction by that agent that everyone is to converge on) the very same stance.[46] This divergence in relevant intersubjectivity constraints on comparative value judgment, on the one hand, and on Frankfurtian commitment, on the other, is at the heart of my response to the Platonic challenge.[47]

Return to the case in which our conscientious objector judges that there is value both in resistance and in loyal military service, but no

45. See especially Frankfurt's "The Faintest Passion." I do not try here to settle the further issue of precisely how to understand such wholeheartedness. For present purposes, the important point is only that wholeheartedness does not require the cited kind of intersubjectively accountable strict comparative evaluation.

46. So our conscientious objector may reflectively decide to reject his inclination toward loyal military service and yet not think, as J. David Velleman puts it, that this "is what anyone would think in response to the relevant practical question, and would think that anyone would think, and so on"; see Velleman's "The Voice of Conscience," *Proceedings of the Aristotelian Society* XCIX (1998): 57–76, at p. 69. And compare Frankfurt's observation that "it is not very likely . . . that what each of us considers most important to himself is exactly the same" ("Autonomy, Necessity, and Love," at p. 132).

47. And it is related to Allan Gibbard's distinction between an "existential commitment" and acceptance of "a norm as a requirement of rationality"—see *Wise Choices, Apt Feelings* (Cambridge, MA: Harvard, 1990), pp. 166–170. See also (in an essay to which Gibbard here refers) P. F. Strawson's discussion of "the natural diversity of human ideals"; "Social Morality and Individual Ideal," in his *Freedom and Resentment and Other Essays* (New York: Methuen, 1974), pp. 26–44, at pp. 42–43.

further truth about which is better. He might reach this judgment concerning circumstances that do not yet include relevant Frankfurtian commitments one way or the other. After all, those may well be the circumstances he is in prior to his decision. He may think that if such commitments are not part of the circumstance, there is no reason to expect appropriate convergence, or its analogue, specifically on one of the options. And he may then proceed, on reflection, to arrive at a Frankfurtian commitment that goes beyond his current evaluative judgments.

7. REFLEXIVITY AND THE VALUE OF LIVING IN ACCORD WITH ONE'S COMMITMENTS

We now need to consider a further Platonic proposal, one that draws on the value of living in accord with one's commitments.[48] The proposal is that ownership of a desire for X consists in a *reflexive* value judgment roughly along the lines of:

> (P) It would be strictly best, in part because of this very judgment that (P), to be a person who acts on the desire for X in relevant circumstances.

One can arrive at such a reflexive judgment even though one does not think that, prior to and independently of that judgment, it would be best to be a person who acts on the desire for X. The reflexive judgment, so to speak, sees itself as part of what determines what would be best. And the proposal is that the agent's relevant commitment consists in such a reflexive value judgment.

How can this evaluative judgment itself help determine what would be best? The idea is that the existence of the judgment brings to bear the value of acting in accord with such judgments. But why does that have

48. This proposal is broadly in the spirit of a suggestion of Velleman about how Davidson's theory of intending might be developed to respond to Buridan cases. Velleman made this suggestion in his contribution to a symposium on my *Intention, Plans, and Practical Reason* at the 1988 meetings of the Central APA. A related idea is in Wolf, "Two Levels of Pluralism," *Ethics* CII (1992): 785–98, at p. 796.

value? Because the judgment is the agent's commitment, and there is value in living in accord with one's commitments.

This proposal remains vulnerable to concerns about weakness of will and the like; for even if one arrives at (P), one may still fail, out of weak will or "perversity," to endorse the cited desire. However, the Platonic challenger might still propose that, barring such breakdowns, desire ownership is in general constituted by judgments along the lines of (P).

This proposal does provide a more subtle treatment of some examples. Nevertheless, it remains in tension with our observations about intersubjectivity. Granted, intersubjectivity constraints may be easier for a judgment that (P) to satisfy given that the relevant circumstances now include the making of the judgment itself. It seems, however, that an agent might own or identify with a desire without making such an intersubjectively accountable value judgment, and without being guilty of weakness of will or the like. We can see the point by returning to our Smith-like interpretation of the relevant intersubjectivity: the agent might identify with her desire without supposing that there would be relevant convergence among rational advisors, even with respect to the situation in which she identifies with that desire. She may have little confidence that there would be such convergence; she may even believe, to the contrary, that reasonable advisors would indeed diverge in their preferences concerning whether or not, given that one has identified with this desire, one is to act on it.

Suppose, for example, the desire in question is the agent's desire not to help people in need. Suppose she identifies with this desire after reading a novel by Ayn Rand. She might nevertheless recognize that this is quite controversial and so not be confident that all rational advisors would converge. She might even think that some (though not all) such advisors would favor her acting rather on a desire to help, even given that she identifies with her desire not to help.[49] This need not, however, prevent *her* from identifying with her desire not to help. And this can be explained by a Frankfurtian theory: for neither the absence of a belief in convergence nor even a belief in nonconvergence need stand in the way of a

49. Such an advisor would favor something analogous to what Nomy Arpaly and Timothy Schroeder call "inverse akrasia"; see their "Praise, Blame and the Whole Self," *Philosophical Studies* XCIII (1999): 161–88.

Frankfurtian attitude that endorses the desire not to help. Either of these would, however, stand in the way of her arriving at a relevant version of (P)—at least, they would stand in the way if she were reflective about the Smith-like convergence constraints we are now supposing to apply to such a value judgment. So, our Randian agent may endorse her desire not to help even though she does not arrive at a version of (P) concerning that desire. She aims at fashioning a coherent life of her own, within constraints of the good. So long as she does not think it strictly better to abandon her commitment to selfishness, she can shape her life of selfishness within these constraints (as she understands them).

A response might be that in such cases the value of living in accord with one's commitments is always sufficient decisively to tilt the evaluative scales in favor of living in accord with one's commitments. So our agent is at least in a position to arrive at a version of (P) concerning her desire not to help, since she is in a position to see that her arriving at this judgment ensures its truth. This does not, however, seem in general quite right. That one's commitments organize and structure one's life over time is, I think, part of what gives them authority to speak for the agent. It does not follow, however, that living in accord with those commitments either has, or must be thought of by the agent as having, a value that, in such cases, is always sufficient decisively to tilt the intersubjective evaluative scales. Authenticity has its limits, even in the eyes of an authentic agent.[50]

8. A FINAL PLATONIC CHALLENGE

There is, then, reason to see Frankfurtian attitudes as essential to important cases of desire ownership in which a relevant strict comparative value

---

50. So the agent in our example may believe, roughly, that prior to her identification neither selfishness nor selflessness was superior to the other, that her selfishness after her identification is superior to her selfishness prior to her identification, but that even after her identification neither her selfishness nor her selflessness would be superior to the other. Raz would say that by her lights her case bears "the mark of incommensurability"; see *The Morality of Freedom*, pp. 325–26. Ruth Chang would offer a different way of conceptualizing such a case; see her "Introduction" to *Incommensurability, Incomparability, and Practical Reason*, pp. 23–27. What matters for my purposes here, however, is only that our agent does not arrive at a relevant instance of (P) even though she identifies with the selfish desire.

judgment is not available to a well-functioning agent. Further, once these Frankfurtian structures are in place, we have the resources for a plausible model of the kinds of weakness of will and Watsonian "perversity" noted earlier. For me to build into my life a commitment to the expression of reactive anger—even though I think it best not to—is for me to arrive at a Frankfurtian commitment to my angry desires despite my value judgment to the contrary. My ownership of those desires is constituted by my Frankfurtian commitment, not by my evaluative judgment. Yet further, we can extend the account to agents who, in certain contexts, simply refrain from making intersubjectively accountable judgments about the good, but nevertheless put themselves fully behind certain desires by way of relevant Frankfurtian attitudes.[51]

So we have a fairly uniform story to tell about ownership of desire in underdetermination cases, in cases of weak will and "perversity," and in cases in which the agent refrains from relevant judgments about the good. Further, we can see the risk of Watsonian perversity as built into the very psychic machinery that enables us to respond, as we frequently must, in underdetermination cases.[52] But now we need to ask: What about those cases in which, by the agent's own lights, the evaluative judgment does fully settle the issue of ownership of relevant desires, and on the basis of this the agent is fully behind, or fully rejects, those desires? Perhaps it is clear to you that it is a very good thing to build mercy into your life, and a very bad thing not to; and that is why you are fully behind your desires to act mercifully. Again, perhaps—in contrast with our earlier case—you see no value at all in reactive anger and its expression, and that is why you fully reject your angry desires. In each case, as you see it, your ownership or rejection is not a response to underdetermination by value, but rather to an important, determining value. Call such cases *value-judgment-determined* cases. Does the possibility of value-judgment-determined cases challenge the centrality of Frankfurtian attitudes to desire ownership and rejection?

51. Here I have benefited from discussion with Sayre-McCord. See also Frankfurt, "Reply to Susan Wolf," in *Contours of Agency: Essays on Themes from Harry Frankfurt*, pp. 245–52, at p. 249.

52. Here I have benefited from related remarks of Velleman in his "What Good Is a Will?" (unpublished manuscript). See also R. Jay Wallace's remarks about "a hazardous by-product of the capacity for self-determination" in his "Normativity, Commitment, and Instrumental Reason," *Philosophers' Imprint* I, 3 (2001): 1–26, at p. 10.

Well, it is common ground at this point in the discussion that Frankfurtian commitments are involved in a wide range of cases. With these Frankfurtian structures in place it will be plausible to infer that even in value-judgment-determined cases, the ownership or rejection of desire involves a Frankfurtian commitment, albeit a Frankfurtian commitment that, by the agent's lights, is made uniquely reasonable by relevant value judgment.[53] By focusing our philosophical microscopes on cases of underdetermination—as well as on cases of weak will, "perversity," and simple absence of evaluative judgment—we uncover Frankfurtian structures that we then infer to be generally involved in desire ownership or rejection. In this way we arrive at a fairly uniform model of desire ownership and rejection across all cases.[54]

But at this point the Platonic challenger might still propose that it is only in value-judgment-determined cases that there is, as it were, full-blown desire ownership or rejection. The other cases I have emphasized are possible; but as cases of desire ownership or rejection they are, so to speak, second (or, in breakdown cases, third) best. So in the end—and this is the final Platonic challenge—we cannot avoid a Platonic picture of the centrality of evaluative judgment, rather than Frankfurtian attitude, to full-blown desire ownership or rejection.

Why believe this? The underlying idea is that value-judgment determined cases have a feature that is not present in the other cases I have emphasized, a feature that is fundamental to full-blown desire ownership or rejection. What feature? The natural candidate here is a kind of

53. Indeed, it is important to note that even when the agent does judge it strictly best to build, say, mercy into his life there may well still be significant underdetermination of just how important this is to be in his life. So there will continue to be a need to respond to this underdetermination.

54. As I say, this inference is plausible; but perhaps it is not required. An alternative picture might be that for certain kinds of agents all there need be in a value-judgment-determined case is the value judgment and its guidance of the role of relevant desire in action. For such agents in such cases the value judgment on its own constitutes the relevant commitment at the heart of ownership or rejection. (Both Frances Kamm and Derek Parfit pointed toward such a view in conversation.) But even this alternative picture would grant the significance of Frankfurtian attitudes for all agents in underdetermination cases, as well as for many other cases of desire ownership for some kinds of agents. The crucial issue for present purposes will then be whether these Frankfurtian cases are somehow less full-blown cases of ownership or rejection. And that is the issue I proceed to address in the main text.

reasonable stability. Desire ownership or rejection involves the agent's stable commitment concerning the desire. And a Platonic challenger might claim that ownership or rejection that is value-judgment-determined will be reasonably stable, whereas ownership or rejection anchored in commitment in the face of underdetermination will not.

I think, however, that this last claim rests on a mistake; for commitments in the face of underdetermination by value judgment may well be stable, and reasonably so. Your commitment to resist military service may have arisen in a context of underdetermination by value judgment. Once your commitment is there, however, you may well be, as Frankfurt would say, wholehearted about it, and in such a case you will normally need some further reason to change it.[55] Normally, you will not have such a further reason. After all, the evaluative case on the other side was, by your lights, already less than conclusive; and once your commitment is in place, values of integrity and the like can now argue in its favor.[56] Your commitment can be reasonably settled and stable and can play its characteristic roles in your practical thought and action, even in the face of underdetermination by intersubjectively accountable value judgment. So your commitment can have, as I have put it, agential authority. So Frankfurtian ownership or rejection of desire in such underdetermination cases need not be a second-class citizen. And that answers the final Platonic challenge.[57]

---

55. On my account this is a special case of the general phenomenon that prior intention-like commitments can reasonably function as a stable (though defeasible) default, given their central role in cross-temporal organization. See, for example, my "Shared Valuing and Frameworks for Practical Reasoning," in Wallace, Philip Pettit, Samuel Scheffler, and Michael Smith, eds., *Reason and Value: Themes from the Moral Philosophy of Joseph Raz* (Oxford: Oxford University Press, 2004); 1–27 [this volume, essay 13]. (Shelly Kagan, in correspondence, suggested a parallel here with the judicial doctrine of *stare decisis*.) See also Barbara Herman's insightful characterization of Frankfurt's views in her "Bootstrapping," in., *Contours of Agency: Essays on Themes from Harry Frankfurt*, pp. 253–74, at p. 259. In "Are Intentions Reasons? And How Should We Cope with Incommensurable Values?"—in Christopher W. Morris and Arthur Ripstein, eds., *Practical Rationality and Preference: Essays for David Gauthier* (New York, Cambridge, 2001), especially pp. 114–19—John Broome explores the potential role of prior intentions in incommensurability cases; but Broome is skeptical about the idea that intentions and the like have the cited kind of reasonable stability.

56. Though see section 7 for relevant qualification.

57. My remarks in this paragraph have benefited from discussions with Nadeem Hussain.

9. CONCLUSION

I think, then, that the Platonic Challenge does not succeed. In at least a wide range of cases, ownership or rejection of desire goes beyond inter-subjectively accountable value judgment and involves distinctive Frank-furtian commitments concerning whether and how to build that desire, and what it is for, into one's practical life.[58]

Now, in the cases of rejection of desire to which Frankfurt originally drew our attention—his unwilling addict, for example—it seems plausible to say that the rejection goes with a judgment that what the desire is for has no positive value, and perhaps also with distinctive feelings of alien-ation and the like. I have, in contrast, not focused on such feelings and have emphasized cases in which an agent rejects a desire even though she takes it that what the desire is for has some value. Perhaps she sees the value of the pleasures of alcohol, or—to change examples—of sexual activity, but is herself committed to a life of abstinence in which these pleasures are given no weight. On my account, she thereby rejects her desires for these pleasures even though she sees these pleasures as having a certain value. This does not mean that she is completely insensitive to the value of alcohol, or of sex. She may, for example, still buy her friend a drink of wine (but not a dose of heroin). She may respect her friend's way of life, while being clear that this way of life is not her own. In buying her friend a drink she is guided by her commitment to building friendship, and a certain kind of respect for and toleration of her friend, into her own life. But this is not to build into her life her own pursuit of the pleasures of alcohol.[59]

In classifying these different cases—including both the unwilling addict and the person committed to abstinence—as ones that involve rejection, I am, then, extending this idea beyond the cases to which Frankfurt's early discussions most directly call our attention. What all these cases have in

---

58. A further issue is whether a full theory will need somehow to limit the etiologies of these Frankfurtian commitments. Perhaps we should say that at least in central cases of ownership, the commitments are to some appropriate extent an issue of the ongoing exercise of the kinds of basic capacities cited in footnote 3. We do not, however, need to settle this here.

59. My remarks in the second half of this paragraph owe a great deal to probing queries from Terence Irwin and to help in responding to those queries provided by Carl Ginet.

common, however, is that the agent is committed not to give the target desire, and what it is for, certain central roles in her practical life. If she nevertheless, in relevant ways, reasons from and/or acts on that desire she thereby violates her commitment concerning (to return to Taylor's phrase) the shape of her life. In extreme cases this would amount to a kind of self-betrayal or a failure of self-respect or self-esteem.[60]

This commonality seems to me to justify a notion of rejection that applies to all such cases. One might perhaps balk here and claim that, despite this commonality, only the first kind of case—in which the agent sees no value at all in what she desires, and perhaps also experiences feelings of alienation—merits the label of rejection. But so long as one grants the commonality I have emphasized, the dispute may be merely verbal. The important point is that appeal to this commonality helps clarify structures involved in strong forms of human agency and autonomy; and it does this in ways that are responsive to important phenomena of underdetermination by value judgment. In my judgment, it is such structures toward which our concerns with ownership and rejection of desire are most fruitfully directed.

60. Concerning self-esteem, see Frankfurt's "Reply to Barbara Herman," in *Contours of Agency: Essays on Themes from Harry Frankfurt*, pp. 275–78, at p. 277–78.

Chapter 8

AUTONOMY AND HIERARCHY

I. THE AUTONOMY-HIERARCHY THESIS

In autonomous action, the agent herself directs and governs the action. But what is it for the agent herself to direct and to govern? One theme in a series of articles by Harry G. Frankfurt is that we can make progress in answering this question by appeal to *higher-order conative attitudes*.[1] Frankfurt's original version of this idea is that in acting of one's own free will, one is not acting simply because one desires so to act. Rather, it is also true that this desire motivates one's action because one desires that this desire motivate one's action. This latter desire about the motivational role of one's desire is a second-order desire. It is, in particular, what Frankfurt calls a second-order "volition." And, according to Frankfurt's original proposal, acting of one's own free will involves in this way such second-order, and sometimes yet higher-order, volitions.[2]

Thanks to William Brewer, Alisa Carse, John Fischer, Nadeem Hussain, Margaret Little, Alfred Mele, Elijah Millgram, Henry Richardson, Neil Roughley, Ralph Wedgewood, and audiences at the Georgetown University Philosophy Department and the Social Philosophy and Policy Center, Bowling Green State University. Special thanks to Gideon Yaffe for a series of very helpful discussions. Work on this essay was supported by a fellowship from the John Simon Guggenheim Memorial Foundation.

1. See Harry G. Frankfurt, *The Importance of What We Care About* (Cambridge: Cambridge University Press, 1988). See also Gerald Dworkin, "Acting Freely," *Nous* 4 (1970): 367–83; Wright Neely, "Freedom and Desire," *Philosophical Review* 83 (1974): 32–54; and Keith Lehrer, "Freedom, Preference, and Autonomy," *The Journal of Ethics* 1, no. 1 (1997): 3–25.

2. Frankfurt, "Freedom of the Will and the Concept of a Person," in Frankfurt, *The Importance of What We Care About*, 11–25.

Frankfurt's hierarchical proposal has met with a number of challenges and has been subject to clarification and emendation.[3] I myself have elsewhere tried to map out some details of this debate.[4] My concern here, however, is with the very idea that there is a close connection between autonomous agency and motivational hierarchy.

Of course, much depends on what kind of close connection one has in mind. Some might argue that all cases of human autonomous agency essentially involve motivational hierarchy. But I will focus on a somewhat weaker claim. As I see it, talk of autonomous agency and of autonomous action is talk of a highly abstract property of agents and actions, one that involves agential direction and governance of action. We can ask, what kinds of psychological functioning in human agents are such that they can constitute or realize this abstract property?[5] And we can consider the view that at least one central kind of psychological functioning that can constitute or realize human autonomous agency involves motivational hierarchy. That is, it involves the functioning of higher-order conative attitudes that concern the presence and/or functioning of conative attitudes. Perhaps there are other forms of functioning that could also claim to realize a kind of human autonomy. If there are, then we will want to understand their relation to the hierarchical model. But, at the least,

3. For an important, early response to Frankfurt's original essay, see Gary Watson, "Free Agency," *Journal of Philosophy* 72 (1975): 205–20. Watson offers an alternative approach, one that replaces appeal to motivational hierarchy with an appeal to a distinction between motivational and evaluative orderings. Watson also points to at least two potential concerns for the hierarchical approach: (1) a concern about the grounds for seeing higher-order desires as having a stronger claim to speak for the agent than do lower-order desires, without embarking on an unacceptable regress; and (2) a concern about the idea that, in deliberation, we reflect on our desires rather than directly on our options. I discuss this second concern below, in the main text of this essay.

4. Michael E. Bratman, "Identification, Decision, and Treating as a Reason," in Bratman, *Faces of Intention* (New York: Cambridge University Press, 1999), 185–206.

5. Here I am, broadly speaking, following both Frankfurt and J. David Velleman. See, in particular, J. David Velleman, "What Happens When Someone Acts?" in Velleman, *The Possibility of Practical Reason* (Oxford: Oxford University Press, 2000), 123–43. In speaking of functioning that realizes such an abstract property, however, I am making room for the possibility of multiple realizations. I am unsure whether Frankfurt or Velleman would also want to do so. (My appeal in the text to a "central kind of functioning" signals that my concern is with the limited claim that one theoretically important realization involves motivational hierarchy.) Let me also note here that, as I understand the notion of functioning, not all causal impacts will be included in an attitude's functioning.

a central kind of functioning that can realize human autonomy involves conative hierarchy. Or so it may be claimed. Let us call this the *autonomy-hierarchy (AH) thesis*. And let us ask why we should accept this thesis.[6]

Gary Watson points to reasons to be skeptical about accepting the AH thesis.[7] Watson notes that agents "do not (or need not usually) ask themselves which of their desires they want to be effective in action; they ask themselves which course of action is most worth pursuing. The initial practical question is about courses of action and not about themselves."[8] It seems to me that Watson is right in arguing that the "initial practical question" that is explicitly and consciously raised in one's practical reasoning is ordinarily about "courses of action" and not about ourselves. But it is one thing to acknowledge this point about the "initial practical question" and another thing to reject the idea that, in at least one central kind of case, autonomy involves motivational hierarchy.

Indeed, I believe that higher-order conative attitudes play a significant role in central cases of autonomous agency, and so we should accept the AH thesis. In support of this view I offer here two lines of argument. One line of argument (the one that will be my main focus here) derives from the role of valuing in central cases of autonomy and from pressures on such valuing to involve hierarchy. This argument draws on the idea that an autonomous agent not only governs her actions but also governs the practical reasoning from which those actions issue. A second line of argument for the AH thesis derives from the idea that an autonomous agent's governance of her own practical reasoning involves her understanding of this reasoning as so governed. In each case, there are reasons to think that a central model of psychological functioning that can at least partly constitute or realize human autonomous agency will make essential appeal to motivational hierarchy. The first step in advancing these arguments is to reflect on the phenomenon of valuing.

6. In Michael E. Bratman, "Reflection, Planning, and Temporally Extended Agency," *Philosophical Review* 109, no. 1 (2000): 35–61 [this volume, essay 2], I explore the role, in strong forms of human agency, of higher-order policies concerning the functioning of first-order desires in one's motivationally effective practical reasoning. A number of individuals have asked whether such policies about practical reasoning need to be higher order. (Samuel Scheffler once raised this question in a particularly helpful way in correspondence.) The present essay responds to these concerns.

7. Watson, "Free Agency," 205–20.

8. Ibid., 219.

2. VALUING AND TWO PROBLEMS
FOR HUMAN AGENTS

It is sometimes useful in the philosophy of action to see certain features of human agency as (at least, implicit) responses to pervasive and systematic problems that human agents face. I think that this strategy is especially useful when we consider what it is to value something. In particular, I think that we can see valuing as a response to two different, though related, problems that reflective human agents face. I shall describe what these problems are, how valuing constitutes a response to them, and what light this sheds on the higher-order structure of valuing. I shall then explain why it is plausible to see such valuing as central to autonomy.

Many problems that we face as human beings are faced by a wide range of nonhuman agents as well; but some problems that we face are limited to agents who are, like us, reflective in certain ways. Here, I highlight two problems of the latter sort. The first concerns reflective self-management. We are creatures who are affected and moved by complex forms of motivation, and we sometimes find ourselves needing to reflect on, and respond to, these forms of motivation.[9] Suppose that I find myself angry, resentful, and desiring retribution. I am, however, reflective: I ask myself whether, as we say, I "really want" to pursue retribution or, rather, to turn the other cheek. I thereby face a problem of reflective self-management.

The second problem begins to arise once we make judgments of value, judgments that we see as intersubjectively accountable in characteristic ways.[10] On reflection, we can reasonably come to judge that there are

9. This is a central Frankfurtian theme. The idea of casting this problem together with the problem, noted below in the text, of underdetermination by value judgment parallels aspects of Marth C. Nussbaum's discussion in her *The Fragility of Goodness: Luck and Ethics in Greek Tragedy and Philosophy* (Cambridge: Cambridge University Press, 1986), chap. 4.

10. In "A Desire of One's Own" (*Journal of Philosophy*, 2003): 221–42 [this volume, essay 7], I note several different ways of interpreting this constraint of intersubjectivity. We might, for example, see a judgment of value as made from a Humean "common point of view," or as a judgment that those who are appropriately rational and informed would converge in a relevant way, or as involving the expression of a demand on others to converge in relevant ways. And other interpretations are possible. For our present purposes, we do not need to settle on a specific interpretation, though for ease of exposition I will sometimes write in ways that fit most naturally with the second of these interpretations. For a version of this second interpretation see Michael Smith, *The Moral Problem* (Oxford: Basil Blackwell, 1994), 151–77.

many things that have value. We can also reasonably come to believe that a coherent human life frequently involves decisions and/or the assignment of weights, priorities, or other forms of significance that go beyond and are underdetermined by these prior, intersubjectively accountable judgments of value.[11] A dramatic case can be found in a version of Sartre's famous example.[12] A young man sees the value of fighting with the Free French, and he also sees the value of staying with his mother. With respect to these judgments, he may expect an appropriate form of intersubjective convergence. The young man also, however, believes that a coherent, temporally extended life requires some sort of specific, wholehearted commitment to one of these valuable activities over the other, a commitment with respect to which he may well not expect relevant intersubjective convergence. Granted, he may suppose that after he has arrived at a commitment to, say, the Free French, the value of loyalty to his commitment becomes salient; and about *this* value he may expect relevant intersubjective convergence. But this does not undermine the observation that there was underdetermination of the contours of the young man's life by his value judgments prior to arriving at his commitment.

I will call these two problems, respectively, problems of *self-management* and problems of *underdetermination (of the contours of one's life) by value judgment*. These are not only problems that philosophers have in theorizing about human agency. They are pervasive, practical problems faced by ordinary human agents.

This is not to say that these problems are normally ones with which we are explicitly and consciously concerned in our everyday practical thinking. Rather, much of our ordinary, day-to-day practical thinking takes for granted background structures that help constitute our solutions to these problems. Watson may well be right in noting that we ordinarily do not

---

11. A number of philosophers have emphasized ways in which such judgments of value can underdetermine the specific contours of an individual life. For present purposes I will take it for granted, without further argument, that there frequently is some such underdetermination. See, e.g., Isaiah Berlin, *Four Essays on Liberty* (Oxford: Oxford University Press, 1969); Robert Nozick, *Philosophical Explanations* (Cambridge, MA: Harvard University Press, 1981), esp. 446–50; and Joseph Raz, *The Morality of Freedom* (Oxford: Oxford University Press, 1986), chap. 14. Consider also T. M. Scanlon's remark that "one cannot respond to every value or pursue every end that is worthwhile, and a central part of life for a rational creature lies in selecting those things that it will pursue." T. M. Scanlon, *What We Owe to Each Other* (Cambridge, MA: Harvard University Press, 1998), 119.

12. Jean-Paul Sartre, "Existentialism Is a Humanism," in W. Kaufmann, ed., *Existentialism from Dostoevsky to Sartre* (1956; reprint, rev. and expanded, New York: Meridian/Penguin, 1975), 354–56.

reflect explicitly and directly on our motivation. Instead, the direct target of our explicit practical reasoning frequently concerns what to do. Nevertheless, our management of our motivation is one of the problems that needs to be addressed by the structures that help shape our practical reasoning. More generally, our coordinated responses to problems of self-management and of underdetermination by value judgment are, so to speak, part of the deep structure of our ordinary practical thinking. Or so I propose.

When we see our practical thinking in this way, we can ask the question: what features of such thinking enter into our solutions to the problems of self-management and underdetermination by value judgment? My conjecture is that human agents tend to incorporate into their practical thinking a unified—as it were, simultaneous—solution to this pair of problems. This unified solution is valuing.

3. VALUING AND POLICIES ABOUT PRACTICAL REASONING

I propose that human agents tend to incorporate into their practical thinking valuing understood in a certain way. What I have in mind is this: Policies are intentions that are general in relevant ways.[13] We have policies of action. We also have policies, or policy-like attitudes,[14] that concern the significance that is to be given to certain considerations in our motivationally effective practical reasoning concerning our own conduct.[15] I might, for example, have a policy that gives no weight at all to revenge, another policy that gives great weight to family, and yet another policy that gives little or no weight to my own contribution to political goals. On the one hand, such policies partly constitute my stance with respect to relevant motivation, such as

13. My discussion throughout this essay assumes the approach to intention that I have called "the planning theory" and that I present in Michael E. Bratman, *Intention, Plans, and Practical Reason* (Cambridge, MA: Harvard University Press, 1987; reissued by CSLI Publications, 1999). I discuss policies, esp., at 87–91. I also discuss policies in Michael E. Bratman, "Intention and Personal Policies," *Philosophical Perspectives* 3 (1989): 443–69.

14. Concerning this qualification, see my discussion of what I call "quasi-policies" in Michael E. Bratman, "Reflection, Planning, and Temporally Extended Agency," 57–60 [this volume, pp. 42–44]. In most of my discussion here I will not keep repeating this qualification (though I will return to it briefly below in note 51).

15. Cp. Nozick, *Philosophical Explanations*, 446–49.

a desire for revenge, that might come up for reflective assessment. On the other hand, some policies of this sort constitute my response to the problem of fashioning a life with a coherent shape in the face of underdetermination by value judgment. Such policies, or policy-like attitudes, about practical reasoning are a kind of valuing, one that constitutes a unified response to problems of self-management and of underdetermination by value judgment.

I have touched on some of these themes elsewhere. In "Valuing and the Will," I pursue a project of Gricean "creature construction."[16] This project introduces forms of valuing as steps in the "construction" of a series of fictional creatures, in pursuit of a (partial) model of actual human agents. We begin with a creature who has certain broadly conative attitudes—desires in a broad sense—and certain belief-like cognitive attitudes. Early in the project of creature construction, we envision a creature whose desires have been suitably exposed to its relevant beliefs and in that sense are "considered." We then turn to a creature who engages in a primitive form of deliberation, in which its considered desires determine the weight that is given to various factors, where the weight that is given matches the degree to which these considered desires tend to move the creature to action. The considered desires of such a creature can be thought of as a primitive kind of valuing.

A more complex creature, however, might be more reflective about her desires, including her considered desires, and might ask herself how she "really wants" such desires, and what they are for, to enter into her deliberation and motivation. An intelligible output of such reflection would be a higher-order policy, or policy-like attitude, about that creature's treatment of her desires as providing, for her motivationally effective deliberation, *justifying* considerations for action.[17] In "Valuing and

16. The basic idea of creature construction comes from Paul Grice. Grice aimed to "construct (in imagination, of course) according to certain principles of construction, a type of creature, or rather a sequence of types of creature, to serve as a model (or models) for actual creatures." See Paul Grice, "Method in Philosophical Psychology (From the Banal to the Bizarre)," Presidential Address, *Proceedings and Addresses of the American Philosophical Association* 68 (1974–75): 37. My discussion is in Michael E. Bratman, "Valuing and the Will," *Philosophical Perspectives* 14 (2000): 249–65 [this volume, essay 3].

17. For some intermediate steps in this construction see "Valuing and the Will," 252–57 [this volume, pp. 52–60].

the Will," I call such policies *self-governing* policies, and I argue that they constitute an important kind of valuing.[18]

It is helpful, here, to distinguish two different ways in which a first-order desire may enter into practical reasoning.[19] Suppose, for example, that my desire for revenge motivates action by way of associated practical reasoning. In one case, the content of my (defeasible) reasoning might be expressed as follows:

Model 1
(a) I desire revenge.
    Action *A* would promote revenge.
    So I have a justifying reason for *A*-ing.
    So I will *A*.

Here (a) is, as is said, the major premise.[20] In a second case, in contrast, my reasoning has as its major premise an appropriate expression of my desire, or of a thought involved in my having that desire. So, for example, we might in the second case see the major premise as:

(b) Revenge is a justifying consideration

where (b) is an expression of my desire, or of a thought involved in my having that desire.[21] The content of my (defeasible) reasoning would then be along the lines of:

Model 2
(b) Revenge is a justifying consideration.
    Action *A* would promote revenge.

18. In the central case that I consider in "Valuing and the Will," the self-governing policy concerns first-order motivation that is already present. I also note, however, that there can be cases in which the policy involves, rather, a commitment to acquiring certain desires; and such a policy might concern one's treatment of certain desires, were one to acquire them.

For a related but different conception of a connection between valuing and policies, see David Copp, *Morality, Normativity, and Society* (New York: Oxford University Press, 1995), 177–78.

19. For a closely related distinction see Philip Pettit and Michael Smith, "Backgrounding Desire," *Philosophical Review* 99 (1990): 565–92. In what follows, my first case corresponds to cases in which, in their terminology, the desire is in the "foreground." My second case is similar to one kind of case in which, in their terminology, the desire is in the "background."

20. We might also see (a) as alluding to further conditions that the desire fulfills, for example, that it is a considered desire.

21. Appeal to an evaluative expression of the desire is characteristic of Donald Davidson's views about practical reasoning. See, e.g., Donald Davidson, "Intending," reprinted in Donald Davidson, *Essays on Actions and Events* (Oxford: Oxford University Press, 1980), 85–86. John Cooper

So I have a justifying reason for *A*-ing.
So I will *A*.

(Here [b] is understood in the indicated way.)[22]

Now, a self-governing policy that eschews my treating my desire for re-venge as reason-providing in my motivationally effective practical reasoning will eschew practical reasoning of both sorts. Indeed, it might do this even in some cases in which my desire really does involve a thought or judgment along the lines of (b). A self-governing policy that supports my treating my desire as reason-providing in my motivationally effective practical reasoning will support practical reasoning of one or both of these sorts. Note that even in the case in which such a policy concerns only practical reasoning along the lines of Model 2, the policy still concerns the cited functioning of the relevant desire in that reasoning. The policy is a higher-order policy about that functioning of the desire, even though the relevant premise in the policy-supported reasoning—premise (b)—does not itself refer to that desire, but is, rather, an expression of that desire or of an involved thought.[23]

Now, as they emerge from the story of creature construction as so far developed, higher-order, self-governing policies are primarily a response

---

emphasizes how, on Aristotle's theory of virtues of character, even appetites and forms of anger and grief involve judgments about the good or what ought to be done, although these judgments are not themselves based on reasoning that aims at determining what is good or what ought to be done. Cooper also emphasizes the permanence of these nonrational desires even in a human being of Aristotelian virtue of character. See John M. Cooper, "Some Remarks on Aristotle's Moral Psychology," reprinted in Cooper, *Reason and Emotion: Essays on Ancient Moral Psychology and Ethical Theory* (Princeton, NJ: Princeton University Press, 1999), 237–52.

22. We might try to see (b), when it is an expression of (a thought involved in) my desire, as sometimes involving an implicit indexical element: Revenge is a justifying consideration (from *my* point of view).

We would then need to address the broadly Frankfurtian issue of which point of view is *mine*. This is the issue of agential authority that I turn to briefly below in section 5. A conse-quence of the approach to agential authority sketched in section 5 (see also note 39) is that there are desires that are not appropriately expressed in this way.

23. Let me note two complexities. The first concerns Model 2. In some cases, the desire for *X* will, even prior to an endorsing policy, already involve a thought of *X* as a justifying consideration or will at least be plausibly expressible along the lines of (b). But there are, I think, also cases that do not fit well into such a picture: for some cases of prereflective anger, for example, this will seem to be an overly intellectualistic picture. Nevertheless, if in a case of this latter sort one does arrive at a self-governing policy in support of treating the anger as reason-providing, then this policy may infuse or shape the anger so that it becomes (or involves a thought that is) expressible in this way. So the reasoning supported by the policy can be Model 2 reasoning.

to concerns with reflective management of one's motivational system. In contrast, in "A Desire of One's Own," I highlight not only these issues of self-management, but also the problem that is posed for our agency by our judgments about multiple, conflicting values that, at least so far as we can see, underdetermine what particular, coherent shape our lives are to take.[24] I suggest that our response to this problem will consist, in one important type of case, in policies, or policy-like attitudes, that say what justifying significance to give to various considerations in our motivationally effective deliberations and practical reasoning about our own action.[25] So, to use an example from "A Desire of One's Own," consider a person—let us call her Jones—who sees the value in sexual activity and who also sees the value of a certain kind of life of abstinence. Jones might then arrive, on reflection, at a policy of giving no positive weight to her sexual activity. She sees that there are alternative, nonabstaining ways of living that have value, but in creating for herself a life of abstinence she puts the value of her sexual activity aside, so to speak. Although she does not expect relevant intersubjective convergence on living such a life, she arrives at a policy, or policy-like attitude, concerning her own motivationally effective practical reasoning. And given the role of such a policy (or policy-like attitude) in her practical reasoning and action, it seems reasonable to see it as constituting a kind of valuing.

A second complexity concerns motivation in the absence of either kind of practical reasoning. An agent who rejects her desire for revenge has a self-governing policy of not allowing that desire to lead to action by way of Model 1 or Model 2 practical reasoning. I think we can also suppose that the agent's policy rejects an effective motivational role for that desire, even if that role does not involve such practical reasoning—perhaps the desire of a Frankfurtian "unwilling addict" could in some cases motivate action in this latter way. However, it is policies specifically about the roles of desires in motivationally effective practical reasoning that are central to autonomous action; or so I will be claiming below in the text. These policies will be my main concern here.

24. Bratman, "A Desire of One's Own." For such talk about the "shape" of our lives see Charles Taylor, "Leading a Life," in Ruth Chang, ed., *Incommensurability, Incomparability, and Practical Reason* (Cambridge, MA: Harvard University Press, 1997), 183.

25. I discuss this idea further in Michael E. Bratman, "Shared Valuing and Frameworks for Practical Reasoning," in R. Jay Wallace, Philip Pettit, Samuel Scheffler, and Michael Smith, eds., *Reason and Value: Themes from the Moral Philosophy of Joseph Raz* (Oxford: Oxford University Press, 2004): 1–27 [this volume, essay 13]. Note that the idea is *not* that such policies directly change what is valuable—though there is room for an indirect impact by way of the value of living in accord with such policies, once they are adopted.

4. TWO PROBLEMS, ONE SOLUTION?

A salient response to the problem of self-management and to the problem of underdetermination by value judgment involves policies concerning one's own motivationally effective practical reasoning. Such policies say what significance to give to certain considerations in this reasoning. Such policies constitute an important kind of valuing. Valuing in this sense is related to, but is to be distinguished from, judging what is good.[26] Indeed, this distinction lies at the heart of the usefulness of such valuing as a response to the problem of underdetermination by value judgment.

One might, however, question whether this is really a single solution to our pair of problems. After all, although our respective responses to these problems involve policies about practical reasoning, there seems to be a difference in the kind of policy that is cited. The policies that are cited as a response to problems of self-management are primarily higher-order responses to separable forms of motivation: desires for revenge or for sexual activity, for example. The policies about practical reasoning that are a response to concerns about underdetermination by value judgment do not need to be about separable forms of motivation, though they may be. Perhaps in response to his dilemma, the young man in Sartre's example settles on a policy of giving weight to helping the Free French, but not to helping his mother. So described, this policy does not seem to be about the functioning of separable forms of motivation. It seems rather directly to support (defeasible) reasoning along the lines of:

Model 3
(c) Helping the Free French is a justifying consideration.
  A would help the Free French.
  So I have justifying reason to do *A*.
  So I will *A*.

26. For this distinction see David Lewis, "Dispositional Theories of Value," in Lewis, *Papers in Ethics and Social Philosophy* (New York: Cambridge University Press, 2000), 68–94; Gary Watson, "Free Action and Free Will," *Mind* 96 (1987): 150; and Gilbert Harman, "Desired Desires," in Harman, *Explaining Value and Other Essays in Moral Philosophy* (Oxford: Oxford University Press, 2000), 117–36, esp. 129–30.

At the same time, this policy seems to reject analogous reasoning concerning the young man helping his mother. Here, premise (c)—in contrast
with premise (b) in Model 2—need not be an expression of (a thought
involved in) a separable desire. So, we might wonder how policies of
practical reasoning that are involved in our solution to problems of self-
management are related to policies that constitute our solution to problems of underdetermination by value judgment. Do we really have a single
solution to our pair of problems?

I think that the basic point to make here is that we need to respond
to both problems, and there will be, at the least, a requirement that an
agent's responses to these problems mesh with one another. There will be
pressure on our young man, for example, not to have policies that give
predominant weight to helping the Free French but that nevertheless
encourage the effective influence on his relevant Model 1 or Model 2
practical reasoning of his powerful desire to stay with his mother. In
pursuit of a model of autonomy, we want a model of a more or less unified agent, one whose agency involves both reflective management of his
motivation and a response to underdetermination by value judgment. As
reflective human agents, we have both a problem of self-management and
a problem of responding to underdetermination by value judgment with a
form of, so to speak, limited self-creation.[27] I have been assuming that the
latter problem is pervasive. The pervasiveness of the former problem is ensured by the pervasiveness of forms of motivation—including appetites and
forms of anger and grief—that can pose problems of self-management.[28]
We seek coordinated solutions to both problems: as we might say, the self
that emerges from self-management should be coordinated with the self
that emerges from limited self-creation.

We can develop the point further by returning to creature construction.
My discussion in "Valuing and the Will" ends with a creature who has
self-governing policies concerning which desired ends to treat as justifying

27. For such talk of self-creation see Raz, *The Morality of Freedom*, 385–90; and Joseph Raz, "The
Truth in Particularism," in Raz, *Engaging Reason: On the Theory of Value and Action* (Oxford: Oxford
University Press, 1999), 242–45.

28. See Cooper, "Some Remarks on Aristotle's Moral Psychology," esp. 247–50, where
Cooper highlights the contrast with the Stoics.

considerations in (as I have here described it) her motivationally effective Model 1 or Model 2 deliberation. Such policies play central roles in the organization of the agent's own thought and action over time. They also play central roles in various forms of social organization, coordination, and cooperation. After all, much of our ability to work with and to coordinate with others depends on our grasp of the justifying significance that they give to various considerations in their practical thinking.

This role in social coordination points to the enormous significance of these forms of coordination in the creature's life, a point that Allan Gibbard has emphasized with great insight.[29] As Gibbard might say, pressures for social coordination will lead to pressure on our creature to try to articulate, explain, and, to some extent, defend and justify her self-governing policies to others in her social world. This suggests that we can expect to emerge—in a later stage of creature construction—some sort of intersubjectively accountable views about values and/or reasons.[30] But at that point we can also expect that these further views will have a feature highlighted by our second problem: given the need for intersubjective accountability, these views will tend to leave unsettled many questions about the particular contours of an individual agent's life. These views will tend, by themselves, to underdetermine, to underspecify, how one is to live.[31] At least, this is reasonable to expect, given the assumption that such underdetermination is common. So a creature's self-governing policies, formed initially in response to problems of self-management, may be in a position to do "double duty" in this later stage of creature construction. They also may be in a position to help constitute her response to underdetermination by her intersubjectively

29. Allan Gibbard, *Wise Choices, Apt Feelings* (Cambridge, MA: Harvard University Press, 1990). While I think that Gibbard's focus on issues about social coordination is of great importance, I see my discussion here as neutral concerning the debate between Gibbard's expressivist understanding of value judgment and certain more cognitivist approaches. This is part of an overall strategy—a kind of method of avoidance, to use John Rawls's terminology—of trying to articulate important structures of human agency in ways that are available to a range of different views in metaethics.

30. I think that we can also expect forms of shared *valuing* (in contrast with shared judgments of value) to emerge. See Bratman, "Shared Valuing and Frameworks for Practical Reasoning."

31. I think that this is implicit, for example, in Gibbard's effort to distinguish between an "existential commitment" and accepting "a norm as a requirement of rationality." See Gibbard, *Wise Choices, Apt Feelings*, 166–70.

accountable value judgments.[32] In this way the creature's responses to our pair of problems can be expected to mesh.

We can also consider matters from the other direction, by beginning with policies of practical reasoning that are a direct response to under-determination by value judgment. Let us here return to Jones. Jones has arrived at a policy of abstinence, a policy that precludes giving positive deliberative weight in her life to her sexual activity. This is her own, distinctive response to underdetermination of the contours of her life by her prior judgments about the good in a human life of sexual activity, on the one hand, and of abstinence as a part of a certain kind of religious observance, on the other hand. Now, this policy seems to be directly about how to weigh certain considerations in her Model 3 practical reasoning, and not about the functioning of separable first-order motivation. But it is likely that in order for this policy to be effective, it will need to involve or be associated with a policy, or policy-like attitude, of putting to one side in her motivationally effective practical reasoning considerations provided by her felt sexual desires. It will need to involve or be associated with a policy of not treating those desires as providing justifying considerations for her Model 1 or Model 2 practical deliberation.

Or consider the young man who settles on a life of fighting with the Free French. This will "mesh" (in the way that I mentioned above) only if he has a way of managing the impact on his deliberation and motivation both of his inclinations not to fight—that is, his affections and concerns for his mother, his fears of battle—and of his affections and concerns for the Free French. A policy of giving weight in his motivationally effective Model 3 practical reasoning to his work with the Free French, but not to his mother's needs for his attention, will likely be effective only if it involves or is associated with such forms of self-management. So there will be pressure on the young man for associated higher-order policies of self-management, policies that concern relevant practical reasoning along the lines of Models 1 and/or 2.

If we begin with problems of self-management, then we arrive first at self-governing policies that are, in part, about the management of the

---

32. Which is not to say that these self-governing policies may not themselves be responsive to the creature's judgments of value.

functioning of one's first-order motivations. We arrive later at the idea that such policies can also constitute (part of) a response to under-determination by intersubjectively accountable value judgments. If, in-stead, we begin with the latter problem about underdetermination, then we arrive first at policies about the significance of certain considerations in one's motivationally effective practical reasoning, and second at associated higher-order policies about the management of the impact of relevant forms of motivation on one's effective motivation and practical reasoning. I surmise that the differences are not differences in the basic model of human agency, but in our route to that model. At the heart of the model in each case are policies about what is to be given significance in one's motivationally effective practical reasoning. And given the kind of crea-tures that human agents are, these policies will normally involve or be associated with policies that concern the management of relevant forms of motivation in practical reasoning and action.[33]

This is not yet to identify these two kinds of policies concerning practical reasoning. The AH thesis does not depend on such identification. The thesis needs only to insist that hierarchical policies are an element in a central case of human autonomy. Nevertheless, I think that there is normally reason for a kind of identification. What we have seen is that in reflective agents like us there is substantial pressure toward a unified cluster of forms of functioning—a cluster that involves coordinated, cross-temporal, policy-like control of practical reasoning along the lines of Models 1, 2, and 3. This suggests that we see the underlying source of this cluster as a single, complex policy or policy-like attitude. In a central case, such a policy will be something like this:

It will be a policy of giving justifying significance to consideration X in motivationally effective Model 3 reasoning, in part by way of appropriate control of associated motivationally effective practical reasoning along the lines of Models 1 and/or 2.

33. A fuller discussion also would consider both "quasi-policies" (see note 14 above) and "singular commitments." See Michael E. Bratman, "Hierarchy, Circularity, and Double Re-duction," in Sarah Buss and Lee Overton, eds., Contours of Agency: Essays on Themes from Harry Frankfurt (Cambridge, MA: MIT Press, 2002), 65–85 [this volume, essay 4]. These complexities can be put to one side here, however, since our primary concern is with a kind of hierarchy involved in all of these phenomena.

In a central case, this will be the form that a self-governing policy will take. Although the genesis of such a policy might only sometimes include explicitly higher-order reflection on first-order motivation, its function and content will be, in part, higher order in the indicated ways.[34] Such (to some extent) higher-order policies are an important form of valuing.

5. VALUING AND AUTONOMY

And they are a form of valuing whose control of action can partly realize or constitute a human agent's direction and governance of action, and thus the agent's autonomy. Or so I maintain. It is time to say why.

In autonomous action, as I have said, an agent directs and governs her action. Note that there are two different ideas here: agential *direction* and agential *governance*. As I see it, in agential direction, there is sufficient unity and organization of the motives of action for their functioning to constitute direction by the agent.[35] Agential governance is a particular form of such agential direction: agential governance is agential direction that appropriately involves the agent's treatment of certain considerations as justifying reasons for action. Autonomous action involves a form of agential direction that also constitutes agential governance. And I want to describe what these phenomena of agential direction and agential governance consist in without appealing to a homunculus account, that is, to a "little person in the head who does the work."

Without appealing to a homunculus account, my strategy is to see agential direction and governance as being realized by appropriate forms of psychological functioning.[36] There is agential direction of action when action is under the control of attitudes whose role in the agent's psychology gives them authority to speak for the agent, to establish the agent's point of view—gives them, in other words, agential authority. This agential direction of action is, furthermore, a form of agential governance

---

34. I consider in the text below, in section 6, the objection that there may be a gap here between function and content.

35. See Frankfurt's work on wholeheartedness in, for example, Harry G. Frankfurt, "The Faintest Passion," reprinted in Frankfurt, *Necessity, Volition, and Love* (Cambridge: Cambridge University Press, 1999), 95–107.

36. See note 5 above.

of action only when these attitudes control action by way of the agent's treatment of relevant considerations as justifying reasons for action, that is, as having subjective normative authority for her.[37]

When we approach autonomous action in this way, valuing of the sort that we have been discussing seems to be a natural candidate for an attitude whose control of action can, in part, realize the agent's direction and governance of action. On the one hand, self-governing policies play central roles in supporting and constituting important forms of cross-temporal organization and coordination in an agent's life. As long as an agent's self-governing policies are not involved in conflict that undermines these cross-temporal organizing roles, we have reason to see such policies as having agential authority.[38] Hence, we likewise have reason to see their control of action as realizing agential direction of action. On the other hand, such policies function, in particular, by way of helping shape the agent's operative, background framework of justifying reasons.[39] To borrow terminology from J. David Velleman, the policies' control of action is part of a story not only of motivation, but also of rational guidance.[40] This is why agential direction of action that is realized by the controlling role of such policies constitutes, at least in part, agential *governance* of action. Taken together with the arguments that I have just offered, that such self-governing policies involve (or bring with them) motivational hierarchy, this leads us to the view that motivational hierarchy is at the heart of at least one important realization of human autonomy. This leads us, that is, to the AH thesis.

37. Concerning these two kinds of authority, see Michael E. Bratman, "Two Problems about Human Agency," *Proceedings of the Aristotelian Society* 101 (2001): 309–26 [this volume, essay 5].

38. I expand on these matters, and their relation to ideas about personal identity, in Bratman, "Reflection, Planning, and Temporally Extended Agency." In pages 48–51 of that essay [this volume, pp. 33–37], I describe the cited nonconflict condition as a version of what Frankfurt calls "satisfaction." In my discussion of higher-order policies (below in the text), I will take it for granted that some such satisfaction condition is realized. A full account of satisfaction would also need to consider the significance of conflict with singular commitments concerning what to treat as justifying (see note 33 above).

39. We might say that such self-governing policies help constitute the agent's justificatory point of view. So if such a self-governing policy were to reject a desire for X, and that desire were nevertheless to involve the thought that X is a justifying consideration from that agent's point of view, that thought would be false.

40. Velleman, "The Guise of the Good," in *The Possibility of Practical Reason*, 99–122.

This argument for the AH thesis has two main steps. The first step is to articulate what we might call design specifications for an autonomous agent.[41] I have, so far, cited two design specifications: sufficient organization of motivation to constitute agential direction, and motivation that involves rational guidance in a way that further qualifies this agential direction as agential governance. The second step in defending the AH thesis is to argue that a model in which higher-order, self-governing policies function in the indicated ways would satisfy these design specifications.[42]

Must the kind of rational guidance that is needed for autonomy also involve sufficient responsiveness to what is judged to be good and/or is good?[43] My response here is to leave this question open, since either answer is compatible with the present argument for the AH thesis.

A final point on valuing and autonomy is that there might be actions that are not the direct issue of the kinds of policy-directed practical reasoning that I have cited, but that are sufficiently related to such reasoning to be candidates for autonomous action in an extended sense. Once we have in hand our basic model of autonomous agency, we can allow for such extensions in our account of autonomous action.

6. TWO OBJECTIONS AND THE AUTONOMY-TRANSPARENCY THESIS

I now consider a pair of closely related objections to this way of defending the AH thesis. Each objection acknowledges the role of reasoning-guiding policies in an important realization of human autonomy. Each objection nevertheless goes on to challenge the idea that such policies need be hierarchical.

---

41. Cp. Velleman, "Introduction," in *The Possibility of Practical Reason*, 11.

42. On this account, autonomous action is compatible with the persistence of first-order motivation that diverges from what is supported by one's self-governing policies. Within the proposed model, what autonomy requires is that one's self-governing policies actually do guide one's relevant reasoning and action. Further, there can be cases—e.g., our case of principled sexual abstinence—in which one's self-governing policy rejects a desire for *X* even though one acknowledges the value of *X*.

43. See Susan Wolf, *Freedom Within Reason* (Oxford: Oxford University Press, 1990); but see also Gary Watson, "Two Faces of Responsibility," *Philosophical Topics* 24 (1996): 240. Relatedly, we might also consider a constraint that, at the least, the relevant self-governing policies not favor one's own loss of autonomy or complete domination by others. Here, again, we need not settle the issue in order to argue for the AH thesis.

The first objection concerns self-management. Suppose you find your-self desiring revenge. You stop to reflect, and you arrive at a commitment not to give weight in your practical reasoning to revenge. This commit-ment, or policy, is certainly a response to an antecedent desire for revenge, but why must its *content* make explicit reference to the functioning of that desire? Why can't its content simply reject forms of Model 3 reasoning that give positive weight to revenge? Granted, for such a commitment to be effective, it must somehow involve management of the impact on one's practical reasoning and action of one's desire for revenge. But this does not show that the content of the guiding policy must refer somehow to the functioning of one's desire and cannot simply be the rejection of Model 3 reasoning that gives positive weight to revenge. So it is not clear that what is needed are higher-order policies of the sort highlighted by the AH thesis.

The second objection concerns limited self-creation (responding to underdetermination by value judgment). Recall Jones's policy of sexual abstinence, which I discussed in section 4. I have said that, to be effective, this policy will likely need to involve a policy of eschewing the demands of felt sexual desires on her motivationally effective deliberations. The second objection to the AH thesis grants that for Jones's policy of sexual absti-nence to be effective, there will normally need to be management of the impact on her deliberation and action of felt sexual desires. However, this objection claims that it does not follow that the *content* of her policy of abstinence will need to refer explicitly to this management of contrary desires. Her policy can simply eschew appeal in her Model 3 deliberation to her sexual activity as a justifying consideration. So it does not follow that her policy is higher order in its content.

Both objections to the way that the AH thesis has been defended thus far grant that the psychological functioning that issues from the reasoning-guiding policies whose control can partly realize human autonomy will normally include some form of management of the impact of relevant first-order motivation on practical reasoning and action. But both ob-jections insist that it does not follow that the reasoning-guiding policies must themselves be higher order in their content.

Now, we might simply respond that there are cases and cases. As long as there are common cases in which autonomy is realized by the functioning of reasoning-guiding policies that are higher order, the AH thesis stands. But I think that we can make a stronger claim than that here.

Our concern is, after all, with *autonomous* agency. For such agency, some sort of modest condition of *transparency* seems apt in characterizing the relation between, on the one hand, known significant functioning that is supported by a reasoning-guiding policy and, on the other hand, the content of that policy. We can put the idea this way:

> If one knows that the effective functioning of the practical reasoning that is supported by one's reasoning-guiding policy at the same time significantly involves management of the roles of relevant motivation, and if one's ensuing action is self-governed, then the content of one's reasoning-guiding policy will refer to, and support, this management of motivation.

The idea here is that, in the absence of such transparency, the functioning of the reasoning-guiding policy would not be sufficient to ensure an agent's governance of her ensuing action. Let us call this the *autonomy-transparency (AT) thesis.* The AT thesis helps block the current pair of objections. These objections depend on driving a wedge between the psychological functioning that issues from the reasoning-guiding policy and the content of that policy. The AT thesis blocks this wedge for cases of autonomy in which the agent has the requisite self-knowledge. And since the requisite self-knowledge need only be a fairly general knowledge of the need for management of motivation—a kind of self-knowledge that is compatible with only partial knowledge of the specific complexities of one's actual motivation—it seems plausible to suppose that an autonomous agent will be knowledgeable in this way.

7. TRANSPARENCY AND SELF-GOVERNED PRACTICAL REASONING

I believe that, if accepted, the autonomy-transparency (AT) thesis effectively blocks the cited two objections to the autonomy-hierarchy (AH) thesis, but why should we accept the AT thesis? My answer appeals to pressures on an autonomous agent to govern not only her action but also the practical reasoning from which her action issues.[44]

Let us begin by noting that the fact that there is practical reasoning leading to action, and that this reasoning has normative or evaluative content, does not yet ensure that the agent governs the reasoning. There can be cases of motivationally effective practical reasoning about which we will want to say—borrowing a phrase from Gibbard—that the agent is not governing the reasoning, but is instead in the "grip" of concerns that drive the reasoning.[45] This might happen, for example, in a case involving a strong desire for revenge and associated thoughts about what degree or type of revenge is deserved. One's motivationally effective practical reasoning might be in the grip of this desire and these normative thoughts.

So the model of (a central case of) autonomous agency that we have been developing—a model that appeals to the role of self-governing policies in guiding reasoning and action—needs to include psychological functioning that ensures that the agent is not in the grip of relevant concerns but is, rather, governing her own relevant, practical reasoning. Suppose, then, that relevant, practical reasoning, and its control of action, involves in an important way psychological functioning of type *F*. And suppose that the agent does govern that reasoning and knows that it involves this *F*-type functioning. We can except that the agent's governance of her reasoning will extend to that known functioning. And the natural way, within the model, to ensure agential governance of that *F*-type functioning is to build support for such functioning into the content of a self-governing policy that guides her reasoning. And this is a condition that will be violated when the agent's reasoning is, instead, in the grip of a certain consideration.

Return now to the AT thesis. This thesis, which I described at the end of the preceding section, concerns cases of self-governed actions that are the issue of practical reasoning that is guided by a relevant self-governing policy,

44. As I understand her views, this is a theme in Christine M. Korsgaard's *The Sources of Normativity* (Cambridge: Cambridge University Press, 1996), chap. 3. It appears here in my discussion as, in effect, a third design specification on autonomous agents.

45. Gibbard, *Wise Choices, Apt Feelings*, 60. I discuss the significance of such cases also in Bratman, "Hierarchy, Circularity, and Double Reduction," and in Bratman, "Two Problems about Human Agency."

P. According to the AT thesis, if the agent in such a case knows that the effective functioning of that practical reasoning significantly involves management of her relevant motivation, then the content of *P* will refer to and support this management of motivation. We have now observed that if, in such a case, the action is self-governed, then so is the practical reasoning from which it issues. And we have also observed that if an agent is to govern her practical reasoning in such a case, then she must govern known, important *F*-type functioning involved in that reasoning and its control of action. We have, further, provided a model of psychological functioning that would realize such agential governance of that reasoning. And within this model, the agential governance of this *F*-type functioning will involve guidance by a policy whose content supports this *F*-type functioning. The AT thesis is, then, a special case of this general feature of this model of self-governed practical reasoning—a special case in which *F* is the management of the cited functioning of relevant motivation. This means that at least a central case of autonomous agency will involve the kind of transparency that is needed to complete our first argument for the AH thesis.

Related concerns about transparency also suggest a second line of support for the AH thesis; or so I now proceed to argue.

8. THE SECOND LINE OF ARGUMENT: POLICIES ABOUT SELF-GOVERNED PRACTICAL REASONING

According to the model that we have been developing, an autonomous agent's reasoning-guiding policies guide practical reasoning that is, in part because of this guidance, governed by the agent. That this reasoning is agentially governed is, I take it, something that the autonomous agent will normally know and endorse. But then a natural extension of our reflections on transparency suggests that the agent's guiding policy will be a policy that favors practical reasoning that is governed by herself. Within the model, however, in order to be governed by the agent, the reasoning needs to be guided by a relevant self-governing policy. So it will be plausible to expect that the reasoning-guiding policy is, in part, about its own role in guiding the reasoning. This is to build into the content of the policy that guides the practical reasoning the condition that this same practical reasoning be appropriately guided by that very policy. And this is to draw on work by Gilbert Harman and others on forms of *reflexivity in intentions*.[46]

Harman, in particular, has argued that a "positive" intention in favor of an action will be "an intention that something will happen in a way that is controlled or guided by" that very intention. In this sense, a positive intention "is reflexive or self-referential—it refers to itself."[47] Harman cautions that this does not require that the agent have "an explicit mental representation of her intention."[48] What is required, however, is that what the intention favors is that there be a certain process that is suitably dependent on, and responsive to, that intention itself.

Consider, then, a case in which one knowingly governs practical reasoning in which one gives positive weight to revenge. The idea now is that one's policy of giving weight in one's reasoning to revenge will be a policy that one's reasoning give such weight to revenge, in part, *because of* this very policy. It will be a policy of giving such weight as a matter of this very policy.

This suggests that, at least in certain central cases of autonomous action, the self-governing policies that guide the underlying practical reasoning will be reflexive;[49] that is, they will be in part about their own guidance of the practical reasoning.[50] Such a reflexive self-governing policy will be a higher-order conative attitude. It will be a policy about the functioning in reasoning

46. Gilbert Harman, "Practical Reasoning," in Harman, *Reasoning, Meaning and Mind* (Oxford: Oxford University Press, 1999), chap. 2; Harman, *Change in View* (Cambridge, MA: MIT Press, 1986), chap. 8; and Harman, "Desired Desires." See also Alan Donagan, *Choice: The Essential Element in Human Action* (London: Routledge & Kegan Paul, 1987), 88; John Searle, *Intentionality* (New York: Cambridge University Press, 1983); J. David Velleman, *Practical Reflection* (Princeton, NJ: Princeton University Press, 1989); and Abraham Roth, "The Self-Referentiality of Intentions," *Philosophical Studies* 97 (2000): 11–52. For an important critique of these ideas, see Alfred Mele, *Springs of Action: Understanding Intentional Behavior* (New York: Oxford University Press, 1992), chap. 11; Harman's response is in Harman, "Desired Desires."

47. Harman, "Desired Desires," 121. Let me note that I am not here endorsing Harman's general view that all positive intentions are reflexive. I am only using his idea of reflexive intentions to make progress with the special case of self-governed practical reasoning.

48. Ibid., 124. Harman notes here a parallel with John Perry's observation that (as Harman writes) "a child can have the thought that 'it is raining' without having any concepts of places or times and without any inner mental representations of particular places and times, even though the content of the child's thought concerns rain at a particular place and a particular time."

49. Related ideas about reflexivity can be found in Keith Lehrer, *Self-Trust: A Study of Reason, Knowledge, and Autonomy* (New York: Oxford University Press, 1997), 100–102.

50. I offer a related argument for seeing such policies as reflexive in Bratman, "Two Problems about Human Agency," 323 [this volume, pp. 102–103].

of a certain policy, namely, itself. So we arrive again, as promised, at a form of motivational hierarchy.

Note, however, that this form of motivational hierarchy is different from that at stake in our first line of argument. According to our first line of argument, valuing involves policies that are, in part, about the role of desires, and/or of what they are for, in providing justifying premises in motivationally effective Model 1 or Model 2 practical reasoning. According to the second line of argument that I have just sketched, the practical reasoning of an autonomous agent, at least in a central case, involves policies that are, in part, supportive of their very own functioning in guiding practical reasoning. The functioning of these self-governing policies, which is reflexively supported in this way, is their very own guidance of practical reasoning along the lines of any of Models 1 through 3.

9. CONCLUSION

Recall Watson's observation that in normal cases of practical reasoning "the initial practical question" is "about courses of action and not about ourselves." My defense of the autonomy-hierarchy (AH) thesis is consistent with this view. My claim is not about the initial practical question, but about the background structures that are brought to bear in trying to answer this question. I have argued that, in central cases of autonomous action, these background structures involve higher-order self-governing policies. While we frequently take for granted such structures in our practical reasoning, we have seen reason to think that they are present in at least certain central cases of autonomy.

Granted, I have left open the possibility that other kinds of background structures might also satisfy our design specifications for autonomy. Faced with such an alternative proposal, we would want to see whether our design specifications are indeed satisfied, and, if so, whether there are, at bottom, significant similarities with our model of self-governing policies.[51] But such prospects can be left open here.

Now, recall that Frankfurt's original appeal to motivational hierarchy— to what he called higher-order "volitions"—was an appeal to higher-order

---

51. And, if so, whether the idea of a quasi-policy can usefully capture these similarities.

conative support for the functioning of a first-order desire as an effective motive of action.[52] I have been led here to higher-order policies not only in support of forms of functioning (along the lines of Models 1 or 2) of first-order motivation in one's practical reasoning and action, but also in reflexive support of their own framework-providing role. Both of these forms of policy-supported functioning in practical reasoning go beyond the bare motivational role of first-order desires, which is the concern of (at least, the original version of) Frankfurtian higher-order volitions. Nevertheless, the approach to autonomy that has emerged here shares with Frankfurt's approach the basic idea that some hierarchical structures provide an important element of at least one central case of autonomous human agency.

The AH thesis is a thesis about important kinds of contemporaneous psychological functioning that can partly realize human autonomous agency. Certain issues about the history of elements in this functioning remain open. In particular, it may be that, in the end, a full story about human autonomy will also need to appeal to some sort of historical condition that blocks certain extreme cases of manipulation, brainwashing, and the like.[53] This is not an issue to be settled here.[54] But before we can settle this issue, we need the best account available of the structural conditions involved on the occasion of autonomous action. My concern here has been to argue that our account of such structural conditions should endorse a version of the autonomy-hierarchy (AH) thesis.

52. Frankfurt, "Freedom of the Will and the Concept of a Person," 16. But see the modification of this idea in Harry G. Frankfurt, "Identification and Wholeheartedness," in Frankfurt, *The Importance of What We Care About*, 159–76.

53. See John Martin Fischer and Mark Ravizza, *Responsibility and Control: A Theory of Moral Responsibility* (New York: Cambridge University Press, 1998); and Keith Lehrer, "Reason and Autonomy," in Ellen Frankel Paul, Fred D. Miller, Jr., and Jeffrey Paul, eds., *Autonomy* (New York: Cambridge University Press, 2003): 177–198. See also Bratman, "Fischer and Ravizza on Moral Responsibility and History," *Philosophy and Phenomenological Research* 61, no. 2 (2000): 453–58. Note, though, that the present issue is autonomy, not the related but different idea of moral responsibility. (See Gary Watson's distinction between "attributability" and "accountability" in Watson, "Two Faces of Responsibility.")

54. Of course, if the specification of the content of the relevant attitudes is ineluctably historical (for reasons developed by, among others, Tyler Burge and Hilary Putnam), then we would need to appeal to such content-fixing historical considerations. But that is a different matter.

Chapter 9

THREE FORMS OF AGENTIAL COMMITMENT: REPLY TO CULLITY AND GERRANS

Human agents are purposive agents who are also capable of stronger forms of agency, including forms of self-governance. Or so it seems. A central problem in the philosophy of action is how to understand these stronger forms of agency and what further philosophical commitments are required for their understanding. Recent work in Frankfurt-influenced philosophy of action on ownership, identification, internality, authority, and endorsement are, at least in large part, efforts to develop a sufficiently rich theoretical apparatus for this task. At bottom is the idea that strong forms of agency that are of interest can be modelled within, as Cullity and Gerrans put it, a "nonhomuncular causal account of agency."[1] Self-governance is constituted by forms of psychological functioning that appropriately involve identification and the like. And we explain these phenomena within a "nonhomuncular causal account."

If this is our project, then our main concern will be whether any such model can provide sufficient conditions for self-government and related phenomena, or whether these come with a higher philosophical cost. If we do

---

1. "Agency and Policy," *Proceedings of the Aristotelian Society* 104 (2004): 317–29, p. 317. (Parenthetical page references are to this paper.)

succeed in providing such sufficient conditions, but also conclude there are several different kinds of functioning that are each sufficient for these strong forms of agency (but neither of which is necessary),[2] or that some actions inherit their status as autonomous by way of their relation to more basic cases and capacities, these would be important but nonthreatening insights.

The essays of mine that are the concern of Cullity and Gerrans's probing discussion aim to contribute to this project by bringing together Frankfurtian hierarchy and the planning theory.[3] In a central case, the agent acts on a desire for X by way of deliberation in which X is given weight, weight that does not merely depend on the fact that this is a way of removing the desire for X. Further, this motivationally effective deliberation is in accordance with and in part explained by a background self-governing policy with which the agent is satisfied.[4] This self-governing policy favors such motivationally effective deliberation reflexively, as a matter of (this very) policy. This self-governing policy has a claim to agential authority—a claim to speak for the agent—in large part because of its role in the cross-temporal organization of the agent's thought and action by way of Lockean connections and continuities. The authority of the self-governing policy to speak for the agent is in this way grounded in its structuring role in temporally extended agency. And the claim is that this model gives us the resources to provide sufficient conditions for self-government and related phenomena of identification and the like.

The idea is not that there is a single attitude involved in all self-governed activity. The idea is only that in central cases of self-governed activity, one or more self-governing policies plays a role. Nor need the relevant self-governing policies be ones the agent could not reject. What needs to be true is that she does not reject them.[5] The content of the

2. See my "Autonomy and Hierarchy," *Social Philosophy & Policy* 20 (2003): 156–76, at 157, n. 5 [this volume, essay 8, p. 163, n.5].

3. Cullity and Gerrans cite essays 2–5 in this volume, as well as my "Identification, Decision, and Treating as a Reason," in my *Faces of Intention* (New York: Cambridge University Press, 1999). In addition to these essays, I would add my "Autonomy and Hierarchy," "A Desire of One's Own," *Journal of Philosophy* 100 (2003): 221–242 [this volume, essay 7], and "Nozick on Free Will," in David Schmidtz, ed., *Robert Nozick* (Cambridge University Press, 2002): 155–74 [this volume, essay 6].

4. More than one self-governing policy may be involved; but here I keep things simple.

5. In both respects there is a contrast with J. David Velleman's appeal to the aim of knowing what you are doing. See his "Introduction," in *The Possibility of Practical Reason* (Oxford: Oxford University Press, 2000).

self-governing policies primarily concerns what to treat as a reason, with what weight or significance, in one's motivationally effective deliberation. The relation of these policies to personal identity is, in the first instance, by way of their role in constituting and supporting Lockean ties; though a reflective agent may be aware of this role and incorporate it into the content of the policy. Finally, once the model is in place we can consider extensions that involve other policy-like attitudes.[6]

Cullity and Gerrans challenge this model primarily by appeal to their self-opaque agent and self-managing addict. Before turning to these examples, though, let me consider two other concerns they raise.

The first is that singular commitments—rather than policy-like commitments—may sometimes suffice. Now, as Cullity and Gerrans note, I too have emphasized the significance of such singular commitments. But the fact that such commitments involve weaker connections to temporally extended agency does, on the theory, entail that they have a weaker claim to agential authority. Once that is said, and once we note that the basic issue concerns the possibility of providing sufficient conditions for strong forms of agency, I do not see a deep disagreement here.

The second preliminary concerns the supposed reflexivity of the self-governing policies. (This is different from the issue of whether they are higher-order policies that concern first-order motivation.) I think there are two different reasons to see these policies as reflexive.[7]

The first begins by noting that the primary target of self-governing policies—the act of treating a desire as reason-providing—is itself a strong form of agency, involving something like identification. So when we appeal to a policy in favor of such treatment of a desire, in order to explain identification with that desire, we risk circularity. My response was to appeal to a weaker form of functioning of the desire—its functioning as end-setting in practical reasoning—such that to treat the desire as reason-providing is, roughly, for that functioning to be guided by a policy in its favor. For the self-governing policy to favor treating the desire as

---

6. See my remarks about self-governing *quasi*-policies in "Reflection, Planning, and Temporally Extended Agency," *Philosophical Review* 109 (2000): 35–61, at 57–60 [this volume, essay 2, pp. 42–44].

7. Cullity and Gerrans suggest (322–23) that my reason for seeing these policies as reflexive is to ensure that the agent is aware of them; but that is not my argument.

reason-providing, it is not enough for it to favor that desire's functioning as end-setting in practical reasoning. It needs to favor, roughly, that desire's functioning as end-setting by way of that very policy. And this is to see the self-governing policy as reflexive.[8]

There is also a further pressure in favor of reflexivity as a condition for self-governed action. I turn to that below, after I consider the two central examples.

The self-managing addict hates his addiction but still concludes it would be best to take the drug as a way of managing his addiction. He does not, however, identify with or endorse his desire for the drug.

I agree. This was why I insisted that the self-governing policy not favor treating the desire as providing only what Cullity and Gerrans call a "*merely desire-removing* reason" (321).[9] On my view, the self-managing addict does not identify with his desire for the drug, though he may identify with his desire for survival and that may be in part why he acts as he does in the face of his addiction.[10]

Cullity and Gerrans's objection to my treatment of this case is not that I misclassify it as one of identification with the desire for the drug, but that I do not provide a deeper account of why it is "necessary that [an agent's] commitment to acting on her desire does not come from the recognition of a merely-desire-removing reason" (323). Why should we limit the relevant commitments in this way? The answer I pointed to in "Reflection, Planning, and Temporally Extended Agency" was that we need to do this to exclude those cases in which the desire provides a reason only in the sense in which "an itch or a potential cause of future harm" provides a reason for its elimination.[11] The self-managing addict sees his desire for the drug as something

---

8. See "Two Problems about Human Agency," *Proceedings of the Aristotelian Society* 101 (2001): 309–26, at 323 [this volume, essay 5, pp. 102–103] and "Hierarchy, Circularity, and Double Reduction," in S. Buss and L. Overton (eds.) *Contours of Agency: Essays on Themes from Harry Frankfurt* (Cambridge, MA: MIT Press, 2002) [this volume, essay 4]. I note complications in "Hierarchy, Circularity, and Double Reduction," section 8.

9. See "Reflection, Planning, and Temporally Extended Agency," at 51–53 [this volume, pp. 37–39].

10. Cullity and Gerrans say their "self-managing addict" would meet Frankfurt's description of the "unwilling addict," (note 14) but I am not convinced, Indeed, Frankfurt's view in "Freedom of the Will and the Concept of a Person" is in danger of entailing that the self-managing addict identifies with his desire for the drug, since he desires that it be his "will."

11. p. 51 [this volume, p. 37].

to be removed or whose harmful effects need to be managed, just as one might see an itch. Granted, an itch does not have a content, whereas the desire for the drug does. And, as it happens, what the self-managing addict thinks will best manage his desire is what is specified in its content. Nevertheless, the rationale he sees for taking the drug is like the rationale for scratching an itch. After all, if he could better manage the desire in a way that had no relation to its content—hypnosis, perhaps—that is what he'd favor. The self-managing addict no more identifies with his desire than I identify with the itch I am scratching. Perhaps this can be deepened;[12] but in any case it seems to me to be roughly on track. And we should not suppose that the difference between the self-managing addict and one who does identify with a desire for the drug is that the self-managing addict does not think getting the drug a good thing. He does, after all, think it instrumentally good; and to think something noninstrumentally good is not yet to identify with the desire for it.[13]

Turn now to the self-opaque agent. He is systematically moved in his deliberation and action by his attraction to conciliation and a policy in favor of this,[14] a policy with which he is satisfied; but he does not know this about himself and would not endorse it if he did.[15] He is "someone who does not give endorsement or authority to central elements of his own personality" (324). So it seems that he satisfies all the conditions of the model and yet neither identifies with his desire to be conciliatory nor acts autonomously.

The example is somewhat puzzling, though, since given that the agent insists this is not his policy, it is not clear that his effective intentions to

---

12. I tried to do that in "Hierarchy, Circularity, and Double Reduction," at 77 [this volume, p. 84]. Cullity and Gerrans (note 17) say that what I say there "rules out an agent's endorsement of desires for goods that are only instrumentally valuable." I disagree. My policy in favor of, say, a desire for money is held in part because the relevant functioning of that desire will tend to get me money; so it is *not* held, as I say in the cited passage, "solely because such functioning of the desire is seen as a causal means to some further end distinct from the end specified by the desire." My policy is not solely a response to "autonomous benefits" of the desire's functioning. That said, I no longer think what I say there helps with the self-managing addict, since his policy also is in part a response to the benefits of getting the drug.

13. On this last point see my "A Desire of One's Own."

14. Here I make it explicit that the policy is higher-order.

15. Indeed, he insists this is not his policy. We might also consider an intermediate case in which the agent does not know of the policy but does not have a false belief that it is not her policy.

treat conciliation as a reason are intentions to do that as a matter of his policy. So it is not clear these intentions make reference to the policy.[16] But such cross-temporal referential connections are central to the agential authority of such policies.[17]

However, bracketing these qualms and allowing Cullity and Gerrans their description of the case, we can say that given the systematic role of the self-governing policy, the agent needs to know of this role if the policy is to have agential authority and he is to identify with the desire.[18] Such a self-knowledge condition is weaker than a requirement that the agent have arrived at his policy by way of a conscious resolution, or even that he be consciously aware of the policy.[19] Such self-knowledge does not seem especially uncommon; so I don't think that this would be, as Cullity and Gerrans say, "to err in the other direction" (322). Indeed, such self-knowledge helps ensure that the policy enters into important cross-temporal referential connections.

Granted, there is also a notion of identification—in the sense in which one is, whether one knows it or not, identified with aspects of one's personality that substantially shape one's temporally extended thought and action—that does not require such self-knowledge.[20] It may be enough for identification in this sense that the relevant self-governing policy is central to the personality in ways highlighted by the theory, even in the absence of the cited self-knowledge. But there is also a stronger form of identification—suggested by talk of strong reflective endorsement—that does seem to require such self-knowledge. And it is this stronger form of identification that seems involved in central cases of self-government.

I think, though, that Cullity and Gerrans would insist that even after we add such a self-knowledge condition we miss something essential

16. I was helped here by Agnieszka Jaworska.

17. See "Reflection, Planning, and Temporally Extended Agency," at 44–45 and 47 [this volume, pp. 29–32].

18. I discuss related self-knowledge conditions on autonomous action in "Autonomy and Hierarchy," 171–73 [this volume, pp. 181–183].

19. Cullity and Gerrans do not seem to make these distinctions.

20. Agnieszka Jaworska forcefully emphasizes something like this notion, which she calls internality, in her "Caring and Internality," *Philosophy and Phenomenological Research* (forthcoming). My remarks here have benefited from this paper and from discussion with Jaworska.

about the relevant "kind of *commitment*" (323). I suspect there are two pressures at work here.

First, there is the idea—one that Cullity and Gerrans attribute to me[21]—that to solve the authority problem within a Frankfurtian theory we need to "identify a higher-order attitude for which doubting whether that attitude speaks for me is itself ceasing to hold that attitude" (316). But the self-opaque agent may newly come to know of the role of his self-governing policy of conciliation, doubt that it speaks for him, but still continue to have that policy. So even if we add self-knowledge, we haven't solved the authority problem.

The reply sketched in "Reflection, Planning, and Temporally Extended Agency" is that if this self-governing policy continues to play—and (we are adding) is known to play—the cited roles in the agent's psychology, then a doubt on the agent's part that it speaks for him is confused.[22] It may, however, be possible to have this doubt without "ceasing to hold that attitude." Of course, given his new self-knowledge, the agent might well change the policy or cease to be relevantly satisfied. But if all that the self-knowledge brings in its wake is the bare judgment that that is not where he stands, that judgment, while possible, is nevertheless a confused failure of self-understanding.

That said, it may be that such confusion does prevent the activity from being fully self-governed. If we do say this—and I will leave this issue open here—we can easily adjust the model to include, as a condition for self-governed action, that there is not this sort of confusion.

This takes us to the second pressure. Here the worry is that once the agent knows of the functioning of the self-governing policy, she must, to be self-governing, go on to endorse the policy; and this takes us back on the path to regress. My initial answer is that if the agent is satisfied with the self-governing policy, and if it does play the cross-temporal, Lockean role I have emphasized, and if there is also the cited self-knowledge, then the agent identifies with the desire. Identification does not require a further, yet-higher-order endorsing attitude in favor of that policy. This is

---

21. But see the next paragraph.
22. See "Reflection, Planning, and Temporally Extended Agency," 60–61 [this volume, pp. 45–46].

a version of a Frankfurtian strategy:[23] we block regress by embedding the attitudes within larger structures of satisfaction and role in cross-temporal organization (and self-knowledge).

There remains, however, an intuitive pull in favor of the idea that even if this suffices for identification, self-government requires some further endorsement of the self-governing policy. If we are to understand this without appeal to a little person in the head, we need to appeal to an appropriate attitude that favors this functioning of the policy; and we need to do that without courting unacceptable regress. But, in fact, this requirement has already been met: for the self-governing policies reflexively favor their own functioning. We were initially led to this idea by a concern with circularity. But now we see a second reason for reflexivity, one that has independent force: it helps ensure higher-order endorsement of the self-governing policy, higher-order endorsement involved in self-governed activity.[24] This reflexivity by itself would not explain the authority of the self-governing policy to speak for the agent.[25] To explain that, we need to appeal to role in cross-temporal organization and to satisfaction. But once the policy is embedded in this psychological context, its reflexive structure allows us to answer this final challenge.

I can now explain my title. An agent is committed to a desire in an initial sense when that desire is supported by a self-governing policy in favor of treating that desire as reason-providing, a policy with which she is satisfied. A stronger form of this commitment requires, further, the cited self-knowledge. Finally, the commitment needed for central cases of autonomy brings with it a distinctive pressure in favor of higher-order endorsement of the self-governing policy (and perhaps also the absence of the cited kind of confusion). This requirement of higher-order endorsement is already satisfied if, concerned with circularity, we see the relevant policies as reflexive. If, however, we do not introduce reflexivity initially, we will want to introduce it when we come to say what constitutes human autonomy.[26]

---

23. See "Two Problems about Human Agency," 318–20 [this volume, pp. 93–100].

24. See "Autonomy and Hierarchy," 173–75 [this volume, pp. 183–85].

25. Contrast Keith Lehrer, *Self-Trust* (New York: Oxford University Press, 1997) at 100–102. The theory of autonomy needs, then, both a kind of Frankfurtian psychological embedding and a kind of reflexivity emphasized by Lehrer and others.

26. Thanks to Agnieszka Jaworska and Gideon Yaffe for extremely helpful discussions.

Chapter 10

PLANNING AGENCY, AUTONOMOUS AGENCY

I. PLANNING AND CORE ELEMENTS
OF AUTONOMY

Humans seem sometimes to be autonomous, self-governed agents: their actions seem at times to be not merely the upshot of antecedent causes but, rather, under the direction of the agent herself in ways that qualify as

This chapter is to a significant extent an overview of themes I have discussed in a recent series of essays. For further details, see "Identification, Decision, and Treating as a Reason," as reprinted in my *Faces of Intention* (New York: Cambridge University Press, 1999): 185–206; "Reflection, Planning, and Temporally Extended Agency," *Philosophical Review* 109 (2000): 35–61 [this volume, essay 2]; "Valuing and the Will," *Philosophical Perspectives: Action and Freedom* 14 (2000): 249–65 [this volume, essay 3]; "Hierarchy, Circularity, and Double Reduction," in S. Buss and L. Overton, eds., *Contours of Agency: Essays on Themes from Harry Frankfurt* (Cambridge, MA: MIT Press, 2002): 65–85 [this volume, essay 4]; "Nozick on Free Will," in David Schmidtz, ed., *Robert Nozick* (New York: Cambridge University Press, 2002): 155–74 [this volume, essay 6]; "Two Problems about Human Agency," *Proceedings of the Aristotelian Society* 101 (2001): 309–26 [this volume, essay 5]; "Autonomy and Hierarchy," in Ellen Frankel Paul, Fred D. Miller, Jr., and Jeffrey Paul, eds., *Autonomy* (New York: Cambridge University Press, 2003): 156–76 [this volume, essay 8]; "Shared Valuing and Frameworks for Practical Reasoning," in R. Jay Wallace et al., eds., *Reason and Value: Themes from the Moral Philosophy of Joseph Raz* (Oxford: Oxford University Press, 2004): 1–27 [this volume, essay 13]; "A Desire of One's Own," *Journal of Philosophy* (2003): 221–42 [this volume, essay 7]; "Three Forms of Agential Commitment: Reply to Cullity and Gerrans," *Proceedings of the Aristotelian Society* 104 (2004): 329–37 [this volume, essay 9]; and "Temptation Revisited," this volume, essay 12. The present essay benefited from written comments from Alfred Mele and Manuel Vargas, and from extremely helpful discussion in a meeting of the Stanford Social Ethics and Normative Theory discussion group and in a colloquium at the University of Miami. It was completed while I was a Fellow at the Center for Advanced Study in Behavioral Sciences. I am grateful for financial support provided by the Andrew W. Mellon Foundation.

a form of governance by that agent. What sense can we make of this apparent phenomenon of governance by the agent herself?[1]

Well, we can take as given for present purposes that human agents have complex psychological economies and that we frequently can explain what they do by appeal to the functioning of these psychological economies. She raised her arm because she wanted to warn her friend; she worked on the chapter because of her plan to finish her book; she helped the stranger because she knew this was the right thing to do; he left the room because he did not want to show his anger. These are all common, everyday instances of explaining action by appeal to psychological functioning. In doing this, we appeal to attitudes of the agent: beliefs, intentions, desires, and so on. The agent herself is part of the story; it is, after all, her attitudes that we cite. These explanations do not, however, simply refer to the agent; they appeal to attitudes that are elements in her psychic economy. The attitudes they cite may include attitudes that are themselves about the agent and her attitudes—desires about desires, perhaps. But what does the explanatory work is, in the end, the functioning of (perhaps in some cases higher-order) attitudes. These explanations are, I will say, nonhomuncular.

When we come to self-governance, however, it is not clear that we can continue in this way. The image of the agent directing and governing is, in the first instance, an image of the agent herself standing back from her attitudes and doing the directing and governing. But if we say that this is, in the end, in what self-governance consists, we will be faced with the question whether the agent who is standing back from these attitudes is herself self-governing. And it is not clear how such an approach can answer that question. Further, if this is, in the end, what we say constitutes self-governance, then it will be puzzling how self-governing human agents can be part of the same natural world as other biological species. Granted, there is already a problem in understanding how the kind of

---

1. As indicated, I understand self-governance of action to be a distinctive form of self-direction or self-determination (I do not distinguish these last two) of action. Autonomy—that is, personal autonomy—is self-direction that is, in particular, self-governance. Or anyway, that is the phenomenon that is my concern here. (See my "Autonomy and Hierarchy," 156–57, 168 [this volume, pp. 162–63, 177].) Autonomy is related in complex ways to moral responsibility and accountability, but I do not consider these further issues here.

psychological functioning cited in ordinary action explanation can be part of that natural world. But here I assume that we can, in the end, see such explanatory appeals to mind as compatible with seeing ourselves as located in this natural order. But if, in talking of self-governance, we need to see the agent as playing an irreducible role in the explanation of action, we have yet a further problem in reconciling our self-understanding as autonomous with our self-understanding as embedded in a natural order.[2]

These reflections lead to the question of whether there are forms of psychological functioning that can be characterized without seeing the agent herself as playing an irreducible role and that are plausible candidates for sufficient conditions for agential governance. It is also an important question, of course, whether certain forms of functioning are necessary for self-governance. But given the structure of the problem as I have characterized it, the basic issue is one about sufficient conditions for autonomy; and we should be alive to the possibility that there are, at bottom, several different forms of functioning, each of which is sufficient, but no one of which is necessary for self-governance.[3]

In response to this question, the first thing to say is that relevant psychological functioning will involve, but go beyond, purposive agency. Autonomous agents are purposive agents, but they are not simply purposive agents. Many nonhuman animals are purposive agents—they act in ways that are responsive to what they want and their cognitive grasp of how to get it—but are unlikely candidates for self-governance. A model of our autonomy will need to introduce forms of functioning that include but go beyond purposiveness.

In earlier work, I have emphasized that it is an important feature of human agents that they are not only purposive agents; they are also

2. See J. David Velleman, "What Happens When Someone Acts?" in his *The Possibility of Practical Reason* (Oxford: Oxford University Press, 2000): 123–43; and R. E. Hobart, "Free Will as Involving Determination and Inconceivable without It," as reprinted in Bernard Berofsky, ed., *Free Will and Determinism* (New York: Harper & Row, 1966): 63–95, esp. 65–66.

3. As for the provision of fully sufficient conditions, though, see my qualifications below in remarks about core elements of autonomy. Alfred R. Mele also pursues a strategy of seeking sufficient (but perhaps not necessary) conditions for certain forms of autonomy. And Mele addresses issues about the historical background of autonomy, issues that, as I explain below, I put aside here. See Mele, *Autonomous Agents: From Self-Control to Autonomy* (New York: Oxford University Press, 1995): 187.

planning agents.[4] Planning agency brings with it further basic capacities and forms of thought and action that are central to our temporally extended and social lives. Indeed, our concept of intention, as it applies to adult human agents, helps track significant contours of these planning capacities. I call my efforts to characterize these features of human agency, and the associated story of intention, the "planning" theory."

As important as it is, however, the step from purposive to planning agency is not by itself a step all the way to self-government. After all, one's planning agency may be tied to the pursuit of ends that are compulsive or obsessive or unreflective or thoughtless or conflicted in ways incompatible with self-government.

This may suggest that though the step from purposive to planning agency is an important step, it is a side step: It does not help us provide relevant sufficient conditions for self-governance. I believe, however, that this suggestion is mistaken, that important kinds of self-governance involve planning attitudes and capacities in a fundamental way.

J. David Velleman once remarked that "an understanding of intention requires an understanding of our freedom or autonomy." And he argued that my 1987 planning theory of intention "falls short in some respects because [it] tries to study intention in isolation from such questions about the fundamental nature of agency."[5] On one natural interpretation of these remarks, the claim is that a theory of intention needs itself to be a theory of autonomy. And this seems too strong to me. There can be intending, planning agents who are not autonomous. A theory of intention should not suppose that only autonomous agents have the basic capacities involved in intending and planning. Nevertheless, I do think that the planning theory of intention has a significant contribution to make to a theory of autonomy.

Let me try to articulate more precisely the kind of contribution I have in mind.[6] We seek models of psychological structures and functioning

---

4. See my *Intention, Plans, and Practical Reason* (Cambridge, MA: Harvard University Press, 1987; reissued by CSLI Publications, 1999); and my *Faces of Intention*.

5. See his review of my *Intention, Plans, and Practical Reason* in *Philosophical Review* (1991): 283.

6. See my "Autonomy and Hierarchy," 157 [this volume, pp. 163–64].

that, in appropriate contexts, can constitute central cases of autonomous agency. We should not assume there is a unique such model, but we can consider it progress if we can provide at least one such model. Further, to make progress in this pursuit, we do well, I think, to focus initially on psychological structures and forms of functioning that are more or less current at the time of action, broadly construed. In the end, we will want to know whether there are further constraints to be added, constraints on the larger history of these structures and forms of functioning. Perhaps, for example, certain kinds of prior manipulation or indoctrination need to be excluded. But before we can make progress with that question of history, we need plausible models of important and central structures and functioning on (roughly) the occasion of autonomous action. I will call a model of such important and central structures and functioning a "model of core elements of autonomy." A model of core elements need provide neither necessary nor fully sufficient conditions for autonomy. It need not provide necessary conditions, for it may be that there is more than one way to be autonomous. And it need not provide fully sufficient conditions, for it may be that to ensure autonomy we need also to impose conditions on the larger history. Nevertheless, a plausible model of core elements would help us understand autonomy and its possible place in our natural world.[7] And I want to argue that the planning theory has an important contribution to make to a plausible model of core elements of autonomy.

My argument will take the following form. I will examine two prominent models of relevant forms of psychological functioning: (1) hierarchical models that highlight responsiveness to higher-order conative attitudes; and (2) value-judgment-responsive models that highlight responsiveness to judgments about the good. Although each of these models points to an important form of functioning, each faces problems when offered as a model of core elements of self-governance. My proposal will be that we solve these problems by drawing on the planning theory.

---

7. And it would be a model of what I have called "core features of human agency." See my "Reflection, Planning, and Temporally Extended Agency," 35–36 [this volume, pp. 21–22]. I point to a similar idea in talking about "strong forms of agency" in "A Desire of One's Own," 222 n. 3 [this volume, p. 138, n. 3].

2. THE HIERARCHICAL MODEL AND WATSON'S THREE OBJECTIONS

Let's begin with hierarchy. Here the idea is that the basic step we need to get from mere purposiveness to self-government is the introduction of higher-order conative attitudes about the functioning of first-order motivating attitudes. One main source of this idea is a complex series of papers by Harry Frankfurt.[8] In his classic early essay, Frankfurt wrote that "it is in securing the conformity of his will to his second-order volitions, then, that a person exercises freedom of the will."[9] Here, by "will," Frankfurt means, roughly, "desire that motivates action"; and a second-order volition is a second-order desire that a certain desire motivate. When the effective motivation of action (the "will") conforms to and is explained by[10] an uncontested second-order volition, the agent exercises freedom of the will. And when Frankfurt later turns explicitly to autonomy and self-government (which he sees as the same thing), it seems fairly clear that something like this hierarchical story is built into his approach.[11]

Now, we have observed that self-government seems to involve the agent's standing back and doing the governing. The hierarchical model acknowledges the power of this picture, a picture that highlights the agent's reflectiveness about her motivation. But the model goes on to understand such reflectiveness by appeal to certain higher-order attitudes— in the simplest case that Frankfurt initially emphasized, an uncontested

---

8. See Harry Frankfurt, *The Importance of What We Care About* (Cambridge: Cambridge University Press, 1988); and *Necessity, Volition, and Love* (Cambridge: Cambridge University Press, 1999). For related ideas, see also Gerald Dworkin, "Acting Freely," *Noûs* 4 (1970): 367–83; Wright Neely, "Freedom and Desire," *Philosophical Review* 83 (1974): 32–54; and Keith Lehrer, "Reason and Autonomy," in Paul, Miller, and Paul, eds., *Autonomy*, 177–98.

9. Frankfurt, "Freedom of the Will and the Concept of a Person," in his *The Importance of What We Care About*, 20. (It is interesting to note that in this passage Frankfurt appeals to something the agent is doing—namely, securing the cited conformity.)

10. Frankfurt points to this condition of explanatory role in his "Identification and Wholeheartedness," in *The Importance of What We Care About*, 163.

11. See esp. Frankfurt's "Autonomy, Necessity and Love" in his *Necessity, Volition, and Love*, 129–41. For a helpful discussion of some issues of Frankfurt interpretation that I am skirting over here, see James Stacey Taylor, "Autonomy, Duress, and Coercion," in Paul, Miller, and Paul, eds., *Autonomy*, 129 n. 5.

second-order volition. In this way, it tries to see self-governance as involving reflectiveness without a homunculus.

Note that the theory need not claim that the very same higher-order attitude is involved in all cases of hierarchical self-governance. It need only claim that all cases of hierarchical self-governance involve some such higher-order conative attitude.

This basic idea has been developed in a number of different ways in recent years both by Frankfurt and by others, and I will later advert to some elements from this literature. But enough has been said about the hierarchical model to see the force of an important trio of objections that were proffered by Gary Watson in response to Frankfurt's initial paper.[12]

Watson's first objection begins with an idea that is central to the hierarchical model, the idea that when a relevant, uncontested higher-order conative attitude favors a certain first-order motivation, the *agent* endorses, or identifies with, that motivation. In the terms of Frankfurt's early version of hierarchy, my uncontested second-order volition in favor of my desire to turn the other cheek constitutes my endorsement of, or identification with, that desire. That is why it is plausible to say that when that desire motivates action, in part because of my second-order volition, *I* am directing my action. But, Watson observes, the hierarchical model does not seem to have the resources to explain this. After all,

> since second-order volitions are themselves simply desires, to add them to the context of conflict is just to increase the number of contenders; it is not to give a special place to any of those in contention.[13]

We can express the point by saying that there is nothing in the very idea of a higher-order desire that explains why it has authority to speak for the agent, to constitute where the agent stands. For all that has been said, when action and will conforms to a higher-order desire, it is simply

12. Gary Watson, "Free Agency," *Journal of Philosophy* 72 (1975): 205–20. R. Jay Wallace endorses similar objections in his "Caring, Reflexivity, and the Structure of Volition," in Monika Betzler and Barbara Guckes, eds., *Autonomes Handeln* (Berlin: Akademie Verlag, 2000): 218–22.

13. Watson, "Free Agency," 218.

conforming to one attitude among many of the wiggles in the psychic stew. The hierarchical model does not yet have an account of the *agential authority* of certain higher-order attitudes.[14] But it needs such an account in order to provide a nonhomuncular model of agential governance. And that is Watson's first objection.[15]

Watson's second objection is built into the alternative model he offers, a model that highlights responsiveness to judgments of the good. Watson sees such judgments as an "evaluational system" that "may be said to constitute one's standpoint."[16] If we are looking for attitudes that speak for the agent, that constitute where the agent stands, then the natural candidates are not higher-order volitions, but evaluative judgments about what "is most worth pursuing."[17] I will call this idea, that the agent's standpoint is constituted by evaluative judgment rather than by higher-order conative attitude, the "Platonic challenge" to the hierarchical model.

Watson's third objection draws on but goes beyond this. He writes:

> [Agents] do not (or need not usually) ask themselves which of their desires they want to be effective in action; they ask themselves which course of action is most worth pursuing. The initial practical question is about courses of action and not about themselves.[18]

Here Watson is emphasizing his Platonic model; but he is also pointing to a further objection, one that involves a claim about the structure of ordinary deliberation. The basic idea is that ordinary deliberation is first-order

---

14. Talk of agential authority comes from my "Two Problems about Human Agency"; talk of wiggles in the psychic stew comes, I admit, from my "Reflection, Planning, and Temporally Extended Agency," 38 [this volume, p. 24].

15. Watson notes that there are elements in Frankfurt's essay—in particular, Frankfurt's talk of an agent who "identifies himself *decisively* with one of his first-order desires"—that suggest that it is not conative hierarchy that is doing the main theoretical work but, rather, the idea of decisive identification. But, Watson remarks, if "notions of acts of identification and of decisive commitment . . . are the crucial notions, it is unclear why these acts of identification cannot themselves be of the first order." (The quote from Frankfurt is in Watson's "Free Agency," at 218, while the quote from Watson is at 219.) I discuss this exchange between Frankfurt and Watson in "Identification, Decision, and Treating as a Reason," in my *Faces of Intention*, 188–90.

16. Watson, "Free Agency," 216.

17. Ibid., 219.

18. Ibid.

deliberation about what to do, not higher-order reflection about one's desires. And the objection is that the hierarchical model misses this point and mistakenly sees deliberation as primarily a matter of higher-order reflection on motivating attitudes. Let us call this the "objection from deliberative structure."

So we have a trio of objections to the hierarchical model: the objection about agential authority, the Platonic challenge, and the objection from deliberative structure. Taken together, these constitute a serious challenge to the hierarchical model.

3. THE PLATONIC MODEL AND UNDERDETERMINATION BY VALUE JUDGMENT

I want to give the hierarchical model something to say in response to this challenge. My strategy is to do this by bringing together elements from the hierarchical model with elements from the planning theory. Before proceeding with this strategy, however, I want to reflect on the Platonic alternative that Watson sketches, one that highlights responsiveness to judgments about the good.

An initial observation is that it seems possible for one to judge that, say, turning the other cheek is best, but still be alienated from that judgment in a way that undermines its agential authority.[19]

We can clarify one way this can happen by turning to one of Frankfurt's later developments of the hierarchical model. In response to concerns about what I have called "agential authority," Frankfurt introduced an important idea: satisfaction.[20] Satisfaction is not a further attitude, but rather a structural feature of the psychic system. For me to be satisfied with my higher-order desire in favor of my desire to turn the other cheek is not for me to have an even-higher-order desire. It is, rather, for my higher-order desire to be embedded in a psychic system in which there is no relevant tendency to change: "Satisfaction is a state of the entire psychic system—a state constituted just by the absence of any tendency or

19. Frankfurt made this point in conversation. Also see Velleman, "What Happens When Someone Acts?" 134.

20. Frankfurt, "The Faintest Passion," in his *Necessity, Volition, and Love*, 103–5.

inclination to alter its condition."[21] Frankfurt's idea—expressed in the terms I have introduced here—is that such a higher-order desire has agential authority when the agent is satisfied with it.

I have elsewhere noted that satisfaction with such a desire may be grounded in depression, and in such cases satisfaction with desire does not seem to be enough to guarantee agential authority.[22] Nevertheless, I think that this idea of satisfaction is important in two ways. First, a version of it will be of use later, as one part of a more adequate account of agential authority. Second, it helps us see that one may be dissatisfied with, and for that reason alienated from, one's evaluative judgment in a way that undermines its agential authority. This is one way in which the Platonic proposal is faced with a problem of agential authority.

However, a defender of the Platonic proposal can, in response, focus on evaluative judgments with which the agent is, in an appropriate sense, satisfied. She may then propose that it is such evaluative judgments that constitute the agent's standpoint. A full defense of this proposal would need to say more about the roles of such evaluative judgments in our agency and why these help establish agential authority. Nevertheless, this does show how the Platonic model can, like the hierarchical model, draw on the idea of satisfaction.

But now we need to consider a different kind of alienation from value judgment, one that was emphasized by Watson himself in a later essay.[23] One might have a settled judgment that turning the other cheek would be best, might be satisfied with that as one's settled evaluative judgment, but nevertheless be fully committed, rather, to revenge. As Watson says, "I might fully 'embrace' a course of action I do not judge best." Watson calls such situations "perverse cases." In such cases, the agent's "standpoint" is not captured by his evaluative judgment but rather by his "perverse" commitment.

However, while Watson was right to emphasize such cases, a defender of the Platonic model does have a response. She can say that such cases

---

21. Frankfurt, "The Faintest Passion," 104.

22. Bratman, "Identification, Decision, and Treating as a Reason," 194–95. And see Bratman, "Reflection, Planning, and Temporally Extended Agency," 49 [this volume, p. 35], for my strategy for avoiding this difficulty within my own account.

23. Watson, "Free Action and Free Will," *Mind* 96 (1987): 150. Also see my "A Desire of One's Own," 227 [this volume, p. 144].

involve a rational breakdown and that in the absence of rational breakdown an agent's standpoint consists of relevant evaluative judgments.
Because we are seeking conditions for self-government and because the
kind of rational breakdown at issue can plausibly be seen as blocking self-
governance, this proposal keeps open the idea that self-governance consists primarily of rational responsiveness to relevant evaluative judgments.

This takes me to a third concern—namely, that even in the absence of
rational breakdown, the agent's evaluative judgments frequently underdetermine important commitments. Faced with difficult issues about what
to give weight or significance to in one's life, one is frequently faced with
multiple, conflicting goods: Turning the other cheek is a good, but so is an
apt reactive response to wrongful treatment; resisting the use of violence
by the military is good, but so is loyalty to one's country; human sexuality
is a good, but so are certain religious lives of abstinence. In many such
cases, the agent's standpoint involves forms of commitment—to draft
resistance, say—that have agential authority but go beyond his prior
evaluative judgment. This may be because the agent thinks that, though
he needs to settle on a coherent stance, the conflicting goods are more or
less equal. Or perhaps he thinks he simply does not know which is more
important. (He is, after all, like all of us, a person with significant limits in
his abilities to arrive at such judgments with any justified confidence.) Or
perhaps he thinks that the relevant goods are in an important way
incommensurable.[24] In such cases, there need not be a rational breakdown
but rather a sensible and determinative response to ways in which one's
value judgments can underdetermine the "shape" of one's life.[25] One may
be committed to building into the fabric of one's own life some things one
judges good, but not others. And even in a case in which one judges that,
say, a life of helping others is strictly better than a life in which one does
not help others, one's judgment will typically leave in its wake significant

24. For this last point, see Joseph Raz, "Incommensurability and Agency," as reprinted in
his *Engaging Reason* (Oxford: Oxford University Press, 1999): 46–66. I discuss this trio of possibilities
in "A Desire of One's Own."

25. See, for example, Robert Nozick, *Philosophical Explanations* (Cambridge, MA: Harvard
University Press, 1981): 446–50. Talk of the shape of a life comes from Charles Taylor, "Leading a
Life," in Ruth Chang, ed., *Incommensurability, Incomparability, and Practical Reason* (Cambridge, MA:
Harvard University Press, 1997): 183.

underdetermination of the exact extent to which this value is to shape one's life, the exact significance this value is to have in one's deliberations.

In these cases of underdetermination by prior value judgment, the hierarchical model seems to be in a better position than the Platonic model. The hierarchical model has room for the view that these elements of the agent's standpoint—elements of commitment in the face of underdetermination by prior value judgment—are constituted by relevant higher-order conative attitudes.[26] Granted, we are still without a full account of the agential authority of those higher-order attitudes. But that is not a defense of the Platonic model. Rather, it is an observation that, so far, neither model solves the problem of agential authority.

It is here that we do well to turn to the planning theory.

4. PLANNING, TEMPORALLY EXTENDED AGENCY, AND AGENTIAL AUTHORITY

A basic feature of adult human agents is that they pursue complex forms of cross-temporal and social organization and coordination by way of planning. They settle on—commit themselves to—prior and typically partial and hierarchically structured[27] plans of action, and this normally shapes later practical reasoning and action in ways that support cross-temporal organization, both individual and social. Such plan-like commitments can involve settling matters left indeterminate by prior evaluative judgment, as when one decides on one of several options, no one of which one sees as clearly superior. Indeed, one can be settled on certain intentions, plans, or policies without reflecting at all on whether they are for the best or making an explicit decision in their favor.[28]

According to the planning theory, our planning agency brings with it distinctive norms of plan consistency, plan coherence, and plan stability.

---

26. For a somewhat similar view, see Keith Lehrer, *Self Trust: A Study of Reason, Knowledge, and Autonomy* (Oxford: Oxford University Press, 1997): chap. 4.

27. The hierarchies I allude to here are, roughly, ones of ends and means, not the conative hierarchies on which I have so far been focusing.

28. In a version of this sort of case emphasized by Nadeem Hussain, an agent in a strongly traditional society unreflectively internalizes certain general policies passed down by the tradition.

To intend to do something in the future or to have a policy concerning certain recurring types of circumstances is to have an attitude that is to be understood in terms of such planning capacities and norms. Such intendings and policies are importantly different from ordinary desires. But they are no more mysterious than the familiar phenomena and norms involved in planning. In this way, the planning theory is a modest, nonmysterious theory of the will.[29]

An agent's plan-like attitudes support cross-temporal organization of her practical thought and action, and they do this in a distinctive way. Prior plans involve reference to later ways of acting; and in filling in and/or executing prior plans one normally sees oneself in ways that refer back to those prior plans. Such plans are, further, typically stable over time. So planning agency supports cross-temporal organization of practical thought and action in the agent's life in part by way of cross-temporal referential connections and in part by way of continuities of stable plans over time. So it supports such organization in part by way of continuities and connections of a sort that are highlighted by Lockean accounts of personal identity over time.[30] And this is no accident: It is a characteristic feature of the functioning of planning in our temporally extended lives.

This opens up an approach to agential authority. The problem of agential authority is the problem of explaining why certain attitudes have authority to constitute the agent's practical standpoint. So far, we have been thinking of this as a problem about the agent at a particular time. But the human agents for whom this problem arises are ones whose agency extends over time: They begin overlapping, and interwoven plans and projects, follow through with them, and (sometimes) complete them. Such temporal extension of agency involves activities at different times performed by the very same agent. A broadly Lockean story of that sameness of agency over time will emphasize relevant psychological connections and continuities. In particular, our planning agency constitutes and supports the cross-temporal organization of this temporally extended agency by way of Lockean connections and continuities—by way of Lockean ties. And this gives relevant

29. See my "Introduction," *Faces of Intention,* 5.
30. See Derek Parfit, *Reasons and Persons* (New York: Oxford University Press, 1984): 206–8; and my "Reflection, Planning, and Temporally Extended Agency," 43–45 [this volume, pp. 28–30].

plan-type attitudes a claim to speak for the temporally persisting agent. As I once wrote, the idea is that "we tackle the problem of where the agent stands *at a time* by appeal to roles of attitudes in creating broadly Lockean conditions of identity of the agent *over time*."[31] And central among the relevant attitudes are plan-type attitudes.

If this is right, then it is good news for the hierarchical theorist. She can see the relevant higher-order conative attitudes—those that constitute the agent's practical standpoint—not merely as desires but rather as plan-type attitudes. She can then cite the Lockean roles of these plan-type attitudes to explain their agential authority. Or, at least, this will be the basic step in such an explanation. In this way, the planning theory can give the hierarchical theorist something more to say in response to the objection from agential authority. And given that intentions and plans are sometimes formed in the face of underdetermination by prior value judgment, such plan-type attitudes are natural candidates to respond to the issues raised by such cases of underdetermination.

5. SELF-GOVERNING POLICIES

But what plan-type attitudes are these? Given the role they need to play within the theory we are developing, they need to be higher-order plan-like attitudes. And they need to be higher-order plan-like attitudes that speak for the agent because they help constitute and support the temporal extension of her agency. They will do this in large part by being plan-type attitudes whose primary role includes the organization of practical thought and action over time by way of Lockean ties. This makes it plausible that in the clearest cases the relevant attitudes will be policy-like: They will concern, in a more or less general way, the functioning of relevant conative attitudes over time, in relevant circumstances.[32]

31. Bratman, "Reflection, Planning, and Temporally Extended Agency," 46 [this volume, p. 32].
32. Granted, there will be cases in which a relevant intention-like attitude will be a "singular commitment" to treat a certain desire in a relevant way on *this* occasion. (See my "Hierarchy, Circularity, and Double Reduction," 78–79 [this volume, pp. 68–88].) Such intention-like attitudes will have some claim to agential authority. Given the singularity of the commitment, however, these intention-like attitudes will have a less extensive tie to temporally extended agency and thus a lesser claim to authority. Because our concern is primarily with sufficient conditions for autonomy, I will here put such cases to one side.

What the hierarchical theorist will primarily want to appeal to, then, are higher-order policy-like attitudes. Which higher-order policy-like attitudes? Here we need to reflect further on the very idea of self-governance.

Autonomous actions, I have said, are under the direction of the agent in ways that qualify as a form of governance by that agent. But what forms of agential direction constitute agential governance? Well, the very idea of governance brings with it, I think, the idea of direction by appeal to considerations treated as in some way legitimizing or justifying. This contrasts with a kind of agential direction or determination that does not involve normative content. And this means that the higher-order policy-like attitudes that are cited by the hierarchical theorist should in some way reflect this distinctive feature of self-governance.

Recall Frankfurt's notion of a second-order volition: a desire that a certain desire motivate. The content of such a second-order volition concerns a process of motivation, not—at least not directly—a process of reasoning that appeals to legitimizing, justifying considerations. So such a higher-order attitude does not seem to reflect the way in which self-governance is a kind of governance, not a kind of direction that involves no normative content.

Consider now a higher-order policy concerning a desire for X. One such policy will say that this desire is to influence action by way of practical reasoning in which X, and/or the desire for X, is given justifying weight or significance. Call such a higher-order policy—one that favors such functioning of the desire in relevant motivationally effective practical reasoning—a *self-governing policy*. Our reflections about self-governance—in contrast with nonnormative self-direction—suggest that self-governing policies can play a basic role in hierarchical theories of self-governance.[33] For reasons we have discussed, such policies have a presumptive claim to agential authority, to speaking for the temporally persisting agent. And such policies will concern which desires are to be treated as providing justifying considerations in motivationally effective practical reasoning. They will in that

---

33. There will also be room for attitudes that play the higher-order policy-like roles in one's temporally extended agency that I have been emphasizing, though they are not general intentions. I call these "quasi-policies." See my "Reflection, Planning, and Temporally Extended Agency," 57–60 [this volume, pp. 42–44].

sense say which desires are to have for the agent what we can call "subjective normative authority"; and they will constitute a form of valuing that is different from, though normally related to, judging valuable.[34]

Can the hierarchical theory, then, simply appeal to such self-governing policies in its model of self-governance? Well, if the guidance by these policies is to constitute the agent's governance, then we should require that the agent knows about this guidance.[35] Does that suffice? Not quite. Although such policies have a presumptive claim to agential authority, it still seems possible to be estranged from a particular self-governing policy. This is a familiar problem for a hierarchical theory. But we have already noted a further resource available to such a theory: a version of the Frankfurtian idea of satisfaction. To have agential authority, we can say, a self-governing policy must be one with which the agent is, in an appropriate sense, satisfied.[36]

But what if the satisfaction is grounded in depression? Depression might substantially undermine the normal functioning of these self-governing policies. Such a case would not challenge the present account. But what if these self-governing policies continue to play their characteristic roles in Lockean cross-temporal organization—by way of shaping temporally extended deliberation and action—but the absence of pressure for change in those policies is due to depression? Well, in this case, the self-governing policies remain settled structures that play these central Lockean roles in

34. For the point about valuing, see my "Valuing and the Will" and "Autonomy and Hierarchy." For the idea of subjective normative authority, see my "Two Problems about Human Agency." (In section 7, I will be extending this notion of subjective normative authority.) Note that these policies concern the agent's practical *reasoning*. So we need to understand the reasoning that is the focus of these policies in a way that does not reintroduce worries about a homunculus. See my "Hierarchy, Circularity, and Double Reduction," 70–78 [this volume, pp. 74–85]; and "Two Problems about Human Agency," 322–23 [this volume, pp. 90–92].

35. See Garrett Cullity and Philip Gerrans, "Agency and Policy," *Proceedings of the Aristotelian Society* 104 (2004): 317–27, and my "Three Forms of Agential Commitment: Reply to Cullity and Gerrans." This self-knowledge requirement is doubly motivated, by the way. It is a straightforwardly plausible condition on self-governance that the agent know what higher-order policies are guiding her thought and action. But, as Agnieszka Jaworska has noted, it is also unlikely that an unknown policy will have the kinds of referential connections to prior intentions and later action that are central to our Lockean account of agential authority.

36. My efforts to spell out an appropriate sense appear in my "Reflection, Planning, and Temporally Extended Agency," 49–50, 59–60 [this volume, pp. 35–36, 44].

temporally extended, deliberative agency, and they do that in the absence of relevant pressure for change. So it seems to me that they still have a presumptive claim to establish the (depressed) agent's standpoint.

Can we stop here? Can we say that in a basic case self-governance consists primarily in the known guidance of practical thought and action by self-governing policies with which the agent is satisfied? Well, there does remain a further worry: Does self-governance require not just that the agent know about this functioning of the self-governing policy and be satisfied with it, but, further, that the agent *endorse* it in a way that is not just a matter of being satisfied with it? But what could such further endorsement be? Some yet further, distinct, and yet-higher-order attitude? But that way lies a familiar regress.

I think that a natural move for the hierarchical theorist to make at this point is to appeal to reflexivity: The self-governing policies that are central to the model of autonomy that we are constructing will be in part about their own functioning.[37] Such a policy will favor treating certain desires as reason-providing as a matter of this very policy.[38] The idea is not that such reflexivity by itself establishes the agential authority of the policy. Agential authority of such attitudes is, rather, primarily a matter of Lockean role and satisfaction. But in a context in which these conditions of authority are present, a further condition of reflexivity ensures, without vicious regress, the endorsement of self-governing policy that seems an element in full-blown self-governance.

The proposed model, then, appeals to practical reasoning and action that are appropriately guided by known, reflexive, higher-order self-governing policies with which the agent is satisfied. By combining the resources of the hierarchical and the planning theories in this way, we arrive at a nonhomuncular model of core elements of autonomy.

---

37. I think there is also another reason for such reflexivity, one associated with the concern about reasoning to which I allude in note 34 and the essays cited there.

38. A closely related idea is in Keith Lehrer, *Self-Trust,* 100–102; and also in his "Reason and Autonomy," 187–91. For the basic idea of seeing intentions as reflexive, see Gilbert Harman, *Change in View* (Cambridge, MA: MIT Press, 1986): 85–88. However, my appeal here to reflexivity is not part of a view that, like Harman's, sees *all* "positive" intentions in this way. Further, because my appeal to reflexivity is against a background of a Lockean story of agential authority, together with a Frankfurtian appeal to satisfaction, the job of such reflexivity within my account of autonomy is considerably more limited than its job within Lehrer's.

6. REPLIES TO WATSON'S THREE OBJECTIONS

How does this proposed model respond to the cited trio of objections to the hierarchical theory? Well, the response to the objection from agential authority has already been front and center. Higher-order self-governing policies have an initial claim to speak for the temporally persisting agent given their systematic role in constituting and supporting the cross-temporal organization of practical thought and action by way of Lockean ties. This claim is relevantly authoritative when the agent is satisfied with these policies and they have the cited reflexive structure.

What about the Platonic challenge? Here the answer is that we need to be able to appeal to a central and important kind of commitment that goes beyond prior value judgment, given phenomena of underdetermination of the shape of one's life by such judgments. We need to be able to appeal to commitments in the face of judgments of roughly equal desirability or of incommensurability; and we need to be able to appeal to commitments in the face of reasonable inability to reach, with confidence, a sufficiently determinative judgment of value. Indeed, such commitments may arise even in an agent who does not much go in for value judgment. The appeal to self-governing policies provides for such commitments— commitments that will normally have a kind of stability over time that is characteristic of such attitudes.[39]

One way to see what is going on here is to suppose, with a wide range of philosophers, that evaluative judgments are in some important sense subject to intersubjectivity constraints. In contrast, the commitments that constitute an agent's own standpoint need not be subject to such constraints.[40] In cases of underdetermination by value judgment, the agent may sensibly arrive at further commitments that he does not see as intersubjectively directed or accountable in ways characteristic of value

---

39. I should emphasize that the relevant notion of stability here is in part a normative one: it will involve norms of reasonable stability. It is an important question how exactly to understand such reasonable stability. For some efforts in this direction, see my "Toxin, Temptation, and the Stability of Intention," in my *Faces of Intention* and "Temptation Revisited," this volume, essay 12. Note that the appeal to reasonable stability is *not* an appeal to "volitional necessities" in the sense invoked by Frankfurt in his "Autonomy, Necessity, and Love," 138.

40. For references and further discussion, see my "A Desire of One's Own."

judgment. This leaves open the idea that self-governance precludes a severe breakdown between evaluative judgments with which the agent is satisfied and the commitments that constitute the agent's standpoint. Such a breakdown—as in a Watsonian "perverse" case—is a significant kind of internal incoherence. So it is plausible to say that there is not the kind of unity of view that is needed for self-governance. Nevertheless, and contrary to the Platonic challenge, a model that appeals only to evaluative judgment does not yet provide the resources to characterize forms of agential commitment that are central to self-governance.

What about the objection from deliberative structure? Should our hierarchical model reject Watson's suggestion that "the initial practical question is about courses of action"? Well, sometimes in deliberation one does reflect directly on one's motivation. Nevertheless, I think that Watson is right that frequently in deliberation what we explicitly consider is, rather, what to do. But this need not be an objection to our hierarchical model. We can understand that model as one of background structures that bear on an agent's efforts to answer this "initial practical question": when a self-governing agent grapples with this question, her thought and action are structured in part by higher-order self-governing policies.[41] Or, at least, this is one important case of self-governance.

Those, anyway, are the basic responses to the three objections. But these responses do point to a further issue. We have seen why appeal to higher-order conative attitudes need not be incompatible with the typically first-order structure of ordinary deliberation. We have seen how to explain why certain kinds of higher-order conative attitudes can have agential authority. And we have seen reason for a model of central cases of self-governance to include forms of commitment, to modes of practical reasoning and action,

---

41. In seeing deliberation as primarily first-order, but also seeing the valuings that enter into deliberation as involving conative hierarchy, my view is in the spirit of certain aspects of Simon Blackburn's approach to these matters. (I provide a different treatment of the relevant hierarchy, however. And my view remains neutral with respect to the basic debate between cognitivist approaches and expressivist approaches of the sort championed by Blackburn.) See Blackburn, *Ruling Passions: A Theory of Practical Reasoning* (Oxford and New York: Clarendon/Oxford University Press, 1998). (Blackburn's remarks about a "staircase of practical and emotional ascent" are at 9; his remarks about valuing are at 67–68; and his remarks about deliberation are at 250–56.)

that go beyond evaluative judgment. But none of these points as yet fully explains the basic philosophical pressure for the introduction of hierarchy into the model. They do show that once hierarchy is introduced, we can respond to challenges concerning agential authority and the structure of deliberation. And they do show that appeal to hierarchical conative attitudes is one way to resolve issues raised by underdetermination by value judgment. But they do not yet fully clarify why we should appeal to such hierarchical attitudes in the first place. Perhaps, instead, we should appeal only to certain first-order plan-like commitments that resolve the problems raised by underdetermination by value judgment, guide first-order deliberation, and also allow for a story of agential authority.

We might respond by reminding ourselves that our fundamental concern is with nonhomuncular sufficient conditions for self-governance. So we need not claim that hierarchy is necessary for self-governance. And this response is correct as far as it goes. But even after noting the availability of this response, there is an aspect of the objection to which we need to respond directly. We need to explain why we should see conative hierarchy as even one among perhaps several different models of core elements of autonomy; and to do that, we need to say more about the pressures for introducing such hierarchy.

This is a salient issue in part because it may seem that the account of self-governance as so far developed lends itself to a modification that leaves the account pretty much intact, but in which conative hierarchy drops out.[42] The idea here would be to appeal to policies simply to give weight or significance to consideration X in one's motivationally effective practical reasoning. Such policies seem to be first-order: Their target is a certain activity of reasoning. But in other respects, it seems they could have the features of self-governing policies that have been exploited by the model: Lockean role in cross-temporal organization, targets of self-knowledge and satisfaction, agential authority, and commitments concerning subjective normative authority that do not require determination by value judgment. So we may wonder why hierarchy should be built into the account. Why not throw away the ladder?

---

42. As Samuel Scheffler and others have noted in correspondence and conversation.

7. REASONS FOR HIERARCHY

We can begin by recalling one reason we have already seen for introducing a kind of conative hierarchy into a model of autonomy: relevant policies about practical reasoning will reflexively support themselves. This is a kind of conative hierarchy. But it is only a limited form of hierarchy, one that does not yet include the idea that such policies are generally about further, distinct forms of first-order motivation. In contrast, hierarchical theories of the sort we have been discussing involve these broader hierarchies of conative attitudes about conative attitudes.[43] So we are still faced with the question of why we should see such broader hierarchies as central to our model of core elements of autonomy.[44]

In at least one strand of his work, Frankfurt's appeal to conative hierarchy is driven by what he takes to be a reflective agent's project of self-constitution. Frankfurt seeks a notion of "internal" that fits with Aristotle's idea that "behavior is voluntary only when its moving principle is inside the agent." And Frankfurt's idea is that "what counts . . . is whether or not the agent has constituted himself to include" a certain "moving principle."[45] The reflective agent's effort at self-constitution is a response to the question, "with respect to each desire, whether to identify himself with it or whether to reject it as an outlaw and hence not a legitimate candidate for satisfaction."[46] In this way, conative hierarchy is seen as involved in the kind of self-constituted internality that is basic to reflective agency.

43. Gilbert Harman argues that (1) "positive intentions are self-referential," so (2) all creatures who have positive intentions have higher-order conative attitudes, and so (3) "Frankfurt's appeal to second-order volitions is not the key to distinguishing autonomy from nonautonomy." Though I would not defend a simple appeal to second-order volitions as this "key," my remarks in the text do point to a response on Frankfurt's behalf to this criticism. Frankfurt can say that what provides the key is the capacity for *broad* conative hierarchy, a capacity that goes beyond the hierarchy built into the purported reflexivity of positive intentions. See Gilbert Harman, "Desired Desires," as reprinted in his *Explaining Value and Other Essays in Moral Philosophy* (Oxford: Oxford University Press, 2000): 122–26.

44. For ease of exposition, in the discussion to follow of reasons for broad hierarchy, I will simply speak of hierarchy where I mean broad hierarchy. Also, I do not claim that the pressures to be discussed exhaust the field. There may be other pressures for conative hierarchy that would need to be considered in a more extensive discussion.

45. Frankfurt, "Identification and Wholeheartedness," 171.

46. Frankfurt, "Reply to Michael E. Bratman," in Sarah Buss and Lee Overton, eds., *Contours of Agency* (Cambridge, MA: MIT Press, 2002): 88.

A second pressure in the direction of conative hierarchy comes from a picture of deliberation as reflection on one's desires, reflection aimed at choosing on which desire to act.[47] Such a model of deliberation, coupled with a search for a nonhomuncular story, can lead straightway to conative hierarchy.

Granted, these two different pressures can interact. Given such a model of deliberation, one may be led to think of deliberation as concerned with self-constitution. And given a Frankfurtian, hierarchical story of self-constitution, one may want to extend it to a model of deliberation.[48] Nevertheless, it is useful to keep these two ideas apart.

One reason this is useful is that these different approaches interact differently with Watson's objection to a model of deliberation as higher-order reflection. Here my strategy has been to argue that—though some deliberation does have this higher-order structure—the hierarchical model of self-governance need not see this as the central case of deliberation. Does this mean that our basic reason for building hierarchy into our model of self-governance should be a metaphysical concern with internality and self-constitution?

Although the issues are complex, I believe that if we stop here we may miss an important practical pressure in the direction of conative hierarchy.

An initial point—from Agnieszka Jaworska—is that the Lockean model of agential authority points to an account of internality (in the sense relevant to the cited Aristotelian idea) that does not make hierarchy essential.[49] There can be important attitudes—a young child's love for her father, say—that do not involve conative hierarchy but nevertheless play the kind of Lockean roles in cross-temporal organization of thought and action that establish

---

47. Though Christine Korsgaard shares with Frankfurt an interest in self-constitution, she also embraces such a model of deliberation when she writes: "When you deliberate, it is as if there were something over and above all your desires, something which is *you*, and which *chooses* which desire to act on" (*The Sources of Normativity*, 100). For Korsgaard's concerns with self-constitution, see her "Self-Constitution in the Ethics of Plato and Kant," *Journal of Ethics* 3 (1999): 1–29.

48. Though Frankfurt himself does not seem so inclined. (See his "Reply to Michael E. Bratman," 89–90.)

49. See her "Caring and Internality," *Philosophy and Phenomenological Research* (forthcoming). The example to follow comes (with a change in gender) from that paper.

internality. So the concern with internality does not, on its own, provide sufficient philosophical pressure for conative hierarchy.

A Frankfurtian response would grant the point but insist that, *for agents who are sufficiently reflective to be self-governing*, internality of first-order motivation is (normally?) the product of higher-order reflection and higher-order endorsement or acceptance. And this brings with it conative hierarchy. So, while conative hierarchy need not be involved in all cases of internality, internality within the psychology of reflective self-governance needs conative hierarchy.

But now consider an alternative model of reflectiveness. This model highlights first-order policies about what to treat as a reason in one's motivationally effective practical reasoning; and it says that such policies are reflectively held when they are appropriately tied to (even if underdetermined by) evaluative reflection. Here we have a central role for plan-type commitments concerning practical reasoning (to which we can extend our account of agential authority); and we have a kind of reflectiveness; but we do not yet have conative hierarchy.

What this alternative model fails fully to recognize, however, is that human agents have a wide range of first-order motivating attitudes in addition to such first-order policies about practical reasoning and that these other motivating attitudes threaten to undermine these policies. The point is related to an aspect of Aristotle's moral psychology that has been highlighted by John Cooper. Cooper emphasizes that a central Aristotelian theme is that human agents are subject to significant motivational pressures that do not arise from reflection on what is worth pursuing.[50] For our purposes here, what is important is the related idea that human agents are subject to a wide range of motivational pressures that do not arise primarily from their basic practical commitments. Indeed, as we all learn, these motivational pressures may well be contrary to those commitments. The clearest cases include (but are not limited to)

---

50. John Cooper, "Some Remarks on Aristotle's Moral Psychology," reprinted in his *Reason and Emotion: Essays on Ancient Moral Psychology and Ethical Theory* (Princeton, NJ: Princeton University Press, 1999): 237–52. As Cooper puts the view, "non-rational desires will be desires no part of the causal history of which is ever any process (self-conscious or not) of investigation into the

certain bodily appetites and certain forms of anger, rage, humiliation, indignation, jealousy, resentment, and grief. It is an important fact about human agents—one reflected in our commonsense self-understanding—that such motivating attitudes are part of their psychology and that human agents need a system of self-management in response to the potential of these forms of motivation to conflict with basic commitments. In the absence of such self-management, human agents are much less likely to be effectively guided by their basic commitments.[51]

Once our model of reflective, self-governing agency explicitly includes these further, wide-ranging, first-order motivating attitudes, however, there is pressure for higher-order reflectiveness and conative hierarchy. After all, we can suppose that a self-governing agent will know of these first-order attitudes and of her need for self-management. And we can suppose that she will, other things being equal, endorse forms of functioning that serve this need. So it is plausible to suppose that her basic commitments will themselves include a commitment to associated management of relevant first-order desires and thus include such self-management as part of their content. And that means these commitments will be higher-order. In particular, given the centrality of practical reasoning to self-governed agency, we can expect that these commitments will include policy-like attitudes that concern the justifying significance to be given (or refused) to various first-order desires, and/or what they are for, in her motivationally effective practical reasoning. Such policies will say, roughly: give (refuse) justifying significance to consideration X in motivationally effective practical reasoning, in part by giving (refusing) such significance to relevant first-order

---

truth about what is good for oneself" (242). Cooper notes that this is compatible with holding, as Aristotle did, that "non-rational desires carry with them value judgments framed in (at least some of) the very same terms of good and bad, right and wrong, etc., that also reappear in our rational reflections about what to do and why" (247). (In contrast, I would want to allow for some nonrational desires that do not involve such value judgments.) What is central, Cooper indicates, is "the permanence in human beings and the independence from reason . . . of the nonrational desires" (249).

51. For a similar focus on this practical problem—though not in the service of a hierarchical model—see Martha C. Nussbaum, *The Fragility of Goodness: Luck and Ethics in Greek Tragedy and Philosophy* (Cambridge: Cambridge University Press, 1986): chap. 4. Note that the commitments that need to be supported by self-management will include shared commitments—for example, our shared commitment to a certain project.

desires and/or what they are for (and do this by way of this very policy).[52] Such policies will help shape what has subjective normative authority for the agent.[53]

This means that a basic pressure for conative hierarchy derives from what is for human agents a pervasive practical problem of self-management. In particular, reflective, self-governing agents will have a wide range of first-order motivating attitudes that will need to be managed in the pursuit of basic commitments. This practical problem exerts pressure on those commitments to be higher-order. And once we recognize this point, we can go on to see such higher-order commitments as potential elements in a Frankfurtian project of self-constitution. If, in contrast, we were to try to model reflectiveness, internality, and self-government without appeal to conative hierarchy, we would be in danger of failing to take due account of this pervasive practical problem.

The idea is not that individual agents reflectively decide to introduce conative hierarchy into their psychic economies in response to the need for self-management.[54] Rather, we can agree with Frankfurt that human agents are in fact typically reflective about their motivation in ways that involve conative hierarchy. Our question is: What can we say to ourselves to make further sense to ourselves of this feature of our psychic lives? This question is part of what T. M. Scanlon calls our "enterprise . . . of self-understanding."[55] And the claim is that we can appeal here to the role of higher-order reflection and conative hierarchy as part of a reasonable response to fundamental,

---

52. See my "Autonomy and Hierarchy." Note that I do not claim that these are the only policies that may be relevant here. For example, as Alfred Mele has noted, the agent may also have a policy in favor of simply trying to remove a certain desire.

53. In including in some such policies a direct concern with X, as well as with associated desires and what they are for, I am extending (as anticipated earlier) what it is that is accorded subjective normative authority.

54. Though we, as theorists, can reason in this way, as part of what Paul Grice called "creature construction." See Grice's "Method in Philosophical Psychology (from the Banal to the Bizarre)" (Presidential Address), in *Proceedings and Addresses of the American Philosophical Association* (1974–75): 23–53. I pursue such a methodology in "Valuing and the Will" and in "Autonomy and Hierarchy." In "Autonomy and Hierarchy," I see self-governing policies as a solution to a pair of pervasive human problems: the need for self-management and the need to respond to underdetermination by value judgment.

55. T. M. Scanlon, "Self-Anchored Morality," in J. B. Schneewind, ed., *Reasons, Ethics, and Society: Themes from Kurt Baier with His Responses* (Chicago: Open Court, 1996): 198. As I see it, one use

pervasive, and (following Cooper's Aristotle) permanent human needs for self-management in the effective pursuit of basic commitments.

This is not to argue that self-governance *must* involve conative hierarchy. It is, rather, to argue that there is a pervasive and permanent practical problem that human agents face and with respect to which conative hierarchy is a reasonable and common human response, at least for agents with relevant self-knowledge. The claim is, further, that when the hierarchical response to this pervasive and permanent practical problem takes an appropriate form— one we have tried to characterize—we arrive at basic elements of a central case of self-governance. Because the cited form of hierarchy essentially involves plan-type attitudes—in particular, self-governing policies—we arrive, as promised, at a model of core elements of human autonomy that involves in basic ways structures of planning agency. And because the planning theory is, as I have said, a modest theory of the will, this is a model of central roles of the will in autonomy.[56]

8. SOME FINAL QUALIFICATIONS

In discussing Watsonian "perverse" cases, I indicated that self-governance precludes certain kinds of severe incoherence between evaluative judgment and basic commitments. This does not entail that self-governance requires evaluative judgment; nor does it entail that self-governance requires that the agent who does make such evaluative judgments gets them right. Indeed, I think that it is not essential to the basic commitments I have emphasized—those that take the form of self-governing policies and have agential authority—that they derive from intersubjectively accountable value judgments. But it still might be urged that there is a further demand

of Gricean creature construction is to help us achieve such self-understanding. Note that in locating this question about conative hierarchy within the enterprise of self-understanding, I do not suppose that the basic concern to which our answer to this question appeals must be a concern with self-understanding. Indeed, the relevant concern to which my answer appeals is a concern with the effective pursuit of basic commitments. For a view that sees this basic concern as, in contrast, a concern with self-understanding, see J. David Velleman, "Introduction," *The Possibility of Practical Reason*, 1–31.

56. These roles are multiple and interconnected: they include the organization of thought and action over time, related forms of agential authority, and roles in shaping what has subjective normative authority. This contrasts with a thin conception of the will as primarily a matter of deciding what to do in present circumstances.

specifically on autonomy, that relevant self-governing policies be to some extent grounded in evaluative judgment—though they may also be underdetermined by, and go beyond, such judgments. And it might also be urged that there is a further demand specifically on autonomy, that the agent at least have the ability to arrive at evaluative judgments that get matters right.[57] These are not, however, issues I will try to adjudicate here. For our present purposes, it suffices to note that whatever we say on these further proposals is compatible with, and could be added to, the proposed model of core elements of autonomy.

Finally, there are traditional and perplexing issues about the compatibility of autonomy and causal determination. The features of agency I have highlighted here as core elements seem to me to be ones that could be present in a deterministic world, which is not to deny that certain forms of causal determination (for example, as the argument frequently goes, certain forms of manipulation) can undermine self-governance. Nevertheless, whether there is a persuasive reason for insisting that autonomy preclude any kind of causal determination of action (because, as the argument might go, causal determination of action is incompatible with self-determination of action) is a matter of great controversy, one that I also will not address here.[58]

57. See, e.g., Susan Wolf, *Freedom within Reason* (Oxford: Oxford University Press, 1990); Nozick, *Philosophical Explanations*, 317–32; and Gideon Yaffe, "Free Will and Agency at Its Best," *Philosophical Perspectives* 14 (2000): 203–29. We need to be careful, though, to remember that our concern here is with autonomy and not directly with moral accountability. [For a related caveat, see Gary Watson, "Two Faces of Responsibility," *Philosophical Topics* 24 (1996): 240–41.]

58. Though see my "Nozick on Free Will."

Chapter 11

THREE THEORIES OF SELF-GOVERNANCE

I want to revisit the important exchange between Harry Frankfurt and Gary Watson concerning the psychological structures involved in significant forms of free agency. In his 1971 paper, Frankfurt proposed that we can best model important aspects of human freedom—in particular, what he called acting of one's own free will—by appeal to hierarchies of desires: desires about desires.[1] Watson's reply aimed to establish that neither desire nor hierarchy is basic for this purpose. Rather, free action is action that is motivated in ways that are responsive to value judgment.[2]

Frankfurt's focus in his essay was on what it is for one's will to be free, and for one to act of one's own free will; Watson's focus was on free agency. Both turned more explicitly to autonomy and self-government in later work. Here I will treat the initial debate about desire, hierarchy, and value judgment as part of the debate about the psychological structures and forms of functioning that are central to human self-governance.[3] And

1. Harry Frankfurt, "Freedom of the Will and the Concept of a Person," in his *The Importance of What We Care About* (Cambridge: Cambridge University Press, 1988), pp. 11–25.
2. Gary Watson, "Free Agency," *Journal of Philosophy* 72 (1975): 205–20.
3. The debates are, then, about a strong form of agency, self-governance, and not about less demanding forms of agency, as in, say, cases of acting but not of one's own free will. A complication is that I would want to leave open the possibility of multiple forms of self-governance. See my "Autonomy and Hierarchy," *Social Philosophy & Policy* 20 (2003): 156–76, at 157 and note 5 [this volume, essay 8, p. 163 and n.5]; and my "Planning Agency, Autonomous Agency," in James Stacey Taylor, ed., *Personal Autonomy: New Essays on Personal Autonomy and Its Role in Contemporary Moral Philosophy* (New York: Cambridge University Press, 2005), 33–57, at 35–36 [this volume, essay 10, pp. 198–99].

I will take the liberty of appealing also to later work of both Frankfurt and Watson in understanding this debate. In the end, I will be led to consider a third theory, one with complex relations to the views both of Frankfurt and of Watson.

This third theory is one I sketched in a recent essay, an essay that was the beneficiary of Watson's characteristically insightful comments.[4] One of my aims here is to put myself in a position to answer a probing question that Watson raised toward the end of those comments, a question about the relation between value judgment and the agent's practical standpoint.

But first things first. So let's begin with Frankfurt.

I.

We can present the view in Frankfurt's original paper along roughly the following lines: A person acts of her own free will just when (1) she acts on the basis of a desire so to act, (2) this desire (which is, in Frankfurt's technical sense, the agent's "will") motivates in part because she desires that this desire be her will, and (3) this latter, second-order desire (which is, in Frankfurt's terminology, a "second-order volition") is itself either uncontested by higher-order volitions or, if contested, the top element of the actual hierarchy of such volitions supports this second-order volition.[5]

Several observations are in order. First, Frankfurt's talk of "will" and "volition" is talk of certain kinds of desires, not of a kind of volitional attitude that contrasts with desire. Second, it follows from all this that if at the highest level of actual hierarchy there remains conflict, then there is not sufficient volitional unity for acting of one's own free will. Third, what matters is the actual desiderative hierarchy. This will be limited in extent even though there is always a logical (and frequently, though not always, a psychological) possibility of stepping back from that so-far-highest-order

4. See my "Planning Agency, Autonomous Agency," and Gary Watson, "Hierarchy and Agential Authority: Comments on Michael Bratman's 'Planning Agency, Autonomous Agency,'" Pacific APA 2004. Watson's comments (together with a reprint of my essay) appear in John Fischer, ed., *Free Will: Critical Concepts in Philosophy* volume IV (New York: Routledge, 2005), 90–97. My thanks to Watson for these extremely helpful and insightful comments, though if he had known they would trigger yet another paper defending the third theory he might have thought better of it or, anyway, valued it differently.

5. Concerning (3) see "Freedom of the Will and the Concept of a Person," at 21.

volition and asking whether one wants that to be determining. Fourth, there is no assumption that the very same higher-order attitude is involved in all cases of acting of one's own free will.[6] The idea is only that all cases of acting of one's own free will involve some highest-order volitional attitude. And, fifth, I think it is reasonable to see Frankfurt's later developments of his views about autonomy and self-government as involving, as a proper part, some such hierarchical model—though, as we will see, the role accorded to hierarchy does change somewhat.

Watson, in his 1975 paper, argues both that this hierarchical model has deep problems and that an alternative model—one that appeals instead to responsiveness to value judgment—gets us closer to what is central to free agency. We can see Watson as making three basic points in this essay.

The first point concerns the apparent claim of the hierarchical theory that such an uncontested highest-order volition constitutes (what Frankfurt later comes to describe as) where the *agent* himself stands.[7] The claim is that when a relevant, uncontested highest-order volition favors a certain first-order motivation, that highest-order volition determines what is the agent's *own* will; and when it plays an appropriate role in action, the agent acts of her *own* free will. In this sense, as I will say, it has *agential authority*.[8] Or so the hierarchical model seems to claim. Watson argues, however, that the hierarchical model does not have the right to make this claim. Speaking in particular of a case in which the relevant highest-order volition is second-order, Watson writes:

> Since second-order volitions are themselves simply desires, to add them to the context of conflict is just to increase the number of contenders; it is not to give a special place to any of those in contention.[9]

6. For a view that seeks to identify a specific element involved in all cases of self-governed agency, see J. David Velleman's appeal to the "sub-agential aim of knowing what [one is] doing" in his "Introduction" in his *The Possibility of Practical Reason* (New York: Oxford University Press, 2000), at 22. And see also Velleman, "What Happens When Someone Acts?" in his *The Possibility of Practical Reason,* at 139.

7. Harry Frankfurt, "Identification and Wholeheartedness," in his *The Importance of What We Care About,* at 166.

8. See Harry Frankfurt, "The Faintest Passion," in his *Necessity, Volition, and Love* (Cambridge: Cambridge University Press, 1999), at 105; and Michael E. Bratman, "Two Problems about Human Agency," *Proceedings of the Aristotelian Society* 101 (2001): 309–26, [this volume, essay 5].

9. Gary Watson, "Free Agency," at p. 218.

An uncontested highest-order desire is, after all, itself another desire, another wiggle in the psychic stew. We have as yet no explanation of why that desire—in contrast with other desires in the stew—has authority to speak for the agent, to constitute, in the metaphysics of agency, where the agent stands. Nor can we solve this problem by appeal to a yet higher-order desire in its favor; that way lies regress. So we are so far without an account of agential authority. This is Watson's first point.

Watson's second point concerns what he sees as the model of deliberation that is implicit in Frankfurt's appeal to hierarchy. Watson supposes that Frankfurt's view is that in deliberation we normally focus not directly on what to do, but on which desire is to be our will. But deliberation, according to Watson, is, rather, normally focused directly on what to do; it need not—though it may—involve higher-order reflection on one's motivation. As Watson says:

> [Agents] do not (or need not usually) ask themselves which of their desires they want to be effective in action; they ask themselves which course of action is most worth pursuing. The initial practical question is about courses of action and not about themselves.[10]

So we have two criticisms of the hierarchical model: the appeal to hierarchies of desire both fails to explain why certain attitudes have agential authority and involves a false view of deliberation. Watson's third point is that we do better in modeling free agency by appealing not primarily to desire and hierarchy but, rather, to valuing. And I think it is fair to say that in this essay, though there are some suggestions to the contrary, Watson understands valuing as, at bottom, judging valuable. Such judgments constitute an "evaluational system" that "may be said to constitute one's standpoint."[11] According to Watson in this 1975 essay, it is this evaluational system—in contrast with a system of desires of various orders—that has (as I have put it) agential authority, that structures deliberation, and that is central to free agency (and so to self-government).

10. "Free Agency," p. 219.
11. "Free Agency," p. 216.

Let me say something about evaluative judgment. Watson indicates in a 2003 essay that he is inclined toward some sort of "cognitivism" about such judgments: they are full-blown beliefs about reasons and the good, beliefs that are susceptible of truth and of falsity.[12] Watson also says, however, that "nothing crucial" in his essay depends on this; and that seems to me an appropriate stance concerning this intersection between the philosophy of action and metaethics. In particular, it is plausible to suppose that the issues here about the role of evaluative judgment in important forms of human agency can be understood in a way that is neutral with respect to debates in metaethics between such cogntivism and forms of expressivism in the spirit of "quasi-realism."[13] In the present context of theorizing about human agency, what we need from a metaethics is the ability to talk coherently about evaluative judgment and to note those features of such judgments that matter to self-government. And this is a standard of adequacy to which both cognitivist and quasi-realist expressivist views should aspire. So for present purposes I will bracket these difficult issues in metaethics.

Returning to Watson's 1975 discussion, we can say that its three main points are that the hierarchical model lacks an account of agential authority, that it presupposes a false view of deliberation, and that it should be replaced by an alternative model that highlights an evaluational system constituted by relevant evaluative judgments. We can call this trio of points *Watson's initial challenge*.

In a later paper, however, Watson qualifies the third element of this initial challenge. While he continues to hold that "valuing cannot be reduced to desiring (at any level)," he now thinks that his appeal to value judgment

> is altogether too rationalistic. For one thing, it conflates valuing with judging good. Notoriously, judging good has no invariable

---

12. Gary Watson, "The Work of the Will," in Sarah Stroud and Christine Tappolet, *Weakness of Will and Practical Irrationality* (Oxford: Clarendon Press, 2003), 172–200, at 176.

13. See Simon Blackburn, *Essays in Quasi-Realism* (New York: Oxford University Press, 1993) and *Ruling Passions* (Oxford: Oxford University Press, 1998); and Allan Gibbard, *Wise Choices, Apt Feelings* (Cambridge: Harvard University Press, 1990) and *Thinking How to Live* (Cambridge: Harvard University Press, 2003).

connection with motivation. . . . One can in an important sense fail to value what one judges valuable.[14]

This suggests that we should see the agent's standpoint as constituted not primarily by the agent's judgments of value but, rather, by what that agent *values*. We would then need to know what it is to value something and how that is related to judging good. But Watson thinks such a revision would still run into a problem:

> But even if this conflation [of valuing with judging good] is rectified by construing valuing as caring about something because (in as much as) it is deemed to be valuable, what one values in a particular case may not be sanctioned by a more general evaluational standpoint that one would be prepared to accept. When it comes right down to it, I might fully "embrace" a course of action I do not judge best. . . .
>   Call such cases, if you like, perverse cases. . . . There is no estrangement here. One's will is fully behind what one does.[15]

I agree with Watson that we need a notion of valuing that is not the same as that of judging good, of value judgment. This poses a hard problem of explaining what valuing is, a problem that Watson briefly addresses in his remark about caring. We should note, though, an important ambiguity in this remark. The parenthetical phrase indicates that one values something just to the extent that one judges it valuable. But simply saying—as is said outside the parenthesis—that to value something is to care about it "because" one judges it valuable does not yet entail that the extent to which one values it matches the degree to which one judges it to be valuable. On either reading, value judgment remains central to a model of self-governance that gives a basic role to valuing. But a reading that drops the parenthetical addition—in contrast with a reading that takes into account that addition—allows for the possibility of

14. Gary Watson, "Free Action and Free Will," *Mind* 96 (1987): 145–72, at 150.
15. "Free Action and Free Will," 150.

valuing something to an extent that diverges from the degree to which one judges it valuable. I will return to this ambiguity below.

Putting this ambiguity aside for now, what exactly is Watson's remaining worry? One worry in this passage is that there can be a breakdown between one's *general* system of valuings and the specific option one most values in a *particular* case. A second worry in this passage is that what one values in a particular case might diverge from one's evaluative *judgment* about the best.[16] In each case, according to Watson, it can nevertheless be true that "one's will is fully behind what one does." There may be "no estrangement" even though the particular valuing is at odds either with one's general system of valuings or one's value judgments or both. And this leads Watson to worry that we will need to characterize such cases by appeal to

> a rather elusive notion of identification and thereby an elusive no-tion of self-determination. The picture of identification as some kind of brute self-assertion seems totally unsatisfactory, but I have no idea what an illuminating account might be.[17]

Did Watson intend these worries about "brute self-assertion" to be a retraction of the third element of his challenge—of, that is, the proposed alternative model in which valuing that is closely tied to value judgment plays a central role? Or did he intend this as, rather, only a statement of an as-yet unsolved challenge to his proposed alternative? I am inclined toward the latter reading, and, in any case, interpreting Watson in this way helps clarify the structure of the larger debate. So that is what I will do. This allows us to express Watson's challenge to the hierarchical model as follows: First, it does not provide, in its metaphysics of agency, an account of agential authority. Second, it presupposes a false view of de-liberation. And third, we do better to turn to a model that gives pride of

---

16. In my earlier discussions of these remarks of Watson, I had focused only on cases of incoherence between value judgment and valuing or decision. See in particular my "A Desire of One's Own," *Journal of Philosophy* 100 (2003): 221–42, at 227 [this volume, essay 7, p. 144]. Here let me add that incoherence within one's valuings seems a more direct threat to the organization of practical thinking that is central to autonomy.

17. 150–51.

place to valuing rather than desiderative hierarchy. In the absence of incoherence, valuing involves, but is not the same as, value judgment. Whether one values things just to the extent one judges them valuable remains an open question; and there also remain puzzles about how to understand "perverse" cases. The first two elements survive from Watson's initial challenge; the third element is a qualified version of the initial positive proposal but still a version that gives pride of place to value judgment by way of its normal role in valuing and by way of the role of valuing in self-government.

2.

What should we say about Watson's challenge? Let's begin with the appeal to the structure of deliberation. Frankfurt's theory highlights higher-order reflection on first-order motivational attitudes. This is, according to Frankfurt, a distinguishing feature of persons.[18] But such higher-order reflection need not be the same thing as ordinary deliberation. A hierarchical theory in the spirit of Frankfurt's could agree that ordinary deliberation is normally first-order deliberation about what to do. It could then say that higher-order reflection on first-order motivating attitudes helps, as it were, to set the stage for such ordinary deliberation: it helps provide the framework within which that deliberation takes place. In ordinary deliberation, "the initial practical question is about courses of action," just as Watson maintains. But, for persons, the psychological background of the deliberation is normally shaped by higher-order structures that are themselves the issue of a characteristic form of reflection.

What about the objection that the hierarchical theory does not have an account of agential authority? This was an insightful objection to Frankfurt's initial essay; and I think that something like this objection helps lead Frankfurt to his later view that satisfaction and whole-heartedness are fundamental to the metaphysics of agential authority. I'll turn to that view below. Here I want to raise a question that was once posed by David Velleman: how is Watson's own proposal supposed to

18. "Freedom of the Will and the Concept of a Person," at 12.

solve this problem? What is it about Watsonian valuings that explains their agential authority?[19] Watson objects that Frankfurt has not explained why certain higher-order volitions—that is, certain higher-order desires—"can have, among all of a person's 'desires,' the special property of being peculiarly his 'own'."[20] But we can also ask why Watsonian valuings have "the special property of being peculiarly [one's] 'own.'" Why, according to Watson, do valuings speak for the agent?

Watson's answer seems to be suggested in his remarks, in his 1975 essay, about the limits on the possibilities of dissociation from one's evaluative system:

> The important feature of one's evaluational system is that one cannot coherently dissociate oneself from it *in its entirety.* . . . One can dissociate oneself from one set of ends and principles only from the standpoint of another such set that one does not disclaim. In short, one cannot dissociate oneself from all normative judgments without forfeiting all standpoints and therewith one's identity as an agent.[21]

But this does not answer our question. After all, a hierarchical theorist could make an analogous remark: one can, he might say, only dissociate oneself from a given hierarchy of desires from the standpoint of some other, higher-order desires. So the question remains: why does the evaluational system speak for the agent in a way in which such a hierarchy of desires would not?

Well, a central role of value judgment is to be responsive to—to track—the good.[22] Valuing is tied more or less tightly to evaluative judgment, and so to this good-tracking role. And it seems likely that it is this aspect of valuing that lies behind Watson's apparent assumption that valuings—in contrast with hierarchies of desire—do speak for the agent.

---

19. See J. David Velleman, "What Happens When Someone Acts?" in his *The Possibility of Practical Reason,* at 134.

20. "Free Agency," 218–19.

21. "Free Agency," 216. Thanks to Watson for reminding me of this passage and its potential relevance to the present discussion.

22. If we wanted to say this within an expressivist metaethics, we would need an expressivist story about good-tracking role. But I take it that this is something that quasi-realists would

So perhaps the view is that valuings have agential authority—they have authority to establish the *agent's* standpoint—because they are, or essentially involve, attitudes whose central function or role is that of *tracking the good*. Call this the *Platonic account of agential authority*.

While I am not sure that this is Watson's account of the agential authority of valuings, this Platonic account does seem to fit a lot of what he says.[23] So I will proceed with the tentative conjecture that this is, broadly speaking, how Watson would understand the agential authority of valuings.

It is clear that Frankfurt would balk at this Platonic approach. You can see this by thinking about what he later went on to say about these matters. In later work Frankfurt proposed that what is central to identification—and so to what I am calling agential authority—is the agent's "satisfaction" with relevant higher-order conative attitudes. Satisfaction with a given higher-order attitude is a structural feature of the psychic system within which that attitude is embedded. You are satisfied with that attitude just when there is no relevant "tendency or inclination to alter" it.[24] Forms of reflection issue in higher-order attitudes, but the agential authority of those attitudes is not ensured by their being higher-order. Agential authority requires satisfaction.

On this later view, does hierarchy have any role to play as a ground of agential authority? Frankfurt remarks that

> It is possible, of course, for someone to be satisfied with his first-order desires without in any way considering whether to endorse them. In that case, he is identified with those first-order desires. But insofar as his desires are utterly unreflective, he is to that extent not genuinely a person at all. He is merely a wanton.[25]

---

want to provide. One strategy might be to appeal to claims of the form "Subject tends to judge that X is good only when X is good." Another strategy might be to appeal to a norm: judge that X is good only when X is good. But these are matters we can put to one side here.

23. This includes, as we will see, Watson's 2004 comments on my APA paper. And see also Watson's endorsement of a "conception of freedom as the capacity to respond to reasons" in his "Introduction" to Gary Watson, ed., *Free Will* (second edition) (Oxford: Oxford University Press, 2003), at 18.

24. Harry Frankfurt, "The Faintest Passion," in his *Necessity, Volition, and Love*, 104.

25. "The Faintest Passion," at 105–6. I discuss this passage also in my "Identification, Decision, and Treating as a Reason," in my *Faces of Intention: Selected Essays on Intention and Agency* (Cambridge: Cambridge University Press, 1999), 185–206, at 204.

I understand this as follows: agential authority is primarily a matter of satisfaction. But the conative attitudes whose agential authority is of central interest in a theory of persons (and, I take it, self-government) will be reflective in ways that (according to Frankfurt) involve hierarchy.

Note how this approach aims to solve the problem of agential authority by articulating certain forms of psychological organization and functioning, specified in a way that does not itself presuppose assumptions about what has such authority.[26] Agential authority is a matter of playing a certain role in the psychic economy. We can call this background idea the *psychological account of agential authority*. Frankfurt's version of such a psychological account appeals to a kind of settledness and stability within the psychic economy. But we could stay within the broad outlines of the psychological account while still modifying this appeal to satisfaction.

Indeed, we can see the Platonic approach as a special case of the psychological approach, one that says that the role or functioning relevant to agential authority is, in particular, tracking the good. But the important point is that within the psychological approach, it is an open question just what forms of functioning are central: the approach leaves open the possibility of a significant alternative to the Platonic approach. And Frankfurt's appeal to satisfaction is one such non-Platonic alternative.

Suppose that within the psychological approach we identify a role, R, playing, which is the ground of agential authority. And suppose R does not essentially involve tracking the good: this is a non-Platonic version of the psychological approach. It still might turn out that certain kinds of evaluative judgments play role R in our psychic economy and thereby have a claim to agential authority. And it may continue to be true that a role of these judgments is to track the good. Nevertheless, it is R, and not this good-tracking role, that is, according to this non-Platonic psychological approach, the basis of the agential authority of these judgments.

Let us take stock so far. The objection from the structure of deliberation can, I think, be met by a suitably qualified hierarchical theory. The concerns about agential authority are concerns for both theories, and each has available a strategy of response—in the one case (or so I conjecture),

26. See my "Two Problems about Human Agency," at 315 [this volume, p. 95].

a Platonic account, in the other case, a non-Platonic psychological account. This takes us to the third element of Watson's challenge, his positive proposal (as qualified). What should we say about this proposal?

3.

An initial point is that our model of self-government will need to appeal to commitments that are significantly underdetermined by the agent's judgments of value. Here is what I said about this in the essay to which I have alluded:

> Faced with difficult issues about what to give weight or significance to in one's life, one is frequently faced with multiple, conflicting goods: turning the other cheek is a good, but so is an apt reactive response to wrongful treatment; resisting the use of violence by the military is good, but so is loyalty to one's country; human sexuality is a good, but so are certain religious lives of abstinence. In many such cases the agent's standpoint involves forms of commitment— to draft resistance, say—that have agential authority but go beyond his prior evaluative judgment. This may be because the agent thinks that, though he needs to settle on a coherent stance, the conflicting goods are more or less equal. Or perhaps he thinks he simply does not know which is more important. . . . Or perhaps he thinks that the relevant goods are in an important way incommensurable.[27]

In many such cases self-government involves—indeed, needs to involve— commitments to significance or weight in deliberation that in their specificity go beyond, though they are not incoherent with, such underdetermining judgments of value. In the background here is the idea that judgments of value are subject to pressures of inter-subjectivity in a way in which commitments to weights, in the face of under-determination by such value judgments, need not be.[28] The agent arrives, for example, at a commitment to eschewing sexuality in his life as part of a religious ideal; but he does

---

27. "Planning Agency, Autonomous Agency," at 40, [this volume, p. 205].
28. See "A Desire of One's Own," 235, [this volume, p. 153].

not suppose that there would be intersubjective agreement on this, nor does he commend this way of life to all reasonable agents. Accordingly, he does not see his commitment to abstinence as a judgment that this is the best way to live, a judgment that would be subject to characteristic intersubjective pressures. But this does not mean that he is not personally committed to this ideal in a way that can enter substantially into his self-governance.

Can Watson's model accommodate this point? If so, how? The answer depends in part on the ambiguity noted earlier. If, on the one hand, one values something just to the extent one judges it valuable, then in such cases of conflicting goods one's commitment to giving more weight to one of those goods cannot be solely a matter of valuing. So if Watson's model is to provide for such cases, it will need to acknowledge that self-government can be shaped both by valuing and by such further commitments concerning weights and significance. If, on the other hand, one can value something in a way that in its specificity goes beyond the extent to which one judges it valuable, though valuing is always to some extent grounded in some judgment of value, then Watson's model can provide for such cases while still seeing valuing as the central attitude in self-government. It can do this by seeing valuing as itself potentially involving determinations that go beyond value judgment.

That Watson would want to provide for such cases is to some extent suggested in a 2003 paper. Here he considers

> circumstances of normative uncertainty or indeterminacy. In these contexts, the question "What shall I do?" is clearly different from the question "What should I do?" The issue here is not "Shall I comply with my judgment?" but "What shall I do in view of the fact that the reasons, all things considered, are not decisive?" Here there is a need for volitional commitment.[29]

Watson's concern here is with underdetermination of a specific decision by "reasons, all things considered." This is not the same as the underdetermination of significance or weight in deliberation by value judgment. But if

---

29. "The Work of the Will," 181–82. And in "Hierarchy and Agential Authority: Comments on Michael Bratman's 'Planning Agency, Autonomous Agency,'" Watson remarks, in a similar vein, that "often one must decide among options that are left open by evaluative judgment" (92).

we think—as do I—that such underdetermination of significance or weight also is a real phenomenon, to be provided for within a model of self-governance, we can perhaps read Watson as suggesting that we provide for it by allowing here as well a kind of "volitional commitment."

These commitments are in the domain of the will, broadly speaking. They are commitments to weights or significance in deliberation, commitments that are not simply matters of evaluative judgment, though they are also not merely matters of desire. Such commitments can, and sometimes need to, go beyond evaluative judgment in their specificity, without being incoherent with evaluative judgment. And, given the role of these commitments in structuring practical thinking with normative content, it will be natural to see them as a form of valuing.

I want to turn now to a related but different argument for the idea that our model of self-governance needs to appeal to a form of valuing that is different from intersubjectively accountable value judgment. The argument I have in mind begins with Joshua Cohen's appeal, in his interpretation of work of John Rawls, to the "idea of reasonable pluralism." Here is how Cohen describes this idea:

> The idea of reasonable pluralism is that there are distinct understandings of value, each of which is fully reasonable. An understanding of value is fully reasonable just in case its adherents are stably disposed to affirm it as they acquire new information and subject it to critical reflection. The contention that there are a plurality of such understandings is suggested by the absence of convergence in reflection on issues of value, which leaves disagreements, for example, about the value of choice, welfare, and self-actualization; about the value of contemplative and practical lives; about the value of devotions to friends and lovers as distinct from more diffuse concerns about abstract others; and about the values of poetic expression and political engagement.[30]

30. Joshua Cohen, "Moral Pluralism and Political Consensus," in David Copp, Jean Hampton, and John E. Roemer, eds., *The Idea of Democracy* (Cambridge: Cambridge University Press, 1993), 270–91, at 281–82. And see John Rawls, "The Domain of the Political and Overlapping Consensus," in *The Idea of Democracy*, 245–69. In discussing Cohen's remarks directly I hope to bypass the question of whether he has accurately interpreted Rawls. For some remarks of

236 PLANNING AND SELF-GOVERNANCE

According to Cohen, in acknowledging—as we should—such reasonable pluralism, "we are acknowledging the scope of practical reason."[31]

The second step in the argument concerns the nature of judgment and belief. This is the idea that it is distinctive of judgment or belief—in contrast with, for example, only taking something as given for the purposes of some argument or endeavor—that in judging or believing that p one is thereby committed to a convergence of rational inquirers on p. John Skorupski expresses this idea in defending what he calls "the *convergence thesis*":

> When I judge that p, I enter a commitment that inquirers who scrutinized the relevant evidence and argument available to them carefully enough would agree that p—unless I could fault their rationality or their evidence.[32]

The purported commitment to convergence is not, on Skorupski's view, a matter of the *content*, p; it is, rather, a matter of the nature of the *attitude* of, as he says, "full belief, judgment."[33]

Now, the argument I have in mind puts Cohen's idea of reasonable pluralism together with Skorupski's convergence thesis. This is, I grant, a bit delicate. Skorupski appeals to rationality, not reasonableness. And the convergence Skorupski is concerned with is convergence in an ideal setting: failure of convergence in the real and messy world does not yet show that there would not be convergence in this ideal setting. Nevertheless, the impact of conjoining these two ideas seems clearly to be in the direction of a kind of humility in arriving at evaluative judgment.[34] If

Rawls that probably point away from this interpretation, see John Rawls, *Political Liberalism* (New York: Columbia University Press, 1993), at 62–63. (Thanks to Blain Neufeld for help in thinking about these aspects of Rawls's views.)

31. "Moral Pluralism and Political Consensus," at 272.

32. John Skorupski, "Value Pluralism," in his *Ethical Explorations* (Oxford: Oxford University Press, 1999), 65–81, at 73.

33. John Skorupski "Reasons and Reason," in his *Ethical Explorations*, 26–48, at 35; and "Value Pluralism," at 77. In contrast, on Michael Smith's view, the *content* of evaluative judgment is about rational convergence. See his *The Moral Problem* (Oxford: Blackwell, 1994), chap. 5. I reflect on the relation of such a Smith-type view about the content of value judgment to the present distinction between value judgment and commitments to weights in my "A Desire of One's Own," *Journal of Philosophy* 100 (2003): 221–42, at 233–36, [this volume, pp. 151–54].

34. My talk here of humility draws from Andrea Westlund's remarks about humility in her "Selflessness and Responsibility for Self: Is Deference Compatible with Autonomy?" *Philosophical*

evaluative judgments involve the commitment cited in the convergence thesis, if Cohen is right about reasonable pluralism, and if one is aware of these things, then one will recognize pressure against treating at least some of one's attitudes concerning weights and significance as value judgments, strictly speaking. This is because one will be attuned to the real possibility that relevant convergence is not to be expected.

The convergence thesis might, however, be too strong. Perhaps one can sensibly hold onto an evaluative judgment even while recognizing, as Cohen puts it, borrowing from Quine, "irresoluble rivalry." Again borrowing from Quine, Cohen calls this "the *sectarian* route of affirming one's own view, that is, believing it as a matter of faith." Taking the sectarian route, one believes "even with full awareness of the fact of reflective divergence."[35]

Even if we grant the possibility of such sectarianism in the realm of evaluative judgment, we might still invoke a tie to intersubjective convergence by seeing such judgments as involving a commitment to *commend* to all. In any case, even if sectarian value judgment is a real possibility, I do nevertheless think *non*sectarianism in this domain would remain a possible and attractive (though in some ways quite demanding) ideal, especially in the domain of judgments of comparative value. It would be an ideal of a kind of humility in judgment. So I think we at least need a philosophical psychology that can make sense of the basic commitments of a humble, nonsectarian evaluator to weights and other kinds of significance, even in the face of "full awareness of the fact of reflective divergence," and so even in the absence of corresponding evaluative judgment. We need this even if it turns out that not all evaluators are nonsectarian. And if we follow Cohen on reasonable pluralism and the limits of practical reason, we will

---

Review 112 (2003): 483–524, at 508. Westlund, however, focuses on "a kind of *humility* about the practical judgments one makes, which takes the form of a standing disposition to be engaged by critical challenges to the commitments that underlie those judgments." The humility of interest to me here is, rather, one that limits the judgments one is willing to make. Humility, for Westlund, is a stance with respect to judgments made; humility for me is a stance of an agent who refrains from making a judgment in the face of (to use Cohen's phrase) "full awareness of the fact of reflective divergence."

35. These quotes are from Cohen, "Moral Pluralism and Political Consensus," at 282. Cohen here draws on W. V. O. Quine, *Pursuit of Truth* (Cambridge: Harvard University Press, 1990), 98–101. The real possibility of sensible sectarian evaluative judgment would also pose a challenge for Smith's account of evaluative content.

need to appeal to a wide range of commitments, on the part of a non-sectarian evaluator, to weights and forms of significance, commitments that go beyond value judgment.

The next point is that these commitments in a nonsectarian evaluator are most naturally described as themselves a form of valuing, rather than a volitional add-on to valuing. After all, these commitments are likely to constitute broad stretches of the agent's attitudes concerning weight and significance in deliberation. So I think we should say that these commitments are a form of valuing that is in the domain of the will, broadly speaking. To value in this sense is to be committed to relevant weights or other forms of significance in deliberation.[36] And these commitments to weights need not conform to the intersubjective pressures articulated in the convergence thesis.

So the situation so far is as follows. Watson's objection from deliberative structure can be met by a suitably qualified hierarchical theory. Both hierarchical theories and a Watsonian theory need to devise strategies for understanding agential authority; and here there is an important distinction between a Platonic account and a non-Platonic psychological account. Finally, cases of underdetermination by value judgment, taken together with issues about reasonable pluralism and convergence, point toward the need, in a model of self-government, for commitments to significance or weight that are broadly in the domain of the will. And these commitments are candidates for an important form of valuing.

What is the relation between these last observations about valuing and the two theories we have been considering? It seems to me that Watson could agree with much of what has been said so far about valuing, though I do not know whether he does. Later, though, we will articulate an approach to the agential authority of such valuing that may not be available to Watson.

What about the hierarchical model? Frankfurt's versions of the hierarchical model have focused on attitudes concerning what is to motivate,

---

36. So we should include in (again to use Cohen's phrase) "understandings of value" both value judgments and valuings in the sense specified. The distinction between these two kinds of "understandings" is central to a moral psychology that is adequate for modeling self-governing agents in a world of reasonable pluralism.

not attitudes concerning what is to have weight or significance in deliberation. Nevertheless, it may be that the kind of commitments to weight
or significance that are involved in valuing and are needed for self-
government will also be higher-order volitional attitudes.

I'll return to these complexities below. First I want to describe a theory
that responds to these observations by highlighting intention-like commitments to weights and other forms of significance.

4.

The theory I have in mind is an *intention-based* theory. It agrees with Watson
that a form of valuing is central to self-government. It then goes on to
see this form of valuing as, in a basic case, a kind of intending. In particular,
it sees it as, in a basic case, a kind of *policy*—where policies are intentions
that are appropriately general, and intentions are understood along the
lines of what I have called the *planning theory*.[37] According to the planning
theory, we understand intentions, and intention-like attitudes, largely in
terms of their roles in cross-temporal and social coordination. We pursue
these forms of coordination in large part by way of settling on prior, partial
plans that then shape later practical reasoning and action. Intentions and
policies are (typically, partial) planning structures, structures whose central roles are those of organization and coordination, both individual and
social. And an important kind of valuing is itself a kind of policy, a policy
about weights and other forms of significance in practical reasoning.

According to the intention-based theory, then, a kind of valuing that is
at the heart of self-governance consists in policies (that is, general intentions) of giving weight or other forms of significance to certain considerations in practical reasoning and action. Call these *self-governing policies*. One's
self-governing policies may fairly closely match one's evaluative judgments;
but they may not—though certain kinds of incoherence between valuings
and value judgments will be, other things equal, rationally criticizable.

A self-governing policy need not be subject to the constraints of intersubjectivity to which value judgments are subject and, in particular, need not

37. See my *Intention, Plans, and Practical Reason* (Cambridge, MA: Harvard University Press, 1987;
reissued by CSLI Publications, 1999), and my *Faces of Intention: Selected Essays on Intention and Agency*.

involve a commitment to rational intersubjective convergence. This helps explain how, in cases of underdetermination by value judgment, one's self-governing policies can sensibly go beyond value judgment in articulating forms of commitment that shape one's practical thought and action. It also helps explain why, even if we grant both reasonable pluralism and Skorupski's convergence thesis, we can sometimes wholeheartedly embrace a self-governing policy "even with," as Cohen says, "full awareness of the fact of reflective divergence." Nonsectarianism together with a recognition of reasonable pluralism, while they can baffle certain evaluative judgments, need not stand in the way of wholehearted self-governing policies.[38]

A self-governing policy of giving consideration C weight W provides an associated premise for one's practical reasoning, a premise along the lines of: C has weight W. This premise is not the same as the content of the policy. The content of the policy concerns one's practical thinking. It says: in one's relevant practical reasoning, treat C as having this weight. The policy is a commitment to treating C in this way in relevant practical reasoning. That content of the policy is not itself the premise provided for that practical reasoning. As noted, that premise is: C has this weight. The policy is a commitment to a form of acceptance, within the context of one's relevant practical reasoning, that C has this weight. It is a commitment to a kind of context-relative acceptance of a normative content, a context-relative acceptance that is to be distinguished from belief and judgment.[39] And such a policy-like commitment to treating C in this way can help constitute the agent's practical standpoint.

The intention-based theory highlights policies concerning weights and significance, rather than hierarchies of desire. Nevertheless, as noted earlier, it still may be that the relevant policies are higher-order. If that were so, then there would be a partial agreement between the intention-based theory and a Frankfurtian hierarchical theory. And, indeed, it does seem to me that, at least for normal human agents, there will be strong pressures on self-governing policies to be higher-order policies.

38. My talk here of wholeheartedness is in the spirit of Frankfurt's work. See, e.g., his "Identification and Wholeheartedness."

39. In these remarks about context-relative acceptance I draw on my "Practical Reasoning and Acceptance in a Context," in my *Faces of Intention*. And see L. J. Cohen, "Belief and Acceptance," *Mind* 98 (1989): 367–89, and Skorupski, "Value-Pluralism," 77.

What pressures? I do not think we should appeal here simply to ordinary deliberation. Here I agree with Watson that in ordinary deliberation, we normally ask ourselves a first-order question about what to do.
Conative hierarchy for Frankfurt primarily derives, however, not from a
hierarchical model of ordinary deliberation but, rather, from a picture of
the reflective agent who is concerned with constituting himself to include,
or to eschew, various first-order motivations with which he finds himself.[40] And this picture of reflective self-constitution need not be challenged by Watson's point about ordinary first-order deliberation. However,
I also think that there are important pressures in the direction of conative
hierarchy that do not depend on such a metaphysical concern on the part
of the agent with self-constitution, though they are compatible with—
and support a response to—that concern. In particular, I think we can
identify two pervasive, practical pressures in the direction of conative
hierarchy, pressures that interact with our intention-based theory.

First, we are creatures who are subject to forms of motivation that are
independent of, and can frequently challenge and/or diverge from, our
commitments to weights and other forms of significance. We are, after
all, subject to various bodily appetites, as well as to forms of rage, indignation, anger, humiliation, grief, resentment, jealousy, self-pity, and self-
indulgence. It is an element in our commonsense self-understanding that
such motivating attitudes are a part of our (as it were, nonangelic) psychic
economies and that we need systems of self-management in response to
the various interactions and conflicts between these forms of motivation
and our various commitments to weights and significance.[41] For our self-
governing policies to be effective in guiding our practical thought and
action, they need to be embedded in some such system of self-management.
Since this is something a self-governing agent will know of and support, it
is reasonable to suppose that her self-governing policies will be in part
about such self-management. So her self-governing policies will be in part
higher-order. They will say, roughly: give (refuse) such-and-such weight or

40. See, e.g., "Identification and Wholeheartedness," 171.
41. In using the label "self-management," I am issuing a promissory note that we can
provide an account of the agential authority of self-governing policies. I turn to this matter in
the next section.

significance to X in part by appropriately shaping the role in practical thought and action of relevant motivating attitudes. This pressure on self-governing policies to be, in part, higher-order derives from the pervasive practical problem of self-management.[42]

A second practical pressure in the direction of hierarchy derives from the basic cross-temporal organizing roles of intentions, plans, and policies.[43] In particular, self-governing policies—like intentions generally—play central roles in the cross-temporal coordination of thought and action. Since this is something a self-governing agent will know of and support, it is reasonable to suppose that her self-governing policies will be in part about such cross-temporal organization of her practical thinking. Her self-governing policy in favor of giving C weight W will be in part in support of practical thinking over time in accordance with and/or supportive of giving C weight W. Since much of this practical thinking will involve relevant self-governing policies, including this one, her policy will concern in part the roles of relevant self-governing policies, including this very policy. So it will be in part a higher-order policy about her self-governing policies, including itself.

Self-governing policies are embedded in a psychic economy that needs to address issues of self-management and that has as a central role the support of basic forms of cross-temporal organization of thought and action. Given that a self-governing agent will both know of and support these basic features of her psychology, we can expect her self-governing policies to be supportive of these features. And this exerts pressure toward hierarchy. The pressure in each case is broadly practical: it derives from basic practical problems of self-management and coordination, taken together with agential awareness and support.[44] But once the machinery of hierarchy is built into these self-governing policies, they can also serve as

---

42. See "Autonomy and Hierarchy," 170–73 [this volume, pp. 179–83], where I discuss further the idea that is in the background here about transparency, in self-governance, of such functioning to content.

43. Here I was helped by Peter Gärdenfors.

44. I do not say that these are the only pressures toward hierarchy. In particular, I think there are two further pressures in the direction of a specific form of hierarchy, namely, reflexivity of self-governing policies. One of these pressures derives from a concern about a potential circularity. The concern is that an appeal to policies to treat as a reason builds into the content of the policies appeal to a strong form of agency we are trying to understand.

a basic element in the efforts at reflective self-constitution that are Frankfurt's main concern.

There is reason, then, to expect that the intention-based theory of self-governance will share with the Frankfurtian theory an appeal to conative hierarchy, though in the case of the intention-based theory, the fundamental higher-order attitude will be intention rather than desire (in the sense of desire that contrasts with intention), and it will concern what to treat as a justifying consideration. The intention-based theory also stands in a complex relation to Watson's theory as so far discussed. Watson himself points to cases of underdetermination by "reasons, all things considered" and to the resulting needs for "volitional commitment." And we have seen that a conception of valuing in the domain of the will may be available to Watson. When we return to the matter of agential authority, however, an important potential contrast emerges.

5 .

Recall that one of Watson's initial challenges to desiderative hierarchy was that it did not yet provide an account of (what I am calling) agential authority. This is a fundamental issue for a theory of self-government. When attitudes with agential authority guide, the agent is "fully behind"[45] and directs; and this is an essential aspect of agential governance. But what constitutes agential authority? What makes it true of certain psychological structures that when they guide, the agent is fully behind and directs? Well, we have noted two strategies for understanding such authority: a Platonic strategy that sees agential authority as deriving from a role in tracking the good; and a non-Platonic psychological strategy that sees agential authority

---

A solution is to see the policy as reflexively favoring its own role in guiding a form of functioning that does not itself presuppose that strong form of agency. I discuss this in "Hierarchy, Circularity, and Double Reduction," in S. Buss and L. Overton, eds., *Contours of Agency: Essays on Themes from Harry Frankfurt* (Cambridge, MA: MIT Press, 2002), 65–85, [this volume, essay 4], and in "Three Forms of Agential Commitment: Reply to Cullity and Gerrans," *Proceedings of the Aristotelian Society* (2004): 329–37, at 331–32 [this volume, essay 9, pp. 191–92], but here I put this matter to one side.

A second pressure toward reflexivity of self-governing policies comes from a strong form of endorsement of those policies that is involved in self-governance. I turn to this matter below, in section 6.

45. To borrow Watson's useful phrase ("Free Action and Free Will," 150).

as rooted in a non-Platonic psychological role. Which strategy should an intention-based theory take?

As I see it, it is most persuasive to develop the intention-based theory along the lines of a non-Platonic psychological account. After all, even when self-governing policies cohere with one's value judgments, they frequently introduce forms of organization of practical thought and action that go beyond—and in some cases, well beyond—what is introduced by those judgments. This will be in particular true for reflective, nonsectarian evaluators who know they are in a world of reasonable pluralism. Further, once the machinery of self-governing policies is in hand, we can see the real possibility of agents who value things in the sense of having such policies, but do not much go in for evaluative judgment. Perhaps—to use an example from Nadeem Hussain—they are unreflective agents in a tradition-oriented society who internalize various self-governing policies without arriving at judgments about the good. The explanation of the authority of self-governing policies to speak for the agent in these various cases seems most naturally understood along the lines of a non-Platonic psychological model.

How, in particular, should we proceed with this non-Platonic psychological strategy? What roles should we appeal to as central to agential authority? Here I think we can draw on a general feature of intention-type attitudes: they have it as a central role to support cross-temporal organization of the agent's practical thought and action; and they characteristically do this in ways that involve the constitution and support of psychological, semantic, and causal ties that are, on a broadly Lockean view of such matters, partly constitutive of the identity of the agent over time.[46] I proceed to explain.

Prior intentions refer to later forms of action; and when one later fills in and follows through with one's prior intentions, one refers back to those prior intentions. One's system of intention-like attitudes is at any one time embedded in a system of referential connections across time, from now to later, from now to the past, from the past forward to now, and from the future back to now. Further, one's system of intention-like

---

46. See my "Reflection, Planning, and Temporally Extended Agency," *The Philosophical Review* 109 (2000): 35–61 [this volume, essay 2]. My thinking about these Lockean ideas has benefited greatly from numerous, temporally extended interactions with Gideon Yaffe. Yaffe discusses connections between Lockean ideas about personal identity and free agency in his *Liberty Worth the Name: Locke on Free Agency* (Princeton, NJ: Princeton University Press, 2000), chap. 3.

attitudes will normally be stable in various ways, and reasonably so, and thereby constitute and support associated psychological continuities. In these ways, one's system of intention-like attitudes supports cross-temporal organization of thought and action in part by way of cross-temporal referential connections and in part by way of associated psychological continuities. And these are the sorts of cross-temporal connections and continuities that play a central role in broadly Lockean models of the persistence of one and the same person over time.

This is true, in particular, of self-governing policies. They support the cross-temporal organization of basic forms of practical thought and action in ways that involve associated Lockean ties of cross-reference and continuity. And this is part of their characteristic functioning. In this characteristic functioning, they help organize the practical life of the agent: they help organize, over time, the agent's practical thinking (including forms of deliberation and planning), the agent's activity, and the complex interrelations between such thought and action; they help constitute and support a temporally extended, interwoven, interlocking structure of coordinated practical thought and action. And they do all this in part by way of constituting and supporting relevant Lockean ties, Lockean ties that help constitute the persistence of that agent as one and the same over time. In functioning in these ways, they help constitute the metaphysical backbone of our temporally extended practical thought and action. And it seems to me reasonable to say that it is in playing these Lockean roles in organizing the temporally extended practical thought and action of one and the same agent, that these attitudes earn the authority to speak for that agent. These attitudes have agential authority *at* a time in virtue of their roles in constituting and supporting the interwoven, interlocking structures of agency of that very person *over* time.[47]

The idea is that for attitudes to help constitute the agent's standpoint is for them to play appropriate roles in the psychic economy, roles that we

---

47. There are parallels here with the interpersonal interlocking of intentions that, as I see it, is central to important forms of shared agency. See my "Shared Cooperative Activity," in *Faces of Intention*: 93–108, and my "Shared Valuing and Frameworks for Practical Reasoning," in R. Jay Wallace, Philip Pettit, Samuel Scheffler, and Michael Smith, eds., *Reason and Value: Themes from the Moral Philosophy of Joseph Raz* (Oxford: Oxford University Press, 2004), 1–27 [this volume, essay 13].

can specify without first settling on what has agential authority. And the idea is, further, that the central authority-grounding roles are the cited Lockean coordinating, organizing roles in temporally extended practical thought and action.[48] This is, it is important to note, a claim about the metaphysics of agency, not a normative ideal of integrity or the like (though we may, of course, also value some such ideal).[49] Our primary target is the metaphysics of a strong form of agency, not—as Gideon Yaffe helpfully puts it—"agency-at-its-best."[50] And the proposal on the table is, in particular, a version of the non-Platonic psychological account of agential authority, though a version that does not, like Frankfurt's, appeal primarily to stability and satisfaction.[51] I do think, though, that the proposal will need to be supplemented by something like Frankfurt's idea of satisfaction: for a self-governing policy to have agential authority, it needs to play, as it characteristically does, the cited Lockean roles in temporally extended agency; and it needs also to be an attitude with which there is an appropriate form of satisfaction on the part of the agent.

Such self-governing policies, I have said in partial agreement with Frankfurt, will normally be higher-order. Recall, however, that when Frankfurt goes beyond conative hierarchy to appeal to satisfaction in his account of agential authority, there is only a loose connection between hierarchy and satisfaction. As he notes, one can be satisfied with first-order, as well as with higher-order attitudes. On my theory, in contrast, there is a closer connection between the hierarchical structure of self-governing policies and the roles that ground their agential authority. This is because this higher-order structure helps realize and support the basic cross-temporal Lockean organizing roles that are, on my view, at the

---

48. This approach agrees with Frankfurt—in contrast with Velleman (see above note 6)—in rejecting the idea that there is a specific, single attitude in the background of all self-governance. On the present approach, different self-governing policies can play the roles characteristic of agential authority in different agents, or in the same agent at different times.

49. This is my answer to one of the other questions Watson raised in his cited comments.

50. *Liberty Worth the Name: Locke on Free Agency*, at 72.

51. Frankfurt notes the cross-temporal organizing roles of decisions when he writes that "a function of decision is to integrate the person both dynamically and statically" ("Identification and Wholeheartedness," 175). But his account of agential authority highlights satisfaction and does not highlight this cross-temporal organizing role.

heart of agential authority.[52] This hierarchical structure itself involves referential connections within the mind at a time, will normally induce referential connections and continuities of motivation over time, and will normally thereby help support organization of thought and action over time.[53] Conative hierarchy by itself does not provide a sufficient ground for agential authority;[54] but the hierarchical aspects of self-governing policies— aspects that are in part a response to the cited practical pressures—help realize and support the forms of Lockean cross-temporal functioning that do ground agential authority.

Return now to Watson's theory. I have noted that there might be room in that theory for a view of valuing that is broadly like the one I have proposed, a view that responds to underdetermination by value judgment and to issues about pluralism and convergence by seeing valuing as, at least in a basic case and to some extent, in the domain of the will. Valuing, so understood, would build in relevant volitional commitments to weights and significance, all within the constraints of (perhaps, limited) value judgment. But if this story of valuing were located within Watson's approach, it would need also to take on a Platonic account of the agential authority of such valuings. At least, it would need to take this on if my tentative conjecture was right in attributing some such account to Watson.

52. This contrast between my account of agential authority and Frankfurt's derives from our different theoretical decisions concerning the relative significance to agential authority of cross-temporal organizing role and satisfaction. I place cross-temporal organizing role front and center but appeal to satisfaction in the background; and hierarchy contributes to cross-temporal organizing role. Frankfurt places satisfaction front and center, though he also notes the cross-temporal organizing role of relevant decisions.

53. The cited relation between hierarchy and Lockean referential connections within the mind at a time is close to a central idea in Gideon Yaffe's discussion of Locke's answer to what Yaffe calls the "Where's the Agent Problem." According to Yaffe, Locke would say that it is an essential feature of choice that the agent is consciously aware of her choices, and "the agent is where choices are, because where there is choice, there is the kind of self-conscious awareness that defines the boundaries of the person" (*Liberty Worth the Name: Locke on Free Agency*, 131). The hierarchy involved in the awareness of choice brings with it a referential relation that is central to Locke's account of "the boundaries of the person." Yaffe also explores the extension of this idea to cross-temporal ties in his discussion of Locke on "contemplation of (temporally) absent pleasure and pain," at 134–39. Note though that the hierarchy involved in self-conscious awareness of a choice is not a *conative* hierarchy, whereas the hierarchy I am emphasizing in my appeal to hierarchical self-governing policies is.

54. For an insightful discussion of the idea that hierarchy is not needed for broadly Lockean role, see Agnieszka Jaworska, "Caring and Internality," *Philosophy and Phenomenological Research* (forthcoming). My discussion of these matters has benefited both from that essay and from discussions with Jaworska.

This issue of interpretation reemerges in a somewhat different context in Watson's 2003 essay, "The Work of the Will." Watson there agrees with me and others that "practical commitment has a planning and coordinating role that is needed for coherent action over time." He then notes in an accompanying footnote that this role can be associated with an "identity constituting function." And he goes on to say that "this identity constituting function can be seen as serving the interests of reason, since without it one lacks any standpoint as a practical reasoner."[55]

One way to understand this is that practical commitments play the cited coordinating role and thereby help constitute the agent's "standpoint as a practical reasoner." So understood, the claim is about the metaphysics of a certain kind of agency. And this is in the spirit of the non-Platonic psychological account of agential authority provided by the intention-based theory.

However, another way to understand Watson's comment is that "this identity constituting function [of these practical commitments] can be seen as serving the interests of reason" by constituting a standpoint whose role is to be responsive to reason and the good. Seen in this way, the remark coheres with a Platonic account of the agential authority of these practical commitments.

The intention-based theory sees the agential authority of volitionally infused valuings as a matter of their organizing roles in our temporally extended agency, and not primarily as a matter of a good-tracking role. (This is not, of course, to deny that it is desirable to track the good.) In this respect, it is in the spirit of Frankfurt's focus on satisfaction, though Frankfurt's theory does not appeal to commitments about weights in deliberation, and satisfaction stands in a less organic relation to hierarchy than do the cross-temporal roles to which I have appealed. On the assumption that Watson's theory would indeed embrace a Platonic account of agential authority, this is an important difference between us.

This interacts with the contrast, already noted, between a claim about the metaphysics of our agency and a normative ideal of "agency-at-its-best." If we were seeking to articulate such an ideal, it would be natural to cite not simply the existence of a coherent standpoint but also the ideal that the

55. "The Work of the Will," at 182 and note 31. Watson's talk here of an "identity constituting function" is in response to related ideas of Frankfurt.

standpoint be responsive to the good. But the problem of agential authority is a problem about the metaphysics of certain forms of agency; it is not, in the first instance, a problem about what kind of agency is most desirable.

Let me return now to a complexity anticipated earlier. The psychological approach to agential authority that I have been sketching highlights Lockean roles in temporally extended agency. It does not directly highlight roles in tracking the good. Nevertheless, it might turn out that there are attitudes that include in their characteristic roles both the cited Lockean roles and tracking the good. If so—and this is the point anticipated earlier—the theory will say that those attitudes have agential authority *and* that those attitudes include in their roles tracking the good; but the theory will *not* say that they have agential authority *because* they have a good-tracking role. So the theory will still not be Platonic.

Now it may be that certain kinds of value judgments, for certain kinds of agents, will in fact play both such roles. To be sure, we have seen reasons for saying both that not all value judgments play these Lockean roles and that not only value judgments play these Lockean roles. And we have seen reasons for our model of self-government to provide a central place for forms of valuing that are not reducible to value judgment. But it does not follow that value judgments never play those Lockean roles.[56] And if and when they do play those roles, they can thereby have agential authority, though this will not be directly because they play a good-tracking role, even if they do and even though success in tracking the good is a good thing.

I can now turn, as promised, to Watson's question.

---

56. There are different ways of conceptualizing cases in which value judgment plays these organizing roles. In such cases, we might say that value judgments are in part constituted by associated valuings. Or we might say that there is in the psychic economy a systematic connection between value judgments that settle some issue and corresponding intentions or self-governing policies. Or we might say in such cases that there is a background policy of conforming to value judgments that settle some issue. Or we might try saying in such cases that value judgments that fully determine some issue themselves directly play these organizing roles: they are judgment-policies or, perhaps, "quasi-policies." (For the idea of a quasi-policy see my "Reflection, Planning, and Temporally Extended Agency," at 57–60 [this volume, pp. 42–44].) There are complex issues here, but we need not settle them in the present context. The important point here is that, on the theory, if such value judgments do have agential authority, the ground of that authority is the same as that of relevant self-governing policies, namely, Lockean cross-temporal organizing role.

6.

In response to my discussion of what I am here calling the intention-based theory, Watson indicates that he is skeptical that on this theory

> higher-order commitments are the *source* of autonomy, self-government, agential authority and the like; that they define the standpoint that speaks uniquely for the agent, rather than deriving from something more basic, namely from planning agency exercised against the background of evaluative judgment. The way Bratman builds hierarchical attitudes into the planning theory . . . seems similar to the way I acknowledged . . . that hierarchical desires are indeed often implicated in evaluative judgments: their authority is a reflection of something else. Specifically, in this case, the authority of higher order policies deriving from the need for self-management is explained by the authority of the individual's other practical judgments.[57]

And I take it that the "other practical judgments" to which Watson alludes in the last sentence are the agent's evaluative judgments.

Now, I agree that on my theory, the agential authority of the higher-order aspects of self-governing policies is derivative. What we need to ask is: from what is it derivative? On Frankfurt's later view—at least as I have interpreted it—the agential authority of higher-order attitudes that are an issue of reflection is grounded in the condition of satisfaction. On Watson's present suggestion, the agential authority of higher-order policies would derive from the authority of evaluative judgment where, I take it, that authority is grounded in its good-tracking role. Now, one may wonder how this Watsonian suggestion would explain the agential authority of commitments that go beyond evaluative judgment.[58] But, in any case, the basic point here is that, on my view, what the agential authority of higher-order policies derives from is the agential authority of the basic structure of policies about weights and other forms of significance. I have emphasized certain

---

57. "Hierarchy and Agential Authority: Comments on Michael Bratman's 'Planning Agency, Autonomous Agency,'" 96.
58. As Agnieszka Jaworska noted in conversation.

systematic practical pressures on these policies to be higher-order. But it is not their higher-order structure that, by itself, provides the basic explanation of their agential authority, though that higher-order structure helps realize and support important forms of functioning that are themselves a part of that explanation. Nor is the agential authority of self-governing policies a matter of good-tracking role. As I see it, the agential authority of these policies is, rather, primarily a matter of their broadly Lockean role in the cross-temporal organization of practical thought and action.[59]

There is an important complication, however. While the agential authority of self-governing policies is primarily a matter of Lockean role in cross-temporal organization, when we turn specifically to self-governance, a distinctive pressure for a kind of hierarchy appears. This pressure comes from the idea that in self-governance, it is not enough to be guided by commitments with agential authority; it is also needed that the agent in some more explicit way endorse those guiding commitments. And the natural way within the theory to capture this idea, without appeal to a little person in the head who endorses, is to say that the guiding, authoritative self-governing policies reflexively support their own guidance. This reflexivity is not essential to agential authority and does not itself explain that authority. If an attitude that did not have agential authority reflexively supported itself, it would not thereby bootstrap its way to agential authority. (Suppose, for example, that the desire for the drug in Frankfurt's famous example was a desire to take the drug because of this very desire.) But once we establish the agential authority of self-governing policies primarily by appeal to cross-temporal role, we can model the further agential endorsement that seems characteristic of self-governance by seeing these policies as reflexive.[60]

---

59. Agnieszka Jaworska argues that a Lockean story of "internality" that is in the spirit of my account of agential authority need not suppose that the attitudes that are "internal" are higher-order; and this leads her to a Lockean treatment of internality without hierarchy. See her "Caring and Internality." My view is that the attitudes that have agential authority and are characteristic of self-governance are, at least in a central case, higher-order, that their agential authority is grounded in Lockean role not in their hierarchical structure, but that their hierarchical structure helps realize and support their capacity to play those Lockean roles. Further, and as I go on to say, I also think that self-governance brings with it pressure for authoritative self-governing policies to be reflexive.

60. I expand a bit on the point of this paragraph in my "Three Forms of Agential Commitment: Reply to Cullity and Gerrans," at 335–36 [this volume, p. 194]. And see also "Autonomy and Hierarchy," 173–75 [this volume, pp. 183–85].

This intention-based theory can acknowledge that certain kinds of incoherence between valuing and value judgment are rationally criticizable, other things equal, and may sometimes undermine satisfaction in ways that matter to agential authority. This intention-based theory is also compatible with (though it does not require) the further idea that our concept of self-governance brings with it the further condition—one that goes beyond the metaphysics of agential authority—that one have the capacity to bring one's attitudes with agential authority into conformity with the constraints of the good.[61] What is crucial to the present version of the intention-based theory is that it is Lockean organizing role in temporally extended agency, not role in tracking the good, that is the primary ground of agential authority.

Return to our nonsectarian evaluator who is impressed with the extent of reasonable pluralism. I am supposing that she may well be wholehearted about various self-governing policies that shape her life even while not expecting relevant convergence, and so even while eschewing corresponding evaluative judgments. These self-governing policies play fundamental Lockean organizing roles in her practical life, roles at the heart of agential authority, even in the face of "full awareness of the fact of reflective divergence." I do not say this will be easy. There is, I suppose, a common human tendency to move in thought from "this is where I stand" to "standing elsewhere is unreasonable." But our job here is not to pretend that self-government in the face of the recognition of reasonable pluralism is easy. Rather, our job here is, in part, to provide a theory of our agency that is compatible with, and sheds light on, such self-government.

In any case, it is here—in differing approaches to agential authority and its relation to cross-temporal organization of practical thought and action, on the one hand, and good-tracking role, on the other—that we arrive at a basic difference between my view and Watson's view, at least if my conjecture about Watson's broadly Platonic view of agential authority is on target.[62] We

---

61. See, e.g., Susan Wolf, *Freedom within Reason* (Oxford: Oxford University Press, 1990). It is important, however, to keep in mind here that our concern is with self-governing agency, not directly with accountability. These are close to the two faces of responsibility that Watson explores in his "Two Faces of Responsibility," *Philosophical Topics* 24 (1996).

62. It is also my response to a related challenge from R. Jay Wallace in his review of S. Buss and L. Overton, eds., *Contours of Agency: Essays on Themes from Harry Frankfurt*, in *Ethics* 14 (2004): 810–15, at 812–13.

also arrive at a fundamental commonality between my view and Frankfurt's view, even given other significant differences. I agree with Watson's original critique of what seemed to be Frankfurt's initial suggestions about agential authority. I agree with Watson that neither desire nor hierarchy is the most basic element of self-governance, though I have emphasized both the need for hierarchy in self-governing agents like us and the contribution of hierarchy to forms of functioning that are central to agential authority. And I agree with Watson about the importance of valuing to a model of self-governance, though my understanding of valuing probably differs from his. But when it comes to the fundamental issue of agential authority—the issue of why it is that when certain psychological structures guide, the agent is fully behind and directs—my non-Platonic psychological approach diverges from what seems to be Watson's Platonic approach and is, at least in this respect, Frankfurtian in spirit.[63]

63. Thanks to Sarah Buss, John Fischer, Harry Frankfurt, Agnieszka Jaworska, Kasper Lippert-Rasmussen, Manuel Vargas, Susan Wolf, Gideon Yaffe, and participants in the Stanford University discussion group on Social Ethics and Normative Theory, and the UCR Conference on "Action and Values, in Honor of the Publication of Gary Watson's *Agency and Answerability*." I want especially to thank Dan Speak for his thoughtful responses as the commentator on this essay when it was presented at the UCR Conference. Some of this essay was written while I was a Fellow at the Center for Advanced Study in Behavioral Sciences. I am grateful for financial support provided by The Andrew W. Mellon foundation.

PART II

Extending the Theory

Chapter 12

TEMPTATION REVISITED

I. TEMPTATION AND RATIONAL WILLPOWER

Suppose you value both pleasant dinners and productive work after dinner. One pleasant aspect of dinner is a glass of wine. Indeed, two glasses would make the dinner even more pleasant. The problem is that a second glass of wine undermines your efforts to work after dinner. So you have an evaluative ranking concerning normal dinners: dinner with one glass of wine over dinner with two glasses. So far so good. The problem is that when you are in the middle of dinner, having had the first glass of wine, you frequently find yourself tempted. As you see it, your temptation is not merely a temporary, felt motivational pull in the direction of a second glass: if it were merely that we could simply say that, in at least one important sense, practical reason is on the side of your evaluative ranking.[1] Your temptation, however, is more than that; or so, at least, it seems to you. Your temptation seems to involve a kind of evaluation, albeit an evaluation that is, you know, temporary. For a short period of time you seem to value the second glass of wine more highly than refraining from that second glass. It is not that you have temporarily come to value, quite generally, dinner with two glasses of wine over dinner with one glass. You still value an overall pattern of one glass over an overall pattern of two glasses; after all, productive after-dinner work remains of great importance to you. But in the middle of dinner, faced with the vivid and immediate prospect of a second glass this one time, you value two glasses over one glass just this one time.

---

1. Why, exactly? That is a matter I aim to sort out below.

But what kind of valuing is this? Does the fact that your relevant attitude is temporary, and is limited to present options and circumstances, mean that it is not, in the end, a form of valuing but only a felt inclination in favor of the second glass? This treatment of the case would make matters more straightforward, for we would then be faced only with a conflict between a general evaluative attitude in favor of a regular one-glass pattern and a temporary motivational push. This seems, however, a fairly rigid form of philosophical legislation. In some such cases, it really will seem to you that you are not simply inclined in favor of the second glass: rather, you value it more highly than refraining—though, to be sure, only this once. So I propose that we take seriously the possibility of such cases of conflict with a just-this-once valuing in favor of the second glass. Granted, this is a non-standard case of valuing: valuing is, normally, a more general attitude—for example, a general attitude about the relative importance of wine and work. But who said moral psychology would be simple?

So let us return to you and the tempting second glasses of wine. These temptations, when they arise, are no surprise. You know yourself well enough to predict that this will happen quite frequently. So, in a calm moment well before your next dinner, you reflect. You could, you know, make a side bet that you will only have one glass of wine, a side bet in light of which you would, when the time comes, continue to value, on balance, having only a single glass. "But," you ask yourself, "perhaps I can proceed more directly, by adopting a general policy—a general intention—of having only one glass of wine at dinner, a policy supported by my stable evaluative ranking of an overall pattern of one glass over an overall pattern of two glasses. When the time of temptation arrives, I can simply follow through with this policy and thereby resist temptation."

Let us suppose that you do adopt this one-glass policy, that the time for follow-through at your next dinner arrives, and that you do indeed at that time come to value having the second glass of wine just this once. And let us consider the proposition that it would nevertheless be rational of you to follow through with your one-glass policy: following through would be a rational exercise of willpower. Might this proposition be true? And if so, why?

I think the answer is: yes, it might well be true, and the explanation takes us to central issues about practical reason and structures of agency.[2]

2. INSTRUMENTAL REASON AND THE AGENT

The claim of interest here is that it may be rational for you to follow through with your one-glass policy even in the face of your evaluative ranking to the contrary. How should we understand this talk of rationality? One idea would be that there are reasons for stopping at one glass that are grounded in an ideal of moderation, or in your long-term good. Such reasons may be reflected in your present valuings, plans, ends, desires, or the like; but they need not.

Whether there are such reasons is a deep issue, one I will not discuss here. It seems to me, though, that there is another deep issue that will remain whatever we think about such reasons. This is the issue of whether it will be *instrumentally* rational of you to follow through with your one-glass policy. Instrumental rationality, as I understand it here, is rationality relative to the agent's current valuings, policies, ends, cares, commitments, desires, preferences, or the like.[3] We might go on to challenge those valuings, ends, and the like as failing to track important goods or reasons; but such a challenge would go beyond a judgment of instrumental rationality relative to those attitudes. And, armed with this notion of instrumental rationality, we can ask whether it would, in this sense, be rational for you to follow through with your one-glass policy.

2. The explanation I focus on here goes beyond and bears a complex relation to my earlier discussions of related matters—thus the title of this paper. See my "Planning and Temptation" and my "Toxin, Temptation, and the Stability of Intention," both reprinted in my *Faces of Intention* (New York: Cambridge University Press, 1999). (In "Planning and Temptation," I discuss work of George Ainslie that is also a backdrop for my present discussion.)

3. The intended sense of "instrumental" is quite broad and goes beyond the ordinary notion of a causal means. In particular, it is intended to include what Bernard Williams calls "constitutive solutions" in his "Internal and External Reasons," in his *Moral Luck* (Cambridge: Cambridge University Press, 1981), p. 104. Indeed, we might speak here of "internal" rationality, rather than instrumental rationality. But the latter terminology is common in the literature about willpower and resolute choice that I am trying to address; so for present purposes, it is less likely to mislead to retain this terminology. (I return briefly to Williams's views about internal reasons below in note 53.)

I believe this is a good question to ask in part because I think it helps us uncover basic issues about the relations between practical reason and the metaphysics of planning agency. Donald Davidson famously emphasized that "incontinence is not essentially a problem in moral philosophy, but a problem in the philosophy of action."[4] I want to make a similar proposal that temptation is primarily a problem about the interaction between instrumental rationality and structures of agency. In any case, this is the problem I will address here.

Instrumental rationality is relative rationality: it is rationality relative to an agent's ends, valuings, plans, policies, preferences, and the like. But, of course, human agents are complex, and in many cases of interest, there is conflict among relevant practical attitudes. Our temptation case is such a case: at dinner there is, in particular, a conflict between your present valuing of a second glass this once and your one-glass policy. So we have available different relativized judgments of instrumental rationality: relative to your one-glass action policy, it is rational to refrain from the second glass; relative to your present-directed valuing, it is rational to drink the second glass this time. It is, however, typically supposed that we can also go on to an *on-balance, all-considered* judgment that says what, relative to all your relevant ends, valuings and the like, it is rational to do.[5]

Can we always reach such a judgment? Are there certain preconditions for such all-in judgments? I think the answer to the latter question may well be: yes, there are such preconditions. And if this is so, our answer to the former question should be: not always. My discussion of this will depend, however, on issues that will emerge in the course of our discussion of temptation cases. So I will, for now, put these questions to one side and focus on the following question: assuming that we can arrive at some such all-considered judgment of instrumental rationality, how are we to understand the relative significance of various conflicting practical attitudes to that judgment? Later I will come back to the issue of preconditions for such judgments and of the connection of those preconditions to puzzles about temptation.

---

4. Donald Davidson, "How Is Weakness of the Will Possible?" in his *Essays on Actions and Events*, second edition (Oxford: Oxford University Press, 2001), 21–42, at p. 30n.

5. This supposition seems to be built into Davidson's talk about "all things considered" evaluative judgments in his "How Is Weakness of the Will Possible?"

It is important to see that in approaching these matters we cannot limit our attention to a narrow notion of instrumental rationality relative to specific, intended (or, in a more Kantian spirit, "willed") ends. This is the narrow notion of instrumental rationality I have elsewhere tried to get at by appeal to a norm of means-end coherence on one's intentions and plans.[6] While of the first importance, such a narrowly focused norm of instrumental reason is not all that we need here. What we need here is, rather, a broader notion of rationality relative to a potentially complex cluster of intentions, ends, valuings, policies, desires, and the like.[7]

Our question about instrumental rationality broadly construed—as I will sometimes say, instrumental rationality in the *thick* sense—may not seem all that difficult. After all, it is common and natural to assume that the answer is that instrumental rationality in the thick sense is rationality relative to the agent's evaluative ranking at the time of action of options she takes to be currently available. And that is why it can seem puzzling to suggest that it might be instrumentally rational on-balance for you to follow through with your one-glass policy in the envisaged circumstances.

But why make this assumption? Why think that it is always the present evaluative ranking of present options that anchors such on-balance judgments of instrumental rationality?

An initial idea is that this priority of evaluative ranking is grounded in a broadly Platonic picture of the relation between our agency and the good.

6. See my *Intention, Plans, and Practical Reason* (Cambridge, MA: Harvard University Press, 1987; reissued by CSLI Publications, 1999). Important, related discussions include: John Broome, "Are Intentions Reasons? And How Should We Cope with Incommensurable Values?" in Christopher Morris and Arthur Ripstein, eds., *Practical Rationality and Preference* (Cambridge: Cambridge University Press, 2001); R. Jay Wallace "Normativity, Commitment, and Instrumental Reason," *Philosophers' Imprint* 1, no. 3 (2001); and Gilbert Harman's groundbreaking 1976 essay, "Practical Reasoning," reprinted in his *Reasoning, Meaning, and Mind* (New York: Oxford University Press, 1999).

7. Wallace interprets talk of means-end coherence as aiming at a wider notion of instrumental rationality relative to one's "overall system of plans and values." ("Normativity, Commitment, and Instrumental Reason," pp. 23–24) This contrasts with the way in which I had understood such talk as getting at a narrowly focused norm of instrumental rationality. However, the idea I am focusing on here of instrumental rationality in a broad sense is close to this idea of Wallace's of instrumental rationality relative to one's "overall system of plans and values." Wallace notes this wider idea primarily to distinguish it from the narrower demand of instrumental reason, which is his main concern in the cited essay. My project here requires that we come to terms with this wider idea; and this will lead us to issues about the structure of planning agency.

These evaluative rankings aim at tracking what is good. When they succeed, they put us into contact with what is good. This aim and potential connection with the good explains why evaluative rankings anchor on-balance judgments of instrumental rationality.

One problem here is that a person may be not very good at tracking the good but nevertheless have a system of evaluative rankings relative to which we can nevertheless make on-balance judgments of instrumental rationality. Further, there is in any case a complex relation between, on the one hand, our judgments about what is good and, on the other hand, our valuings and evaluative rankings (which I take to be modes of valuing). I might think something good but not value it in a way that gives it weight in my deliberations about what to do. And I might think that neither X nor Y is better than the other and still, sensibly, value X over Y. It is not unusual to be faced with a need to choose in one's life between X and Y, even though one thinks they are (roughly) equally desirable or one thinks they are in some ways incommensurable or one thinks one is simply not in an epistemic position to reach a judgment about which is better. One may, nevertheless, need to settle on one of them in ways that involve valuing one over the other.[8] This means that there will frequently be valuings and evaluative rankings that have only at most a complex relation to judgments about the good. These valuings and evaluative rankings will nevertheless play a central role in thick instrumental rationality, a central role that the Platonic story does not seem to explain.

I propose, then, to consider an alternative approach, one that appeals more broadly to the roles of evaluative rankings in the psychic economy of our agency. Such roles need not entail (though they should not preclude) success in tracking the good. We need to say what those roles are, and why they support, when they do, a priority for on-balance judgments of instrumental rationality. And we need to see whether the associated view of instrumental reason makes room for rational willpower.

8. I discuss some of these matters in "A Desire of One's Own," *The Journal of Philosophy* 100 (2003): 221–42 [this volume, essay 7]. I discuss valuing in "Valuing and the Will," *Philosophical Perspectives* 14 (2000): 249–65, [this volume, essay 3], and in "Autonomy and Hierarchy," in Ellen Frankel Paul, Fred D. Miller, Jr., and Jeffrey Paul, eds., *Autonomy* (New York: Cambridge University Press, 2003), 156–76 [this volume, essay 8].

3. TWO STRATEGIES: STABILITY AND AUTHORITY

Begin by distinguishing two different strategies for understanding the inter-relations between instrumental reason, rational willpower, and structures of agency.

The first strategy has three steps. It begins by taking it for granted that on-balance judgments of instrumental rationality are normally anchored in the agent's evaluative ranking, at the time of action, of present options. Some account is needed of this assumption, but this issue is initially put aside. We then go on to note that intentions to act are normally grounded in one's evaluative rankings. So, to treat such intentions as an independent anchor for on-balance judgments of instrumental rationality normally would in-volve an odd kind of double counting. And such double counting would make possible an odd kind of bootstrapping in which a decision to act makes instrumentally rational an action that was, prior to the decision, irrational.[9]

But now we turn to the third step of this strategy. This step emphasizes the complex, cross-temporal, and social coordinating roles of intentions, plans, and policies. Such cross-temporal and social organization is ex-tremely useful: it is, for cognitively limited agents like us, a more-or-less all-purpose or universal means, a means to an enormously wide range of human ends.[10] A breakdown in such organization will frequently frustrate many of a planning agent's most important ends. Intentions, plans, and policies, in playing these cross-temporal and social organizing roles, need to have a certain stability: they need to have a certain resistance to recon-sideration and revision.

We will want to assess various forms of such stability as reasonable or not. Since for present purposes we are limiting our direct concern to instrumental reason, we will want to limit our assessments of reasonable stability in a corresponding way. But we are also concerned, in particular,

9. I first discussed this issue in "Intention and Means-End Reasoning," *Philosophical Review* 90 (1981): 252–65.

10. See my "Taking Plans Seriously," *Social Theory and Practice* 9 (1983): 271–87, p. 275. For a discussion of related ideas see Crystal Thorpe, "A Puzzle about Humean Theories of Practical Reason," unpublished MS. I first learned of the idea of a universal means from Joel Feinberg, who emphasized that the idea can be traced at least to John Stuart Mills's discussion of the utility of security in his *Utilitarianism*, chapter 5.

with stability within planning agency; so we will want to be alive to the implications for reasonable stability of basic features of such agency.

Returning to our example, then, we want to know whether a one-glass action policy might have a kind of reasonable stability such that it might be instrumentally rational to stick with it even in the face of a temporary evaluative ranking to the contrary, and even given the ability to diverge from that policy.[11] If so, we would have identified a way in which, at least in certain temptation cases, on-balance instrumental rationality may be anchored primarily in action policy rather than present but temporary evaluative ranking.

So this first approach takes it for granted that on-balance judgments of instrumental rationality are normally anchored in the agent's evaluative ranking. But it also proposes that, given relevant standards of reasonable stability of intention-like attitudes, action-directed policies can themselves sometimes provide such an anchor, and they can perhaps do this even in certain cases of conflict with the agent's present evaluative ranking of present options. Call this the *intention stability* strategy.

A second strategy begins with the idea that when we see certain attitudes as anchoring on-balance judgments of instrumental rationality, we are seeing them as constituting a point of view that is in a strong sense the *agent's* point of view. On-balance instrumental rationality is rationality relative to a framework that is, in a strong sense, the agent's own framework.[12] So, in particular, your current evaluative rankings have priority for thick judgments of instrumental rationality (when they do have such priority) because they have authority to articulate, in the face of conflict, *your* relevant perspective on your present options—they have authority to establish where *you* currently stand on a salient practical

---

11. In my *Intention, Plans, and Practical Reason,* I treated reasonable stability as primarily a matter of reasonable (and frequently nonreflective) nonreconsideration. In "Toxin, Temptation, and the Stability of Intention," I include in reasonable stability both reasonable nonreconsideration and certain forms of reasonable retention. For a somewhat similar emphasis on the importance of such normative questions about the stability of prior intentions, an emphasis that highlights reasonable resistance to reconsideration, see Richard Holton, "Intention and Weakness of Will," *The Journal of Philosophy* (1999): 241–62. Holton pursues related matters in his "How Is Strength of Will Possible?" in S. Stroud and C. Tappolet, eds., *Weakness of Will and Practical Irrationality* (Oxford: Clarendon Press, 2003), 39–67.

12. This is why, if *X* is on-balance instrumentally rational for me, then I favor *X*. See related remarks about "presumptive normative authority" in my "Two Problems about Human Agency," *Proceedings of the Aristotelian Society* (2000–2001): 309–26 [this volume, essay 5].

matter.[13] At the bottom of the issue about the relative significance to instrumental rationality in the thick sense of various conflicting practical attitudes is this broadly Frankfurtian issue of what most clearly speaks for where "the person himself stands."[14] Or so it is maintained by a defender of this second strategy.

Let us say that attitudes that establish where the person himself stands— that establish the agent's practical framework—have "agential authority."[15] And let us call this second approach the *agential authority* strategy.

So we have two different strategies for investigating the relative priority of evaluative ranking and of conflicting action policy to on-balance judgments of instrumental rationality in the thick sense: the intention stability strategy and the agential authority strategy. Now, in my earlier essays on temptation, I pursued a version of the strategy of intention stability.[16] In more recent work on agency, I have turned to issues about agential authority.[17] What I want to do here is to see to what extent issues of agential authority, and the approach I have taken to them, can help us with our questions about temptation. This will lead to a version of the agential authority strategy, to a restatement of the intention stability approach, and to a complex understanding of the interrelations between these two approaches.

I begin with agential authority.

4. THE STRATEGY OF AGENTIAL AUTHORITY

The idea behind the agential authority strategy is that thick judgments of instrumental rationality involve a relativization to the *agent's* framework of relevant attitudes. This means that we need to ask which attitudes are not

13. For such talk about where you stand see Harry Frankfurt, "Identification and Whole-heartedness," in his *The Importance of What We Care About* (Cambridge: Cambridge University Press, 1988).

14. Ibid., p. 166.

15. For this terminology see my "Two Problems About Human Agency."

16. See "Planning and Temptation" and "Toxin, Temptation, and the Stability of Intention."

17. See, e.g., my "Reflection, Planning, and Temporally Extended Agency," *Philosophical Review* 109 (2000): 35–61, [this volume, essay 2], and "Two Problems about Human Agency."

merely wiggles in the psychic stew[18] but rather help constitute what is to serve as the *agent's* relevant framework. And, as noted, this takes us to Frankfurtian issues about the authority of various attitudes to establish the agent's point of view.

Now, recent philosophy of action has included two subliteratures that have tended not to interact very much: a literature on resolute choice, the toxin problem, and related matters;[19] and a Frankfurt-inspired literature on the constitution of the agent. The agential authority strategy tries to bring these literatures into contact with each other by way of the idea that behind debates about instrumental practical reason lurk (among other things) broadly Frankfurtian issues about the constitution of the agent.

Once we see things along these lines, however, we need to address the question of whether or not it is always the agent's evaluative ranking that has relevant agential authority in the kinds of temptation cases of interest here. In particular, we need to consider whether in some versions of our temptation case it is not the cited evaluative ranking in favor of a second glass this time but, rather, the agent's one-glass action policy that has the stronger claim to such agential authority. If it were the action policy that had the stronger claim to agential authority, we would have an explanation of why it is on-balance instrumentally rational to follow through with that policy.

Now, I think we do normally see an agent's current valuings, or evaluative rankings, as having a dominant claim to agential authority. (I will return below to the question why this is so.) The point to be made here, however, is that sometimes we do not see valuings in this way. As J. David Velleman notes:

> A person can be alienated from his values, too; and he can be alienated from them even as they continue to grip him and to influence his behavior.[20]

---

18. "Reflection, Planning, and Temporally Extended Agency," p. 38 [this volume, p. 24].

19. See, for example, Edward F. McClennen, *Rationality and Dynamic Choice: Foundational Explorations* (Cambridge: Cambridge University Press, 1990); David Gauthier, "Resolute Choice and Rational Deliberation: A Critique and a Defense," *Nous* 31 (1997): 1–25; and Joe Mintoff, "Rational Cooperation, Intention and Reconsideration," *Ethics* 107 (1997): 612–43.

20. "What Happens When Someone Acts?" in *The Possibility of Practical Reason* (Oxford: Oxford University Press, 2000), p. 134. I assume here that Velleman's talk of a person's "values" matches my talk of valuings; but the story I sketch below of nonauthoritative valuing is not Velleman's story.

What we need to understand is why valuings, or evaluative rankings, normally, even if perhaps not universally, have agential authority and whether this rationale may fail to apply in certain special cases, including, perhaps, our case of temptation.

5. AGENTIAL AUTHORITY AND TEMPORALLY EXTENDED AGENCY

Issues about agential authority arose immediately in the literature spawned by Frankfurt's seminal 1971 essay.[21] Why think Frankfurtian second-order volitions, as Gary Watson put it, "have, among all of a person's 'desires,' the special property of being peculiarly his 'own' "?[22] The answer cannot in general be an appeal to a further, yet-higher-order co-native attitude: that way lies regress. At some point we need a different kind of answer. Frankfurt saw this clearly in his presidential address.[23] His basic insight there was to appeal not to a further, yet-higher-order, attitude but to a relevant form of psychological functioning. Frankfurt appealed, in particular, to what he called "satisfaction" with relevant higher-order attitudes. Roughly, one is satisfied with a relevant higher-order attitude when there is an "absence of any tendency or inclination to alter" it.[24]

In my own work I have developed the point somewhat differently. I have argued that a basic role or function to appeal to here is the role in the cross-temporal coordination and organization of one's practical thought and action. In particular, what is central is the support of such cross-temporal organization, in part, by way of the kinds of continuities and connections central to a broadly Lockean view of personal identity over time. We are agents who persist over time and whose agency is extended over time; and it is the role in supporting and constituting cross-temporal organizing structures central to our persistence over time that is at the heart of agential

---

21. "Freedom of the Will and the Concept of a Person" in his *The Importance of What We Care About.*

22. "Free Agency," *Journal of Philosophy* 72 (1975): 205–20, at p. 108.

23. "The Faintest Passion," in his *Necessity, Volition, and Love* (New York: Cambridge University Press, 1999).

24. "The Faintest Passion," p. 104.

authority.[25] Where the agent stands at a time is substantially shaped by attitudes whose role it is to structure the agent's life over time.[26] This is not to say that we can do without something like Frankfurtian satisfaction. What is needed for agential authority is a substantial role in supporting and constituting central cross-temporal organizing structures, together with something like satisfaction with the attitudes that play this role. And we can say that one is satisfied with such attitudes when, roughly, other relevant attitudes of that agent at that time do not exert significant pressure on that agent for change of those attitudes.[27]

For present purposes, anyway, I am going to assume without further argument that something like this approach to agential authority—an approach that highlights role in Lockean cross-temporal organization of practical thought and action, together with associated satisfaction—is more or less right. What we want to know is how it is within such an approach that valuings normally have agential authority. We need, then, to reflect further on what valuing is.

6. VALUING

Valuing, I take it, is a pro attitude, one that bears a complex relation to value judgment. I can recognize a wide range of goods, judge that they are good, but still only incorporate some of them, or even none of them, into

---

25. See for example "Reflection, Planning, and Temporally Extended Agency," and "Two Problems about Human Agency." (The terminology of continuities and connections is drawn from Derek Parfit, *Reasons and Persons* [Oxford: Oxford University Press, 1984], 206–8. My discussion of this is in "Reflection, Planning, and Temporally Extended Agency," at pp. 43–45 [this volume, pp. 29–30], where I note an important difference between Parfit's terminology and my terminology.)

26. This focus on such identity-constituting cross-temporal organization of practical thought and action is not itself a focus on what Christine Korsgaard calls the agent's conception of her practical identity. (See her *The Sources of Normativity* [Cambridge: Cambridge University Press, 1996], lecture 3.) The present approach to agential authority tries to identify forms of functioning that make it the case that certain attitudes establish the agent's point of view. These attitudes may be—but need not be—Korsgaardian conceptions of one's practical identity; and in any case, given any such conception, we will still need to know if it has agential authority. For discussion of these points see my "Reflection, Planning, and Temporally Extended Agency," at 56–57 [this volume, pp. 41–42], and my "Two Problems about Human Agency" at 317–18 [this volume, pp. 100–02].

27. This is a rough gloss on what I say, in developing Frankfurt's idea, in "Reflection, Planning, and Temporally Extended Agency," 49–50, 59–60 [this volume, pp. 35–36, 44].

my practical reasoning and action in ways that constitute valuing them. To value something is, at least in part, to be set to give it justifying significance in one's motivationally effective practical reasoning.

I agree, then, with Gary Watson when he observes that "to value is also to want."[28] But what kind of wanting is this? We might try saying that valuing is constituted by preferences that have been fully exposed to consideration in light of one's relevant beliefs.[29] And such considered preferences may be thought to involve not only motivation but also a kind of endorsement.

There is a problem, however, with this supposed element of endorsement. It seems possible to acknowledge that one's considered preference in fact favors (or would favor), say, smoking, but nevertheless, in an important and relevant sense, not endorse smoking.[30] So we need a notion of valuing that retains the connection to wanting, but also better captures the connection with a kind of endorsement.[31] And here I have proposed that we see valuing, at least in a basic case, as a policy about one's motivationally effective practical deliberation. I value X when I have a policy of treating X as a justifying consideration in my motivationally effective practical reasoning.[32] The relevant practical reasoning here is, in the central case, reasoning in which one weighs various pros and cons

28. Watson, "Free Agency," p. 215. And see also his "Free Action and Free Will," *Mind* (1987): 145–72. And see also Gilbert Harman, "Desired Desires," in his *Explaining Value and Other Essays in Moral Philosophy* (Oxford: Oxford University Press, 2000), 117–36, at 129–30; and Bernard Berofsky, "Identification, the Self, and Autonomy," in Ellen Frankel Paul, Fred D. Miller, Jr., and Jeffrey Paul, eds., *Autonomy* (New York: Cambridge University Press, 2003), 199–220, at 207.

29. See David Gauthier, *Morals by Agreement* (New York: Oxford University Press, 1986), 29–33. A related but different idea is in Richard Brandt, *A Theory of the Good and the Right* (New York: Oxford University Press, 1979). Robert Brandom also examines this aspect of Gauthier's view in his "What Do Expressions of Preference Express?" in Morris and Ripstein, eds., *Practical Rationality and Preference: Essays for David Gauthier*, 11–36. And see my discussion of Creature 3 in my "Valuing and the Will."

30. The example is, pretty much, Gauthier's, in *Morals by Agreement*, at p. 32; but he does not draw the same conclusion. The basic point about endorsement is due to Allan Gibbard, *Wise Choices, Apt Feelings* (Cambridge, MA: Harvard University Press, 1990), 18–22. Gibbard proposes that we need to "pursue the element of endorsement that full-information accounts leave out" (p. 22). See also J. David Velleman, "Brandt's Definition of 'Good'," *Philosophical Review* 97 (1988): 353–71.

31. Though we need to do this in a way that still leaves open the possibility of valuings without agential authority. More on this below.

32. See the discussion of Creature 8 (and its relation to Creature 3) in my "Valuing and the Will." Such policies, as I understand them, are intentions that are appropriately general. In "Valuing and the Will," I supposed that such a policy about practical reasoning would normally be a higher-order policy. I return to the issue of whether such a policy needs to be

concerning alternative options. Valuing of this sort helps specify which considerations to treat as such pros or cons.

Now, though one may judge something good without in this sense valuing it, there will nevertheless frequently (though not universally) be a close relation between what one judges good and what one values. It is, for example, because I judge forgiveness to be good that I value it. In such a case we can wonder whether my judgment itself constitutes, or consists in, or in some way includes or plays the role of, my policy-like valuing. Or should we see the judgment and the valuing as distinct but connected elements? My strategy here will be to leave these difficult issues open. I will focus instead on how valuing—however exactly we resolve these issues about its precise relations to value judgment—enters into on-balance instrumental rationality. In particular, we can ask whether such valuing is normally an anchor for on-balance judgments of instrumental rationality.

For valuing to be such an anchor, it needs to constitute (at least in part) the agent's practical framework: it needs to have agential authority. So we need to ask whether—and if so, why—such valuing normally has agential authority. And on the approach I am taking here, if valuing normally has agential authority, it is in large part because of its central role in cross-temporal organization of our practical thought and action, cross-temporal organization that involves relevant Lockean continuities and connections. And I think we can see that valuing will, indeed, normally support such organization in one's practical thought and action over time.[33] Valuing involves a policy of reasoning in certain ways over time and of shaping one's actions over time in accord with that reasoning. So one's valuing will tend to support and to help constitute important forms of cross-temporal organization, by way of various continuities and connections, of one's practical thought and action. So there is a strong case for saying that a

---

higher-order in my "Autonomy and Hierarchy." I discuss relations between such policies about practical reasoning and judgments about the good both in "Autonomy and Hierarchy" and in my "A Desire of One's Own." And compare Allan Gibbard's talk of "policies for living" in his "Morality as Consistency in Living: Korsgaard's Kantian Lectures," *Ethics* 110 (1999): 140–64.

33. It is important that valuing—like other intentions, plans, and policies—will also play significant *inter*personal organizing roles. But here I am supposing that it is the role in organization within the life of the agent that is central to agential authority.

policy-like valuing with which the agent is appropriately satisfied has agential authority. So there is a strong case for seeing such valuings as anchors for on-balance judgments of instrumental rationality.

This helps explain the presumption that valuing does normally anchor on-balance judgments of instrumental rationality. But now we need to know whether this authority may indeed be defeated in our case of temptation. And this returns us to the question of the sense in which, in the case of temptation, you value two glasses this one time.

7. VALUING, SINGULARITY, AND AGENTIAL AUTHORITY

Faced with a second glass of wine, you value drinking it this time more highly than refraining, though you continue to value an overall one-glass pattern more highly than an overall two-glass pattern. In what does your valuing a second glass this once consist? The approach I have sketched sees valuing as policy-like. But your valuing of two glasses this one time does not seem to be general in the way that policies are.

In response, we might try to uncover implicit generality. Perhaps we can see this valuing as a policy about practical reasoning along the lines of:

> (P) a policy of giving (in motivationally effective deliberation) more weight on this occasion to a second glass of wine than to after-dinner work, while generally giving more weight instead to after-dinner work.

Your valuing would be, then, a policy of practical reasoning with a built-in exclusion concerning the present occasion.

This does seem a way to understand certain cases. Suppose I think today really is very different from other days, and so have a policy that treats today differently. (Why is this day different from all other days? Perhaps today is the anniversary of a special event.) But your temptation case is not like that. Your valuing of the second glass today seems not to be a general policy for the future, though one that treats today differently from later days. It seems rather to be simply a valuing of a second glass this one time.[34] This valuing does then oblige you to reformulate your prior, uniform one-glass policy of not giving relevant weight to a second glass; and you may thereby arrive at a policy along the lines of (P). But your valuing of the second glass this once seems not to consist in (P) but rather in a singular valuing that then exerts pressure in the direction of (P).

This means that to explain in what your valuing two glasses just this once consists, we need to adjust the account of valuing as so far presented. And the needed adjustment seems clear. A policy of practical reasoning is a general intention. Your valuing of two glasses this one time is an intention about practical reasoning, but it is only an intention about present practical reasoning. It is a singular commitment concerning relevant motivationally effective practical reasoning.[35] It is a singular commitment to give relatively more justifying weight on this occasion to a second glass. What we learn from such a temptation case is that valuings, though normally policies (that is, general intentions) concerning practical reasoning, can sometimes be singular commitments to giving something justifying weight in motivationally effective deliberation. Such singular commitments concerning practical reasoning are not merely felt inclinations; but they also are not general policies of reasoning.[36]

And now the point to note is that, given our approach to agential authority, such a singular valuing may have only an attenuated claim to constitute where you stand on this occasion. It is a singular commitment: its role is not to structure your ongoing practical reasoning and action but only to structure your present reasoning and action. In contrast, your general action policy of only having one glass of wine at dinner does have the role of organizing thought and action over time, in part by way of associated continuities and connections. So there is a case for saying that this action policy, in contrast with your singular valuing, has the stronger claim to authority to constitute where you stand.[37] So it may be on-balance

34. Here and in the rest of this paragraph I am much indebted to Agnieszka Jaworska.
35. See my "Hierarchy, Circularity, and Double Reduction," in Sarah Buss and Lee Overton, eds., *Contours of Agency: Essays on Themes from Harry Frankfurt* (Cambridge, MA: MIT Press, 2002): 65–85, at 78–80 [this volume, essay 4, pp. 85–87].
36. Nor need a singular commitment to treat as a reason be a commitment to a singular reason.
37. I do not say that this is the only case that might be available for this claim about authority, as will become clear in my discussion below of the potential significance of anticipated regret.

instrumentally rational for you to follow through with your one-glass action-policy, despite your present-directed evaluative ranking to the contrary.

Note that an analogous argument for following through with a prior intention to drink the distasteful toxin (in Gregory Kavka's example) would not work.[38] In Kavka's case, if one has earlier formed the intention to drink toxin and the time comes to drink, one has already received the financial award for simply having the intention to drink, and one's evaluative ranking now favors not drinking. This evaluative ranking is not merely a singular commitment but, rather, involves a general policy of giving weight to the avoidance of future pain. So we will not be able to argue—in a way that would parallel the argument just mooted in the case of temptation—that the evaluative ranking that favors not drinking toxin has only an attenuated claim to agential authority.

Returning now to our temptation case, we can look at things this way: on the one hand, prior intentions and policies concerning action, while not themselves valuings, play independent and important organizing roles in our temporally extended agency. On the other hand, valuing itself also consists in certain intentions or policies. These are not policies or intentions simply to act in a certain way but, rather, policies or intentions about, roughly, the weighing of pros and cons in one's motivationally effective practical reasoning. In the temptation case, the conflict is, in effect, between an action-focused general policy and a reasoning-focused singular intention. And what we have seen is that there is a substantive question about which more fully speaks for the agent. Agential authority is a status that needs to be earned; and it is not automatically earned solely by being an attitude whose content concerns, in particular, which considerations are to weigh in deliberation. To be sure, evaluative rankings and valuings normally do have agential authority, given that they are normally policy-like and given the fundamental importance to our temporally extended agency of deliberative control of action. Nevertheless, there is reason to suppose that there are special cases in which the general policy of action has more of a claim to agential authority than does a

38. See Gregory Kavka, "The Toxin Puzzle," *Analysis* 43 (1983): 33–36.

conflicting present-directed singular evaluative ranking. Reflection on the metaphysics of agential authority makes theoretical room for the idea that the one-glass action policy may anchor the thick judgment of instrumental rationality in such special cases. And this leads to the idea that it may be on-balance instrumentally rational of you to follow through with your one-glass action policy despite an evaluative ranking that favors the second glass this one time.[39]

8. THE STRATEGY OF INTENTION STABILITY

It is time to return to the strategy of intention stability. The basic idea of this strategy is to articulate principles of intention stability that can, in certain cases, make (instrumental) sense of sticking with a prior action policy in the face of a conflicting evaluative ranking. Now, in my earlier discussions of this strategy, I emphasized two ideas. First, given our important needs for co-ordination over time and socially, the central roles our planning agency plays in responding to these needs, and our significant cognitive limits, there are broad pragmatic pressures in the direction of stability of intention-like attitudes.[40] But, further, a second and important element in our account of plan stability will be a "no regret" principle.[41] I continue to believe that we should appeal to both such elements. But I have also come to believe that we need to refashion the story of the relation between these elements in a way that draws on the idea of agential authority.[42] This refashioning will also lead

---

39. What happens when you do stick with your one-glass action policy despite your present-directed valuing to the contrary? It is not that your one-glass policy adds yet a further consideration to be weighed in your deliberation in which, given your temporary valuing, you are committed to giving weight to the second glass. Rather, your one-glass action-policy displaces or preempts such deliberation and perhaps (in this case) reasonably so. You act by way of the direct application of this policy to your present situation. This is a kind of reasoning: you reason from the general policy of having only one glass, and the observation that you have already had a glass, to a conclusion in favor of refraining from a second glass. But this is not practical reasoning in which you weigh conflicting pros and cons. Such deliberative weighing of pros and cons is, rather, preempted by the policy of action. So the reasoning-focused singular intention that constitutes the cited, singular present-directed valuing does not get relevantly engaged: you do not engage in the kind of deliberation that is the concern of that intention or, at least, your action is not an issue of such deliberation.

40. See "Planning and Temptation," 52–56.

41. See "Toxin, Temptation, and the Stability of Intention," 79–89.

42. In rethinking these matters, I have benefited from Richard Holton's "Rational Resolve," *Philosophical Review* 113 (2004): 507–35, in which he criticizes my account in "Toxin, Temptation, and

to a more complex understanding of the relation between the strategies of
intention stability and of agential authority.

We begin by emphasizing the usefulness of our planning capacities—
they are, for agents like us, more or less all-purpose means. We then ask
what guidance this gives us in formulating principles of instrumentally
reasonable intention stability. Given that we are agents with limited cognitive resources, on many occasions we simply maintain our prior intentions as time goes by and even in the face of new information. Such
processes of nonreconsideration play a central role in our temporally extended agency. When is it instrumentally reasonable simply to maintain
one's prior intention and not stop to reconsider? Here I have proposed a
two-tier pragmatic theory, one that seeks habits and strategies of nonreconsideration that would, in the long run, promote the agent's ends.[43]
Which ends? The relevant ends will include the agent's present ends. They
will also normally include a wide range of actual or potential future ends,
given that a planning agent will normally project her agency into the
future in a way that involves identifying more or less specifically with her
anticipated ends in her planned-for future planning agency.[44]

It is not clear, however, how to extend this approach concerning
nonreconsideration to a temptation case in which you do reflect on
whether or not to stick with your one-glass policy. I take it that in this
case it is clear to you, when you are offered the second glass of wine, that
you really do value drinking it this time more highly than refraining.
What you are wondering is whether you should nevertheless stick with
your prior one-glass policy.[45]

---

the Stability of Intention." While I have learned from Holton's discussion, the way I try here to
connect the no-regret principle both to the broadly pragmatic story of stability and to ideas of
agential authority diverges from his approach.

43. See *Intention, Plans, and Practical Reason*, chap. 5, and "Planning and Temptation," 52–56.

44. In speaking of identification, here I have in mind the approach I have sketched in
"Reflection, Planning, and Temporally Extended Agency": to identify with a desire is, roughly,
to have a policy that says to treat that desire, or what it is for, as a justifying consideration in
deliberation.

45. In "How Is Strength of Will Possible?" Holton sees willpower as a matter of "refusing to
reconsider one's resolutions" (p. 49). Given what I have said about reasonable nonreconsideration of a prior intention, it will be clear that I agree that many times willpower is a matter of nonreconsideration. But I also think that sometimes it is a matter of how
one responds to one's prior intention or policy even once one has embarked upon reconsideration.

Now, the broad usefulness of stability of plan-type attitudes that lies behind the two-tier pragmatic account of reasonable nonreconsideration does, I think, also support some sort of defeasible, default presumption in favor of following through with one's prior intentions and policies even when one does reconsider whether to do so.[46] Or, anyway, there is such a default presumption so long as one does not have reason to distrust the earlier process of intention or policy formation.[47] (If one knew, for example, that this had been the result of deep depression, matters would be different.) To grant this pragmatically grounded default in favor of the prior intention or policy does not, however, amount to seeing that intention or policy as providing a further (bootstrapping) reason in deliberation. What it amounts to is, rather, seeing it as establishing a certain burden of proof on a challenge to that intention or policy.[48]

Given this default presumption, it can be reasonable to stick with one's prior intention or policy in the face of reconsideration even if one values certain alternatives no less highly (but also, no more highly). Normally, though, this default presumption will be overridden by a present evaluative ranking strictly to the contrary—a present evaluative ranking that ranks a specific alternative strictly higher than what one had intended. After all, your prior intentions and policies concerning action are themselves normally formed primarily on the basis of your evaluative rankings. To give such action-focused intentions or policies priority over such an evaluative ranking would normally seem a criticizable prior-policy "worship."[49]

If, however, we suppose for this reason that the pragmatic argument for stability of prior intention or policy is in general blocked by an eval-

---

46. In correspondence, Shelly Kagan has suggested a parallel here with the judicial doctrine of *stare decisis*. And for a similar idea see Robert Nozick, *Philosophical Explanations* (Cambridge, MA: Harvard University Press, 1981), at 297.

47. See Edward S. Hinchman, "Trust and Diachronic Agency," *Nous* 37 (2003): 25–51.

48. There is here a parallel with Frederick Schauer's idea that certain rules impose an associated "presumption or burden of persuasion . . . in a particular decisional environment." See his *Playing by the Rules: A Philosophical Examination of Rule-Based Decision-Making in Law and in Life* (Oxford: Clarendon Press, 1991): 203–6.

49. See "Planning and Temptation," at 54–55. The problem here is analogous to the problem about "rule worship" frequently raised for rule-utilitarian theories. See J. J. C. Smart, "Extreme and Restricted Utilitarianism," in Philippa Foot, ed., *Theories of Ethics* (Oxford: Oxford University Press, 1967).

uative ranking that is strictly to the contrary, we are so far without resources to explain why it might be instrumentally rational for you to stick with your prior one-glass action policy despite your present ranking in favor of a second glass. What is needed, then, is an explanation of what may be special about such a temptation case such that—in contrast with many other cases—the cited evaluative ranking does *not* override the pragmatically grounded default in favor of the prior policy of action.

It is here that I have wanted to appeal to anticipated future regret. In the temptation case you know, let us suppose, that if you were to be guided by your evaluative ranking in favor of a second glass, you would later regret that, and if instead you were to stick with your one-glass policy, you would later be glad that you did. For a planning agent—one who projects her agency into the future in ways that involve plan-type attitudes—such anticipated regret will normally have a prima facie significance. Our planning agency is future-oriented in a way that normally brings with it a present identification with how one will see matters—including one's now present actions—in the relevant future. This is part of the characteristic future-oriented focus of plans and policies.[50] And this provides a ground for giving prima facie significance to one's present anticipation that one will, at an appropriate later time, be glad if one did follow through with one's prior plan or policy and regret it if one didn't.[51]

What kind of significance? This is the point at which I now want to draw on the idea of agential authority. A planning agent's agency is, and is understood by her to be, temporally extended in characteristic ways. Her anticipation of relevant regret is an anticipation of a breakdown in the cross-temporal coherence of this temporally extended agency: she is, over time, not of a single mind about this matter. So there is pressure in the direction of saying that this present evaluative ranking has only an attenuated authority to speak for this agent, given that she is, and knows

50. See "Toxin, Temptation, and the Stability of Intention," 86–87. (I note there a complex relation between this idea and Thomas Nagel's discussion in his *The Possibility of Altruism* [Oxford: Oxford University Press, 1971].)

51. See "Toxin, Temptation, and the Stability of Intention," pp. 83–85, for discussion of the relevant notion of regret.

herself to be, an agent whose agency is temporally extended, and given her expectation of later regret.

This can help us understand why it may be rational to stick with the prior one-glass policy despite the evaluative ranking to the contrary. Because of concerns with policy worship, we need to see the pragmatically grounded default in favor of a prior action policy as defeasible and, in particular, as normally defeated by a present evaluative ranking to the contrary. If, however, one knows one would regret acting on that ranking, and would be glad if one stuck with the prior action policy, then this can sometimes disqualify this ranking from defeating the pragmatically grounded default in favor of stability. The anticipated future regret can sometimes undermine the agential authority of that normally overriding evaluative ranking in favor of the second glass and, so to speak, delegitimize it.

Once this is granted, we can see why it may sometimes be instrumentally rational of you to follow through with your one-glass action policy, despite your present-directed evaluative ranking to the contrary; for we can suppose that you know that you would later regret giving in to your present temptation, and so (defeasibly) that your present ranking in favor of a second glass does not fully speak for you. Note, however, that it does not follow that in Kavka's case it would, for this reason, be instrumentally rational to follow through with an intention to drink toxin. This is because it is not true that you would later regret acting on your present evaluative ranking in favor of not drinking.[52] So these considerations of regret support the presumption of stability of the one-glass action policy, but not the presumption of stability of the prior intention to drink toxin, in the face of the conflicting, present evaluative ranking. In this way we develop an approach to instrumentally reasonable intention stability that

52. In "Toxin, Temptation, and the Stability of Intention," I claimed, further, that we could not use this no-regret argument to explain why a person in certain special kinds of reciprocation cases would be instrumentally rational to reciprocate. My claim was not that there is no account to be given of the rationality or reasonableness of reciprocation, only that the theoretical resources solely of individual planning agency and instrumental rationality would not suffice in these special cases. And in other work, I have tried to provide theoretical resources for characterizing the very phenomenon of cooperative activity; see, e.g., "Shared Cooperative Activity," reprinted in my *Faces of Intention*.

distinguishes—as it seems to me we should—between stability in our temptation case and stability in Kavka's toxin case. And we do this in a way that avoids plan worship—for we continue to hold that the pragmatically grounded default presumption in favor of the prior intention or policy is normally overridden by a present evaluative ranking to the contrary.

9. AUTHORITY, STABILITY, AND INSTRUMENTAL RATIONALITY

How is this version of the intention stability strategy related to our version of the agential authority strategy? Well, consider how these different strategies treat the two main elements of our case of temptation: the general one-glass action policy, and the conflicting ranking in favor of a second glass this one time. Begin with the general action policy. The agential authority strategy focuses on the presumptive agential authority of this general policy. The intention stability strategy, in contrast, focuses on the pragmatically grounded reasonable stability of this policy. Turn now to the conflicting evaluative ranking in favor of a second glass this time. The agential authority strategy supports a challenge to the agential authority of that ranking, a challenge that, as I have developed it so far, is grounded in the singularity of that ranking (in contrast with the generality of the action policy). The intention stability strategy shares this concern with the authority of that evaluative ranking; but, as I have developed this strategy so far, this challenge to the authority of that evaluative ranking highlights not its singularity but its relation to anticipated future regret.

So while these strategies highlight different aspects of the one-glass action policy—in one case, its authority; in the other case, its reasonable stability—both strategies concern themselves with the agential authority of the conflicting evaluative ranking. As presented so far, however, they highlight different lines of argument for the diminished authority of that singular evaluative ranking: an appeal to its singularity in one case, and an appeal to anticipated future regret in the other. But once this is clear, there seems no deep reason why both forms of argument for the attenuated authority of the conflicting evaluative ranking—the ranking in favor of drinking the second glass this once—are not available to both strategies. In this respect, then, there is a potential convergence in the basic ideas underlying the two strategies. (There remains an issue about what happens if these two different lines of argument for attenuated authority come apart. I turn to this issue below.)

Where the strategies continue to diverge, however, is in what they highlight about the general action policy: in one case, it's presumptive agential authority; in the other case, it's pragmatically grounded stability. So, despite the partial convergence on the significance of the authority of the conflicting evaluative ranking, there remains this important difference between the two strategies.

In both cases, the strategies are responding, though in different ways, to the temporally extended structure of our planning agency. Both strategies aim to track significant interactions between instrumental reason and these structures of agency.[53] And, as developed so far, these two strategies converge, despite their differences, in their judgments about our temptation case. Nevertheless, it seems that things could fall apart, and this in two different ways. First, it seems that the singularity of valuing does not ensure that one will later regret acting on it; and future regret might not track the difference between singular and general attitude. So it seems that the two lines of argument for the attenuated authority of the singular evaluative ranking might come apart. Second, we can wonder if the appeal to the presumptive authority of the action policy might in some

---

53. At this point it may be useful briefly to locate my discussion within the context of the exchange between Bernard Williams and Christine Korsgaard about internalism about practical reasons. In "Skepticism about Practical Reason" (*Journal of Philosophy* [1986]: 5–25), Korsgaard argues that Williams's claim that all practical reasons are internal reasons is compatible with the ideas, first, that there are structural features of practical reason that will be reflected in the "subjective motivational set" of any rational agent, and, second, that these structural features induce substantive demands on any rational agent. Williams, in turn, acknowledges the first point. And he says that if a theory could establish the second point—that there are such resulting substantive demands—"what it would yield would be a limiting version of internalism." ("Postscript: Some Further Notes on Internal and External Reasons" in Elijah Millgram, ed., *Varieties of Practical Reasoning* [Cambridge, MA: MIT Press, 2001], 91–97, at 94.) But Williams is also skeptical that such structural features will yield substantive reasons. My essay aims to understand and to highlight features of authority and stability of elements of the agent's "subjective motivational set" by drawing on structural features of our temporally extended planning agency. In this respect, my approach to rational willpower is to some extent in the spirit of Korsgaard's first observation, though my focus is, more specifically, on rational planning agency. I do not, however, claim to uncover the kinds of substantive reasons for action for all rational agents that are at stake in Korsgaard's second point.

cases have a different force than the appeal to the pragmatically grounded stability of that action policy. What to say?

The second potential divergence in the strategies will, I think, be, somewhat attenuated by complex relations between agential authority and stability. First, the satisfaction involved in agential authority induces a kind of stability. Second, the agential authority of an attitude itself provides grounds for its reasonable stability, given the role of cross-temporally stable attitudes with agential authority in temporally extended forms of self-government and integrity that we value.[54] There is more to say about these matters than I can say here. But what we can say is that if there are these kinds of interrelations between agential authority and reasonable stability over time, the second of the two threats of divergence between our two strategies will be less forceful.

In any case, we are left with the first threat, which seems real enough. It does seem that the two lines of argument for the attenuated authority of the conflicting evaluative ranking—one that appeals to singularity, one that appeals to anticipated future regret—can come apart in certain temptation cases. And if they do come apart, it remains unclear whether we can arrive at an univocal on-balance judgment of instrumental rationality.

This returns us to the very idea of an on-balance judgment of instrumental rationality and to the question of whether there are preconditions for such judgments. And my tentative conjecture is that in our temptation case, a univocal on-balance judgment of instrumental rationality will depend on there being a convergence of the different concerns highlighted by our two strategies. This will require a convergence in the impact on the authority of present evaluative ranking of appeals to singularity, on the one hand, and to regret, on the other. And it will require a convergence in the significance of appeals to the authority and the stability of action policy. In the absence of such convergence, a precondition for such an on-balance judgment may not be met. In

54. I explore this idea in more detail in my "Anchors for Deliberation," in Christopher Lumer and Sandro Nannini, eds., *Intentionality, Deliberation and Autonomy* (Aldershot, etc.: Ashgate, forthcoming). There are related themes in in Jed Rubenfeld, *Freedom and Time: A Theory of Constitutional Self-Government* (New Haven, CT: Yale University Press, 2001). See e.g., pp. 143–44.

contrast, for those temptation cases in which there is such convergence, our two strategies, taken together, succeed in what we have been trying to do. By drawing on basic features of our temporally extended planning agency, they make theoretical room for instrumentally rational will-power.[55]

55. An earlier version of this essay was written for and presented at the 2002 Amsterdam Workshop on Intention and Rationality. This final version was written for and is forthcoming in a volume of essays associated with that workshop, edited by Bruno Verbeek and tentatively titled *Reasons and Intentions* (Aldershot, etc.: Ashgate, forthcoming). It appears here first. I presented a brief synopsis of some of the arguments of this essay, in a talk entitled "Personal Rules and Rational Willpower," at the symposium "The Rationality of Rule-Following" at the 2004 meetings of the Association of American Law Schools. "Personal Rules and Rational Will-power" subsequently appeared in *San Diego Law Review* 42 (2005): 61–68. Many thanks to Jonathan Shemmer, Allen Wood, and participants in the 2002 Amsterdam Workshop on Intention and Rationality, and the Stanford Social Ethics and Normative Theory discussion group, for helpful discussions, and to Chrisoula Andreou, Govert den Hartogh, Elijah Millgram, and Jed Rubenfeld for helpful correspondence. Special thanks to Agnieszka Jaworksa and Gideon Yaffe for extensive and very helpful discussions. This essay was revised while I was a Fellow at the Center for Advanced Study in Behavioral Sciences. I am grateful for financial support provided by The Andrew W. Mellon Foundation.

SHARED VALUING AND FRAMEWORKS FOR PRACTICAL REASONING

I. FRAMEWORKS

Intentions, plans, and policies provide background frameworks that structure deliberation and practical reasoning. These background frameworks have a characteristic stability over time. They shape practical reasoning, sometimes by shaping what options are to be considered, sometimes by shaping what is to count as a consideration of significance in favor of or contrary to options considered. In providing such frameworks, our intentions, plans, and policies help constitute and support important forms of cross-temporal coordination and organization both within the life of an individual agent and socially, across different lives. These forms of organization—both intra- and interpersonal—are central to our ability to achieve complex, temporally extended goals. Our capacities for such intention-like attitudes, and associated structures of planning and practical reasoning, are, for temporally persisting and social agents like us, more or less all-purpose, universal means: they are means to an extremely wide range of potentially divergent human goals.[1]

---

1. So these capacities (and/or the social conditions that support them) are candidates for the role of a Rawlsian primary good. See John Rawls, *A Theory of Justice* rev. ed. (Cambridge, MA: Harvard University Press, 1999), 62, 92–93. Crystal Thorpe explores the implications of a related idea for the idea that there are reasons that we all share (in a sense that differs from that of "shared valuing" to be discussed below). See her "A Puzzle about Humean Theories of Practical Reason" (unpublished MS).

And that is one basic reason why distinctive norms introduced by these organizing and co-ordinating structures have rational force for us.

Or so I have argued on several different occasions in developing what I have called the planning theory, a theory that I have also characterized as a modest theory of the will.[2] My aim in the present essay is to highlight these themes and then to extend them. My hope is that we can thereby arrive at a deeper understanding of a wide range of interrelated practical phenomena. We can, in particular, begin to develop a model of an important range of social phenomena that, because of their framework-providing role, are plausibly understood as forms of *shared valuing*.

2. FOUR KINDS OF FRAMEWORK

Let me begin by briefly noting four kinds of cases in which, as I see it, relevant intentions, plans, and/or policies provide various kinds of background frameworks for practical reasoning. I will then turn to a somewhat more detailed discussion of each of the cases.

In the first—and basic—case, a background framework is provided by an individual's prior intentions and plans concerning her more or less specific future courses of action. Perhaps she has settled on a complex plan for her day, and this structures her ensuing practical thinking and action.

2. Early statements are in "Intention and Means–End Reasoning," *Philosophical Review* 90 (1981): 252–65, and in "Taking Plans Seriously," *Social Theory and Practice* 9 (1983), 271–87. I develop these ideas (and some important qualifications) further in *Intention, Plans, and Practical Reason* (Cambridge, MA: Harvard University Press, 1987; reissued by CSLI Publications, 1999), and *Faces of Intention: Selected Essays on Intention and Agency* (New York: Cambridge University Press, 1999). A more recent development is sketched in "Reflection, Planning, and Temporally Extended Agency," *Philosophical Review* 109 (2000): 35–61 [this volume, essay 2]. In my "Introduction" to *Faces of Intention*, 5, I describe the planning theory as a modest theory of the will, one that does justice to the role of the will in our practical lives while avoiding Davidsonian concerns with "mysterious acts of the will." (See Donald Davidson, "Intending," in his *Essays on Actions and Events* [New York: Oxford University Press, 1980], 83–102, at 83.)

In "Reflection, Planning, and Temporally Extended Agency," I argue further that certain planning structures help constitute and support cross-temporal connections and continuities central to a broadly Lockean view of personal identity, and thereby to (what I call) agential authority. A full story of the norms characteristic of these planning structures would appeal as well to these considerations and their connections to issues of autonomy. But to keep the present discussion manageable, I will mostly put these matters aside here. For a related but different appeal to roles in constituting and supporting Lockean continuities and connections see Agnieszka Jaworska, "Caring and Internality" *Philosophy and Phenomenological Research* (forthcoming).

Her plan poses problems about means and the like, and it filters options inconsistent with the plan. Or anyway, it does this so long as it is not reconsidered and changed; and the role of such plans in organizing our lives—in part in tandem with our limited cognitive resources—exerts rational pressure against such reconsideration and change.

Second, similar frameworks can be provided by *shared* intentions—intentions that involve more than one individual agent and concern shared, coordinated activities of those individual agents. Perhaps you and I share an intention to organize and run a conference together. This shared intention then structures our relevant, interlocking practical reasoning—including relevant bargaining and negotiation—about how to execute our shared intention.

In yet a further kind of case, plan-like frameworks concern not only courses of action, but what considerations are to be given justifying significance or weight in relevant deliberation and practical reasoning. In a central case, this framework is provided by policies about how to treat certain considerations in relevant practical reasoning. Perhaps, for example, you have a policy of discounting in your deliberation concerns with revenge, despite your susceptibility to strong desires for it. In this case the cited policy about practical reasoning is a policy of an individual: namely, you. But it also seems that certain groups can have analogous policies: perhaps, for example, a philosophy department has a policy of not allowing considerations of congeniality to enter into its faculty hiring decisions.

So we have four main cases:

1. *Individual intentions and plans concerning individual action*: Individual S's prior intentions and plans concerning her own future conduct frame her practical reasoning by posing problems and filtering options.
2. *Shared intention concerning shared action*: S_1's and S_2's shared intention to J frames their interlocking deliberation and bargaining by posing problems and filtering options.
3. *Individual policies concerning what to treat as a justifying reason*: Individual S's policies, concerning the justifying significance or weight to be given to consideration C in her own practical reasoning, frame that practical reasoning.

4. *Shared policy concerning what to treat as a justifying reason*: S_1 and S_2 have a shared policy concerning the justifying significance or weight to be given to consideration C in relevant contexts of shared deliberation.

I have discussed (1)–(3) in earlier work. Here I want to highlight certain themes from these earlier discussions. I will then turn to (4) with the hope that ideas from (1)–(3) can be extended in ways that shed light on (4). In this way I hope to shed light on forms of shared valuing.

3. INDIVIDUAL INTENTION CONCERNING INDIVIDUAL ACTION

Begin with intentions and plans of an individual agent concerning more or less specific courses of action of that agent.[3] I intend, let us suppose, to work on this paper for several hours this morning, then finish reading a recent Ph.D. thesis draft, then, if it is sunny, meet Susan for lunch in the park. I arrived at these intentions, and the plan in which they are embedded, for various reasons. Some of these reasons are specific to particular elements of the plan, and some of them concern the overall organization of the plan and its relation to other, larger plans of mine (e.g., to take a vacation next week).

Such intentions and plans engage distinctive norms of consistency, coherence, and stability—norms that go beyond those that apply to ordinary desires. Other things equal, an agent's intentions and plans are to be, taken together, consistent with each other and with her beliefs about the world. Further, one's intentions and plans, while typically partial, need to be filled in appropriately as time goes by. They need to be filled in with subplans concerning means and the like, subplans that are at least as extensive as one believes is (now) needed in order to do what one intends and plans; otherwise these intentions and plans will be threatened with means-end incoherence.[4] And, finally, while such intentions and plans are

---

3. See *Intention, Plans, and Practical Reason*, esp. chaps. 2 and 3.
4. See ibid. 31. Note that this demand for means-end coherence can exert rational pressure in favor of a decision among several means, none of which is, taken individually, a necessary means; for it may be (and frequently is) that what is necessary for one to achieve one's intended end is that one reach some decision or other concerning alternative, nonnecessary but individually sufficient means.

not, of course, irrevocable, they are normally stable: their reconsideration and change—typically (but not always) in light of new information—is itself subject to distinctive norms of reasonable stability. Responsiveness to these demands for consistency, coherence, and stability promotes our general interests in the overall, cross-temporal organization of our lives, both individual and social. These general interests in what is for us the universal means of such cross-temporal organization help give these demands for consistency, coherence, and stability a distinctive rational force.[5]

Do such intentions themselves give the agent yet further reasons for action? Here we face conflicting pressures. On the one hand, we do not want to say simply that my intention to A gives me a new reason to A, a reason that is of the same sort as the reasons for A that will normally have led me to my intention in the first place. We do not want to say this, because we do not want to sanction a simple form of bootstrapping. We do not want to say that simply by forming an intention in favor of an action that, I know, would otherwise not be one I have sufficient reason to perform, I directly give myself a new reason for so acting that can tip the scale of reasons. Irrationally forming an intention to act in a way that is contrary to the balance of one's acknowledged, prior reasons for action does not seem to be a way of making it straightforwardly rational for one to go ahead and act in the way one intends.[6]

On the other hand, even if one's initial intention is itself rationally criticizable, it nevertheless engages demands of means-end coherence: we nevertheless recognize a kind of rational pressure to settle on means and the like and engage in associated practical reasoning.[7] Further, we sometimes settle on a course of action—form an intention in its favor—even though,

5. One way to put the point is that responsiveness to these demands partly constitutes planning agency, and planning agency is, for reasons noted, a universal means for temporally persisting and social agents like us. So means-end reason enters twice: as a norm of means-end coherence on one's intentions and plans; and in an argument that one has reason to be, as one is, a planning agent, since planning agency is, for us, a universal means.

6. For many of the points in this and the next paragraph see "Intention and Means-End Reasoning" and Intention, Plans, and Practical Reason, 23–49.

7. See the discussion of Mondale's intention to challenge Reagan's "Star Wars" plan in the Presidential debate in Intention, Plans, and Practical Reason, 24–49. R. Jay Wallace emphasizes a closely related point in his "Normativity, Commitment, and Instrumental Reason," Philosophers' Imprint vol. 1 no. 3 (2001), www.philosophersimprint.org/001003. Wallace emphasizes that choice, decision, and intention bring with them distinctive demands of instrumental reason, even in the absence of the agent's endorsement of the intended end as good. I am in agreement with Wallace on this point.

so far as we can see, this course of action is not, at least prior to our decision, superior to some conflicting competitor. Sometimes, in what I have called Buridan cases, we suppose that these courses of action are evaluatively on a par.[8] Sometimes we may suspect or know that one course is superior but not know which one.[9] Sometimes we may think that each of several conflicting options has something to be said for it, but these considerations are in a way incommensurable and there is no further fact, or judgment to be made, about which option is better.[10] In any of these cases we nevertheless recognize that once we decide on a particular course of action, we are under rational pressure to settle matters of means and the like. And this suggests that our intention or decision really does provide a new reason for action.

I have tried to do justice to both of these conflicting pressures by appealing to the idea that such prior intentions and plans provide *framework reasons.*[11] This appeal to framework reasons involves four ideas. First, in the absence of reconsideration or abandonment, prior intentions and plans structure further reasoning about means and the like, reasoning that is sensitive to rational demands for consistency and means-end coherence of one's plans. They do this by posing problems for such reasoning, problems of how to fill in one's partial plans in the pursuit of means-end coherence. And they do this by providing a filter on options by way of demands for consistency with prior intentions and plans, taken together with relevant beliefs. Second, we

8. See my "Davidson's Theory of Intention," reprinted in *Faces of Intention,* esp. 219–20. See also Edna Ullmann-Margalit and Sidney Morgenbesser, "Picking and Choosing," *Social Research* 44 (1977): 757–85.

9. See Frank R. Stockton's 1882 story, "The Lady, or the Tiger?" in Thomas K. Parkes (ed.), *The American Short Story* (New York: Galahad Books, 1994), 202–7.

10. See Joseph Raz, "Incommensurability and Agency," in his *Engaging Reason: On the Theory of Value and Action* (Oxford: Oxford University Press, 1999), 65. See also Richard Holton, "Intention and Weakness of Will," *Journal of Philosophy* 96 (1999): 245.

11. See *Intention, Plans, and Practical Reason,* 28–35. John Broome is concerned with a similar tension between avoiding bootstrapping and providing a normative role for intentions. This leads him to distinguish reasons from what he calls "normative requirements". On his view, there is a normative requirement not to intend an end without intending a known, necessary means; but this does not mean that intending the end is a reason for intending those means. My account of the demand for means-end coherence parallels Broome's account of the normative requirement connecting intended ends and necessary means. I think, though, that we differ in the account we would give of what I call reasonable stability of intention. See John Broome, "Are Intentions Reasons? And How Should We Cope with Incommensurable Values?," in Christopher W. Morris and Arthur Ripstein (eds.), *Practical Rationality and Preferences Essays for David Gauthier* (Cambridge: Cambridge University Press, 2001), esp. 114–19.

can nevertheless step back and criticize the entire plan-like structure that emerges—including both intended end and derived, intended means—in light of reasons for and against these larger structures. Even if this larger plan is coherent and consistent, it may nevertheless be insufficiently supported by relevant reasons. Third, there are important, general reasons—reasons grounded in central features of our temporally extended agency—that favor stability of one's framework of prior intentions and plans. But, fourth, such intentions and plans are not irrevocable. They remain open to reconsideration and change, especially in certain cases in which one newly learns that the reasons for which one originally arrived at one's intentions are no longer in force, or one recognizes that one's original reasons were even then, and continue to be, insufficient to justify one's initial decision. And this leads us to recognize an important question: what are appropriate norms of intention and plan stability?[12]

This question about reasonable stability is, I think, quite difficult. It raises deep questions about the interaction between two features of our planning agency. On the one hand, we engage in long-term planning aimed at determining future conduct in ways that are sensitive to our cognitive limitations and achieve important forms of cross-temporal organization that are able to bear scrutiny over the temporally extended stretch of the planned activity. On the other hand, at the time of action it is the agent *at that time* who is in control, not some "past self" who settled on a prior plan or "future self" at, so to speak, plan's end. Different views of stability respond differently to these twin features of our planning agency; and disagreements here are at the bottom of debates about versions of "sophistication" and "resolute choice." These are not, however, matters we need go into in detail here.[13] All

---

12. In his seminal 1976 paper, Gilbert Harman emphasized that "the system of intentions has an inertia that keeps it going when desire fades" ("Practical Reasoning," reprinted in Gilbert Harman, *Reasoning, Meaning, and Mind* [Oxford: Oxford University Press, 1999], at 62). In appealing to the reasonable stability of intention, I am agreeing with this idea of Harman, but I am also emphasizing that this is a phenomenon that can be assessed in light of relevant norms of reasonable stability. I briefly indicate relations between this approach and broadly Deweyian ideas about deliberation and "entanglements" in "Taking Plans Seriously," 277–78. Richard Holton also emphasizes the significance of the normative dimension of stability in his "Intention and Weakness of Will," 247–51.

13. I discuss these issues in "Toxin, Temptation, and the Stability of Intention," in *Faces of Intention*, 58–90, where I defend a view in the space between "sophisticated" and "resolute" choice. The *locus classicus* for the idea of resolute choice is Edward F. McClennen, *Rationality and Dynamic Choice: Foundational Explorations* (Cambridge: Cambridge University Press, 1990).

that is needed for present purposes is the recognition of the theoretical importance of norms of reasonable stability of prior intentions and plans.[14]

This idea of reasonable stability is a key to the relation between demands for consistency and means-end coherence, on the one hand, and framework reasons, on the other. Consistency and means-end coherence are requirements on one's overall package of intentions and plans, given one's beliefs. By themselves, however, these requirements do not fully explain the idea of framework reasons. To explain that idea, we need also to appeal to reasonable stability. For example, given an intention in favor of E, and a belief that to achieve E one must settle on an intention in favor of means M, one is faced with means-end incoherence if one intends E but does not intend M. So one needs either (a) to intend M or (b) to give up one's intention in favor of E. So far there is no presumption in favor of either (a) or (b). Once we add reasonable stability as a feature of the prior intention in favor of E, however, there is a presumption specifically in favor of intending M. One can, of course, override this presumption by abandoning the intention in favor of E; but that will raise issues about potentially unreasonable instability (though, of course, it will sometimes be *unreasonable not* to abandon an ill-formed prior intention). When we in this way tie demands for consistency and coherence of our intentions and plans together with norms of reasonable stability of those intentions and plans, we arrive at a model of intentions and plans as framework reasons.[15]

The picture that emerges is that prior intentions and plans, so long as they are not reconsidered or abandoned, structure further reasoning about means and the like, and they do this in ways that are shaped by requirements for consistency and coherence of those intentions and plans. So long as one does not reconsider or abandon those plans, they are poised to play this framework-providing role in practical reasoning. But we may on occasion—especially in light of relevant, new information— reasonably reconsider and, perhaps, abandon such prior intentions and plans. Here norms of reasonable stability come to the fore. Finally, the

14. See my *Intention, Plans, and Practical Reason*, chap. 5; see also Holton, "Intention and Weakness of Will," 247–51.

15. I briefly consider relations between the idea of a framework reason and Joseph Raz's notion of an exclusionary reason in *Intention, Plans, and Practical Reason*, 180 n. 11. See Joseph Raz, *Practical Reason and Norms* (London: Hutchinson, 1975; reissued by Princeton University Press, 1990).

norms of stability that ground these framework-setting roles are themselves grounded not solely in the particular reasons for the particular intentions and actions at issue. They are also grounded, more broadly,
in our general interest in the overall cross-temporal organization and
coherence of our practical thought and action.

4. SHARED INTENTION CONCERNING
SHARED ACTION

Turn now to shared intention—our shared intention, for example, to
organize a conference together. In a series of papers,[16] I have proposed that
you and I share an intention to J—at least in the basic case—when we each
intend that we J, we each intend that we J in accordance with and because
of each of our intentions that we J and their meshing subplans, and all this
is common knowledge.[17] Further, in the context of the shared intention,
the persistence of each of our intentions that we J is dependent on the
known persistence of the other's intention that we J, and this mutual
interdependence of these intentions of each is common knowledge.[18]

The idea, then, is that such a shared intention consists of a complex
structure of interlocking and interdependent practical attitudes of the
individual participants, in a context of common knowledge. Such shared
intentions lie behind important kinds of shared activity, including what I
have called *jointly intentional activity* and *shared cooperative activity*. I will not
repeat here all the details of these models of shared intention and shared
agency; but I do want to emphasize several points.

First, when two people share an intention to J, they each intend that
their J-ing proceed by way of both of their intentions that they J and their

---

16. See my "Shared Cooperative Activity," "Shared Intention," "Shared Intention and
Mutual Obligation," and "I Intend that We J"—all in *Faces of Intention*.

17. For a qualification see my "I Intend that We J," in *Faces of Intention*, 143–44.

18. See ibid. 153. The claim is only that there is this known mutual interdependence in this
basic case of shared intention. There can be special cases in which I intend that we J even
though my intention is, I know, not dependent on a corresponding intention of yours.
Margaret Gilbert has emphasized related forms of mutual interdependence in her extensive
work on shared agency. On her view, however, the relevant mutual interdependence always
involves an obligation-constituting joint commitment, whereas on my view this need not
always be so. See, e.g., her "What Is It for *Us* to Intend?" in her *Sociality and Responsibility* (Lanham,
Md.: Rowman & Littlefield, 2000), 14–36.

meshing subplans. In this sense their individual intentions interlock, and they each intend that their joint *J*-ing proceed by way of the agency of each. This does not, of course, mean that when there is shared intention the participants must already have arrived at complete, meshing subplans. As in the case of an individual's intentions and plans concerning her own activity, shared intentions will typically be partial and will need to be filled in as time goes by. There will be rational pressure on each participant, when engaged in practical reasoning and bargaining about how to carry out the shared intention, to adjust her subplans in ways that will successfully mesh with those of the other participant in the shared intention. Each person's complex intention—that they *J* by way of interlocking, meshing intentions and subplans of each—provides that person with a framework reason to fill in her own plans with subplans that support the joint activity in ways that mesh with the subplans of her partner.

Second, such shared intentions require neither shared reasons for the intention or the shared activity nor agreement that the shared activity is superior to its alternatives. Two people may share an intention to organize a conference even if they each have very different reasons for this: perhaps one person's reason is the advancement of scholarship, while the other person's reason has more to do with his own professional reputation. Further, even if there were agreement about which reasons are relevant, they may nevertheless disagree about which shared activity would be best. They may arrive at their shared intention by way of bargaining and compromise. However, even given divergence in the reasons for participating in the shared intention and/or divergence in underlying value judgment, their shared intention structures and coordinates their reasoning and bargaining concerning relevant subplans and the like. It structures their planning and bargaining about, for example, when to have the conference, whom to invite, what its main topics will be, and so on. It provides a background framework for such reasoning and bargaining.

This structuring role derives from the fact that the relevant intentions of each participant favor the coordinated, interlocking, meshing execution of each person's intentions and subplans in favor of the shared activity. Demands for coherence and consistency on the intentions of each of the individuals then require each to seek consistency and coherence in the overall package of subplans of both. So each will need to seek subplans that mesh with the other's subplans. These pressures toward meshing subplans will help shape the reasoning and bargaining of each in the pursuit of the shared activity.

This shared framework will be subject to demands for stability. Some of these demands will derive from familiar requirements of reasonable stability on the intentions of each. In this respect, there is a commonality with the case of an individual's prior plans about her own activities. But it is also true that some relevant demands for stability will normally derive also from associated interpersonal obligations, obligations that are normally (though, on my view, not universally) generated in cases of such shared intentions by way of associated assurances, promises, intentionally induced reliance, and the like.[19]

Throughout, a central source of these demands for stability, consistency, and coherence is a general concern with organization and coordination. Even in the case of an individual's plans about her own activities, these concerns with organization have a social dimension: a main reason for constructing plans is to help make oneself a reliable participant in forms of social coordination. But in the case of shared intentions and plans, concerns with interpersonal organization take center stage.

Note that these structures can also arise in cases of shared *policies*—for example, your and my shared policy of meeting weekly to discuss the philosophy of action. This shared policy will frame our relevant reasoning and bargaining about, say, where to meet, what journal article to talk about, and so on. And our shared policy will be subject to analogous pressures—both individually and socially based—for stability.

I will return below to this idea of a shared policy; but first it will be useful to highlight certain commonalities that have emerged from the discussion so far.

5. PARTIALITY AND FRAMEWORKS

We have noted that in both the individual and the shared cases relevant intentions, plans, and policies concerning action are typically partial: they specify certain actions or ends but typically leave certain issues about means, preliminary steps, specifications, and the like to later practical

19. See my "Shared Intention and Mutual Obligation."

reasoning and, especially in the case of shared intention, bargaining. This partiality makes room for important forms of further practical reasoning and bargaining. Relevant intentions provide a background framework, and associated framework reasons, for that further practical reasoning and bargaining. They provide this framework in the following ways:

(1) They pose problems about further means and the like, problems driven by the need for forms of plan coherence.
(2) They constrain solutions to those problems given the needs for plan consistency.
(3) They play roles (1) and (2) in so far as they are not reconsidered or abandoned; and their reconsideration, and potential change, is itself subject to relevant norms of reasonable stability.

In the individual case, the plans whose coherence, consistency, and stability are at stake are those of the individual concerning her own activity. In the shared case, what is of primary interest are the interdependent plans of each concerning the joint activity of both, a joint activity that each intends to issue from interlocking intentions and meshing subplans of each. These distinctive complexities in what is intended by each participant in a shared intention lead, by way of demands of consistency and means-end coherence on the intentions of each, to corresponding rational pressures toward meshing, coordinated subplans among all the participants. In the shared case, further, interactions among the individuals may well, by way of norms about promissory obligations, assurances, and the like, generate further, special grounds for the stability of the shared intentions. (Of course, there is also room for assurances and the like in the case of an individual's plans about her own activity. The point here is only that the roles of assurance-based obligations and the like are particularly salient in the case of shared intention.)

In both individual and shared cases, the grounds for these demands for consistency, coherence, and stability include general concerns with overall organization and coordination, both within a single person's temporally extended life and socially, across lives. And in both cases, these demands do not in general depend on the prior superiority of the relevant course of action: both the individual and the shared cases can, for example, sometimes be Buridan cases, or involve relevant forms of incommensurability or of weakness of will; and shared intentions, and their subplans, can be a compromise in the face of disagreement about the best. In all these cases, prior intentions—individual or shared—provide (albeit, revocable) framework reasons for relevant means, preliminary steps, specifications, and the like.

So there are deep commonalities across the cases of individual and shared intentions. As we will now see, there are also, in many cases of both sorts, important links to relevant policies about what to treat as a justifying reason for action.

6. INDIVIDUAL POLICIES CONCERNING WHAT
TO TREAT AS A REASON

The first step is to turn to a different kind of framework for the practical reasoning of an individual.[20] The basic idea here is that an agent may have policies—as I call them, *self-governing* policies—that say which considerations are to be given what sort of justifying significance or weight in her motivationally effective practical reasoning.[21] A person might, for example, have a policy of discounting or bracketing in her practical reasoning various forms of anger or resentment; another person might have a policy of sexual abstinence, a policy that involves refraining from giving weight in her deliberation to her desires for sexual activity; a third person might have a policy of giving great significance in his deliberation and action to style and verve; a fourth might have a policy that assigns great weight to certain religious practices in her deliberation about what to do; a fifth a policy that gives weight to honesty in her public assessments of the work of her colleagues, even if this is personally difficult.

Such self-governing policies provide a framework for practical reasoning. As I have emphasized, individual or shared intentions and plans concerning

---

20. See my "Reflection, Planning, and Temporally Extended Agency"; "A Desire of One's Own," *Journal of Philosophy* 100 (2003): 221–42 [this volume, essay 7]; and "Autonomy and Hierarchy," *Social Philosophy and Policy* 20 (2003): 156–76 [this volume, essay 8].

21. For some related ideas see T. M. Scanlon, *What We Owe to Each Other* (Cambridge, MA: Harvard University Press, 1998), 45–53, a discussion to which I am indebted. I discuss some of these ideas from Scanlon in "Identification, Decision, and Treating as a Reason," in my *Faces of Intention*, 196–97.

specific activities also provide frameworks for practical reasoning. Let me say a bit about how these frameworks are related to each other.

One's intentions concerning specific activities normally pose, in light of demands for coherence, problems of how to fill in one's associated partial plans of action with specifications of means and the like; and they constrain solutions to those problems by way of demands for consistency. The framework-providing role of these intentions consists in part in posing problems and constraining solutions. In filling in one's plans, however, one will typically need to weigh various pros and cons concerning alternative means or the like. And here one's self-governing policies can provide a relevant background framework of commitments to treating certain considerations as having weight or other kinds of justifying significance in such deliberations.

So, to a first approximation, intentions concerning specific activities and self-governing policies provide different kinds of frameworks that normally interact with one another in the indicated way. However, it should also be noted that self-governing policies may also pose their own, distinctive problems of means. They are, after all, policies about how to reason; and one may find that, in order for one to reason effectively in the way favored by one's policy, one needs to take related steps. Such steps may well include forms of management of the impact of related desires or emotions—for example, of the impact on one's practical reasoning and action of anger or indignation.[22]

As I see it, such self-governing policies will themselves normally be to some extent responsive to and grounded in judgements about value, judgements that are subject to characteristic intersubjective pressures.[23] However, such judgements of value many times leave underdetermined important details about how to live one's life.[24] Self-governing policies are sometimes in part a response to such underdetermination by value judgment and the resulting

---

22. This is a version of a central theme of Harry Frankfurt. See esp. his *The Importance of What We Care About* (Cambridge: Cambridge University Press, 1988).

23. Though in a particular case such policies may in fact not be responsive to any such judgments.

24. See, e.g., Joseph Raz, *The Morality of Freedom* (Oxford: Oxford University Press, 1986), chap. 14, and Robert Nozick, *Philosophical Explanations* (Cambridge, MA: Harvard University Press, 1981), esp. 446–50. My own discussion is primarily in "A Desire of One's Own". And compare John Broome's discussion of the interaction between such issues and the normative role of intention in his "Are Intentions Reasons?," esp. 114–19.

need to go beyond prior judgements concerning multiple, conflicting values in shaping one's own life (while recognizing the value of alternatives). Self-governing policies are, as I have already suggested, also sometimes in part an element in our efforts at self-management, given our need to reflect on and manage various forms of first-order motivation.[25] A person's policy of bracketing forms of anger or resentment can be in part a policy of reflective self-management, and in part a (in some cases and to some extent, life-defining) response to complex and conflicting evaluative pressures concerning the role of the reactive emotions in a human life. And a person's policy of bracketing forms of embarrassment and personal discomfort when it comes to certain kinds of professional assessments may also play an analogous, dual role. Given these characteristic roles in our practical lives—the response to underdetermination by value judgment, the role in self-management, the provision of associated structures to practical reasoning—it seems reasonable to say that such self-governing policies are a kind of *valuing*, a kind of valuing that is related to but different from value judgment.[26]

Our self-governing policies are under pressure to be consistent with one another and to constitute, when taken together, a coherent framework for practical reasoning. One result of such pressures can be that such policies involve significant context relativity. I can, for example, have a policy of not giving weight to certain kinds of considerations of friendliness in job interviews or the like, even though I do give those considerations great weight in other contexts. There are limits here concerning how fine-grained such context relativity can be before it undermines important forms of personal coherence; but this is not a matter we need to resolve here.

Again, it also seems clear that norms of stability will be of great importance in this domain, and this for general reasons about cross-temporal

---

25. I discuss interactions between these two different roles of self-governing policies, and the relevance of these interactions to hierarchical models of autonomous agency, in my "Autonomy and Hierarchy."

26. See also my "Valuing and the Will," *Philosophical Perspectives* 14 (2000): 249–65 [this volume, essay 3], and "Autonomy and Hierarchy." Concerning the distinction between valuing and value judgment see Gary Watson, "Free Action and Free Will," *Mind* 96 (1987): 145–72, at 150; and Gilbert Harman, "Desired Desires," as reprinted in his *Explaining Value and Other Essays in Moral Philosophy* (Oxford: Oxford University Press, 2000), 129–30. Let me note that I think some such distinction, and my treatment of it here, is available to a range of different views in metaethics, including both forms of expressivism and forms of cognitivism.

organization and coherence within one's temporally extended life. While such self-governing policies are normally not irrevocable or, to use an idea from Harry Frankfurt, volitionally necessary,[27] their frequent, significant change would tend toward a seriously fractured life.

Self-governing policies help shape what we treat as having justificatory weight or significance in our reasoning about what to do. In this way they help determine what I have called the "subjective normative authority" of certain considerations.[28] They help provide a framework of justificatory significance that responds, in a coordinated way, to the dual pressures both to manage one's motivational life and to respond to underdetermination by value judgment. The pressure to respond to underdetermination by value judgement is, then, rooted in a kind of partiality—a partiality in one's operative framework of reasons, given only one's intersubjectively account-able judgments of value. So there is here a certain parallel with the partiality of ordinary plans of action. However, whereas the partiality of plans of action is a partiality in their specification of courses of action, the partiality at issue here, and to which self-governing policies are in part a response, is one engendered by underdetermination by value judgment of broad features of significance in a life of one's own.

Brief reflection on related work of Joseph Raz is useful here. Raz sees reasons for action as frequently not determining a uniquely rational course of action. Reasons, rather, frequently only pick out a set of options each of which would be compatible with the reasons there are antecedent to the choice. There remains a need for the agent to choose from these reason-eligible alternatives:

> reasons for action are better characterized as making actions eligible rather than requiring their performance on pain of irrationality. In typical situations, reason does not determine what is to be done. Rather it sets a range of eligible options before agents, who choose among them as they feel inclined . . . the will plays a role in human agency separate from that of reason, a role that neither kowtows to

27. See his "On the Necessity of Ideals," in his *Necessity, Volition, and Love* (Cambridge: Cambridge University Press, 1999).

28. See my "Two Problems about Human Agency," *Proceedings of the Aristotelian Society* 101 (2001), 309–26 [this volume, essay 5].

reason by endorsing its conclusions nor irrationally rebels against it by refusing to endorse them.[29]

Judgements about reasons frequently only identify a number of "eligible" options among which one must choose. It is the latter role that is played by "the will." In acknowledging this role of the will, Raz endorses what he calls the "classical" conception of human action, in contrast with what he calls the "rationalist" conception.[30]

Now, in emphasizing the roles of first-order planning structures, at times in the face of a sort of underdetermination to which Raz points, my view shares an important feature with what Raz calls the classical conception. Does my appeal to the roles of self-governing policies in shaping what has subjective normative authority, at times in the face of underdetermination by value judgment, also correspond to Razian themes? The answer is complicated.

Raz emphasizes ways in which choice of particular actions in the face of underdetermination by reasons helps make "us into who we are."[31] In this way, choices of particular actions can have an indirect impact on an agent's reasons, by way of the values of integrity and self-respect.[32] And Raz suggests that these choices may also have an impact by way of closing off certain options as not possible for that agent.[33] So far, however, it is choices of particular options that are seen as partially shaping one's reasons.

However, Raz also emphasizes that we can choose general goals from among a myriad of potential goods and that such goals provide reasons for action that one did not have prior to having those goals. They provide such reasons because the satisfaction of such goals is part of the agent's well-being.[34]

29. Raz, "Incommensurability and Agency," 65. Elsewhere Raz calls this *"the basic belief"*—the view "that most of the time people have a variety of options such that it would accord with reason for them to choose any one of them and it would not be against reason to avoid any one of them.... The basic belief applies to large as well as to small decisions" ("Explaining Normativity," in *Engaging Reason*, 100). Raz endorses this basic belief in ibid., 101.

30. Raz, "Incommensurability and Agency," 47.

31. Raz, "The Truth in Particularism," in *Engaging Reason*, 242.

32. Ibid., 243.

33. Ibid., 241.

34. Raz, "Incommensurability and Agency," 63–64. See also Raz, *Morality of Freedom*, chap. 12. Thanks to Nadeem Hussain for emphasizing the significance to the present discussion of this aspect of Raz's views.

Such chosen goals, then, seem to function to some extent like self-governing policies, as I understand them.

As I see it, though, a self-governing policy may give significance to considerations that are more like side constraints than goals—for example, a policy of honesty in public assessments of work of colleagues, or of bracketing the impact of retributive desires. Further, my account highlights not primarily a direct relation to well-being but, rather, a relation between self-governing policies and our general interest in the cross-temporal organization of our practical thought and action, a cross-temporal organization that is a kind of universal means for temporally persisting and social agents like us.[35] As Michael Friedman once put it in conversation, the normativity comes from the constraints of cross-temporal organization. And this relation to cross-temporal organization helps make the characteristic functioning of self-governing policies in our practical lives *ceteris paribus* a case of rational, proper functioning.

Return now to the interaction between the different kinds of framework-providing phenomena I have been discussing. Note that these different framework-providing phenomena will many times be part of a unified package of commitments. A commitment to pursue a certain kind of scientific career, for example, is likely to be in part a first-order plan of action and in part a policy about what considerations to treat as justifying in certain professional contexts. Indeed, full participation in the planned activity may well require commitment to some such associated self-governing policy.

Finally, as this last example suggests, these phenomena may well also involve *shared* intentions and plans, and their characteristic, shared frameworks for practical reasoning and bargaining. After all, to continue with the example, a commitment to pursue a certain kind of scientific career is also likely to involve participation in relevant shared intentions and in the shared cooperative activities associated with the pursuit of the science.[36] Participation in scientific research—like many other important human activities—is, at least normally and in part, participation in a distinctive kind of shared activity.[37]

35. And that helps constitute and support important Lockean ties. See n. 2.
36. Here I was helped by conversation with Michael Friedman.
37. This is compatible with recognizing that it is a kind of shared activity that tends to issue in knowledge. See Alvin Goldman, *Knowledge in a Social World* (Oxford: Oxford University Press, 1999).

Here individual intention, shared intention, and individual self-governing policies are intertwined within a complex package of interrelated commitments. And this takes us within a step of the phenomenon of shared policies about what to treat as a reason.

7. SHARED POLICIES CONCERNING WHAT
TO TREAT AS A REASON

We have seen how individuals can participate in shared intentions or policies concerning their shared activities. And we have seen how individuals can have self-governing policies concerning the justifying significance to be given to various considerations in their deliberation about what to do. We can now put these ideas together and arrive at the idea of shared policies concerning what to treat as having justifying significance in contexts of shared activity and associated shared deliberation.

A philosophy department, for example, may have a shared policy about how to take into account issues of subfield in its searches and associated deliberations.[38] This is a matter on which departments may reasonably diverge. One department may have a shared policy of ignoring such issues; another may have a policy of always restricting consideration to candidates in a previously designated subfield. In each case the policies are, we may suppose, grounded to some extent in considerations about what makes a good department, as well as in other shared policies (e.g., about who gets to vote on such matters). It is possible that the members of the department agree about which policy would be (prior to any departmental commitment to a policy) best, and that this is why the department has that policy. But such shared policies may well go beyond such judgments about value, and do not require agreement in those judgments. Such shared policies nevertheless constitute a commitment, on the part of the individuals in the group, to structuring their shared deliberation and planning in a certain way. In participating in such a shared policy, one need not suppose that it is the best such policy. One may think there is no

---

38. For discussions of related examples see J. David Velleman, "How to Share an Intention," as reprinted in his *The Possibility of Practical Reason* (Oxford: Oxford University Press, 2000), 200–220, and Christopher Kutz, "The Judicial Community," *Philosophical Issues* 11 (2001): 442–69.

single best policy; or one may think that a different policy would be best. Indeed, each member of the department may have a different view of what the best policy would be, but nevertheless come to be committed to a shared policy that (prior to the department's commitment to it) no one sees as best.[39]

Again, different universities may have different shared policies about the justifying weight to be given to legacy considerations in deliberations about undergraduate admissions. One may work in the admissions office and be committed to its policy about such issues without thinking it is the best such policy.

In some cases, particular shared policies concerning what to treat as a reason in certain contexts of shared activity are more or less definitive of the group whose policies they are. If you are going to be a member of a certain scientific research group, you may need to participate in a shared policy of giving weight in scientific debate to certain kinds of evidence, but not to whether or not the person offering the evidence is your friend.[40] Central to certain groups may be a shared policy of treating conformity to particular religious texts or traditions or rituals as a justifying reason for action. Again, a club may have a shared policy of giving justifying weight to, say, religious affiliation, or race, in its deliberations about membership; and that may be why you do not want to be a member of that club. And members of a jury may be required to share a policy of refraining from giving justifying weight to their felt empathy with the defendant, or to information not presented at the trial, when deliberating together in their official capacity as jurors.

As these examples suggest, such shared policies about what to treat as justifying will normally be part of a larger package of commitments, one that includes shared intentions in favor of associated shared activities. A group might have both a shared intention to worship together each Saturday and a shared policy to treat associated rituals and traditions as providing justifying reasons for action on those occasions of shared worship.

39. Though I will not argue for this here, it is not even necessary, I think, that each member thinks the actual policy is best given that the department is committed to it.

40. The policy here will probably concern both treating certain considerations as reasons for action and treating certain considerations as evidence for something like belief formation— perhaps for forms of context-relative acceptance, in a sense I discuss in "Practical Reasoning and Acceptance in a Context," in *Faces of Intention*.

And a scientific research group might have shared intentions to engage in a certain line of research, together with shared policies about what is to count as a justifying consideration in the group's associated deliberations about what to publish. In each case, participation in the relevant shared cooperative activities of religious worship or scientific research involves as well participation in related shared policies about what to treat as a justifying reason in the context of those shared activities.

Such shared policies about what to treat as a reason can help frame shared deliberation in ways analogous to ways in which an individual's self-governing policies help frame her individual deliberation. And this may be so even though there is reasonable disagreement about which such policy would be best. The deliberations of different undergraduate admissions committees may be framed by different shared policies about the justifying role of the fact that a candidate's parents attended that university. And the deliberations of different scientific research groups may be framed by different shared policies about the justifying role of the usefulness of secrecy in the pursuit of lucrative patents.

These shared policies bring with them associated demands for consistency, coherence, and stability. The ground of these demands includes, again, general concerns with coordination and organization over time and interpersonally. And, as in the case of shared intentions and policies concerning courses of action, there may well be pressures in favor of stability that arise specifically from associated assurances and the like. Joining a group, for example, may sometimes involve (perhaps, implicit) promises to participate in certain shared policies about what to treat as justifying in relevant shared contexts.

8. THE CORE CASE AND FORMS OF SHARED VALUING

Suppose our committee has a shared policy to give justifying weight to legacy considerations in admissions decisions: we intend to treat such considerations as justifying in our relevant shared deliberation. Our shared policy is, then, a special kind of shared intention, one whose targeted activity is a certain kind of shared deliberation.

This suggests that we try to understand in what such a shared policy consists by appeal to our earlier story about shared intention. According to this earlier story, we intend to J, in the basic case, just when, in a context of common knowledge, we each intend that we J in accordance with and because of each of our intentions that we J and their meshing subplans, and our individual intentions that we J involve an appropriate kind of mutual interdependence.

So let us apply this story to our cited shared policy about our shared deliberation. We have such a shared policy just when, in a context of common knowledge, we each intend that we give justifying weight to legacy considerations in our shared deliberation and that this proceed in accordance with and because of each of our intentions that we give such weight and their meshing subplans; and there is mutual interdependence between each of our intentions that we give such weight.

And now let us generalize. In what I will call the *core case*, the following holds in a context of common knowledge:

(a) We each intend
   (i) that we give weight to R in relevant shared deliberation, and
   (ii) that (i) proceed by way of each of our (a) (i) intentions and their meshing subplans.
(b) There is mutual interdependence between each of our (a) intentions.

Note that in the core case the shared policy concerns shared deliberation. To see the significance of this limitation, consider an example. Suppose that you and I, in a context of common knowledge, each have a policy of giving forgiveness justifying weight in our individual interactions with others. Though in a very weak sense we share a policy about what to treat as justifying, the targeted context is not one of our shared deliberation: each intends only that he or she deliberate in the cited way in contexts of individual deliberation and action. So this is not a core case.

Note also that the core case requires mutual interdependence between the intentions of each concerning what is to be treated as justifying. Indeed, in the absence of appropriate mutual interdependence, each participant would not normally have an intention that *they* give weight to R in shared deliberation.[41] In some cases, such interdependence will be a result of the need to fix on a group policy in the face of divergence in

---

41. See my "I Intend that We J."

relevant value judgements of the individuals. But there will also be cases of such interdependence in the presence of agreement in relevant value judgment. Perhaps, for example, all the members of a committee agree, for similar reasons, that a particular policy about legacy considerations would be best. Nevertheless, it may also be true that, given their recognition of the need for coordination in such matters, they are each committed to the policy in part also because others are.[42]

It does seem, however, that there are possible cases in which participants in a shared activity each have mutually *in*dependent policies about what to give justifying weight in the context of that shared activity. Such cases would not be core cases even if the cited policies favored the same considerations. Here is an example: You and I each have a policy of giving weight, in the context of our joint research project, to seeking out related published works and acknowledging them in our own publications. We recognize that our shared project might break down were we not to agree in this way. Nevertheless, we are each committed to a policy of giving weight to these considerations whether or not the other does, and in each case our reason for our policy does not refer to the other's policy.

While such a case is possible, it is important to see that there will also be significant pressure in the direction of mutual interdependence. This pressure comes from the structure of the targeted shared activity: in this case, the activity of the joint research project. After all, it is required that there be intentions that this activity proceed by way of meshing subplans. And part of the way the activity frequently proceeds is by way of relevant, shared deliberation. When it does proceed in this way, each participant is committed to there being meshing subplans concerning that deliberation. So each participant is committed to there being a mesh in the relevant policies about what to give weight to in that deliberation. So each has *a* reason to adjust her policies about such weights in order to mesh with her partners' corresponding policies. So when there is such mesh—as there is in our case in which each has the same policy about the weight to be given to certain kinds of scholarship—each will have *a* reason for her contribution to that mesh, a

---

42. Scott Shapiro makes a related point in a different context. See his discussion of his example of the ancient Hebrews in his "Law, Plans, and Practical Reason," *Legal Theory* 8 (2002): 387–441. My discussion here has benefited from Shapiro's discussion.

reason that derives from each person's commitment to mesh together with facts about the other's policy. Granted, it remains possible that this reason is not a reason *for which* the person has her relevant policy. So a certain kind of independence remains possible. But it also seems that, given the intentional structure of the shared activity and associated deliberation, there will frequently be the kind of mutual interdependence that is built into the core case.

The core case, then, involves the condition, first, that the target is shared deliberation and, second, that the intentions of the individuals about what is to be given weight in that deliberation are themselves mutually interdependent. The shared policy in a core case will normally be to some extent responsive to relevant judgements of value on the part of the various participants. In this respect, there is a parallel with the case of an individual's valuings. Nevertheless, the shared policy in the core case requires neither agreement nor disagreement in underlying value judgments: the core case is neutral about this matter. Return, for example, to our policy about seeking out related works by others. We might have this policy because we are in agreement that it is required by broad considerations of scholarship. But perhaps, instead, one of us participates in this policy for this reason, while another participates because he thinks it is a good way to win friends.

Further, the core case can allow for the possibility that the participants recognize the value of alternative policies. A department may be committed to a policy about the relevance of sub-field considerations in its searches even while its members recognize that a case can also be made for an alternative policy.

A shared policy in the core case provides a background framework that structures relevant shared deliberation. It helps fix on certain (in some cases, group-defining) modes of shared deliberation, modes of deliberation that can be at the heart of associated shared activities. It plays these framework-providing roles in the shared deliberation of the group in a way that is neutral concerning the presence or absence of agreement in underlying value judgment and that can allow for recognition of the value of alternatives. Such shared policies are related to, but distinguishable from, the value judgments of the individuals, even in cases of agreement in such judgements.

These framework-providing roles of such shared policies in the core case to some extent parallel the roles of self-governing policies in the life of an individual agent. Since it was those roles that supported the proposal that those self-governing policies were a form of valuing, should we say that such shared policies in the core case are a kind of *shared valuing*?

The issues are delicate. On the one hand, a shared policy in favor of giving significance to R in the core case does not ensure either that the individual participants each judge that R is good or that the individual participants each individually value R. The individual participants must, of course, each be committed to a policy that gives significance to R in certain shared deliberative contexts. Nevertheless, it may be that none of the participants has a self-governing policy that gives weight to R in contexts outside this special shared context. In this sense, it may be that none of the participants individually values R even though they are each participants in the shared policy in favor of R. So it may seem strained to say that a shared policy in the core case in favor of R is a kind of shared valuing.

On the other hand, such a shared policy does help determine what is to be treated by the participants as a justifying consideration in relevant shared practical contexts. It plays a basic, structuring role in the normatively guided deliberation and action of the group. In this respect, it seems a reasonable candidate for a form of shared valuing.

My tentative proposal is that we see such shared policies in the core case as a form of shared valuing but also recognize that it may be important whether or not there are also other forms of agreement.[43] Shared valuings that also involve agreement in the valuings and/or value judgments of the participants may have a special significance in certain important contexts—for example, in the context of certain kinds of friendship.[44] This generic model of shared valuing allows us to describe these stronger conditions of agreement but also to highlight the broad

43. As Seana Shiffrin noted in conversation, such a shared policy may also articulate a shared rationale, one that may be useful when we come up against hard cases. For example, we will give weight to legacy considerations as a way of creating donor loyalty. Shiffrin suggested that such further content in the shared policy may be necessary for shared valuing; but here I find it better just to note that this is one common case of shared valuing.

David Copp discusses a related idea of a "society's values" in his *Morality, Normativity, and Society* (New York: Oxford University Press, 1995), 190–91.

44. Several discussants of this paper at the 2003 Moral Psychology Conference at Franklin and Marshall College emphasized this case of friendship.

and important commonality that is captured by the conditions of the core case.[45]

Granted, if I am a participant in a core case in our shared policy to, say, give weight to legacy considerations, but think this is a bad idea and do not value it, then it might be odd for me simply to say, "We value giving weight to legacy considerations." But I am inclined to see the oddity here in terms of a conversational implicature. What I need to do is tell you "But I myself, as an individual, do not value this." Without that qualification my original remark may be true but misleading.

9. INTERCONNECTED FRAMEWORKS AND THE WILL

I have emphasized parallels and interrelations between shared valuing, in the sense of the core case and other framework-providing phenomena noted earlier in this essay. By exploring these parallels and interrelations, we may hope to clarify important features of shared valuing, provide conceptual resources for distinguishing among cases of shared valuing, distinguish shared valuing from related but different phenomena, highlight the significance of such shared valuing to our lives, and provide models of shared valuing that are sufficiently articulated to do serious theoretical work in our understanding of important social phenomena.

I want to conclude by commenting on two general themes. The first is that there is an important range of human activities that involve, in ways that are organically interconnected, all four of these kinds of framework-providing phenomena. As a member of a scientific research team, for example, I have relevant, individual research plans and self-governing policies that apply to these contexts; and I am a participant in shared intentions to engage in a certain shared research project, as well as shared valuings that structure our deliberation in the pursuit of that shared project. Again, to take an example from a different domain, there will likely be analogous, interconnected planning and policy structures when actors join together in a dramatic production.

---

45. In these three paragraphs I benefited from discussion with the Stanford ethics discussion group and with the Bay Area Forum for Law and Ethics.

A final example comes from the law.[46] Jules Coleman argues that legal officials—including judges, legislators, and administrators—can be seen as engaged in a shared cooperative activity aimed, in part, at "making possible the existence of a durable legal practice."[47] Coleman argues that this point is central to a defence of legal positivism; but that is not a matter we need discuss here. What is important for present purposes is that it is plausible that such shared activities in law would normally involve the quartet of framework-providing structures we have been examining. In particular, Coleman emphasizes that these structures include "parameters of reason[s] that are recognized as appropriate or good."[48] And that seems likely to involve shared valuings concerning relevant legal contexts.

The second theme returns us to the very idea of the will. In each of the four kinds of cases outlined at the beginning of this essay, a framework for practical reasoning is provided by intention-like attitudes that bring with them distinctive norms of consistency, coherence, and stability. These intention-like attitudes are frequently grounded to some extent in inter-subjectively accountable value judgment. However, they may well need to go beyond those judgments in order to fix on sufficiently contoured and articulated courses of action or modes of deliberation, both individual and social. Our need to fix on such courses of action or modes of deliberation is grounded in large part in our need for organizing, cross-temporal structure in our practical thought and action, both individual and social. And we have seen reason to believe that a wide range of important human activities involve an interrelated quartet of structures whose function it is to help constitute and support such cross-temporal organization.

I think that it is natural to say that these organizing, intention-like structures are elements of the will.[49] A characteristic, defining function of

---

46. See Jules L. Coleman, *The Practice of Principle* (Oxford: Oxford University Press, 2001), esp. 95–100. Coleman credits Scott Shapiro with the basic idea. Shapiro develops the idea in a somewhat different way, and in fascinating detail, in his "Law, Plans, and Practical Reason." I discuss some of these views of Shapiro in my "Shapiro on Legal Positivism and Jointly Intentional Activity," *Legal Theory* 8 (2002): 511–17.

47. Coleman, *Practice of Principle*, 97.

48. Ibid., 98.

49. This is a further development of the idea that the planning theory is a modest theory of the will.

the will, so understood, is the cross-temporal organization of our individual and shared practical thought and action, in ways that respond to the underdetermination by judgments about value of the specific contours of our lives, both individual and social; in ways that can allow for recognition of, and respect for, the value of alternative modes of thought and action; and in ways that help us achieve a wide range of human ends. Shared valuing, in particular, is a kind of shared willing.[50]

50. Thanks to Talbot Brewer, John Broome, Edward Hinchman, Simon May, Peter Railton, Gideon Yaffe, members of the Stanford ethics discussion group and the Bay Area Forum for Law and Ethics, and participants in discussions of this essay at Georgetown University, the Analytic Legal Philosophy Conference at Yale Law School, the Australian National University, and the Moral Psychology Conference at Franklin and Marshall College. Work on this essay was supported by a fellowship from the John Simon Guggenheim Memorial Foundation.

Index

accountability
  intersubjective, 8–9, 153 n.45, 155,
    157, 159–160, 165–166, 174–176, 212, 220, 235,
    298, 309
  as responsibility, 4, 111, 114, 186 n.53, 196 n.1,
    221 n.57, 252 n.61
action, explanation of, 25, 27, 39, 196–197,
  200
addict, self-managing, 189–191
addict, unwilling, 40, 72, 77, 130–134, 160, 171 n.23,
  190 n.10
addiction, 23, 38, 68, 90, 160, 171 n.23, 189–191
  see also addict, unwilling; addict, self-
  managing
agency
  core features of, 3, 21–22, 25–26, 28, 46, 50,
    63, 125, 199 n.7, 206, 264
  Humean vs. Kantian theory of, 86
  ideals of, 9, 248
  free, 47–48, 109, 130, 223–225, 244 n.46
  full-blown, 91–92, 94, 96, 98, 100–103
  strong forms of, 6 n.5, 8, 11–14, 138 n.3, 143
    n.18, 161, 164 n.6, 187–189, 199 n.7, 222, 242
    n.44, 246
  time slice vs. temporally extended, 28–29,
    31, 45, 59, 83, 98
  see also agency-at-its-best; agential
    direction; planning agency; purposive
    agency; self-governed agency; shared
    agency; temporally extended agency
agency-at-its-best (Yaffe), 9, 246, 248
agent, self-opaque, 189, 191–193
agential authority, 5–10, 12, 14–15
  and agential direction, 177–179
  and hierarchical model, 92–96, 202–203,
    212–220, 224–234, 238
  and Korsgaard, 96–98

and Nozick, 118 n.27, 126 n.37, 129–136
and the Platonic challenge, 138–143, 150, 156,
  159, 203–206, 243–253
problem of, 34, 41, 45–46, 59, 66 n.49, 92,
  94–95, 170 n.22
and its role in the explanation of action,
  25, 36
of self-governing policies, 60, 82–83, 100–105,
  241, 188–189, 192, 194, 209–211
strategy, 265–267, 277–281
and temporally extended agency, 65,
  98–100, 206–208, 267–268, 284 n.2
see also agential endorsement; subjective
  normative authority
agential commitment, 135, 141–142, 151, 213
agential direction, 4, 163, 177–179, 209
agential endorsement, 7, 14, 187, 287 n.7
  of deliberation, 38, 102–103
  of desires, 22–25, 34–35, 38–42, 70, 73–75,
    118 n.27, 141, 155–156, 170 n.23, 201
  and hierarchy, 28, 58–59, 81, 217
  implications for stability, 12, 26 n.15
  and its role in the explanation of action,
    25, 37, 39
  of a self-conception, 96–99
  and self-governing policies, 44, 45 n.61,
    191–192, 194, 211, 243 n.44, 251, 269
  see also identification; reflection; subjective
    normative authority
agential identification, *see* identification
agglomerativity, 147 n.27
Ainslie, George, 55–56, 259 n.2
akrasia, see weakness of will
Allison, Henry, 86 n.48
Anscombe, G. E. M, 108 n.6
Aristotle, 170 n.21, 215–217, 218 n.50, 220
Arpaly, Nomy, 101 n.44, 155 n.49